ESSENTIALS OF ORGANIZATIONAL BEHAVIOR

Seventh Edition

Stephen P. Robbins

San Diego State University

Upper Saddle River, New Jersey 07458

Library of Congress Cataloging-in-Publication Data

Robbins, Stephen P.
   Essentials of organizational behavior / Stephen P. Robbins.—7th ed.
     p. cm.
   Includes bibliographical references and index.
   ISBN 0-13-035309-4
   1. Organizational behavior. I. Title.
HD58.7 .R6 2002
658.3—dc21
                                                     2001055446

Executive Editor: David Shafer
Senior Managing Editor (Editorial): Jennifer Glennon
Editor-in-Chief: Jeff Shelstad
Assistant Editor: Melanie Olsen
Editorial Assistant: Kevin Glynn
Senior Marketing Manager: Shannon Moore
Marketing Assistant: Christine Genneken
Managing Editor (Production): Judy Leale
Production Editor: Keri Jean
Production Assistant: Dianne Falcone
Permissions Coordinator: Suzanne Grappi
Associate Director, Manufacturing: Vincent Scelta
Production Manager: Arnold Vila
Manufacturing Buyer: Diane Peirano
Design Manager: Pat Smythe
Art Director: Janet Slowik
Interior Design: Janet Slowik
Cover Design: Jerry McDaniel
Cover Illustration: Jerry McDaniel
Illustrator (Interior): Matrix Art Services
Manager, Print Production: Christy Mahon
Composition: UG / GGS Information Services, Inc.
Full-Service Project Management: Terri O'Prey, UG / GGS Information Services, Inc.
Printer/Binder: Courier

Credits and acknowledgments borrowed from other sources and reproduced, with permission, in this textbook appear on appropriate pages within text.

Copyright © 2003, 2000, 1997, 1994, 1992 by Pearson Education, Inc., Upper Saddle River, New Jersey, 07458. All rights reserved. Printed in the United States of America. This publication is protected by Copyright and permission should be obtained from the publisher prior to any prohibited reproduction, storage in a retrieval system, or transmission in any form or by any means, electronic, mechanical, photocopying, recording, or likewise. For information regarding permission(s), write to: Rights and Permissions Department.

Pearson Education LTD.
Pearson Education Australia PTY, Limited
Pearson Education Singapore, Pte. Ltd.
Pearson Education North Asia Ltd.
Pearson Education, Canada, Ltd.
Pearson Educación de Mexico, S.A. de C.V.
Pearson Education–Japan
Pearson Education Malaysia, Pte. Ltd.

10 9 8 7 6 5 4 3 2 1
ISBN 0-13-035309-4

*This book is dedicated to my friends and colleagues in
The Organizational Behavior Teaching Society
who, through their teaching research and commitment
to the learning process, have significantly improved
the ability of students to
understand and apply OB concepts.*

Brief Contents

Preface xvii

Part I   PROLOGUE 1
1. Introduction to Organizational Behavior 1

Part II   THE INDIVIDUAL IN THE ORGANIZATION 14
2. Foundations of Individual Behavior 14
3. Personality and Emotions 30
4. Basic Motivation Concepts 42
5. Motivation: From Concepts to Applications 55
6. Individual Decision Making 69

Part III GROUPS IN THE ORGANIZATION 84
7. Foundations of Group Behavior 84
8. Understanding Work Teams 100
9. Communication 113
10. Leadership and Creating Trust 130
11. Power and Politics 150
12. Conflict and Negotiation 163

Part IV   THE ORGANIZATION SYSTEM 178
13. Foundations of Organization Structure 178
14. Technology and Work Design 196
15. Human Resource Policies and Practices 215
16. Organizational Culture 230
17. Organizational Change and Development 248

Epilogue 266
Endnotes 267
Glindex (Index/Glossary) 285

Contents

Preface xvii

Part I   **PROLOGUE**   **1**

1. **Introduction to Organizational Behavior**   1

    The Field of Organizational Behavior   2
    - *Definition*   2
    - *Contributing Disciplines*   3

    Goals of Organizational Behavior   5
    - *Explanation*   5
    - *Prediction*   5
    - *Control*   5

    Challenges and Opportunities for OB: A Managerial Perspective   6
    - *Improving Quality and Productivity*   6
    - *Improving People Skills*   7
    - *Managing Workforce Diversity*   7
    - *Responding to Globalization*   8
    - *Empowering People*   9
    - *Stimulating Innovation and Change*   9
    - *Coping with "Temporariness"*   10
    - *Helping Employees Balance Work/Life Conflicts*   10
    - *Declining Employee Loyalty*   11
    - *Improving Ethical Behavior*   11

    The Plan of This Book   12

Part II   **THE INDIVIDUAL IN THE ORGANIZATION**   **14**

2. **Foundations of Individual Behavior**   14

    Values   14
    - *Types of Values*   15
    - *Values, Loyalty, and Ethical Behavior*   17
    - *Values Across Cultures*   17

Attitudes 19
    Job Satisfaction 19
    Reducing Dissonance 21
    The Attitude/Behavior Relationship 22
Perception 23
    Factors Influencing Perception 23
    Attribution Theory 23
    Shortcuts to Judging Others 25
Learning 26
Implications for Managers 27

3. Personality and Emotions 30

Personality 30
    The Myers-Briggs Type Indicator 31
    The Big-Five Model 31
    Other Key Personality Attributes 32
    Personality and National Culture 33
    Matching Personalities and Jobs 34
Emotions 36
    What Are Emotions? 36
    Felt Versus Displayed Emotions 37
    The Six Universal Emotions 38
    Gender and Emotions 38
    Emotions and National Culture 39
    OB Applications 39
Implications for Managers 41

4. Basic Motivation Concepts 42

What Is Motivation? 43
Early Theories of Motivation 43
    Hierarchy of Needs Theory 43
    Theory X and Theory Y 45
    Two-Factor Theory 45
Contemporary Theories of Motivation 47
    McClelland's Theory of Needs 47
    Goal-Setting Theory 48
    Reinforcement Theory 49
    Equity Theory 50
    Expectancy Theory 52
Don't Forget: Motivation Theories Are Culture-Bound! 53
Implications for Managers 54

5. **Motivation: From Concepts to Applications** 55
    Management by Objectives 55
        What Is MBO? 56
        Linking MBO and Goal-Setting Theory 57
        MBO in Practice 57
    Behavior Modification 58
        What Is OB Mod? 58
        Linking OB Mod and Reinforcement Theory 60
        OB Mod in Practice 60
    Employee Recognition Programs 60
        What Are Employee Recognition Programs? 60
        Linking Recognition Programs and Reinforcement Theory 61
        Employee Recognition Programs in Practice 61
    Employee Involvement Programs 61
        What Is Employee Involvement? 61
        Examples of Employee Involvement Programs 62
        Linking Employee Involvement Programs and Motivation Theories 63
        Employee Involvement Programs in Practice 63
    Variable-Pay Programs 64
        What Are Variable-Pay Programs? 64
        Linking Variable-Pay Programs and Expectancy Theory 65
        Variable-Pay Programs in Practice 66
    Skill-Based Pay Plans 66
        What Are Skill-Based Pay Plans? 66
        Linking Skill-Based Pay Plans to Motivation Theories 67
        Skill-Based Pay in Practice 67
    Implications for Managers 68

6. **Individual Decision Making** 69
    How Should Decisions Be Made? 70
        The Rational Decision-Making Process 70
        Improving Creativity in Decision Making 71
    How Decisions Are Actually Made in Organizations 73
        Bounded Rationality 73
        Intuition 74
        Identifying Problems 75

Developing Alternatives 75
Making Choices 76
Individual Differences 77
Organizational Constraints 80
Cultural Differences 81
Ethics in Decision Making 82
Implications for Managers 83

Part III GROUPS IN THE ORGANIZATION 84

7. Foundations of Group Behavior 84
Defining and Classifying Groups 84
Basic Group Concepts 85
Roles 85
Norms 87
Cohesiveness 90
Size 90
Composition 92
Status 93
Group Decision Making 94
The Individual Versus the Group 94
Groupthink and Groupshift 95
Selecting the Best Group Decision-Making Technique 97
Implications for Managers 98

8. Understanding Work Teams 100
Why Have Teams Become So Popular? 101
Teams Versus Groups: What's the Difference? 101
Types of Teams 102
Problem-Solving Teams 102
Self-Managed Work Teams 103
Cross-Functional Teams 104
Virtual Teams 104
Creating Effective Teams 105
Work Design 105
Composition 106
Context 108
Process 109
Turning Individuals into Team Players 110
The Challenge 110
Shaping Team Players 111
Implications for Managers 112

9. **Communication   113**
   - Functions of Communication   114
   - The Communication Process   114
   - Direction of Communication   115
     - *Downward   115*
     - *Upward   115*
     - *Lateral   116*
   - Interpersonal Communication   116
     - *Oral Communication   116*
     - *Written Communication   117*
     - *Nonverbal Communication   117*
   - Organizational Communication   119
     - *Formal Small-Group Networks   119*
     - *The Grapevine   119*
     - *Computer-Aided Communication   121*
   - Barriers to Effective Communication   123
     - *Filtering   123*
     - *Selective Perception   123*
     - *Information Overload   123*
     - *Gender Styles   123*
     - *Emotions   124*
     - *Language   124*
   - Cross-Cultural Communication   124
     - *Cultural Context   125*
     - *A Cultural Guide   126*
   - Ethics in Communication: Is It Wrong to Tell a Lie?   126
   - Implications for Managers   126

10. **Leadership and Creating Trust   130**
    - What Is Leadership?   130
    - Trait Theories   131
    - Behavioral Theories   131
      - *Ohio State Studies   132*
      - *University of Michigan Studies   133*
      - *The Managerial Grid   133*
      - *Summary of Behavioral Theories   133*
    - Contingency Theories   134
      - *The Fiedler Model   135*
      - *Leader-Member Exchange Theory   137*
      - *Path-Goal Theory   137*
      - *Leader-Participation Model   139*

Gender As a Contingency Variable: Do Males and Females Lead Differently? 139
Trait Theories Updated: Charismatic Leadership 141
Visionary Leadership 142
Team Leadership 142
Is Leadership Always Relevant? 143
Trust and Leadership 144
What Is Trust? 144
Trust and Leadership 146
Three Types of Trust 146
How Do You Build Trust? 147
Implications for Managers 148

11. Power and Politics 150

A Definition of Power 150
Contrasting Leadership and Power 151
Bases of Power 152
Coercive Power 152
Reward Power 153
Legitimate Power 153
Expert Power 153
Referent Power 153
Dependency: The Key to Power 154
The General Dependency Postulate 154
What Creates Dependency? 154
Power in Groups: Coalitions 155
Power and Sexual Harassment 156
Politics: Power in Action 157
A Definition of Political Behavior 157
The Importance of a Political Perspective 158
Factors Contributing to Political Behavior 158
Impression Management 160
The Ethics of Behaving Politically 161
Implications for Managers 162

12. Conflict and Negotiation 163

A Definition of Conflict 163
Transitions in Conflict Thought 164
The Traditional View 164
The Human Relations View 165
The Interactionist View 165

Differentiating Functional from Dysfunctional Conflicts   165
The Conflict Process   166
    Stage I: Potential Opposition   166
    Stage II: Cognition and Personalization   168
    Stage III: Behavior   168
    Stage IV: Outcomes   169
Negotiation   171
    Bargaining Strategies   171
    Issues in Negotiation   173
Implications for Managers   176

Part IV   THE ORGANIZATION SYSTEM   178

13. Foundations of Organization Structure   178

What Is Organization Structure?   178
    Work Specialization   179
    Departmentalization   181
    Chain of Command   182
    Span of Control   183
    Centralization and Decentralization   184
    Formalization   184
Common Organizational Designs   185
    The Simple Structure   185
    The Bureaucracy   186
    The Matrix Structure   187
New Options   188
    The Team Structure   188
    The Virtual Organization   189
    The Boundaryless Organization   190
Why Do Structures Differ?   191
    Strategy   191
    Organization Size   192
    Technology   192
    Environmental Uncertainty   193
Organization Structure and Employee Behavior   193
Implications for Managers   195

14. Technology and Work Design   196

Technology in the Workplace   196
    Continuous Improvement Processes   197
    Process Reengineering   198
    Mass Customization   199

Organizational Behavior in an E-World 200
    What's an E-Organization? 200
    Selected Implications for Individual Behavior 201
    Selected Implications for Group Behavior 203
    Will E-Orgs Redefine Interpersonal Relationships? 205
Work Design 206
    Task Characteristic Theories 206
    Work Redesign 209
    Popular Work Schedule Options 211
Implications for Managers 213

15. Human Resource Policies and Practices 215

Employee Selection 216
    Interviews 216
    Written Tests 217
    Performance-Simulation Tests 217
Training Programs 218
    Types of Training 218
    Training Methods 220
Performance Appraisal 220
    Performance Appraisal and Motivation 221
    What Do We Evaluate? 221
    Who Should Do the Evaluating? 222
    Performance Appraisal Methods 223
    Suggestions for Improving Performance Appraisals 225
    Don't Forget Performance Feedback! 226
    What About Team Performance Appraisals? 227
    Performance Appraisal in a Global Context 228
Implications for Managers 228

16. Organizational Culture 230

Defining Organizational Culture 231
    Culture Is a Descriptive Term 231
    Do Organizations Have Uniform Cultures? 231
    Strong Versus Weak Cultures 233
What Does Culture Do? 233
    Culture's Functions 233
    Culture As a Liability 234
Creating and Sustaining Culture 234
    How a Culture Begins 234
    Keeping a Culture Alive 235
    Summary: How Cultures Form 238

Contents xv

How Employees Learn Culture 239
Stories 239
Rituals 240
Material Symbols 240
Language 241
Managing Cultural Change 241
Creating an Ethical Organizational Culture 242
Spirituality and Organizational Culture 243
What Is Spirituality? 243
Why Spirituality Now? 243
Characteristics of a Spiritual Organization 244
Criticisms of Spirituality 245
Organizational Culture versus National Culture 246
Organizational Culture and the Paradox of Diversity 246
Implications for Managers 247

17. **Organizational Change and Development 248**
Forces for Change 248
Managing Planned Change 250
Two Views of Change 251
The "Calm Waters" Simile 251
The "White-Water Rapids" Simile 252
Putting the Two Views in Perspective 252
Resistance to Change 253
Individual Resistance 253
Organizational Resistance 254
Overcoming Resistance to Change 255
Managing Change Through Organizational Development 257
Sensitivity Training 257
Survey Feedback 258
Process Consultation 258
Team Building 259
Intergroup Development 260
Contemporary Issues in Organizational Change 260
Work Stress 261
Stimulating Innovation 262
Knowledge Management 263
Implications for Managers 264

Epilogue 266
Endnotes 267
Glindex (Index/Glossary) 285

Preface

This book was created as an alternative to the 600- or 700-page comprehensive textbook in organizational behavior (OB). It attempts to provide balanced coverage of all the key elements comprising the discipline of OB, in a style that readers will find both informative and interesting. I'm pleased to say that this text has achieved a wide following in short courses and executive programs and in traditional courses as a companion volume with experiential, skill development, case, and readings books. It is currently used at more than 400 colleges and universities in the United States, Canada, Latin America, Europe, Australia, and Asia. It's also been translated into Bahasa Indonesian, Chinese, Dutch, Japanese, Polish, and Spanish.

RETAINED FROM THE PREVIOUS EDITION

What do people like about this book? Surveys of users have found general agreement about the following features. Needless to say, they've all been retained in this edition.

- *Length*. Since its inception in 1984, I've tried diligently to keep this book to approximately 300 pages. Users tell me this length allows them considerable flexibility in assigning supporting materials and projects.
- *Balanced topic coverage*. Although short in length, this book continues to provide balanced coverage of all the key concepts in OB. This includes not only traditional topics such as personality, motivation, and leadership; but also cutting-edge issues such as emotions, trust, work-life balance, workplace spirituality, knowledge management, and e-organizations.
- *Writing style*. This book is frequently singled out for the fluid writing style and extensive use of examples. Users regularly tell me that they find this book "conversational," "interesting," "student-friendly," and "very clear and understandable."
- *Practicality*. This book has never been solely about theory. It's about *using* theory to better explain and predict the behavior of people in organizations. In each edition of this book, I have focused on making sure that readers see the link between OB theories, research, and implications for practice.
- *Absence of pedagogy*. Part of the reason I've been able to keep this book short in length is that it doesn't include review questions, cases, exercises, or similar teaching/learning aids. This book continues to provide only the basic core of OB knowledge, allowing instructors the maximum flexibility in designing and shaping their course.
- *Integration of globalization, diversity, and ethics*. As shown in Exhibit A, the topics of globalization and cross-cultural differences, diversity, and ethics are discussed throughout this book. Rather than presented in stand-alone chapters, these

Exhibit A Integrative Topics (with specific page references)

Chapter	Globalization and Cross-Cultural Differences	Diversity	Ethics
1	4, 8–9	3, 7–8, 10–11	5, 11–12
2	17–19	16–17, 28	17
3	33–34, 39	38	32
4	53–54		
5	61, 62–63		62
6	81	76	79–80, 82
7	92, 98–99	92	
8	110, 111	107	
9	118, 124–26	123–24	126
10		139–41	145
11		156–57	161–62
12	169, 175–76		
13			
14		198	203
15	216, 228	219	219–20
16	246	246–47	242–43
17	249, 250, 263	249	262

topics have been woven into the context of relevant issues. Users tell me they find this integrative approach makes these topics more fully part of OB and reinforces their importance.

- *Comprehensive supplements.* While this book may be short in length, it's not short on supplements. It comes with a complete, high-tech support package for both faculty and students. This includes a comprehensive instructor's manual and Test Item File; a dedicated Web site (www.prenhall.com/robbins); an Instructor's Resource CD-ROM, including the computerized Test Item File, instructor's manual, and PowerPoint slides; and the Robbins Self-Assessment Library, which provides students with insights into their skills, abilities, and interests. These supplements are described in detail later in this Preface.

NEW TO THE SEVENTH EDITION

This seventh edition has been updated in terms of research, examples, and topic coverage. For instance, you'll find new material in this edition on:

- Organizational citizenship behavior (Chapters 1 and 2)
- Work-life balance (Chapter 1)

- Amabile's model of creativity in decision making (Chapter 6)
- Group demography (Chapter 7)
- Team-effectiveness model (Chapter 8)
- Low- and high-context cultures (Chapter 9)
- Leader-member exchange theory (Chapter 10)
- OB and the e-organization (Chapter 14)
- Mass customization (Chapter 14)
- Flextime and telecommuting (Chapter 14)
- Employee selection and training (Chapter 15)
- Workplace spirituality (Chapter 16)
- Knowledge management (Chapter 17)

SUPPLEMENTS PACKAGE

Essentials of Organizational Behavior continues to be supported with an extensive supplement package for both students and faculty.

For the Student

- The updated and revised Robbins Self-Assessment Library is available with this text as a no-cost option. It contains 50 exercises that provide insights into your skills, abilities, and interests. This is available in both print and CD-ROM formats as well as online.
- Companion Web site—The Companion Web site *www.prenhall.com/robbins* is the industry standard for companion Web sites. Designed by professors for professors and their students, it provides a customized course Web site, including new communication tools, one-click navigation of chapter content, and other valuable resources.

For the Professor

- Instructor's Manual with Test Item File—The instructor's manual portion includes learning objectives, chapter outlines, chapter summaries, discussion questions, and skill exercises; the Test Item File provides true/false, multiple-choice, and essay questions.
- Companion Web site—The Companion Web site provides professors with bimonthly news articles integrated into the text with accompanying discussion questions and group exercises, online delivery of PowerPoint slides and instructor's material, and sample syllabi and teaching suggestions posted on a community chat room.
- Instructor's Resource CD-ROM—The Instructor's Resource CD-ROM contains the computerized Test Item File, PowerPoint Electronic Transparencies, and the instructor's manual. A revised, comprehensive package of text outlines

and figures corresponding to the text, the PowerPoint Electronic Transparencies are designed to aid the educator and supplement in-class lectures. Containing all of the questions in the printed Test Item File, Test Manager is a comprehensive suite of tools for testing and assessment. Test Manager allows educators to easily create and distribute tests for their courses, either by printing and distributing through traditional methods or by an online delivery via Local Area Network (LAN) servers.

- Videos—important topics in organizational behavior are illustrated in the accompanying videos. Real companies are used to highlight organizational behavior practices that work!

Acknowledgments

A number of people played critical roles in helping to produce this revision. Special thanks are extended to the following reviewers for their helpful comments and suggestions: Professor Claudia Harris, North Carolina Central University; Dr. David A. Foote, Middle Tennessee State University; Jeffrey J. Sherwood, Washington State University; Dr. Jenna Lundberg, Ithaca College; Dr. Carol I. Young, Wittenberg University; Dr. Angeline W. McArthur, University of Wisconsin-Parkside.

At Prentice-Hall, I want to thank David Shafer, Jennifer Glennon, Melanie Olsen, Kim Marsden, Shannon Moore, Judy Leale, Keri Jean, and Janet Slowik for overseeing the production and marketing of this book. And, finally, I want to thank my wife, Laura, for her love and support.

STEPHEN P. ROBBINS

PART I: Prologue

CHAPTER 1
Introduction to Organizational Behavior

After reading this chapter, you should be able to

1. Define organizational behavior (OB)
2. Identify the primary behavioral disciplines contributing to OB
3. Describe the three goals of OB
4. List the major challenges and opportunities for managers to use OB concepts
5. Discuss why workforce diversity has become an important issue in management
6. Explain how managers and organizations are responding to the problem of employee ethical dilemmas
7. Discuss how a knowledge of OB can help managers stimulate organizational innovation and change

When I ask managers to describe their most frequent or troublesome problems, the answers I get tend to exhibit a common theme. The managers most often describe _people_ problems. They talk about their bosses' poor communication skills, employees' lack of motivation, conflicts between team members, overcoming employee resistance to a company reorganization, and similar concerns.

Because a manager's job is inherently one of working with and through other people—bosses, peers, and employees—good "people skills" are a valuable, even necessary, asset in solving these problems.[1] This book has been written to help managers, and potential managers, develop these people skills.

THE FIELD OF ORGANIZATIONAL BEHAVIOR

The study of people at work is generally referred to as the study of organizational behavior. Let's begin, then, by defining the term *organizational behavior* and briefly reviewing its origins.

Definition

 Organizational behavior (OB) is the systematic study of the actions and attitudes that people exhibit within organizations. Let's look at the key parts of this definition.

Each of us regularly uses intuition, or our "gut feelings," in trying to explain phenomena. For instance, a friend catches a cold and we're quick to remind him that he "didn't take his vitamins," "doesn't dress properly," or that "it happens every year when the seasons change." We're not really sure why he caught cold, but that doesn't stop us from offering our intuitive analysis. The field of OB seeks to replace intuitive explanations with **systematic study**: that is, the use of scientific evidence gathered under controlled conditions and measured and interpreted in a reasonably rigorous manner to attribute cause and effect. The objective, of course, is to draw accurate conclusions. So the field of OB—its theories and conclusions—is based on a large number of systematically designed research studies.

What does OB systematically study? Actions (or behaviors) and attitudes! But not *all* actions and attitudes. Three types of behavior have historically proved to be important determinants of employee performance: *productivity*, *absenteeism*, and *turnover*. The importance of productivity is obvious. Managers clearly are concerned with the quantity and quality of output that each employee generates. But absence and turnover—particularly excessively high rates—can adversely affect this output. In terms of absence, it's hard for an employee to be productive if he or she isn't at work. In addition, high rates of employee turnover increase costs and tend to place less experienced people in jobs.

More recently, a fourth type of behavior—*organizational citizenship*—has been found to be important in determining employee performance. **Organizational citizenship** is discretionary behavior that is not part of an employee's formal job requirements but that nevertheless promotes the effective functioning of the organization. Examples of good employee citizenship behavior include helping others on one's work team, volunteering for extra job activities, avoiding unnecessary conflicts, and making constructive statements about one's work group and the overall organization.

Organizational behavior is also concerned with employee *job satisfaction*, which is an attitude. Managers should be concerned with their employees' job satisfaction for three reasons. First, there may be a link between satisfaction and productivity. Second, satisfaction appears to be negatively related to absenteeism and turnover. Finally, it can be argued that managers have a humanistic responsibility to provide their employees with jobs that are challenging, intrinsically rewarding, and satisfying.

The last part of our definition of OB that needs elaboration is the term *organization*. Psychology and sociology are well-known disciplines that study behavior, but they do not concentrate solely on work-related issues. In contrast, OB is specifically concerned with work-related behavior—and *that* takes place in organizations. An **organization** is a consciously coordinated social unit, composed of two or more people, that functions on a relatively continuous basis to achieve a common goal or set of goals. It's characterized by formal roles that define and shape the behavior of its members. So OB encompasses the behavior of people in such diverse organizations as manufacturing and service firms; schools; hospitals; churches; military units; charitable organizations; and local, state, and federal government agencies.

Contributing Disciplines

Organizational behavior is applied behavioral science and, as a result, is built upon contributions from several behavioral disciplines. The predominant areas are psychology, sociology, social psychology, anthropology, and political science. As you'll learn, psychology's contributions have been mainly at the individual or micro level of analysis, whereas the latter disciplines have contributed to our understanding of macro concepts—group processes and organization. Exhibit 1-1 provides an overview of the contributions made toward a distinct field of study: organizational behavior.

Psychology **Psychology** is the science that seeks to measure, explain, and sometimes change the behavior of humans and other animals. Psychologists concern themselves with studying and attempting to understand *individual* behavior. Those who have contributed and continue to add to the knowledge of OB are learning theorists, personality theorists, counseling psychologists, and, most important, industrial and organizational psychologists.

Early industrial psychologists, for instance, concerned themselves with problems of fatigue, boredom, and any other factor relevant to working conditions that could impede efficient work performance. More recently, their contributions have been expanded to include learning, perception, personality, workforce diversity, emotions, training, leadership effectiveness, needs and motivational forces, job satisfaction, decision-making processes, performance appraisals, attitude measurement, employee-selection techniques, job design, and work stress.

Sociology Whereas psychologists focus on the individual, sociologists study the social system in which individuals fill their roles; that is, **sociology** studies people in relation to their fellow human beings. Sociologists have made their greatest contribution to OB through their study of group behavior in organizations, particularly formal and complex organizations. Areas within OB that have received valuable input from sociologists include group dynamics, design of work teams, organizational culture, formal organization theory and structure, bureaucracy, communications, status, power, conflict, and work/life balance.

Social Psychology **Social psychology** is an area within psychology, blending concepts from psychology and sociology. It focuses on the influence of people on one another. One of the major areas receiving considerable investigation by social psychologists has been *change*—how to implement it and how to reduce barriers to its acceptance. In addition, social psychologists have made significant contributions in measuring, understanding, and changing attitudes, communication patterns, the ways in which group activities can satisfy individual needs, and group decision-making processes.

Anthropology **Anthropology** is the study of societies to learn about human beings and their activities. It includes their physical character, evolutionary history, geographic distribution, group relationships, and cultural history and practices. The work of anthropologists on cultures and environments, for instance, has helped us understand

EXHIBIT 1–1 Toward an OB Discipline

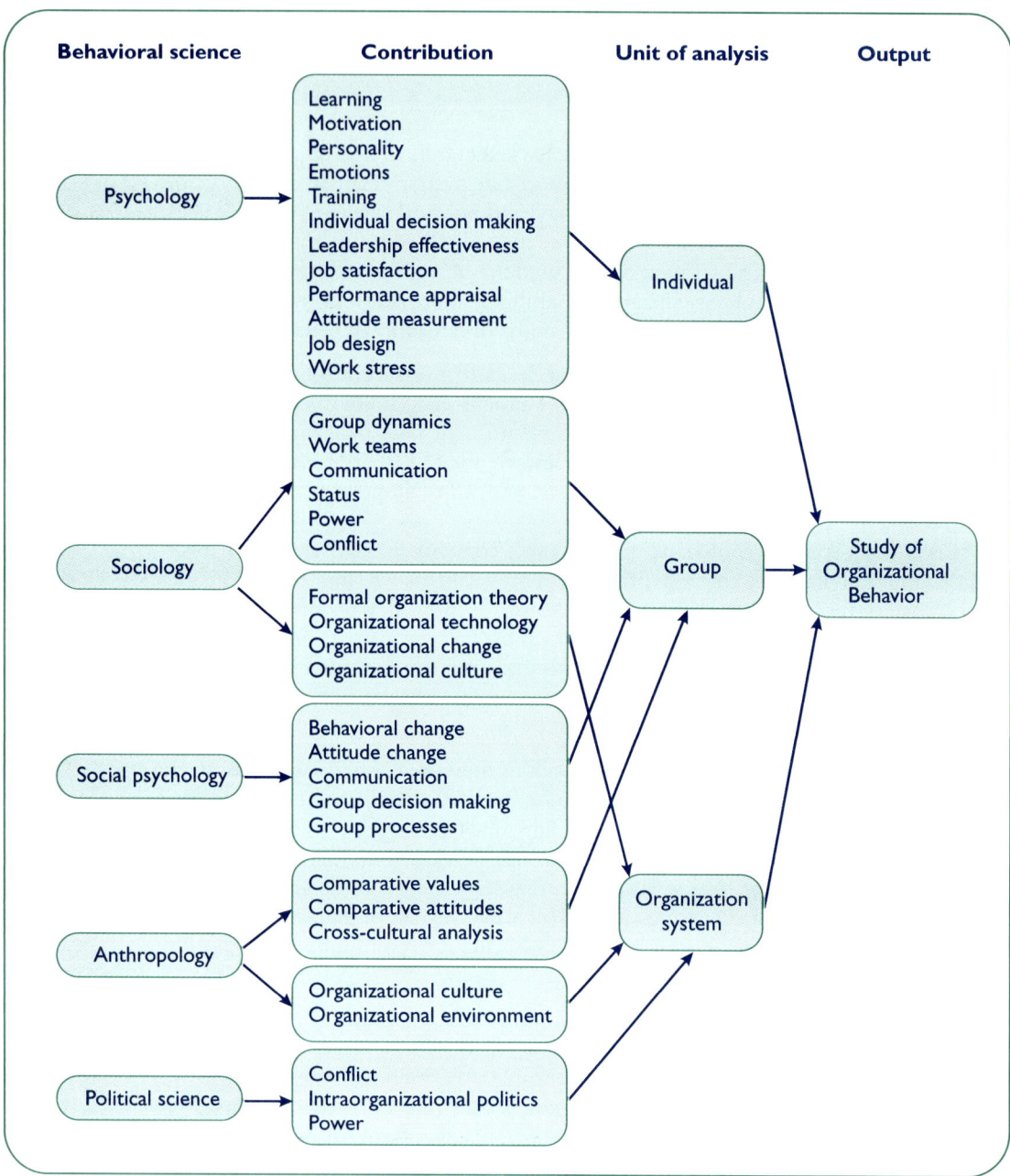

differences in fundamental values, attitudes, and behavior between people in different countries and within organizations. Much of our current understanding of organizational culture, organizational environments, and differences between national cultures is the result of the work of anthropologists or those using their methods.

Political Science Although frequently overlooked, the contributions of political scientists are significant to the understanding of behavior in organizations. **Political**

science is the study of the behavior of individuals and groups within a political environment. Specific topics of concern to political scientists include structuring of conflict, allocation of power, and how people manipulate power for individual self-interest.

GOALS OF ORGANIZATIONAL BEHAVIOR

What does OB seek to do? We know it's concerned with developing people skills, but what precisely are its goals? The goals of OB are to help you to *explain*, *predict*, and *control* human behavior.

Explanation

When we seek answers to why an individual or a group of individuals did something, we are pursuing the explanation objective. It's probably the least important of the three goals, from a management perspective, because it occurs after the fact. Yet, if we are to understand a phenomenon, we must begin by trying to explain it. We can then use this understanding to determine a cause. For example, if a number of valued employees resign, we undoubtedly want to know why, in order to determine if it was something that could have been prevented. Obviously, employees quit their jobs for many reasons, but if the explanation for a high quit-rate is inadequate pay or boring jobs, managers often can take actions that will correct this situation in the future.

Prediction

The goal of prediction focuses on future events. It seeks to determine what outcomes will result from a given action. A manager of a small factory who attempts to assess how employees will respond to the installation of new robotic equipment is engaging in a predictive exercise. On the basis of a knowledge of OB, the manager can predict certain behavioral responses to the change. Of course, there are various ways to implement a major change, so the manager is likely to assess employee responses to several change interventions. In this way, the manager can anticipate which approaches will generate the least degree of employee resistance and use that information in making his or her decision.

Control

The most controversial goal is using OB knowledge to control behavior. When a manager asks, for instance, "What can I do to make Dave put out more effort on his job?" that manager is concerned with control.

Why is control controversial? Most of us live in democratic societies, which are built upon the concept of personal freedom. Therefore, the idea that one person should attempt to get others to behave in a certain way, when the subjects of that control may be unaware that their behavior is being manipulated, has been viewed in some circles as unethical and repugnant. That OB offers technologies that facilitate the control of people is a fact. Whether those technologies should be used in organizations becomes an ethical question. You should be aware, however, that the control objective is frequently seen by managers as the most valuable contribution that OB makes toward their effectiveness on the job.

CHALLENGES AND OPPORTUNITIES FOR OB: A MANAGERIAL PERSPECTIVE

The ability to explain, predict, and control organizational behavior has never been more important to managers. A quick look at a few of the dramatic changes now taking place in organizations supports this claim. For instance, the typical employee is getting older; there are more and more women and minorities in the workplace; global competition is requiring employees to become more flexible and to learn to cope with rapid change and innovation; and the bonds of loyalty that historically held many employees to their employers are being severed.

In short, there are a lot of challenges and opportunities today for managers to use OB concepts. In this section, we'll review some of the most critical issues confronting managers for which OB offers solutions—or at least some meaningful insights toward solutions.

Improving Quality and Productivity

Peter Wood manages in a very competitive business. He's manufacturing-systems manager at the Oak Creek, Wisconsin, plant for Delphi Automotive Systems. The plant makes catalytic converters for more than 40 automobile manufacturers. In 1997 Wood recognized that customers increasingly wanted customized products and they weren't willing to wait 3 weeks for delivery. So Wood led a complete overhaul of the Oak Creek plant.[2] Assembly lines were replaced with team work cells, employees were given total responsibility for quality, and hundreds of wasteful processes were cut from the production system. The overhaul worked. Within 2 years, productivity at Oak Creek has increased by more than 25 percent, quality has improved, and delivery time has been cut to 4 days.

More and more managers are confronting the challenges that Peter Wood is facing. They are having to improve their organization's productivity and the quality of the products and services they offer. To improve quality and productivity, they are implementing programs such as quality management and process reengineering—programs that require extensive employee involvement.

As Exhibit 1-2 describes, **quality management** is driven by the constant attainment of customer satisfaction through the continuous improvement of all organizational processes.[3] It has implications for OB because it requires employees to rethink what they do and become more involved in workplace decisions.

In times of rapid and dramatic change, it's sometimes necessary to approach improving quality and productivity from the perspective of "How would we do things around here if we were starting from scratch?" That, in essence, is the approach of **process reengineering**. It asks managers to reconsider how work would be done and their organization structured if they were starting over.[4] The actions that Peter Wood took at Delphi's Oak Creek plant illustrates process reengineering. Instead of merely making incremental changes in the basic production processes, Wood reinvented the plant's whole production system. Every process was evaluated in terms of its contribution to the plant's goals. Inefficient processes were thrown out. Entire new systems were introduced. And most employees found themselves undergoing training to do entirely new jobs. Rather than try to make small improvements in a system that was too rigid and inflexible to meet changing cus-

EXHIBIT 1–2   What Is Quality Management?

1. *Intense focus on the customer.* The customer includes not only outsiders who buy the organization's products or services but also internal customers (such as shipping or accounts payable personnel) who interact with and serve others in the organization.
2. *Concern for continual improvement.* Quality management is a commitment to never be satisfied. "Very good" is not good enough. Quality can always be improved.
3. *Improvement in the quality of everything the organization does.* The term *quality* applies not only to the final product but also to how the organization handles deliveries, how rapidly it responds to complaints, how politely the phones are answered, and the like.
4. *Accurate measurement.* Quality management uses statistical techniques to measure every critical performance variable in the organization's operations. These performance variables are then compared against standards or benchmarks to identify problems, the problems are traced to their roots, and the causes are eliminated.
5. *Empowerment of employees.* Quality management involves the people on the line in the improvement process. Teams are widely used as empowerment vehicles for finding and solving problems.

tomer needs, Wood completely revamped his plant's production system and the jobs of individual employees. For instance, Oak Creek employees now check for quality, help establish productivity standards, and actively participate in introducing workflow innovations.

Today's managers understand that the success of any effort at improving quality and productivity must include their employees. These employees will not only be a major force in carrying out changes but increasingly will actively participate in planning those changes. OB offers important insights into helping managers work through these changes.

Improving People Skills

We opened this chapter by demonstrating how important people skills are to managerial effectiveness. We said that "this book has been written to help managers, and potential managers, develop these people skills."

As you proceed through this textbook, we"ll present relevant concepts and theories that can help you explain and predict the behavior of people at work. In addition, you'll also gain insights into specific people skills that you can use on the job. For instance, you'll learn a variety of ways to motivate people, how to be a better communicator, and how to create more effective teams.

Managing Workforce Diversity

One of the most important and broad-based challenges currently facing organizations is adapting to people who are different. The term we use for describing this challenge is **workforce diversity**.

Workforce diversity means that organizations are becoming more heterogeneous in terms of gender, race, and ethnicity. The term encompasses women,

African Americans, Hispanic Americans, and Asian Americans. It also includes the physically disabled, gays and lesbians, and the elderly.[5] Moreover, workforce diversity is an issue in Canada, Australia, South Africa, Japan, and Europe as well as the United States. Managers in Canada and Australia, for instance, are having to adjust to large influxes of Asian workers. The "new" South Africa is increasingly characterized by blacks holding important technical and managerial jobs. Women, long confined to low-paying temporary jobs in Japan, are now moving into managerial positions. And the creation of the European Union, which opened up borders throughout much of western Europe, has increased workforce diversity in organizations that operate in countries such as Germany, Portugal, Italy, and France.

Organizations used to take a "melting pot" approach to differences, assuming that people from different cultures and nationalities would somehow automatically want to assimilate. But employees don't set aside their cultural values and lifestyle preferences when they come to work. The challenge for organizations, therefore, is to make themselves more accommodating to diverse groups of people by addressing different lifestyles, family needs, and work styles. The melting pot assumption is being replaced by one that recognizes and values differences.[6]

Haven't organizations always included members of diverse groups? Yes, but they were such a small percentage of the workforce that no one paid much attention to them. Moreover, it was assumed that minorities would seek to blend-in and assimilate. The bulk of the pre-1980s workforce were male Caucasians working full-time to support a nonemployed wife and school-aged children. That's no longer true. Currently, 46 percent of the U.S. labor force are women. And minorities and immigrants make up 23 percent.[7]

Workforce diversity has important implications for management practice. Managers need to shift their philosophy from treating everyone alike to recognizing differences and responding to those differences in ways that will ensure employee retention and greater productivity—while at the same time not discriminating. Diversity, if positively managed, can increase creativity and innovation in organizations as well as improve decision making by providing different perspectives on problems.[8] When diversity is not managed properly, there is potential for higher turnover, more difficult communication, and more interpersonal conflicts.

Responding to Globalization

Management is no longer constrained by national borders. Four of the five highest grossing McDonald's restaurants are in Hong Kong. Prentice Hall, the largest seller of college textbooks in the United States and the publisher of this book, is owned by a British company. ExxonMobil, a so-called American company, receives almost 75 percent of its revenues from sales outside the United States. Toyota makes cars in Kentucky; General Motors makes cars in Brazil; and Ford, which owns Volvo, transfers executives between Sweden and the United States. These examples illustrate that the world has become a global village. In turn, managers have to become capable of working with people from different cultures.

Globalization affects a manager's people skills in at least two ways. First, if you're a manager, you're increasingly likely to find yourself in a foreign assignment. You may be transferred to your employer's operating division or subsidiary in another country. Once there, you'll have to manage a workforce that is likely to be very different in needs, aspirations, and attitudes from the ones you were used to back home. Second, even in your own country, you're going to find yourself working with bosses, peers, and employees who were born and raised in different cultures. For instance, what motivates you may not motivate them. Or your style of communication may be straightforward and open, but they may find this style uncomfortable and threatening. To work effectively with these people, you'll need to understand their culture, how it has shaped them, and how to adapt your management style to their differences. As we discuss OB concepts throughout this book, we'll frequently address how cultural differences might require managers to modify their practices.

Empowering People

If you pick up any popular business periodical nowadays, you'll read about the reshaping of the relationship between managers and those they're supposedly responsible for managing. You'll find managers being called coaches, advisers, sponsors, or facilitators. In many organizations, employees are now called associates. And there's a blurring between the roles of managers and workers.[9] Decision making is being pushed down to the operating level, where workers are being given the freedom to make choices about schedules and procedures and to solve work-related problems. Ten or 15 years ago, managers were encouraged to get their employees to participate in work-related decisions. Now, managers are going considerably further by allowing employees full control of their work. An increasing number of organizations are using self-managed teams, where workers operate largely without bosses.

What's going on? What's going on is that managers are *empowering employees*. They are putting employees in charge of what they do. And in so doing, managers are having to learn how to give up control, and employees are having to learn how to take responsibility for their work and make appropriate decisions. In later chapters, we'll show how **empowerment** is changing leadership styles, power relationships, the way work is designed, and the way organizations are structured.

Stimulating Innovation and Change

Whatever happened to W. T. Grant, Gimbel's, Eastern Airlines, Smith Corona, Montgomery Ward, and J. Peterman? All these giants went bust! Why have other giants, such as Sears and Boeing implemented huge cost-cutting programs and eliminated thousands of jobs? To avoid going bust!

Today's successful organizations must foster innovation and master the art of change or they'll become candidates for extinction. Victory will go to organizations that maintain their flexibility, continually improve their quality, and beat their competition to the marketplace with a constant stream of innovative products and services. Domino's single-handedly brought on the demise of thousands of small pizza parlors whose managers thought they could continue doing what they had been doing for years. Amazon.com is putting a lot of independent bookstores out of business as it proves you can successfully sell books from an Internet Web site. Fox Television has successfully stolen a major portion of the under-25 viewing audience from their much larger network rivals through innovative programming, including *The Simpsons, The X-Files,* and *MAD TV.*

An organization's employees can be the impetus for innovation and change or they can be a major stumbling block. The challenge for managers is to stimulate employee creativity and tolerance for change. The field of OB provides a wealth of ideas and techniques to aid in realizing these goals.

Coping with "Temporariness"

Managing used to be characterized by long periods of stability, interrupted occasionally by short periods of change. Managing today would be more accurately described as long periods of ongoing change, interrupted occasionally by short periods of stability! The world that most managers and employees face today is one of permanent "temporariness." The actual jobs that workers perform are in a permanent state of flux. So workers need to continually update their knowledge and skills to perform new job requirements. For example, production employees at companies such as Caterpillar, Ford, and Alcoa now need to know how to operate computerized production equipment. That was not part of their job descriptions 15 years ago. Work groups are also increasingly in a state of flux. In the past, employees were assigned to a specific department, and that assignment was relatively permanent. There was a considerable amount of security in working with the same people day in and day out. That predictability has been replaced by temporary work groups, teams that include members from different departments and whose members change all the time, and the increased use of employee rotation to fill constantly changing work assignments. Finally, organizations themselves are in a state of flux. They continually reorganize their various divisions, sell off poorly performing businesses, downsize operations, and replace permanent employees with temporaries.

Today's managers and employees must learn to cope with temporariness. They have to learn to live with flexibility, spontaneity, and unpredictability. The study of OB can provide important insights into a work world of continual change, how to overcome resistance to change, and how best to create an organizational culture that thrives on change.

Helping Employees Balance Work/Life Conflicts

The typical employee in the 1960s or 1970s showed up at the workplace Monday through Friday and did his or her job in eight- or nine-hour chunks of time. The workplace and hours were clearly specified. That's no longer true for a large segment of today's workforce. Employees are increasingly complaining that the line between work and nonwork time has become blurred, creating personal conflicts and stress.[10]

A number of forces have contributed to blurring the lines between employees' work and personal lives. First, the creation of global organizations means their world never sleeps. At any time and on any day, for instance, thousands of DaimlerChrysler employees are working somewhere. The need to consult with colleagues or customers 8 or 10 time-zones away means that many employees of global firms are "on-call" 24 hours a day. Second, communication technology allows employees to do their work at home, in their car, or on the beach in Tahiti. This lets many people in technical and professional jobs do their work any time and from any place. Third, organizations are asking employees to put in longer hours. For instance, between 1977 and 1997, the average workweek increased from 43 to 47 hours; and the number of people working 50 or more hours a week jumped from 24 percent to 37 percent.[11] Finally, fewer families have only a single breadwinner. Today's married employee is typically part of a dual-career couple. This makes it increasingly difficult for married employees to find the time to fulfill commitments to home, spouse, children, parents, and friends.

Employees are increasingly recognizing that work is squeezing out personal lives and they're not happy about it. For example, recent studies suggest that employees want jobs that give them flexibility in their work schedules so they can better manage work/life conflicts.[12] In addition, the next generation of employees is likely to have similar concerns.[13] A majority of college and university students say that attaining a balance between personal life and work is a primary career goal. They want "a life" as well as a job! Organizations that don't help their people achieve work/life balance will find it increasingly hard to attract and retain the most capable and motivated employees.

As you'll see in later chapters, the field of OB offers a number of suggestions to guide managers in designing workplaces and jobs that can help employees deal with work/life conflicts.

Declining Employee Loyalty

Corporate employees used to believe that their employers would reward their loyalty and good work with job security, generous benefits, and steady pay increases. But beginning in the mid-1980s, in response to global competition, unfriendly takeovers, leveraged buyouts, and the like, corporations began to discard traditional policies on job security, seniority, and compensation. They sought to become "lean and mean" by closing factories, moving operations to lower-cost countries, selling off or closing down less-profitable businesses, eliminating entire levels of management, replacing permanent employees with temporaries, and substituting performance-based pay systems for seniority-based programs. It is important to note that this is not just a North American phenomenon. European companies are doing the same. For instance, Barclays, the big British bank, recently cut staff levels by 20 percent. And some German firms have trimmed their workforce and management ranks: Siemens, the electronic engineering conglomerate, shed more than 3,000 jobs in one year alone; and steelmaker Krupp-Hoesch cut its management hierarchy from five levels to three.

These changes have resulted in a sharp decline in employee loyalty.[14] Employees perceive that their employers are less committed to them, and, as a result, employees respond by being less committed to their companies.

An important OB challenge will be for managers to devise ways to motivate workers who feel less committed to their employers, while maintaining their organizations' global competitiveness.

Improving Ethical Behavior

In an organizational world characterized by time pressures, expectations of increasing worker productivity, and tough competition in the marketplace, it's not altogether surprising that many employees feel pressured to cut corners, break rules, and engage in other forms of questionable practices.

Members of organizations are increasingly finding themselves facing **ethical dilemmas**, situations in which they are required to define right and wrong conduct. For example, should they "blow the whistle" if they uncover illegal activities taking place in their company? Should they follow orders with which they don't personally agree? Do they give an inflated performance evaluation to an employee whom they like, knowing that such an evaluation could save that employee's job? Do they allow themselves to "play politics" in the organization if it will help their career advancement?

What constitutes good ethical behavior has never been clearly defined. And, in recent years, the line differentiating right from wrong has become even more blurred. Employees see people all around them engaging in unethical practices—elected officials are indicted for padding their expense accounts or taking bribes; successful executives use insider information for personal financial gain; university administrators "look the other way" when a winning coach verbally abuses his athletes; and even the President of the United States distorts the truth under oath. They hear these people, when caught, giving excuses such as "everyone does it," "you have to seize every advantage nowadays," "I never thought I'd get caught," or "it depends on what the meaning of the word 'is' is."

Managers and their organizations are responding to this problem from a number of directions. They're writing and distributing codes of ethics to guide employees through ethical dilemmas. They're offering seminars, workshops, and similar training programs to try to improve ethical behaviors. They're providing in-house advisers who can be contacted, in many cases anonymously, for assistance in dealing with ethical issues. And they're creating protection mechanisms for employees who reveal internal unethical practices.

Today's manager needs to create an ethically healthy climate in which his or her employees can do their work productively and confront a minimal degree of ambiguity regarding what constitutes right and wrong behaviors. In upcoming chapters, we'll discuss the kinds of actions managers can take to create an ethically healthy climate and to help employees sort through ethically ambiguous situations.

THE PLAN OF THIS BOOK

How is this book going to help you better explain, predict, and control behavior? Our approach uses a building-block process. As illustrated in Exhibit 1-3, there are three levels of analysis in OB. As we move from the individual level to the organization system level, we increase in an additive fashion our understanding of behavior in organizations.

Chapters 2 through 6 deal with the individual in the organization. We begin by looking at the foundations of individual behavior—values, attitudes, perception, and

EXHIBIT 1–3 Levels of OB Analysis

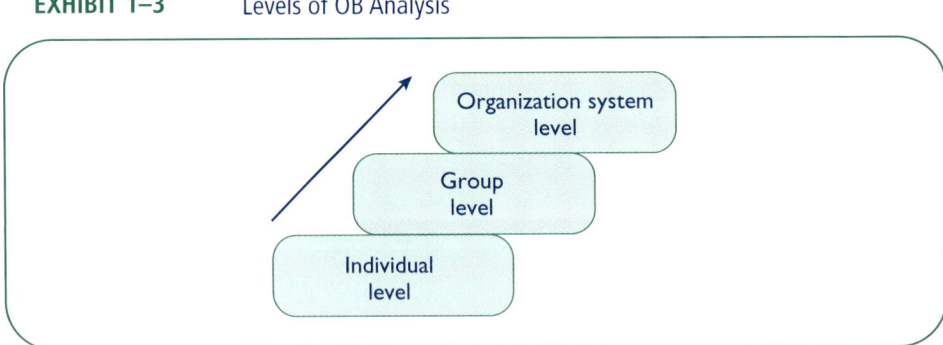

learning. Then we move on to consider the role of personality and emotions in individual behavior. We conclude this section with a discussion of motivation issues and the topic of individual decision making.

The behavior of people in groups is something more than the sum total of each individual acting in his or her own way. People's behavior in groups is different from their behavior when they are alone. Chapters 7 through 12 address group behavior. We introduce a group behavior model, discuss ways to make teams more effective, consider communication issues and group decision making, and then investigate the important topics of leadership, trust, power, politics, and conflict and negotiation.

Organizational behavior reaches its highest level of sophistication when we add the formal organization system to our knowledge of individual and group behavior. Just as groups are more than the sum of their individual members, organizations are not necessarily merely the summation of the behavior of a number of groups. In Chapters 13 through 17, we discuss how an organization's structure, work design, and technology affect behavior; the effect that an organization's human resource policies and practices have on people; how each organization has its own culture that acts to shape the behavior of its members; and the various organizational change and development techniques that managers can use to affect behavior for the organization's benefit.

PART II: The Individual in the Organization

CHAPTER 2

Foundations of Individual Behavior

After reading this chapter, you should be able to

1. List the dominant values in today's workforce
2. Describe the relationship between satisfaction and productivity
3. Explain the theory of cognitive dissonance
4. Summarize the relationship between attitudes and behavior
5. Explain how two people can see the same thing and interpret it differently
6. Summarize attribution theory
7. Outline the learning process

An understanding of individual behavior begins with a review of the major psychological contributions to OB. These contributions are subdivided into the following four concepts: values, attitudes, perception, and learning.

VALUES

Is capital punishment right or wrong? If a person likes power, is that good or bad? The answers to these questions are value-laden. Some might argue, for example, that capital punishment is right because it's an appropriate retribution for crimes such as murder or treason. However, others might argue, just as strongly, that no government has the right to take anyone's life.

Values represent basic convictions that "a specific mode of conduct or end-state of existence is personally or socially preferable to an opposite or converse mode of conduct or end-state of existence."[1] They contain a moral flavor in that they carry an individual's ideas as to what is right, good, or desirable. **Value systems** represent a prioritizing of individual values. They're identified by the relative importance an individual assigns to values such as freedom, pleasure, self-respect, honesty, obedience, and equality.

Types of Values

Can we classify values? The answer is: Yes! In this section, we'll review two approaches to developing value typologies.

Rokeach Value Survey Milton Rokeach created the Rokeach Value Survey (RVS).[2] The RVS consists of two sets of values, with each set containing 18 individual value items. One set, called **terminal values,** refers to desirable end-states of existence. These are the goals that a person would like to achieve during his or her lifetime. The other set, called **instrumental values,** refers to preferable modes of behavior, or means of achieving the terminal values. Exhibit 2-1 gives common examples for each of these sets.

Several studies confirm that RVS values vary among groups.[3] People in the same occupations or categories (e.g., corporate managers, union members, parents, students) tend to hold similar values. For instance, one study comparing corporate executives, members of the steelworkers' union, and members of a community activist group found a good deal of overlap among the three groups,[4] but also some very significant differences. The activists had value preferences that were quite different from those of the other two groups. They ranked equality as their most important terminal value; executives and union members ranked this value 12 and 13, respectively. Activists ranked "helpful" as their second-highest instrumental value. The other two groups both ranked it 14. These differences are important, since executives, union members, and activists all have a vested interest in what corporations

EXHIBIT 2–1   Examples of Terminal and Instrumental Values in the Rokeach Value Survey

Terminal Values	Instrumental Values
A comfortable life (a prosperous life)	Ambitious (hardworking, aspiring)
A sense of accomplishment (lasting contribution)	Capable (competent, effective)
A world of peace (free of war and conflict)	Cheerful (lighthearted, joyful)
A world of beauty (beauty of nature and the arts)	Clean (neat, tidy)
Equality (brotherhood, equal opportunity for all)	Courageous (standing up for your beliefs)
Family security (taking care of loved ones)	Helpful (working for the welfare of others)
Freedom (independence, free choice)	Honest (sincere, truthful)
Happiness (contentedness)	Imaginative (daring, creative)
Inner harmony (freedom from inner conflict)	Logical (consistent, rational)
Pleasure (an enjoyable, leisurely life)	Loving (affectionate, tender)
Salvation (saved, eternal life)	Obedient (dutiful, respectful)
Social recognition (respect, admiration)	Polite (courteous, well mannered)
True friendship (close companionship)	Responsible (dependable, reliable)

Source: Adapted from M. Rokeach, *The Nature of Human Values* (New York: The Free Press, 1973).

do. "When corporations and critical stakeholder groups such as these [other] two come together in negotiations or contend with one another over economic and social policies, they are likely to begin with these built-in differences in personal value preferences... Reaching agreement on any specific issue or policy where these personal values are importantly implicated might prove to be quite difficult."[5]

Contemporary Work Cohorts Your author has integrated several recent analyses of work values into four groups in an attempt to capture the unique values of different cohorts or generations in the U.S. workforce.[6] (No assumption is made that this framework would universally apply across all cultures.) Exhibit 2-2 proposes that employees can be segmented by the era in which they entered the workforce. Because most people start work between the ages of 18 and 23, the eras also correlate closely with the chronological age of employees.

Workers who grew up influenced by the Great Depression, World War II, the Andrews Sisters, and the Berlin blockade entered the workforce through the 1950s and early 1960s believing in hard work, the status quo, and authority figures. We call them *Veterans*. Once hired, Veterans tended to be loyal to their employers. In terms of the terminal values on the RVS, these employees are likely to place the greatest importance on a comfortable life and family security.

Boomers entered the workforce from the mid-1960s through the mid-1980s. Members of this cohort were influenced heavily by the civil rights movement, the Beatles, the Vietnam war, and baby-boom competition. They brought with them a large measure of the "hippie ethic" and distrust of authority. But they place a great deal of emphasis on achievement and material success. They're pragmatists who believe that ends can justify means. Boomers see the organizations that employ them merely as vehicles for their careers. Terminal values like a sense of accomplishment and social recognition rank high with them.

Xers' lives have been shaped by globalization, two-career parents, MTV, AIDS, and computers. They value flexibility, life options, and the achievement of job satisfaction. Family and relationships are very important to this cohort. They also enjoy team-oriented work. Money is important as an indicator of career performance, but Xers are willing to trade off salary increases, titles, security, and promotions for increased leisure time and expanded lifestyle options. In search of balance in their lives, Xers are less willing to make personal sacrifices for the sake of their employer

EXHIBIT 2–2   Dominant Values in Today's Workforce

Cohort	Entered the Workforce	Approximate Current Age	Dominant Work Values
Veterans	1950s or early 1960s	60+	Hard working, conservative, conforming; loyalty to the organization
Boomers	1965 – 1985	40–60	Success, achievement, ambition, dislike of authority; loyalty to career
Xers	1985 – 2000	25–40	Work/life balance, team-oriented, dislike of rules; loyalty to relationships
Nexters	2000 to present	Under 25	Confident, financial success, self-reliant but team-oriented; loyalty to both self and relationships

than previous generations were. On the RVS, they rate high on true friendship, happiness, and pleasure.

The most recent entrants to the workforce, the *Nexters*, have grown up during prosperous times, so they tend to be optimistic about the economy, to believe in themselves, and to be confident about their ability to succeed. Nexters are at ease with diversity and the first generation to take technology for granted. They've lived most of their lives with CD players, VCRs, cellular phones, and the Internet. This generation is very money-oriented and desirous of the things that money can buy. They seek financial success. Like Xers, they enjoy teamwork but they're also highly self-reliant. They tend to emphasize terminal values such as freedom and a comfortable life.

An understanding that individuals' values differ but tend to reflect the societal values of the period in which they grew up can be a valuable aid in explaining and predicting behavior. Employees in their 60s, for instance, are more likely to accept authority than are their co-workers who are 10 or 15 years younger. And workers in their 30s are more likely than their parents to balk at having to work weekends and more prone to leave a job in mid-career to pursue another that provides more leisure time.

Values, Loyalty and Ethical Behavior

Has there been a decline in business ethics? While the issue is debatable, a lot of people think ethical standards began to erode in the late 1970s.[7] If there has been a decline in ethical standards, perhaps we should look to our work cohorts model (see Exhibit 2-2) for a possible explanation. After all, managers consistently report that the action of their bosses is the most important factor influencing ethical and unethical behavior in their organizations.[8] Given this fact, the values of those in middle and upper management should have a significant bearing on the entire ethical climate within an organization.

Through the mid-1970s, the managerial ranks were dominated by Veterans whose loyalties were to their employer. When faced with ethical dilemmas, their decisions were made in terms of what was best for their organization. Beginning in the mid- to late 1970s, Boomers began to rise into the upper levels of management. By the early 1990s, a large portion of middle and top management positions in business organizations were held by Boomers.

The loyalty of Boomers is to their careers. Their focus is inward and their primary concern is with looking out for "Number One." Such self-centered values would be consistent with a decline in ethical standards. Could this help explain the alleged decline in business ethics beginning in the late 1970s?

The potential good news in this analysis is that Xers are now in the process of moving into middle-management slots and soon will be rising into top management. Since their loyalty is to relationships, they are more likely to consider the ethical implications of their actions on others around them. The result? We might look forward to an uplifting of ethical standards in business over the next decade or two merely as a result of changing values within the managerial ranks.

Values Across Cultures

In Chapter 1, we described the new global village and said "managers have to become capable of working with people from different cultures." Because values differ across cultures, an understanding of these differences should be helpful in explaining and predicting behavior of employees from different countries. A comparison of American and Japanese culture can help illustrate this point.[9]

American children are taught early the values of individuality and uniqueness. In contrast, Japanese children are indoctrinated to be "team players," to work within the group, and to conform. A significant part of an American student's education is to learn to think, analyze, and question. Their Japanese counterparts are rewarded for recounting facts. These different socialization practices reflect different cultures and, not surprisingly, result in different types of employees. The average U.S. worker is more competitive and self-focused than the Japanese worker. The obvious conclusion from these observations is that predictions of employee behavior, based on U.S. workers, are likely to be off-target when they're applied to a population of employees—such as the Japanese—who prefer and perform better in standardized tasks, as part of a work team, with group-based decisions and rewards.

A Framework for Assessing Cultures One of the most widely referenced approaches for analyzing variations among cultures was originated by Geert Hofstede.[10] He surveyed more than 116,000 IBM employees in 40 countries about their work-related values. And what did he find? He found that managers and employees vary on five value dimensions of national culture. They are listed and defined as follows:

Power distance—The degree to which people in a country accept that power in institutions and organizations is distributed unequally. Ranges from relatively equal (low power distance) to extremely unequal (high power distance).

Individualism vs. **collectivism**—Individualism is the degree to which people in a country prefer to act as individuals rather than as members of groups. Collectivism is the opposite or the equivalent of low individualism.

Quantity of life vs. **quality of life**—Quantity of life is the degree to which values such as assertiveness, the acquisition of money and material goods, and competition prevail. Quality of life is the degree to which people value relationships, and show sensitivity and concern for the welfare of others.[11]

Uncertainty avoidance—The degree to which people in a country prefer structured over unstructured situations. In countries that score high on uncertainty avoidance, people have an increased level of anxiety that manifests itself in greater nervousness, stress, and aggressiveness.

Long-term vs. **short-term orientation**—People in long-term-orientation countries look to the future and value thrift and persistence. A short-term orientation values the past and present, and emphasizes respect for tradition and fulfilling social obligations.

Exhibit 2-3 provides a summary of how a number of countries rate on these five dimensions. For instance, not surprisingly, most Asian countries are more collectivist than individualistic. On the other hand, the United States ranked highest among all countries surveyed on individualism.

Implications for OB Most of the concepts that currently make up the body of knowledge we call *organizational behavior* have been developed by Americans using American subjects in domestic contexts. A comprehensive study, for instance, of more than 11,000 articles published in 24 management and organizational behavior journals over a 10-year period revealed that approximately 80 percent of the studies were done in the United States and had been conducted by Americans.[12] Follow-up studies continue to confirm the lack of cross-cultural considerations in management and OB

EXHIBIT 2–3   Examples of Cultural Dimensions

Country	Power Distance	Individualism*	Quantity of Life**	Uncertainty Avoidance	Long-term Orientation***
China	High	Low	Moderate	Moderate	High
France	High	High	Moderate	High	Low
Germany	Low	High	High	Moderate	Moderate
Hong Kong	High	Low	High	Low	High
Indonesia	High	Low	Moderate	Low	Low
Japan	Moderate	Moderate	High	Moderate	Moderate
Netherlands	Low	High	Low	Moderate	Moderate
Russia	High	Moderate	Low	High	Low
United States	Low	High	High	Low	Low
West Africa	High	Low	Moderate	Moderate	Low

* A low score is synonymous with collectivism.
**A low score is synonymous with high quality of life.
*** A low score is synonymous with a short-term orientation.
Source: Adapted from G. Hofstede, "Cultural Constraints in Management Theories," *Academy of Management Executive*, February 1993, p. 91.

research.[13] What this means is that (1) not all OB theories and concepts are universally applicable to managing people around the world, especially in countries where work values are considerably different from those in the United States, and (2) you should take into consideration cultural values when trying to understand the behavior of people in different countries.

ATTITUDES

Attitudes are evaluative statements—either favorable or unfavorable—concerning objects, people, or events. They reflect how one feels about something. When I say "I like my job," I'm expressing my attitude about work.

A person can have thousands of attitudes, but OB focuses on a very limited number of job-related attitudes. These include job satisfaction, job involvement (the degree to which a person identifies with his or her job and actively participates in it), and organizational commitment (an indicator of loyalty to, and identification with, the organization). Without question, however, job satisfaction has received the bulk of attention.

Job Satisfaction

Job satisfaction refers to an individual's general attitude toward his or her job. A person with a high level of job satisfaction holds positive attitudes toward the job; a person who is dissatisfied with his or her job holds negative attitudes about the job. When people speak of employee attitudes, more often than not they mean job satisfaction. In fact, the two terms are frequently used interchangeably.

What Determines Job Satisfaction? What work-related variables determine job satisfaction? The evidence indicates that the most important factors conducive to job satisfaction are mentally challenging work, equitable rewards, supportive working conditions, and supportive colleagues.[14]

Employees tend to prefer jobs that give them opportunities to use their skills and abilities and offer a variety of tasks, freedom, and feedback on how well they're doing. These characteristics make work mentally challenging. Jobs that have too little challenge create boredom, but too much challenge creates frustration and feelings of failure. Under conditions of moderate challenge, most employees will experience pleasure and satisfaction.

Employees want pay systems and promotion policies that they perceive as being just, unambiguous, and in line with their expectations. When pay is seen as fair, based on job demands, individual skill level, and community pay standards, satisfaction is likely to result. Similarly, individuals who perceive that promotion decisions are made in a fair and just manner are likely to experience satisfaction from their jobs.

Employees are concerned with their work environment for both personal comfort and facilitating doing a good job. They prefer physical surroundings that are safe, comfortable, clean, and have a minimum degree of distractions.

Finally, people get more out of work than merely money or tangible achievements. For most employees, work also fills the need for social interaction. Not surprisingly, therefore, having friendly and supportive co-workers leads to increased job satisfaction.

Satisfaction and Productivity Few topics have attracted as much interest among students of organizational behavior as the satisfaction/productivity relationship.[15] The question typically posed is: Are satisfied workers more productive than dissatisfied workers?

The early views on the satisfaction/productivity relationship can be essentially summarized in the statement "a happy worker is a productive worker." Much of the paternalism shown by managers in the 1930s through the 1950s—for example, forming company bowling teams and credit unions, holding company picnics, and training supervisors to be sensitive to the concerns of employees—was initiated with the intent to try to make workers happy. But the happy-worker thesis was based more on wishful thinking than on hard evidence.

A more careful analysis indicates that if satisfaction does have a positive effect on productivity, that effect is fairly small. The introduction of moderating variables, however, has improved the relationship. For instance, the relationship is stronger when employees' behavior is not constrained or controlled by outside factors. An employee's productivity on machine-paced jobs, for example, is going to be much more influenced by the speed of the machine than by his or her level of satisfaction.

Currently, on the basis of a comprehensive review of the evidence, we would conclude that productivity is more likely to lead to satisfaction rather than the other way around. If you do a good job, you intrinsically feel good about it. In addition, if we assume that the organization rewards productivity, your higher productivity should increase verbal recognition, your pay level, and probabilities for promotion. These rewards, in turn, will increase your level of satisfaction with the job.

Satisfaction and OCB It seems logical to assume that job satisfaction should be a major determinant of an employee's organizational citizenship behavior (OCB).[16] Satisfied employees would seem more likely to talk positively about the organization, help others, and go beyond the normal expectations in their job. Moreover, satisfied employees might be more prone to go beyond the call of duty because they want to reciprocate their positive experiences. Consistent with this thinking, early discussions of OCB assumed that it was closely linked with satisfaction.[17] More recent evidence, however, suggests that satisfaction influences OCB, but through perceptions of fairness.

There is a modest overall relationship between job satisfaction and OCB.[18] But satisfaction is unrelated to OCB when fairness is controlled for.[19] What does this mean? Basically, job satisfaction comes down to conceptions of fair outcomes, treatment, and procedures.[20] If you don't feel like your supervisor, the organization's procedures, or pay policies are fair, your job satisfaction is likely to suffer significantly. However, when you perceive organizational processes and outcomes to be fair, trust develops. And when you trust your employer, you're more willing to voluntarily engage in behaviors that go beyond your formal job requirements.

Reducing Dissonance

One of the most relevant findings pertaining to attitudes is the fact that individuals seek consistency. **Cognitive dissonance** occurs when there are inconsistencies between two or more of a person's attitudes or between a person's behavior and attitudes. The theory of cognitive dissonance suggests that people seek to minimize dissonance and the discomfort it causes.[21]

In the real world, no individual can avoid dissonance completely. You know that "honesty is the best policy" but say nothing when a store clerk gives you back too much change. Or you tell your children to brush after every meal, but *you* don't. So how do people cope? A person's desire to reduce dissonance is determined by the importance of the elements creating the dissonance, the degree of influence the individual believes he or she has over the elements, and the rewards that may be involved in dissonance.

If the elements creating the dissonance are relatively unimportant, the pressure to correct this imbalance will be low. But, say a factory manager—Mrs. Smith, who has a husband and several children—believes strongly that no company should pollute the air or water. Unfortunately, because of the requirements of her job, Mrs. Smith is placed in the position of having to make decisions that would trade off her company's profitability against her attitudes on pollution. She knows that dumping the company's sewage into the local river (we'll assume the practice is legal) is in the best economic interest of her firm. What will she do? Clearly, Mrs. Smith is experiencing a high degree of cognitive dissonance. Because of the importance of the elements in this example, we can't expect Mrs. Smith to ignore the inconsistency. Besides quitting her job, there are several paths that she can follow to deal with her dilemma. She can reduce dissonance either by changing her behavior (stop polluting the river) or by concluding that the dissonant behavior is not so important after all ("I've got to make a living and, in my role as a corporate decision maker, I often have to place the good of my company above that of the environment or society."). A third alternative would be for Mrs. Smith to change her attitude ("There is nothing wrong with polluting the river."). Still another choice would be to seek out more consonant elements to outweigh the dissonant ones ("The benefits to society from manufacturing our products more than offset the cost to society of the resulting water pollution.").

The degree of influence that individuals believe they have over the elements will have an impact on how they will react to the dissonance. If they perceive the dissonance to be an uncontrollable result—something about which they have no choice—they're not likely to be receptive to attitude change. If, for example, the dissonance-producing behavior is required as a result of the boss's directive, the pressure to reduce dissonance would be less than if the behavior is performed voluntarily. Although dissonance exists, it can be rationalized and justified.

Rewards also influence the degree to which individuals are motivated to reduce dissonance. The tension inherent in high dissonance may be reduced when accompanied by a high reward. The reward acts to reduce dissonance by increasing the consistency side of the individual's balance sheet. Because people in organizations are given some form of reward or remuneration for their services, employees often can deal with greater dissonance on their jobs than off their jobs.

These moderating factors suggest that just because individuals experience dissonance, they will not necessarily move directly toward consistency, that is, toward reduction of this dissonance. If the issues underlying the dissonance are of minimal importance, if an individual perceives that the dissonance is externally imposed and is substantially uncontrollable, or if rewards are significant enough to offset the dissonance, the individual will not be under great tension to reduce the dissonance.

What are the organizational implications of the theory of cognitive dissonance? It can help to predict the propensity to engage in both attitude and behavioral change. For example, if individuals are required by the demands of their job to say or do things that contradict their personal attitude, they will tend to modify their attitude in order to make it compatible with the cognition of what they must say or do. In addition, the greater the dissonance—after it has been moderated by importance, choice, and reward factors—the greater the pressures to reduce the dissonance.

The Attitude/Behavior Relationship

Early research on the relationship between attitudes and behavior assumed them to be causally related; that is, the attitudes people hold determine what they do. Common sense, too, suggests a relationship. Isn't it logical that people watch television programs they like or that employees try to avoid assignments they find distasteful?

In the late 1960s, however, this assumed relationship between attitudes and behavior (A-B) was challenged by a review of the research.[22] On the basis of an evaluation of a number of studies that investigated the A-B relationship, the reviewer concluded that attitudes were unrelated to behavior or, at best, only slightly related. More recent research has demonstrated that there is indeed a measurable relationship if moderating contingency variables are taken into consideration.

One thing that improves our chances of finding significant A-B relationships is the use of both specific attitudes and specific behaviors. It is one thing to talk about a person's attitude toward "being socially responsible" and another to speak of her attitude toward "donating $25 to the National Multiple Sclerosis Society." The more specific the attitude we are measuring and the more specific we are in identifying a related behavior, the greater the probability that we can show a relationship between A and B.

Another moderator is social constraints on behavior. Discrepancies between attitudes and behavior may occur because the social pressures on the individual to behave in a certain way hold exceptional power. Group pressures, for instance, may explain why an employee who holds strong anti-union attitudes attends pro-union organizing meetings.

Of course, A and B may be at odds for other reasons. Individuals can and do hold contradictory attitudes at a given time, though, as we have noted, there are pressures toward consistency. In addition, other things besides attitudes influence behavior. But it is fair to say that, in spite of some attacks, most A-B studies yield positive results—in other words, attitudes *do* influence behavior.

PERCEPTION

Perception is a process by which individuals organize and interpret their sensory impressions in order to give meaning to their environment. Research on perception consistently demonstrates that different individuals may look at the same thing yet perceive it differently. The fact is that none of us sees reality. What we do is interpret what we see and call it reality.

Factors Influencing Perception

How do we explain the fact that people perceive the same thing differently? A number of factors operate to shape and sometimes distort perception. These factors can reside in the *perceiver*, in the object or *target* being perceived, or in the context of the *situation* in which the perception is made.

When an individual looks at a target and attempts to interpret what he or she sees, that interpretation is heavily influenced by the personal characteristics of the individual perceiver. Personal characteristics affecting perception include attitudes, personality, motives, interests, past experiences, and expectations.

Characteristics of the target being observed can affect what is perceived. Loud people are more likely to be noticed in a group than are quiet ones. So, too, are extremely attractive or unattractive individuals. Because targets are not looked at in isolation, the relationship of a target to its background influences perception, as does our tendency to group close things and similar things together.

The context in which we see objects or events is also important. The time at which an object or event is seen can influence attention, as can location, light, heat, or any number of situational factors.

Attribution Theory

Much of the research on perception is directed at inanimate objects. But OB is concerned with human beings, so our discussion of perception should focus on person perception.

Our perceptions of people differ from our perceptions of inanimate objects such as desks, machines, or buildings because we make inferences about the actions of people that we don't make about inanimate objects. Nonliving objects are subject to the laws of nature, but they have no beliefs, motives, or intentions. People do. The result is that when we observe people, we attempt to develop explanations of why they behave in certain ways. Our perception and judgment of a person's actions, therefore, will be significantly influenced by the assumptions we make about the person's internal state.

Attribution theory has been proposed to develop explanations of how we judge people differently depending on what meaning we attribute to a given behavior.[23] Basically, the theory suggests that when we observe an individual's behavior, we attempt to determine whether it was internally or externally caused. That determination, however, depends on three factors: (1) distinctiveness, (2) consensus, and (3) consistency. First, let's clarify the differences between internal and external causation, then elaborate on each of the three determining factors.

Internally caused behaviors are those believed to be under the personal control of the individual. *Externally* caused behavior results from outside causes; that is, the person is seen as forced into the behavior by the situation. If one of your employees was late for work, you might attribute his lateness to his partying into the wee hours of the morning and then oversleeping. This would be an internal interpretation. But if you attributed his arriving late to a major automobile accident that tied up traffic on the road he regularly uses, then you would be making an external attribution. As observers, we have a tendency to assume that others' behavior is internally controlled, while we tend to exaggerate the degree to which our own behavior is externally determined. But this is a broad generalization. There still exists a considerable amount of deviation in attribution, depending on how we interpret the distinctiveness, consensus, and consistency of the actions.

Distinctiveness refers to whether an individual displays different behaviors in different situations. Is the employee who arrives late today also the source of complaints by co-workers for being a "goof-off"? What we want to know is whether this behavior is unusual. If it is, the observer is likely to give the behavior an external attribution. If this action is not unique, it will probably be judged as internal.

If everyone who is faced with a similar situation responds in the same way, we can say the behavior shows *consensus*. Our tardy employee's behavior would meet this criterion if all employees who took the same route to work were also late. From an attribution perspective, if consensus is high you would be expected to give an external attribution to the employee's tardiness; whereas if other employees who took the same route made it to work on time, your conclusion for causation would be internal.

Finally, an observer looks for *consistency* in a person's actions. Does the person respond the same way over time? Coming in 10 minutes late for work is not perceived in the same way if for one employee it represents an unusual case (she hasn't been late for several months), while for another it is part of a routine pattern (she is late two or three times a week). The more consistent the behavior, the more the observer is inclined to attribute it to internal causes.

The preceding explains what you have seen operating for years. All similar behaviors are not perceived similarly. We look at actions and judge them within their situational context. If you have a reputation as a good student yet fail one test in a course, the instructor is likely to disregard the poor exam. Why? He or she will attribute the cause of this unusual performance to external conditions. It may not be your fault! (But the teacher is not likely to ignore the low test score of a student who has a consistent record of being a poor performer.) Similarly, if everyone in class failed the test, the instructor might attribute the outcome to external causes rather than to causes under the students' own control. He or she might conclude that the questions were poorly written, the room was too warm, or that the students didn't have the necessary prerequisites.

Another important finding from attribution theory is that there are errors or biases that distort attributions. For instance, there is substantial evidence that when we make judgments about the behavior of *other* people, we have a tendency to underestimate the influence of external factors and overestimate the influence of internal or personal factors.[24] This is called the **fundamental attribution error** and can explain why a sales manager is prone to attribute poor performance of her sales agents to laziness rather than to the innovative product line introduced by a competitor. There is also a tendency for individuals to attribute their *own* successes to internal factors such as ability or effort while putting the blame for failure on external factors such as luck. This is called the **self-serving bias** and suggests that feedback provided to employees in performance reviews will be predictably distorted by recipients depending on whether it is positive or negative.

Shortcuts to Judging Others

Making judgments about others is done all the time by people in organizations. For example, managers regularly evaluate the performance of their employees, and operatives assess whether their co-workers are putting forth their full effort. But making judgments about others is difficult. To make the task easier, individuals take shortcuts. Some of these shortcuts are valuable—they allow us to make accurate perceptions rapidly and provide valid data for making predictions. However, they can also result in significant distortions.

Individuals cannot assimilate all they observe, so they use **selectivity**. They take in data in bits and pieces. But these bits and pieces are not chosen randomly; they are selectively chosen depending on the interests, background, experience, and attitudes of the observer. Selective perception allows us to "speed read" others but not without the risk of drawing an inaccurate picture.

It's easy to judge others if we assume they are similar to us. **Assumed similarity,** or the "like me" effect, results in an individual's perception of others being influenced more by what the observer is like than by what the person being observed is like. If you want challenge and responsibility in your job, you may assume that others want the same. People who assume that others are like them will be right only in those instances when they judge someone who actually is like them. The rest of the time, they'll be wrong.

When we judge someone on the basis of our perception of the group to which he or she belongs, we are using the shortcut called **stereotyping.** "Married people are more stable employees than singles" or "union people expect something for nothing" are examples of stereotypes. To the degree that a stereotype is a factual generalization, it helps in making accurate judgments. But many stereotypes have no foundation in fact. In these latter cases, stereotypes distort judgments.

When we draw a general impression about an individual on the basis of a single characteristic such as intelligence, sociability, or appearance, a **halo effect** is operating. It's not unusual for the halo effect to occur during selection interviews. An interviewer may perceive a sloppily dressed candidate for a marketing research position as an irresponsible person with an unprofessional attitude and marginal abilities when, in fact, the candidate may be highly responsible, professional, and competent. What has happened is that a single trait—appearance—has overridden other characteristics in the interviewer's general perception of the individual.

LEARNING

The final concept introduced in this chapter is learning. It is included for the obvious reason that almost all complex human behavior is learned. If we want to explain, predict, or control behavior, we need to understand how people learn.

The psychologist's definition of learning is considerably broader than the layperson's view that "it's what we did when we went to school." In actuality, each of us is continuously "going to school." Learning is going on all the time. A more accurate definition of **learning**, therefore, is any relatively permanent change in behavior that occurs as a result of experience.

How do we learn? Exhibit 2-4 summarizes the learning process. First, learning helps us adapt to, and master, our environment. By changing our behavior to accommodate changing conditions, we become responsible citizens and productive employees. But learning is built on the **law of effect**, which says that behavior is a function of its consequences.[25] Behavior that is followed by a favorable consequence tends to be repeated; behavior followed by an unfavorable consequence tends not to be repeated. Consequence, in this terminology, refers to anything a person considers rewarding (i.e., money, praise, promotions, a smile). If your boss compliments you on your sales approach, you're likely to repeat that behavior. Conversely, if you're reprimanded for your sales approach, you're less likely to repeat it. But the keys to the learning process are the two theories, or explanations, of how we learn. One is *shaping* and the other is *modeling*.

When learning takes place in graduated steps, it is shaped. Managers shape employee behavior by systematically reinforcing, through rewards, each successive step that moves the employee closer to the desired behavior. Much of our learning has been done by shaping. When we speak of "learning by mistakes," we are referring to shaping. We try, we fail, and we try again. Through such series of trial and error, we master skills such as riding a bicycle, playing a musical instrument, performing basic mathematical computations, and answering multiple-choice questions on tests.

In addition to shaping, much of what we have learned is the result of observing others and modeling our behavior after them. Whereas the trial-and-error learning process is usually slow, modeling can produce complex behavioral changes quite rapidly. For instance, most of us, at one time or another, when having trouble in school or in a particular class, look to find someone who seems to have the system down pat. Then we observe that person to see what he or she is doing that is different from our approach. If we find some differences, we incorporate them into our behav-

EXHIBIT 2–4   The Learning Process

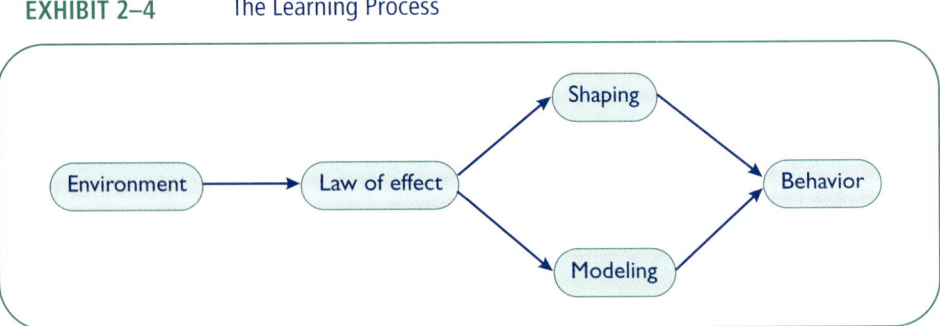

ior repertoire. If our performance improves (a favorable consequence), we're likely to make a permanent change in our behavior to reflect what we've seen work for others. The process is the same at work as it is in school. A new employee who wants to be successful on her job is likely to look for someone in the organization who is well respected and successful and then try to imitate that person's behavior.

IMPLICATIONS FOR MANAGERS

This chapter introduced several psychological concepts. Let's now put them together and demonstrate their importance for the manager who is trying to understand organizational behavior.

Exhibit 2-5 summarizes our discussion of individual behavior. In very simplified terms, we can say that an individual enters an organization with a relatively entrenched set of values and attitudes, and a substantially established personality (a topic in our next chapter). Although they're not permanently fixed, an employee's values, attitudes, and personality are essentially "givens" at the time he or she enters an organization. How employees interpret their work environment (perception) will influence their level of motivation (the topic of Chapters 4 and 5), what they learn on the job, and, eventually, their individual work behavior. We've also added *ability* to our model to acknowledge that an individual's behavior is influenced by the talents and skills that person holds when he or she joins the organization. Learning, of course, will alter this variable over time.

Values

Why should a manager seek to know an individual's values? Though they don't directly influence behavior, values strongly influence a person's attitudes. So knowledge of an individual's value system can provide insight into his or her attitudes.

Given that people's values differ, managers can use the Rokeach Value Survey to evaluate job applicants and determine if their values align with the

EXHIBIT 2–5 Key Variables Affecting Individual Behavior

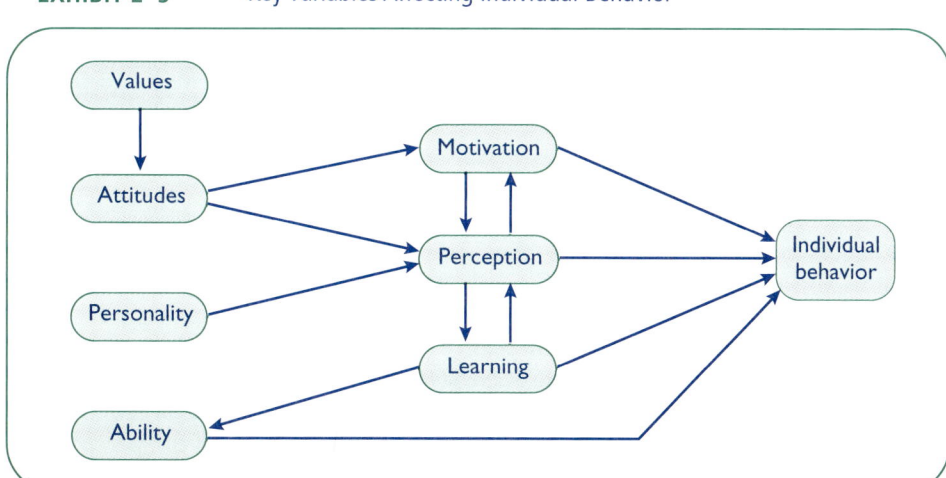

dominant values of the organization. An employee's performance and satisfaction are likely to be higher if his or her values fit well with the organization. For instance, the person who places high importance on imagination, independence, and freedom is likely to be poorly matched with an organization that seeks conformity from its employees. Managers are more likely to appreciate, evaluate positively, and allocate rewards to employees who "fit in," and employees are more likely to be satisfied if they perceive that they do fit. This argues for management to strive during the selection of new employees to find job candidates who not only have the ability, experience, and motivation to perform, but also a value system that is compatible with the organization's.

In addition, while values are certainly not uniform among individuals of the same age, the fact that people of common ages have similar experiences translates into somewhat similar work values. This suggests that people of like generations may find it easier to work together and help explain value conflicts among people from different generations.

Attitudes

Managers should be interested in their employees' attitudes because attitudes influence behavior. Satisfied employees, for instance, have lower rates of turnover and absenteeism than dissatisfied employees. Given that managers want to keep resignations and absences down—especially among their more productive employees—they will want to do things that will generate positive job attitudes.

Research on the satisfaction/productivity relationship has important implications for managers. It suggests that the goal of making employees happy on the assumption that doing so will lead to high productivity is probably misdirected. Managers would get better results by directing their attention primarily to what will help employees become more productive. Successful job performance should then lead to feelings of accomplishment, increased pay, promotions, and other rewards—all desirable outcomes—which then lead to satisfaction with the job.

Managers should also be aware that employees will try to reduce cognitive dissonance. More important, dissonance can be managed. If employees are required to engage in activities that appear inconsistent to them or that are at odds with their attitudes, the pressures to reduce the resulting dissonance are lessened when the employee perceives the dissonance as externally imposed and beyond his or her control or if the rewards are significant enough to offset the dissonance.

Perception

Managers need to recognize that their employees react to perceptions, not to reality. So whether a manager's appraisal of an employee is actually objective and unbiased or whether the organization's wage levels are actually among the highest in the industry is less relevant than what employees perceive. Individuals who perceive appraisals as biased or wage levels as low will behave as if those conditions actually exist, regardless of reality. Employees naturally organize and interpret what they see; inherent in this process is the potential for perceptual distortion.

The message to managers should be clear: They need to pay close attention to how employees perceive both their jobs and management practices. Remember, the valuable employee who quits for an invalid reason is just as "gone" as one who quits for a valid reason.

Learning

The issue isn't whether employees continually learn on the job or not. They do! The only issue is whether managers are going to let employee learning occur randomly or whether they are going to manage learning—through the rewards they allocate and the examples they set. If marginal employees are rewarded with pay raises and promotions, they will have little reason to change their behavior. If managers want behavior A, but reward behavior B, it shouldn't surprise them to find employees learning to engage in behavior B. Similarly, managers should expect that employees will look to them as models. Managers who are constantly late to work, or take two hours for lunch, or help themselves to company office supplies for personal use, should expect employees to read the message they're sending and model their behavior accordingly.

CHAPTER 3

Personality and Emotions

After reading this chapter, you should be able to

1. Describe the eight categories in the MBTI personality framework
2. Identify the "Big Five" personality variables and their relationship to behavior in organizations
3. Describe the impact of job typology on the personality/job performance relationship
4. Differentiate *felt* from *displayed* emotions
5. Identify the six universal emotions
6. Explain gender differences to emotional reactions and reading others
7. Describe ways in which emotions influence work-related behavior

Employees enter the organization with fairly well-established personalities. And their personalities have a strong influence on their behavior at work. In this chapter, we introduce several models for classifying personalities and show the importance of matching personality with jobs to increase employee performance. Then we move to the topic of emotions. While long overlooked in discussions of organizational behavior, we'll show how emotions play a key role in helping to explain and predict employee behavior.

PERSONALITY

Some people are quiet and passive; others are loud and aggressive. When we describe people in terms of characteristics such as quiet, passive, loud, aggressive, ambitious, loyal, or sociable, we're categorizing them in terms of personality traits. An individual's **personality**, therefore, is the combination of psychological traits we use to classify that person.

The Myers–Briggs Type Indicator

One of the most widely used frameworks for classifying personalities is called the **Myers-Briggs Type Indicator (MBTI)**.[1] It's essentially a 100-question personality test that asks people how they usually feel or act in particular situations.

On the basis of the answers individuals give to the test, they are classified as extroverted or introverted (E or I), sensing or intuitive (S or N), thinking or feeling (T or F), and perceiving or judging (P or J). These classifications are then combined into 16 personality types. To illustrate, let's take several examples. INTJs are visionaries. They usually have original minds and great drive for their own ideas and purposes. They're characterized as skeptical, critical, independent, determined, and often stubborn. ESTJs are organizers. They're practical, realistic, matter-of-fact, with a natural head for business or mechanics. They like to organize and run activities. The ENTP type is a conceptualizer. He or she is quick, ingenious, and good at many things. This person tends to be resourceful in solving challenging problems but may neglect routine assignments.

A study that profiled 13 contemporary businesspeople who created super-successful firms such as Apple Computer, FedEx, Honda Motors, Microsoft, Price Club, and Sony found all 13 to be intuitive thinkers (NTs).[2] This finding is particularly interesting because intuitive thinkers represent only about 5 percent of the population.

More than 2 million people a year take the MBTI in the United States alone. Organizations using the MBTI include Apple Computer, AT&T, GE, 3M Co., plus many hospitals, educational institutions, and even the U.S. Armed Forces. There is no hard evidence that the MBTI is a valid measure of personality. But lack of such evidence doesn't seem to deter organizations from using it.

The Big-Five Model

Whereas the MBTI lacks valid supporting evidence, that can't be said for the five-factor model of personality—more typically called the "Big Five."[3]

In recent years, an impressive body of research supports that five basic personality dimensions underlie all others. Factors in the **Big Five Model** are:

Extroversion: This dimension captures one's comfort level with relationships. Extroverts tend to be gregarious, assertive, and sociable. Introverts tend to be reserved, timid, and quiet.

Agreeableness: This dimension refers to an individual's propensity to defer to others. Highly agreeable people are cooperative, warm, and trusting. People who score low on agreeableness are cold, disagreeable, and antagonistic.

Conscientiousness: This dimension is a measure of reliability. A highly conscientious person is responsible, organized, dependable, and persistent. Those who score low on this dimension are easily distracted, disorganized, and unreliable.

Emotional stability: This dimension taps a person's ability to withstand stress. People with positive emotional stability tend to be calm, self-confident, and secure. Those with highly negative scores tend to be nervous, anxious, depressed, and insecure.

Openness to experience: The final dimension addresses an individual's range of interests and fascination with novelty. Extremely open people are creative, curious, and artistically sensitive. Those at the other end of the openness category are conventional and find comfort in the familiar.

In addition to providing a unifying personality framework, research on the Big Five also has found important relationships between these personality dimensions and job performance.[4] A broad spectrum of occupations were examined: professionals (including engineers, architects, accountants, attorneys), police, managers, salespeople, and semiskilled and skilled employees. Job performance was defined in terms of performance ratings, proficiency during training programs, and personnel data such as salary level. The results showed that conscientiousness predicted job performance for all occupational groups.

For the other personality dimensions, predictability depended on both the performance criterion and occupational group. For instance, extroversion predicted performance in managerial and sales positions. This result makes sense because these occupations involve high social interaction. Similarly, openness to experience was found to be important in predicting training proficiency, which, too, seems logical. What wasn't so clear was why emotional stability wasn't related to job performance. Intuitively, it would seem that people who are calm and secure would do better on almost all jobs than people who are anxious and insecure. The researchers suggested that the answer might be that only people who score fairly high on emotional stability retain their jobs. If that is true, then the range among those people studied, all of whom were employed, would tend to be quite small.

Other Key Personality Attributes

Six additional personality attributes have been identified that appear to have more direct relevance for explaining and predicting behavior in organizations. They are locus of control, Machiavellianism, self-esteem, self-monitoring, risk propensity, and Type A personality.

Some people believe they are masters of their own fate. Other people see themselves as pawns of fate, believing that what happens to them is due to luck or chance. **Locus of control** in the first case is internal; these people believe they control their destiny. Those who see their life as being controlled by outsiders are externals. The evidence shows that employees who rate high in externality are less satisfied with their jobs, more alienated from the work setting, and less involved in their jobs than are internals. A manager might also expect to find that externals blame a poor performance evaluation on their boss's prejudice, their co-workers, or other events outside their control. Internals would probably explain the same evaluation in terms of their own actions.

The personality characteristic of **Machiavellianism** (Mach) is named after Niccolo Machiavelli, who wrote in the sixteenth century on how to gain and use power. An individual exhibiting strong Machiavellian tendencies is manipulative, maintains emotional distance, and believes that ends can justify means. "If it works, use it" is consistent with a high Mach perspective. Not surprisingly, high Machs are more likely to engage in behavior that is ethically questionable than are low Machs. Do high Machs make good employees? That answer depends on the type of job and whether you consider ethical implications in evaluating performance. In jobs that require bargaining skills (such as labor negotiator) or where there are substantial rewards for winning (as in commissioned sales), high Machs will be productive. But if the ends can't justify the means or if there are no absolute standards of performance, our ability to predict a high Mach's performance will be severely curtailed.

People differ in the degree to which they like or dislike themselves. This trait is called **self-esteem**. Research finds that self-esteem is directly related to expectations for success. People with high self-esteem, for instance, believe that they possess the ability they need in order to succeed at work. Self-esteem (SE) has also been found to affect susceptibility to outside influences. People with low SE are more susceptible to external influences than are high SEs. Low SEs depend on the receipt of positive evaluations from others; and as a result, they are more likely to seek approval from others and are more prone to conform to the beliefs and behaviors of those they respect than are high SEs. In managerial positions, low SEs will tend to be concerned with pleasing others and, therefore, are less likely to take unpopular stands than are high SEs. In terms of job satisfaction, the evidence indicates that high SEs are more satisfied with their jobs than are low SEs.

Did you ever notice that some people are much better than others at adjusting their behavior to changing situations? This is because they score high in **self-monitoring**. High self-monitors are sensitive to external cues and can behave differently in different situations. They're chameleons—able to change to fit the situation and to hide their true selves. On the other hand, low self-monitors are consistent. They display their true dispositions and attitudes in every situation. The evidence suggests that high self-monitors tend to pay closer attention to the behavior of others and are more capable of conforming than low self-monitors. High self-monitors also tend to be better at playing organizational politics because they're sensitive to cues and can put on different "faces" for different audiences.

People differ in their willingness to take chances. Individuals with a high **risk propensity** make more rapid decisions and use less information in making their choices than individuals with low risk propensity. Managers might use this information to align employee risk-taking propensity with specific job demands. For instance, a high risk-taking propensity may lead to more effective performance for a stock trader in a brokerage firm. This type of job demands rapid decision making. On the other hand, this personality characteristic might prove to be a major obstacle for an accountant who performs auditing activities. This latter job might be better filled by someone with a low risk-taking propensity.

Do you know people who are excessively competitive and always seem to be experiencing a sense of time urgency? If you do, it's a good bet that those people have a **Type A personality**. Type A's are characterized by an incessant struggle to achieve more and more in less and less time. They're impatient, cope poorly with leisure time, and create a life of self-imposed deadlines. In North American culture, such characteristics tend to be highly prized and positively associated with ambition and the successful acquisition of material goods. In terms of work behavior, Type A's are fast workers. They emphasize quantity over quality. In managerial positions, Type A's demonstrate their competitiveness by working long hours and, not infrequently, making poor decisions because they make them too fast. Type A's are also rarely creative. Because of their concern with quantity and speed, they rely on past experiences when faced with problems. They will not allocate the time necessary to develop unique solutions to new problems. It appears that the Type A personality is more likely to lead to high performance in jobs such as sales than it does in senior executive positions.

Personality and National Culture

Do personality frameworks, like the Big Five model, transfer across cultures? Are dimensions such as locus of control and the Type A personality relevant in all cultures? Let's try to answer these questions.

The five personality factors identified in the Big Five model appear in almost all cross-cultural studies. This includes a wide diversity of cultures—such as China, Israel, Germany, Japan, Spain, Nigeria, Norway, Pakistan, and the United States. Differences tend to surface by the emphasis on dimensions. Chinese, for example, use the category of conscientiousness more often and use the category of agreeableness less often than do Americans. But there is a surprisingly high amount of agreement, especially among individuals from developed countries. As a case in point, a comprehensive review of studies covering people from the 15-nation European Community found that conscientiousness was a valid predictor of performance across jobs and occupational groups.[5] This is exactly what U.S. studies have found.

There are no common personality types for a given country. You can, for instance, find high and low risk-takers in almost any culture. Yet a country's culture influences the dominant personality characteristics of its population. We can see this by looking at locus of control and the Type A personality.

There is evidence that cultures differ in terms of people's relationship to their environment.[6] In some cultures, such as those in North America, people believe that they can dominate their environment. People in other societies, such as Middle Eastern countries, believe that life is essentially preordained. Notice the close parallel to internal and external locus of control. We should expect, therefore, a larger proportion of internals in the American and Canadian workforce than in the Saudi Arabian or Iranian workforce.

The prevalence of Type A personalities will be somewhat influenced by the culture in which a person grows up. There are Type A's in every country, but there will be more in capitalistic countries, where achievement and material success are highly valued. For instance, it is estimated that about 50 percent of the North American population is Type A.[7] This percentage shouldn't be surprising. The United States and Canada both have a high emphasis on time management and efficiency. Both cultures stress accomplishments and acquisition of money and material goods. In cultures such as Sweden and France, where materialism is less revered, we would predict a smaller proportion of Type A personalities.

Matching Personalities and Jobs

Obviously, individual personalities differ. So, too, do jobs. Following this logic, efforts have been made to match personalities with the proper jobs. The most researched personality job-fit theory is the **six-personality-types model**. This model states that an employee's satisfaction with and propensity to leave his or her job depend on the degree to which the individual's personality matches his or her occupational environment.[8] Six major personality types have been identified. They are listed in Exhibit 3-1, along with their compatible occupations.

A Vocational Preference Inventory questionnaire has been developed that contains 160 occupational titles. Respondents indicate which of these occupations they like or dislike, and their answers are used to form personality profiles. Utilizing this procedure, research strongly supports the hexagonal diagram in Exhibit 3-2. This figure shows that the closer two fields or orientations are in the hexagon, the more compatible they are. Adjacent categories are quite similar, while those diagonally opposite are highly dissimilar.

What does all this mean? The theory argues that satisfaction is highest and turnover lowest when personality and occupation are in agreement. Social individuals

EXHIBIT 3–1 Holland's Typology of Personality and Sample Occupations

Type	Personality Characteristics	Sample Occupations
Realistic: Prefers physical activities that require skill, strength, and coordination	Shy, genuine, persistent, stable, conforming, practical	Mechanic, drill press operator, assembly-line worker, farmer
Investigative: Prefers activities involving thinking, organizing, and understanding	Analytical, original, curious, independent	Biologist, economist, mathematician, news reporter
Social: Prefers activities that involve helping and developing others	Sociable, friendly, cooperative, understanding	Social worker, teacher, counselor, clinical psychologist
Conventional: Prefers rule-regulated, orderly, and unambiguous activities	Conforming, efficient, practical, unimaginative, inflexible	Accountant, corporate manager, bank teller, file clerk
Enterprising: Prefers verbal activities in which there are opportunities to influence others and attain power	Self-confident, ambitious, energetic, domineering	Lawyer, real estate agent, public relations specialist, small business manager
Artistic: Prefers ambiguous and unsystematic activities that allow creative expression	Imaginative, disorderly, idealistic, emotional, impractical	Painter, musician, writer, interior decorator

Source: Based on J.L. Holland, *Making Vocational Choices: A Theory of Vocational Personalities and Work Environments*, 2nd ed. (Upper Saddle River, NJ: Prentice Hall, 1985).

EXHIBIT 3–2 Hexagonal Diagram of the Relationship among Occupational Personality Types

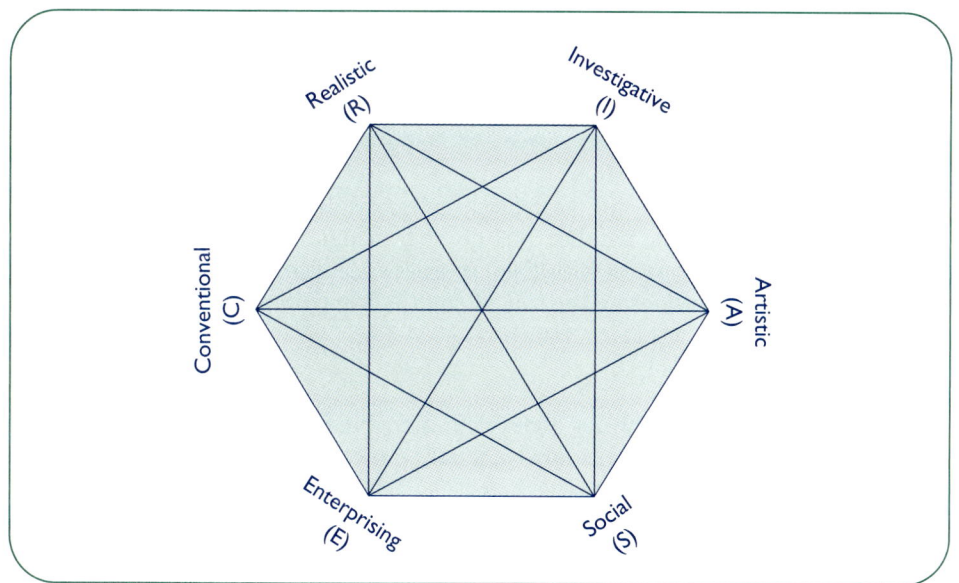

Source: John L. Holland. *Making Vocational Choices: A Theory of Vocational Personalities and Work Environments*, 2nd ed. (Psychological Assessment Resources, Inc., 1985) p. 23. Used by permission. [This model originally appeared in J. L. Holland et al., "An Empirical Occupational Classification Derived from a Theory of Personality and Intended for Practice and Research," ACT Research Report No. 29 (Iowa City): The American College Testing Program, 1969.]

should be in social jobs, conventional people in conventional jobs, and so forth. A realistic person in a realistic job is in a more congruent situation than a realistic person in an investigative job. A realistic person in a social job is in the most incongruent situation possible. The key points of this model are that (1) there do appear to be intrinsic personality differences among individuals, (2) there are different types of jobs, and (3) people in job environments congruent with their personality type should be more satisfied and less likely to resign voluntarily than people in incongruent jobs.

EMOTIONS

On December 26, 2000, a 42-year-old software tester at a Boston-area Internet consulting firm walked into his place of work. Armed with an AK-47 assault rifle, a shotgun, and a semiautomatic handgun, he killed seven of his co-workers. For this worker, anger had led to violence.

Going on a shooting rampage at work is an extreme example, but it does dramatically illustrate the theme of this section: Emotions are an important factor in employee behavior.

Given the obvious role that emotions play in our everyday life, it might surprise you to learn that, until very recently, the topic of emotions had been given little or no attention within the field of OB. How could this be? We can offer two possible explanations. The first is the *myth of rationality*.[9] Since the late nineteenth century, organizations have been essentially designed with the objective of trying to control emotions. It was believed that a well-run organization was one that successfully eliminated frustration, anger, love, hate, joy, grief and similar feelings. Such emotions were seen as the antithesis of rationality. So although researchers and managers knew that emotions were an inseparable part of everyday life, they tried to create organizations that were emotion free. That, of course, was not possible. The second factor that acted to keep emotions out of OB was the belief that *emotions of any kind were disruptive*.[10] When emotions were considered, the discussion focused on strong negative emotions—especially anger—that interfered with an employee's ability to do his or her job effectively. Emotions were rarely viewed as being constructive or able to stimulate performance-enhancing behaviors.

Certainly some emotions, particularly when exhibited at the wrong time, can reduce employee performance. But this doesn't change the reality that employees bring an emotional component with them to work every day and that no study of OB is complete without considering the role of emotions in workplace behavior.

What Are Emotions?

Although we don't want to obsess about definitions, before we can proceed with our analysis, we need to clarify three terms that are closely intertwined—*affect*, *emotions*, and *moods*.

Affect is a generic term that covers a broad range of feelings that people experience. It's an umbrella concept that encompasses both emotions and moods.[11] **Emotions** are intense feelings that are directed at someone or something.[12] Finally, **moods** are feelings that tend to be less intense than emotions, and they lack a contextual stimulus.[13]

Emotions are reactions to an object, not a trait. They're object-specific. You show your emotions when you're "happy about something, angry at someone, afraid of something."[14] Moods, on the other hand, aren't directed at an object. Emotions can turn into moods when you lose focus on the contextual object. So when a work colleague criticizes you for the way you spoke to a client, you might become angry at him. That is, you show emotion (anger) toward a specific object (your colleague). But later in the day, you might find yourself just generally dispirited. You can't attribute this feeling to any single event; you're just not your normal, upbeat self. This affect state describes a mood.

A related affect-term that is gaining increasing importance in organizational behavior is *emotional labor*. Every employee expends physical and mental labor when they put their bodies and cognitive capabilities, respectively, into their job. But most jobs also require **emotional labor**. This is when an employee expresses organizationally desired emotions during interpersonal transactions.[15] The concept of emotional labor originally developed in relation to service jobs. Airline flight attendants, for instance, are expected to be cheerful, funeral counselors sad, and doctors emotionally neutral. But today, the concept of emotional labor seems relevant to almost every job. You're expected, for example, to be courteous and not hostile in interactions with co-workers. And leaders are expected to draw on emotional labor to "charge the troops." Almost every great speech, for instance, contains a strong emotional component that stirs feelings in others. As we proceed in this section, you'll see that the increasing importance of emotional labor as a key component of effective job performance has given understanding of emotion a heightened relevance within the field of OB.

Felt versus Displayed Emotions

Emotional labor creates dilemmas for employees when their job requires them to exhibit emotions that are incongruous with their actual feelings. Not surprisingly, this is a frequent occurrence. For instance, you may find it very difficult to be friendly with everyone at work. Maybe you consider someone's personality abrasive. Maybe you know someone has said negative things about you behind your back. Regardless, your job requires you to interact with these people on a regular basis. So you're forced to feign friendliness.

It can help you to better understand emotions if you separate them into *felt* versus *displayed*.[16] **Felt emotions** are an individual's actual emotions. In contrast, **displayed emotions** are those that are organizationally-required and considered appropriate in a given job. They're not innate; they're learned. "The ritual look of delight on the face of the first runner-up as the new Miss America is announced is a product of the display rule that losers should mask their sadness with an expression of joy for the winner."[17] Similarly, most of us know that we are expected to act sad at funerals regardless of whether we consider the person's death to be a loss and to pretend to be happy at weddings even if we don't feel like celebrating.[18] Effective managers have learned to be serious when giving an employee a negative performance evaluation and to cover up their anger when they've been passed over for promotion. And the salesperson who hasn't learned to smile and appear friendly, regardless of his or her true feelings at the moment, isn't going to last long on most sales jobs.

The key point here is that felt and displayed emotions are often different. In fact, many people have problems working with others simply because they naively assume that the emotions they see others display is what those others actually feel. This is particularly true in organizations, in which role demands and situations often require people to exhibit emotional behaviors that mask their true feelings.

The Six Universal Emotions

There have been numerous efforts to limit and define the fundamental or basic set of emotions. Research has identified six universal emotions: anger, fear, sadness, happiness, disgust, and surprise.[19]

Exhibit 3-3 illustrates that these six emotions can be conceptualized as existing along a continuum.[20] The closer any two emotions are to each other on this continuum, the more people are likely to confuse them. For instance, happiness and surprise are frequently mistaken for each other, while happiness and disgust are rarely confused. In addition, as we'll elaborate on later in this section, cultural factors can also influence interpretations.

Do these six basic emotions surface in the workplace? Absolutely. I get *angry* after receiving a poor performance appraisal. I *fear* that I could be laid off as a result of a company cutback. I'm *sad* about one of my co-workers leaving to take a new job in another city. I'm *happy* after being selected as employee-of-the-month. I'm *disgusted* with the way my supervisor treats women on our team. And I'm *surprised* to find out that management plans a complete restructuring of the company's retirement program.

Gender and Emotions

It's widely assumed that women are more "in touch" with their feelings than men—that they react more emotionally and are better able to read emotions in others. Is there any truth to these assumptions?

The evidence does confirm differences between men and women when it comes to emotional reactions and ability to read others. Women show greater emotional expression than men[21]; they experience emotions more intensely; and they more frequently express both positive and negative emotions, except anger.[22] In contrast to men, women also report more comfort in expressing emotions. Finally, women are better at reading nonverbal cues than are men.[23]

What explains these differences? Three possible answers have been suggested. One explanation is the different ways men and women have been socialized.[24] Men are taught to be tough and brave; showing emotion is inconsistent with this image. Women, on the other hand, are socialized to be nurturing. This may account for the perception that women are generally warmer and friendlier than men. For instance, women are expected to express more positive emotions on the job (for example, by smiling) than men, and they do.[25] A second explanation is that women may have more innate ability to read others and present their emotions than do men.[26] Thirdly, women may have a greater need for social approval and, thus, a higher propensity to show positive emotions such as happiness.

EXHIBIT 3–3   Emotion Continuum

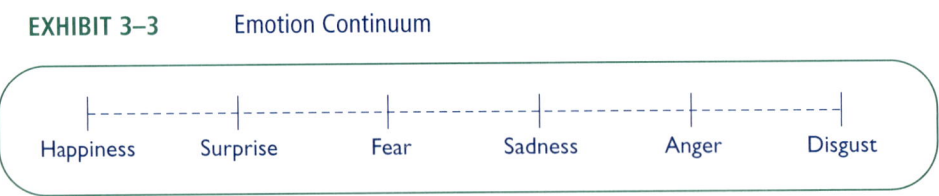

Based on R.D. Woodworth, *Experimental Psychology* (New York: Holt, 1938).

Emotions and National Culture

Cultural norms in the United States dictate that employees in service organizations should smile and act friendly when interacting with customers.[27] But this norm doesn't apply worldwide. In Israel, smiling by supermarket cashiers is seen as a sign of inexperience, so cashiers are encouraged to look somber.[28] In Moslem cultures, smiling is frequently taken as a sign of sexual attraction, so women are socialized not to smile at men.[29]

The above examples illustrate the need to consider cultural factors as influencing what is or isn't considered emotionally appropriate. What's acceptable in one culture may seem extremely unusual or even dysfunctional in another. And cultures differ in terms of the interpretation they give to emotions.

There tends to be high agreement on what emotions mean *within* cultures but not between. For instance, one study asked Americans to match facial expressions with the six universal emotions.[30] The range of agreement was between 86 and 98 percent. When a group of Japanese were given the same task, they correctly labeled only surprise (with 97 percent agreement). On the other five emotions, their accuracy ranged from only 27 to 70 percent. In addition, studies indicate that some cultures lack words for such standard emotions as *anxiety*, *depression*, or *guilt*. Tahitians, as a case in point, don't have a word directly equivalent to sadness. When Tahitians are sad, their peers typically attribute their state to a physical illness.[31]

OB Applications

We conclude our discussion of emotions by considering their application to several topics in OB. In this section, we assess how an understanding of emotions can improve our ability to explain and predict the selection process in organizations, decision making, motivation, leadership, interpersonal conflict, and deviant workplace behaviors.

Ability and Selection People who know their own emotions and are good at reading others' emotions may be more effective in their jobs. That, in essence, is the theme underlying recent studies on *emotional intelligence*.[32]

Emotional intelligence (EI) refers to an assortment of noncognitive skills, capabilities, and competencies that influence a person's ability to succeed in coping with environmental demands and pressures. It's composed of five dimensions:

Self-awareness. The ability to be aware of what you're feeling.
Self-management. The ability to manage one's own emotions and impulses.
Self-motivation. The ability to persist in the face of setbacks and failures.
Empathy. The ability to sense how others are feeling.
Social skills. The ability to handle the emotions of others.

Several studies suggest that EI may play an important role in job performance. For instance, one study looked at the characteristics of Bell Lab engineers who were rated as stars by their peers. The scientists concluded that stars were better at relating to others. That is, it was EI, not academic IQ, that characterized high performers. A second study of Air Force recruiters generated similar findings. Top-performing recruiters exhibited high levels of EI. Using these findings, the Air Force revamped its selection criteria. A follow-up investigation found that future hires who had high-EI scores were 2.6 times more successful than those who didn't.

The implications from the initial evidence on EI is that employers should consider it as a factor in selection, especially in jobs that demand a high degree of social interaction.

Decision Making As you'll see in Chapter 6, traditional approaches to the study of decision making in organizations have emphasized rationality. They have downplayed, or even ignored, the role of anxieties, stress, fears, frustrations, doubts, and similar emotions. Yet it's naive to assume that decision choices aren't influenced by one's feelings at a particular moment. Given the same objective data, for instance, we should expect that people may make different choices when they're angry and under stress than when they're calm and collected.

You can improve your understanding of decision making by considering "the heart" as well as "the head." People use emotions as well as rational and intuitive processes in making decisions. Failure to incorporate emotions into the study of decision processes will result in an incomplete (and often inaccurate) view of the process.

Motivation We'll discuss motivation in Chapters 4 and 5. At this point, we want merely to introduce the idea that, like decision making, the dominant approaches to the study of motivation reflect an overrationalized view of individuals.[33]

Motivation theories basically propose that individuals "are motivated to the extent that their behavior is expected to lead to desired outcomes. The image is that of rational exchange: the employee essentially trades effort for pay, security, promotions, and so forth."[34] But people aren't cold, unfeeling machines. Their perceptions and calculations of situations are filled with emotional content that significantly influences how much effort they exert. Moreover, people who are highly motivated in their jobs are emotionally committed. People who are engaged in their work "become physically, cognitively, *and* emotionally immersed in the experience of activity, in the pursuit of a goal."[35]

Are all people emotionally engaged in their work? No! But many are. And if we focus only on rational calculations of inducements and contributions, we fail to be able to explain behaviors such as the individual who forgets to have dinner and works late into the night, lost in the thrill of her work.[36]

Leadership The ability to lead others is a fundamental quality sought by organizations. We'll discuss the topic of leadership, in depth, in Chapter 10. Here, however, we briefly introduce how emotions can be an integral part of leadership.

Effective leaders almost all rely on the expression of feelings to help convey their messages. In fact, the expression of emotions in speeches is often the critical element that results in individuals accepting or rejecting a leader's message. "When leaders feel excited, enthusiastic, and active, they may be more likely to energize their subordinates and convey a sense of efficacy, competence, optimism, and enjoyment."[37] Politicians, as a case in point, have learned to show enthusiasm when talking about their chances for winning an election, even when polls suggest otherwise.

Corporate executives know that emotional content is critical if employees are to buy into their vision of their company's future and accept change. When new visions are offered, especially when they contain distant or vague goals, change is often difficult to accept. So when effective leaders want to implement significant changes, they rely on "the evocation, framing, and mobilization of *emotions*."[38] By arousing emotions and linking them to an appealing vision, leaders increase the likelihood that managers and employees alike will accept change.

Interpersonal Conflict Few issues are more intertwined with emotions than the topic of interpersonal conflict. Whenever conflicts arise, you can be fairly certain that emotions are also surfacing. A manager's success in trying to resolve conflicts, in fact, is often largely due to his or her ability to identify the emotional elements in the conflict and to get the conflicting parties to work through their emotions. And the manager who ignores the emotional elements in conflicts, focusing singularly on rational and task-focused concerns, is unlikely to be very effective in resolving those conflicts.

Deviant Workplace Behaviors Negative emotions can lead to a number of deviant workplace behaviors.

Anyone who has spent much time in an organization realizes that people often engage in voluntary actions that violate established norms and that threaten the organization, its members, or both. These actions are called **employee deviance**.[39] They fall into categories such as production (e.g., leaving early, intentionally working slowly); property (e.g., stealing, sabotage); political (e.g., gossiping, blaming co-workers); and personal aggression (e.g., sexual harassment, verbal abuse). Many of these deviant behaviors can be traced to negative emotions.

For instance, envy is an emotion that occurs when you resent someone for having something that you don't, and which you strongly desire. It can lead to malicious deviant behaviors. Envy, for example, has been found to be associated with hostility, "backstabbing" and other forms of political behavior, negatively distorting others' successes, and positively distorting one's own accomplishments.[40]

IMPLICATIONS FOR MANAGERS

Personality

The major value of a manager's understanding personality differences probably lies in selection. You are likely to have higher-performing and more-satisfied employees if consideration is given to matching personality types with compatible jobs. In addition, there may be other benefits. For instance, managers can expect that individuals with an external locus of control may be less satisfied with their jobs than internals and also that they may be less willing to accept responsibility for their actions.

Emotions

Emotions are a natural part of an individual's make-up. Where managers often err is in ignoring the emotional elements in organizational behavior and assessing individual behavior as if it were completely rational. As one consultant aptly put it, "You can't divorce emotions from the workplace because you can't divorce emotions from people."[41] Managers who understand the role of emotions will significantly improve their ability to explain and predict individual behavior.

Do emotions affect job performance? Yes. They can *hinder* performance, especially negative emotions. That's probably why organizations, for the most part, try to keep emotions out of the workplace. But emotions can also *enhance* performance. How? Two ways.[42] First, emotions can increase arousal levels, thus acting as motivators to higher performance. Second, emotional labor recognizes that feelings can be part of a job's required behavior. So, for instance, the ability to effectively manage emotions in leadership and sales positions may be critical to success in those positions.

CHAPTER 4

Basic Motivation Concepts

After reading this chapter, you should be able to

1. Outline the basic motivation process
2. Describe Maslow's hierarchy of needs theory
3. Contrast Theory X and Theory Y
4. Differentiate motivators from hygiene factors
5. List the characteristics that high achievers prefer in a job
6. Summarize the types of goals that increase performance
7. Contrast reinforcement and goal-setting theories
8. Explain equity theory
9. Clarify the key relationships in expectancy theory

Referring to their son or daughter, parents have said it for so many years that it has achieved the status of a cliché: "He/she has the ability but just won't apply him/herself." Few of us work to, or even near, our potential, and most of us will admit to that. Thomas Edison underscored his belief in the importance of hard work for achieving success when he said that "genius is one percent inspiration and 99 percent perspiration." The fact is that some people work harder or exert more effort than others. The result is that individuals of lesser ability can, and do, outperform their more gifted counterparts. For this reason, an individual's performance at work or otherwise depends not only on ability but on motivation as well. This chapter considers various explanations of why some people exert more effort on their jobs than others. In the next chapter, we'll build on these explanations to describe a variety of applied motivation techniques.

WHAT IS MOTIVATION?

We might define motivation in terms of some outward behavior. People who are motivated exert a greater effort to perform than those who are not motivated. But such a definition is relative and tells us little. A more descriptive but less substantive definition would say that **motivation** is the willingness to do something and is conditioned by this action's ability to satisfy some need for the individual. A **need**, in our terminology, means a physiological or psychological deficiency that makes certain outcomes appear attractive. This motivation process can be seen in Exhibit 4-1.

An unsatisfied need creates tension, which stimulates drives within the individual. These drives generate a search to find particular goals that, if attained, will satisfy the need and lead to the reduction of tension.

Motivated employees are in a state of tension. In order to relieve this tension, they engage in activity. The greater the tension, the more activity will be needed to bring about relief. Therefore, when we see employees working hard at some activity, we can conclude they are driven by a desire to achieve some goal they value.

EARLY THEORIES OF MOTIVATION

The decade of the 1950s was a fruitful period in the development of motivation concepts. Three specific theories were formulated during this period, which, though now heavily attacked and their validity called into question, are probably still the best-known explanations for employee motivation: the hierarchy of needs theory, Theory X and Theory Y, and the two-factor theory. We have since developed more valid explanations of motivation, but you should know these early theories for at least two reasons: (1) they represent a foundation from which contemporary theories have grown, and (2) practicing managers regularly use these theories and their terminologies in explaining employee motivation.

Hierarchy of Needs Theory

It's probably safe to say that the best-known approach to motivation is Abraham Maslow's **hierarchy of needs theory**.[1] He hypothesized that within every human being there exists a hierarchy of five needs. These are:

1. *Physiological needs*: Include hunger, thirst, shelter, sex, and other bodily needs
2. *Safety needs*: Include security and protection from physical and emotional harm
3. *Social needs*: Include affection, a sense of belonging, acceptance, and friendship
4. *Esteem needs*: Include internal factors such as self-respect, autonomy, and achievement and external factors such as status, recognition, and attention

EXHIBIT 4–1 Basic Motivation Process

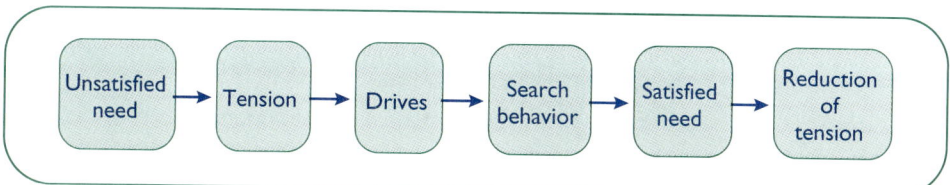

5. *Self-actualization need*: The drive to become what one is capable of becoming; includes growth, achieving one's potential, and self-fulfillment

As each of these needs becomes substantially satisfied, the next need becomes dominant. In terms of Exhibit 4-2, the individual moves up the hierarchy. From the standpoint of motivation, Maslow's theory would say that, although no need is ever fully gratified, a substantially satisfied need no longer motivates.

Maslow separated the five needs into higher and lower orders. Physiological and safety needs were described as lower-order needs; social, esteem, and self-actualization were categorized as higher-order needs. The two orders were differentiated on the premise that higher-order needs are satisfied internally, whereas lower-order needs are predominantly satisfied externally (by things such as wages, union contracts, and tenure). In fact, the natural conclusion to be drawn from Maslow's classification is that, in times of economic plenty, almost all permanently employed workers will have their lower-order needs substantially met.

Maslow's need theory has received wide recognition, particularly among practicing managers. This acceptance can be attributed to the logic and ease with which the theory is intuitively understood. Unfortunately, however, research does not generally validate the theory. For instance, little support is found for the prediction that need structures are organized along the dimensions proposed by Maslow or the prediction that the substantial satisfaction of a given need leads to the activation of the next higher need. So, although the need hierarchy is well known and undoubtedly used by many managers as a guide toward motivating their employees, little substantive evidence exists to indicate that following the theory will lead to a more motivated workforce.

EXHIBIT 4–2   Maslow's Hierarchy of Needs

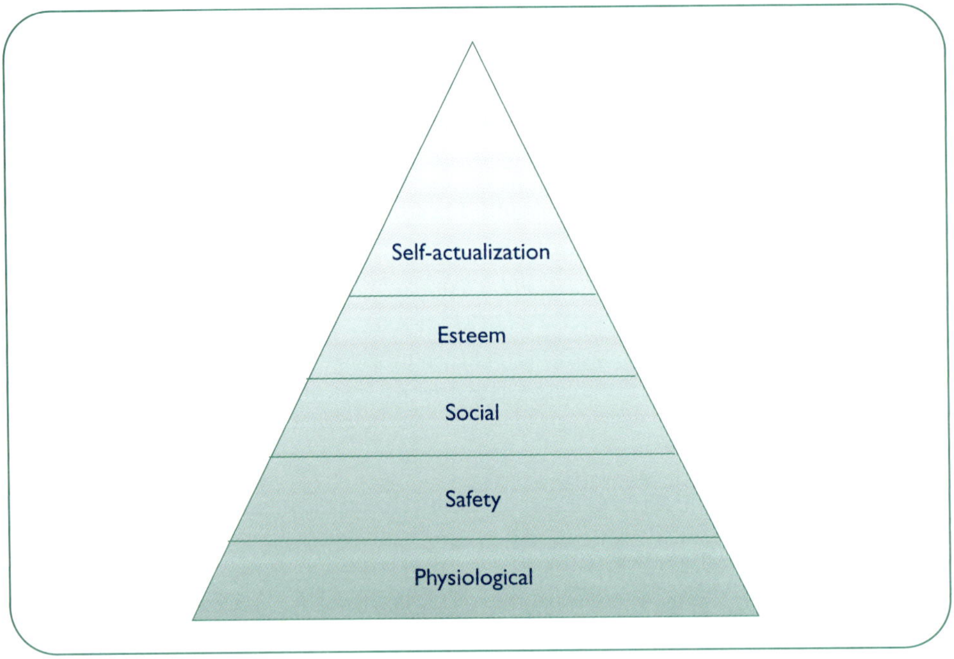

- Self-actualization
- Esteem
- Social
- Safety
- Physiological

Source: A. Maslow, *Motivation and Personality, Second Edition* (New York: Harper & Row, 1970).

Theory X and Theory Y

Douglas McGregor proposed two distinct views of human beings: one basically negative, labeled **Theory X,** and the other basically positive, labeled **Theory Y**.[2] After viewing the way managers dealt with employees, McGregor concluded that a manager's view of the nature of human beings is based on a certain grouping of assumptions and that he or she tends to mold his or her behavior toward employees according to those assumptions.

Under Theory X, four assumptions are held by the manager:

1. Employees inherently dislike work and, whenever possible, will attempt to avoid it.
2. Since employees dislike work, they must be coerced, controlled, or threatened with punishment to achieve desired goals.
3. Employees will avoid responsibilities and seek formal direction whenever possible.
4. Most workers place security above all other factors associated with work and will display little ambition.

Under Theory Y, four contrasting assumptions are held by the manager:

1. Employees can view work as being as natural as rest or play.
2. People will exercise self-direction and self-control if they are committed to the objectives.
3. The average person can learn to accept, even seek, responsibility.
4. The ability to make innovative decisions is widely dispersed throughout the population and is not necessarily the sole province of those in management positions.

What are the motivational implications if you accept McGregor's analysis? The answer is best expressed in the framework presented by Maslow. Theory X assumes that lower-order needs dominate individuals. Theory Y assumes that higher-order needs dominate individuals. McGregor, himself, held to the belief that Theory Y assumptions were more valid than Theory X. Therefore, he proposed ideas such as participation in decision making, responsible and challenging jobs, and good group relations as approaches that would maximize an employee's job motivation.

Unfortunately, there is no evidence to confirm that either set of assumptions is valid or that accepting Theory Y assumptions and altering one's actions accordingly will increase workers' motivation. As will become evident later, either Theory X or Theory Y assumptions may be appropriate in a particular situation.

Two-Factor Theory

The **two-factor theory** (sometimes also called *motivation-hygiene theory*) was proposed by psychologist Frederick Herzberg.[3] In the belief that an individual's relation to work is basic and that one's attitude toward work can very well determine success or failure, Herzberg investigated the question, "What do people want from their jobs?" He asked people to describe, in detail, situations in which they felt exceptionally good or bad about their jobs. These responses were then tabulated and categorized.

From the categorized responses, Herzberg concluded that the replies people gave when they felt good about their jobs were significantly different from the replies given when they felt bad. As seen in Exhibit 4-3, certain characteristics tend to be consistently related to job satisfaction and others to job dissatisfaction.

EXHIBIT 4–3 Herzberg's Two-Factor Theory

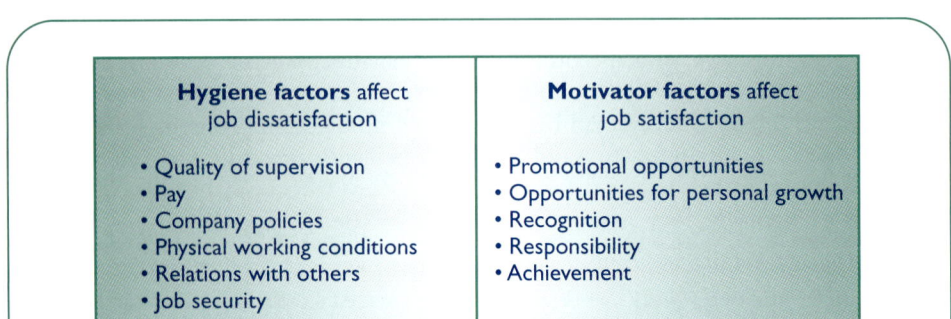

Source: Based on F. Herzberg, "One More Time: How Do You Motivate Employees?" *Harvard Business Review*, January-February 1968, p. 57.

Intrinsic factors, such as advancement, recognition, responsibility, and achievement seem to be related to job satisfaction. Respondents who felt good about their work tended to attribute these factors to themselves. On the other hand, dissatisfied respondents tended to cite extrinsic factors, such as supervision, pay, company policies, and working conditions.

The data suggest, said Herzberg, that the opposite of satisfaction is not dissatisfaction, as was traditionally believed. Removing dissatisfying characteristics from a job does not necessarily make the job satisfying. Herzberg proposed that his findings indicated the existence of a dual continuum: The opposite of "Satisfaction" is "No Satisfaction," and the opposite of "Dissatisfaction" is "No Dissatisfaction."

According to Herzberg, the factors leading to job satisfaction are separate and distinct from those that lead to job dissatisfaction. Therefore, managers who seek to eliminate factors that can create job dissatisfaction may bring about peace but not necessarily motivation. They will be placating their workforce rather than motivating them. As a result, conditions surrounding the job, such as quality of supervision, pay, company policies, physical working conditions, relations with others, and job security were characterized by Herzberg as **hygiene factors**. When they're adequate, people will not be dissatisfied; neither will they be satisfied. If we want to motivate people on their jobs, Herzberg suggested emphasizing factors associated with the work itself or to outcomes directly derived from it, such as promotional opportunities, opportunities for personal growth, recognition, responsibility, and achievement. These are the characteristics that people find intrinsically rewarding.

The two-factor theory is not without detractors. Criticisms of the theory include the following:

1. The procedure that Herzberg used is limited by its methodology. When things are going well, people tend to take credit themselves, but they blame failure on the extrinsic environment.
2. The reliability of Herzberg's methodology is questionable. Raters have to make interpretations, so they may contaminate the findings by interpreting similar responses differently.

3. No overall measure of satisfaction was utilized. A person may dislike part of his or her job yet still find the job acceptable.
4. The theory is inconsistent with previous research. The two-factor theory ignores situational variables.
5. Herzberg assumed a relationship between satisfaction and productivity, but his research methodology looked only at satisfaction, not at productivity. To make such research relevant, one must assume a strong relationship between satisfaction and productivity.

Regardless of criticisms, Herzberg's theory has been widely popularized, and few managers are unfamiliar with his recommendations. As a case in point, much of the initial enthusiasm for vertically expanding jobs to allow workers greater responsibility in planning and controlling their work (which we discuss in Chapter 14) can probably be attributed largely to Herzberg's findings and recommendations.

CONTEMPORARY THEORIES OF MOTIVATION

The previous theories are well known but, unfortunately, have not held up well under close examination. All is not lost, however. Contemporary theories have a reasonable degree of valid supporting documentation. The following theories represent the current state of the art in explaining employee motivation.

McClelland's Theory of Needs

David McClelland and others have proposed three major relevant motives or needs in the workplace. We call this **McClelland's Theory of Needs**[4]:

1. The **need for achievement (nAch)**—The drive to excel, to achieve in relation to a set of standards, to strive to succeed
2. The **need for power (nPow)**—The need to make others behave in a way they would not have behaved otherwise
3. The **need for affiliation (nAff)**—The desire for friendly and close interpersonal relationships

Some people have a compelling drive to succeed, but they are striving for personal achievement rather than the rewards of success. They have a desire to do something better or more efficiently than it has been done before. This drive is the need for achievement. From research into the need for achievement, McClelland found that high achievers differentiate themselves from others by their desire to do things better. They seek situations in which they can attain personal responsibility for finding solutions to problems, receive rapid and unambiguous feedback on their performance, and set moderately challenging goals. They prefer working at a challenging problem and accepting the personal responsibility for success or failure rather than leaving the outcome to chance or the actions of others.

High achievers perform best when they perceive their probability of success as being 0.5, that is, when they estimate that they have a 50–50 chance of success. They dislike gambling with high odds (high probability of failure) because success in such a situation would be more a matter of luck than of ability, and they get no achievement satisfaction from happenstance success. Similarly, they dislike low odds (high probability of success) because there is no challenge to their skills.

They like to set realistic but difficult goals that require stretching themselves a little. When there is an approximately equal chance of success or failure, there is the optimal opportunity to experience feelings of accomplishment and satisfaction from their efforts.

The need for power is the desire to have an impact, to be influential, and to control others. Individuals high in *nPow* enjoy being in charge, strive for influence over others, prefer competitive and status-oriented situations, and tend to be more concerned with gaining prestige and influence over others than with effective performance.

The third need isolated by McClelland is affiliation. This need has received the least attention of researchers. Individuals with a high *nAff* strive for friendship, prefer cooperative situations rather than competitive ones, and desire relationships involving a high degree of mutual understanding.

How do you find out if someone is, for instance, a high achiever? All three motives are typically measured through a projective test in which subjects respond to a set of pictures. Each picture is briefly shown to the subject and then he or she writes a story based on the picture. For example, the picture may show a man sitting at a desk. He is looking pensively at a photograph of a woman and two children that sits at the corner of the desk. The subject will then be asked to write a story describing what is going on, what preceded this situation, what will happen in the future, and the like. The stories become, in effect, projective tests that measure unconscious motives. Each story is scored, and the subject is rated on each of the three motives.

An extensive amount of research indicates that some reasonably well supported predictions can be made on the basis of the relationship between achievement need and job performance. Though less research has been done on power and affiliation needs, there are consistent findings in those areas too. First, individuals with a high need to achieve prefer job situations with personal responsibility, feedback, and an intermediate degree of risk. When these characteristics are prevalent, high achievers will be strongly motivated. The evidence consistently demonstrates, for instance, that high achievers are successful in entrepreneurial activities such as running their own business, managing a self-contained unit within a large organization, and many sales positions. Second, a high need to achieve does not necessarily lead to being a good manager, especially in large organizations. High *nAch* salespeople do not necessarily make good sales managers, and the good manager in a large organization does not typically have a high need to achieve. Third, the needs for affiliation and power tend to be closely related to managerial success. The best managers are high in the need for power and low in their need for affiliation. Last, employees have been successfully trained to stimulate their achievement need. If the job calls for a high achiever, management can select a person with a high *nAch* or develop their own candidate through achievement training.

Goal-Setting Theory

Considerable evidence supports **goal-setting theory**. This theory states that intentions—expressed as goals—can be a major source of work motivation. We can say, with a considerable degree of confidence, that specific goals lead to increased performance and that difficult goals, when accepted, result in higher performance than easy goals.[5]

Specific, difficult-to-achieve goals produce a higher level of output than a generalized goal of "do your best." The specificity of the goal itself acts as an internal stimulus. For instance, when a trucker commits to making 18 round-trip hauls between Baltimore and Washington, D.C., each week, this intention gives him a specific objective to reach for. We can say that, all things being equal, the trucker with a specific goal will outperform his counterpart who operates either with no goals or with the generalized goal of "do your best."

If factors such as ability and acceptance of the goals are held constant, we can also state that the more difficult the goals, the higher the level of performance. However, it's logical to assume that easier goals are more likely to be accepted. But once an employee accepts a hard task, he or she will exert a high level of effort until the goal is achieved, lowered, or abandoned.

If employees have the opportunity to participate in the setting of their own goals, will they try harder? The evidence is mixed regarding the superiority of participation over assigned goals. In some cases, goals that have been set participatively have elicited superior performance; in other cases, individuals have performed best when assigned goals by their boss. A major advantage of participation may be in increasing acceptance of the goal itself as a desirable one to work toward. As we noted earlier, resistance is greatest when goals are difficult. People who participate in goal setting are more likely to accept even a difficult goal than one that is arbitrarily assigned to them, because individuals are more committed to choices in which they have a voice. Thus, although participative goals may have no superiority over assigned goals when acceptance is taken as a given, participation does increase the probability that more difficult goals will be agreed to and acted upon.

Studies testing goal-setting theory have demonstrated the superiority of specific and challenging goals as motivating forces. Although we can't conclude that having employees participate in the goal-setting process is *always* desirable, participation is probably preferable to assignment when you expect resistance to difficult challenges. As an overall conclusion, therefore, we have significant evidence that intentions—as articulated in terms of goals—are a potent motivating force.

The observant reader may have noted what appears to be a contradiction between the findings on achievement motivation and those on goal setting. Is it a contradiction that achievement motivation is stimulated by moderately challenging goals, while goal-setting theory says motivation is maximized by difficult goals? The answer is *no*, for two reasons. First, goal-setting theory deals with people in general. The conclusions on achievement motivation are based only on people who have a high *nAch*, and probably less than 10 to 20 percent of any country's workforce are naturally high achievers. So difficult goals are still recommended for the majority of workers. Second, goal setting's conclusions apply to those who accept, and are committed to, the goals. Difficult goals will lead to higher performance only if they are accepted.

Reinforcement Theory

A counterpoint to goal-setting theory is reinforcement theory. The former is a cognitive approach, proposing that an individual's purposes direct his or her actions. In **reinforcement theory** we have a behavioristic approach, which argues that reinforcement conditions behavior. The two theories are clearly at odds philosophically. Reinforcement theorists see behavior as environmentally caused; internal cognitive events are not matters for concern. What controls behavior are reinforcers—any consequences that, when immediately following a response, increase the probability that the behavior will be repeated.

Reinforcement theory ignores the inner state of the individual and concentrates solely on what happens to a person when he or she takes some action. Because it doesn't concern itself with what initiates behavior, it's not, strictly speaking, a theory of motivation. But it does provide a powerful means of analysis of what controls behavior, and it's for that reason that it's typically considered in discussions of motivation.

Chapter 2 introduced the law of effect (behavior is a function of its consequences) and showed that reinforcers (consequences) condition behavior and help explain how people learn. The law of effect and the concept of reinforcement also help explain motivation. A large amount of research indicates that people will exert more effort on tasks that are reinforced than on tasks that are not.[6] Reinforcement *is* undoubtedly an important influence on work behavior. What people do on their jobs and the amount of effort they allocate to various tasks are affected by the consequences of their behavior. But reinforcement is not the single explanation for differences in employee motivation. Goals, for instance, have an impact on motivation; so, too, do levels of achievement motivation, inequities in rewards, and expectations.

Equity Theory

Employees don't work in a vacuum. They make comparisons. If someone offered you $75,000 a year for your first job on graduation from college, you'd probably grab at the offer and report to work enthused and certainly satisfied with your pay. How would you react, however, if you found out a month or so into the job that a coworker—another recent graduate, your age, with comparable grades from a comparable college—was getting $80,000 a year? You'd probably be upset! Even though, in absolute terms, $75,000 is a lot of money for a new graduate to make (and you know it!), that suddenly isn't the issue. The issue now centers around relative rewards and what you believe is fair. There is ample evidence for us to conclude that employees compare their own job inputs and outcomes with those of others and that inequities can influence the degree of effort that employees exert.[7]

Equity theory says that employees weigh what they put into a job situation (input) against what they get from it (outcome) and then compare their input:outcome ratio with the input:outcome ratio of relevant others. If they perceive their ratio to be equal to that of the relevant others with whom they compare themselves, a state of equity is said to exist. They feel that their situation is fair, that justice prevails. If the ratios are unequal, inequity exists; that is, the employees tend to view themselves as underrewarded or overrewarded. When inequities occur, employees will attempt to correct them.

The referent that employees choose to compare themselves against is an important variable in equity theory. The three referent categories have been classified as "other," "system," and "self." The "other" category includes other individuals with similar jobs in the same organization and also includes friends, neighbors, or professional associates. On the basis of information that employees receive through word of mouth, newspapers, and magazines, on such issues as executive salaries or a recent union contract, employees can compare their pay with that of others.

The "system" category considers organizational pay policies and procedures as well as the administration of this system. It considers organization-wide pay policies, both implied and explicit. Precedents set by the organization in terms of allocation of pay would be a major determinant in this category.

The "self" category refers to input:outcome ratios that are unique to the individual. This category is influenced by criteria such as past jobs or family commitments.

The choice of a particular set of referents is related to the information available about referents as well as to their perceived relevance. Equity theory purports that, when employees envision an inequity, they may make one or more of five choices:

1. Distort either their own or others' inputs or outcomes
2. Behave in some way so as to induce others to change their inputs or outcomes
3. Behave in some way so as to change their own inputs or outcomes
4. Choose a different comparison referent
5. Quit their job

Equity theory recognizes that individuals are concerned not only with the absolute amount of rewards they receive for their efforts but also with the relationship of that amount to what others receive. Inputs such as effort, experience, education, and competence are compared with outcomes such as salary levels, raises, recognition, and other factors. When people perceive an imbalance in their input:outcome ratio relative to others, tension is created. This tension provides the basis for motivation, as people strive for what they perceive as equity and fairness.

Specifically, the theory establishes four propositions relating to inequitable pay:

1. *Given payment by time, overrewarded employees will produce more than equitably paid employees.* Hourly and salaried employees will generate a high quantity or quality of production in order to increase the input side of the ratio and bring about equity.
2. *Given payment by quantity of production, overrewarded employees will produce fewer but higher-quality units than equitably paid employees.* Individuals paid on a piece-rate basis will increase their effort to achieve equity, which can result in greater quality or quantity. Increases in quantity, however, will only increase inequity, since every unit produced results in further overpayment. Therefore, effort is directed toward increasing quality rather than quantity.
3. *Given payment by time, underrewarded employees will produce less or a poorer quality of output.* Effort will be decreased, and the result will be lower productivity or poorer quality of output than that produced by equitably paid employees.
4. *Given payment by quantity of production, underrewarded employees will produce a large number of low-quality units in comparison with equitably paid employees.* Employees on piece-rate pay plans can bring about equity because trading off quality of output for quantity will result in an increase in rewards with little or no increase in contributions.

A review of the research tends to confirm the equity thesis consistently: Employee motivation is influenced significantly by relative rewards as well as by absolute rewards. When employees perceive inequity, they will act to correct the situation. The result might be lower or higher productivity, improved or reduced quality of output, increased absenteeism, or voluntary resignation.

The preceding does not mean that equity theory is without problems. The theory leaves some key issues unclear. For instance, how do employees select who is included in the "other" referent category? How do they define inputs and outcomes? How do they combine and weigh their inputs and outcomes to arrive at totals? When and how do the factors change over time? Regardless of these problems, equity theory has an impressive amount of research support and offers us some important insights into employee motivation.

Expectancy Theory

The most comprehensive explanation of motivation is expectancy theory.[8] Though it, too, has its critics, most of the research evidence supports the theory. Essentially, **expectancy theory** argues that the strength of a tendency to act in a certain way depends on the strength of an expectation that the act will be followed by a given outcome and on the attractiveness of that outcome to the individual. Therefore, it includes these three variables:

1. *Attractiveness*—The importance the individual places on the potential outcome or reward that can be achieved on the job. This variable considers the unsatisfied needs of the individual.
2. *Performance/reward linkage*—The degree to which the individual believes that performing at a particular level will lead to the attainment of a desired outcome.
3. *Effort/performance linkage*—The probability perceived by the individual that exerting a given amount of effort will lead to performance.

Although this theory may sound pretty complex, it really isn't that difficult to visualize. Whether one has the desire to produce at any given time depends on one's particular goals and one's perception of the relative worth of performance as a path to the attainment of those goals.

Exhibit 4-4 is a considerable simplification of expectancy theory but describes its major contentions. The strength of a person's motivation to perform (effort) depends on how strongly she believes she can achieve what she attempts. If she achieves this goal (performance), will she be adequately rewarded and, if she is rewarded by the organization, will the reward satisfy her individual goals? Let us consider the four steps inherent in the theory.

First, what perceived outcomes does the job offer the employee? Outcomes may be positive: pay, security, companionship, trust, fringe benefits, a chance to use talent or skills, or congenial relationships. On the other hand, employees may view the outcomes as negative: fatigue, boredom, frustration, anxiety, harsh supervision, or threat of dismissal. Importantly, reality is not relevant here; the critical issue is what the individual employee perceives the outcome to be, regardless of whether her perceptions are accurate.

Second, how attractive do employees consider these outcomes? Are they valued positively, negatively, or neutrally? This is obviously an internal issue to the individual and considers personal attitudes, personality, and needs. The individual who finds a

EXHIBIT 4–4 Simplified Expectancy Model

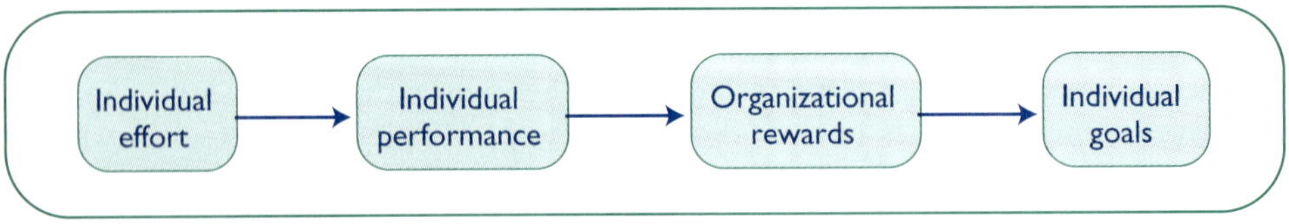

Individual effort → Individual performance → Organizational rewards → Individual goals

particular outcome attractive—that is, positively valued—will prefer attaining it to not attaining it. Others may find it negative and, therefore, prefer not to attain it. Still others may be neutral.

Third, what kind of behavior must the employee exhibit in order to achieve these outcomes? The outcomes are not likely to have any effect on the individual employee's performance unless the employee knows, clearly and unambiguously, what she must do in order to achieve them. For example, what is "doing well" in terms of performance appraisal? On what criteria will the employee's performance be judged?

Fourth and last, how does the employee view her chances of doing what is asked of her? After the employee has considered her own competencies and her ability to control the variables that will determine her success, what probability does she place on successful attainment?

Let's highlight some of the issues that expectancy theory has brought forward. First, it emphasizes payoffs, or rewards. As a result, we have to believe that the rewards the organization is offering align with what the employee wants. It is a theory based on self-interest, wherein each individual seeks to maximize his or her expected satisfaction. We have to be concerned with the attractiveness of rewards; this aspect requires an understanding and knowledge of what value the individual puts on organizational payoffs. We want to reward individuals with the things they value positively. Second, expectancy theory emphasizes expected behaviors. Does the person know what is expected of her and know how she will be appraised? Finally, the theory is concerned with the individual's expectations. What is realistic is irrelevant. The employee's own expectations of performance, reward, and goal satisfaction outcomes, not the objective outcomes themselves, will determine her level of effort.

DON'T FORGET: MOTIVATION THEORIES ARE CULTURE-BOUND!

Most current motivation theories were developed in the United States by Americans and about Americans. So we need to be careful about assuming that recommendations based on motivation theories transfer across cultures.[9] The most blatant pro-American characteristics inherent in these theories is the strong emphasis on individualism and quantity-of-life factors. For instance, both goal-setting and expectancy theories emphasize goal accomplishment as well as rational and individual thought. Let's take a look at how this bias has affected a few of the motivation theories introduced in this chapter.

Maslow's hierarchy of needs theory argues that people start at the physiological level and then move progressively up the hierarchy in this order: physiological, safety, social, esteem, and self-actualization. This hierarchy, if it has any application at all, aligns with American culture. In other cultures, the order of importance might be different. In countries such as Japan, Greece, or Mexico, where uncertainty avoidance characteristics are strong, security needs would be on top of the needs hierarchy. Countries that score high on quality-of-life characteristics—such as Denmark, Sweden, Norway, the Netherlands, and Finland—would have social needs on top. We would predict, for instance, that group work will motivate employees more when the country's culture scores high on the quality-of-life criterion.

Another motivation concept that clearly has a U.S. bias is the achievement need. The view that a high achievement need acts as an internal motivator presupposes two cultural characteristics—a willingness to accept a moderate degree of risk (which excludes countries with strong uncertainty avoidance characteristics) and a concern with performance (which applies almost singularly to countries with strong quantity-of-life characteristics). This combination is found in Anglo-American countries such as the United States, Canada, and Great Britain. On the other hand, these characteristics are almost absent in countries such as Chile and Portugal.

Goal-setting theory is also certainly culture-bound. It is well adapted to the United States because its key components align reasonably well with U.S. culture. It assumes that employees will be reasonably independent (not too high a score on power distance), managers and employees will seek challenging goals (low in uncertainty avoidance), and performance is considered important by both (high in quantity-of-life). Goal-setting theory's recommendations are not likely to increase motivation in countries in which the opposite conditions exist, such as France, Portugal, and Chile.

IMPLICATIONS FOR MANAGERS

Many of the theories presented in this chapter have demonstrated reasonably strong predictive value. How does a manager concerned with motivating employees apply these theories? Certain general suggestions can be extracted for application, at least for managers in North America. For instance, the following recommendations are consistent with the findings in this chapter: (1) recognize individual differences, (2) match people to jobs, (3) use goals, (4) ensure that goals are perceived as attainable, (5) individualize rewards, (6) link rewards to performance, and (7) check the system for equity. These suggestions, of course, would need to be modified to reflect cultural differences outside of North America.

The importance of motivating employees today justifies more specifics than the concepts we've just offered. The next chapter builds on the concepts we've presented here, providing a review of the more popular motivation techniques and programs.

CHAPTER 5

Motivation: From Concepts to Applications

After reading this chapter, you should be able to

1. Identify the four ingredients common to MBO programs
2. Outline the five-step problem-solving model in OB Mod
3. Explain why managers might want to use employee involvement programs
4. Contrast participative management with employee involvement
5. Explain how ESOPs can increase employee motivation
6. Describe the link between skill-based pay plans and motivation theories

It's one thing to be able to recite the principles of motivation theories; it's another to see how, as a manager, you could use them. In this chapter, we focus on how to apply motivation concepts—that is, how to link theories to practice.

In the following pages, we'll review motivation techniques and programs that have gained varying degrees of acceptance in practice. For each of the techniques and programs we review, we'll specifically address how they build on one or more of the motivation theories covered in Chapter 4.

MANAGEMENT BY OBJECTIVES

Goal-setting theory has an impressive base of research support. But as a manager, how do you make goal setting operational? The best answer to that question is: Install a management by objectives (MBO) program.

What Is MBO?

Management by objectives (MBO) emphasizes participatively set goals that are tangible, verifiable, and measurable. It's not a new idea. In fact, it was originally proposed by Peter Drucker nearly 50 years ago as a means of using goals to motivate people rather than to control them.[1] Today, no introduction to basic management concepts would be complete without a discussion of MBO.

MBO's appeal undoubtedly lies in its emphasis on converting overall organizational objectives into specific objectives for organizational units and individual members. MBO operationalizes the concept of objectives by devising a process by which objectives cascade down through the organization. As depicted in Exhibit 5-1, the organization's overall objectives are translated into specific objectives for each succeeding level (that is, divisional, departmental, individual) in the organization. But because lower-unit managers jointly participate in setting their own goals, MBO works from the "bottom up" as well as from the "top down." The result is a hierarchy of objectives that links objectives at one level to those at the next level. And for the individual employee, MBO provides specific personal performance objectives. Each person, therefore, has an identified specific contribution to make to his or her unit's performance. If all the individuals achieve their goals, then their unit's goals will be attained and the organization's overall objectives will become a reality.

There are four ingredients common to MBO programs: goal specificity, participative decision making, an explicit time period, and performance feedback. The objectives in MBO should be concise statements of expected accomplishments. It is not enough, for example, merely to state a desire to cut costs, improve service, or increase quality. Such desires have to be converted into tangible objectives that can be measured and evaluated. To cut departmental costs *by 7 percent*, to improve service by ensuring that all telephone orders are processed *within 24 hours of receipt*, or to increase quality by keeping returns to *less than 1 percent of sales* are examples of specific objectives.

EXHIBIT 5–1 Cascading of Objectives

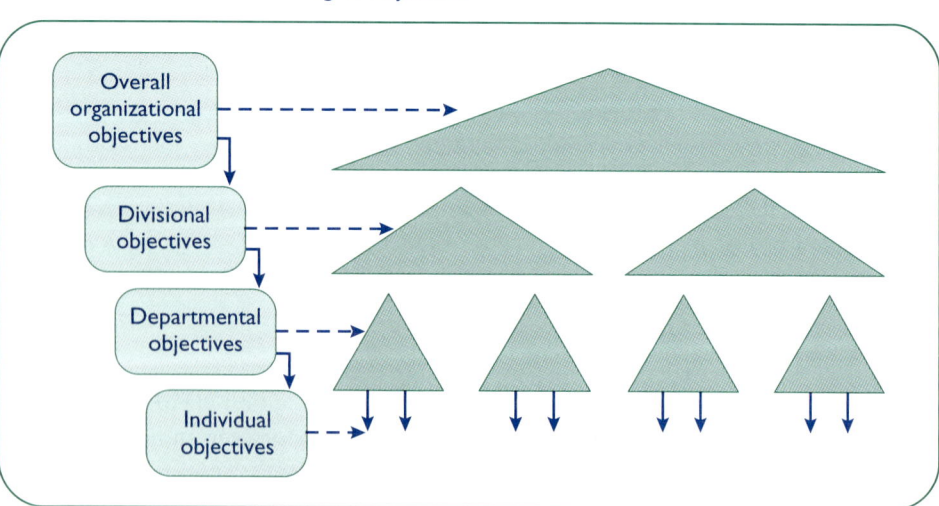

The objectives in MBO are not unilaterally set by the boss and then assigned to employees. MBO replaces imposed goals with participatively determined goals. The manager and employee jointly choose the goals and agree on how they will be measured.

Each objective has a specific time period in which it is to be completed. Typically that period is 3 months, 6 months, or 1 year. So managers and employees have not only specific objectives but also stipulated periods in which to accomplish them.

The final ingredient in an MBO program is feedback on performance. MBO seeks to give continuous feedback on progress toward goals so that individuals can monitor and correct their own actions. Continuous feedback, supplemented by more formal periodic managerial evaluations, takes place at the top of the organization as well as at the bottom. The vice president of sales, for instance, has objectives for overall sales and for each of his or her major products. He or she will monitor ongoing sales reports to determine progress toward the sales division's objectives. Similarly, district sales managers have objectives, as does each salesperson in the field. Feedback in terms of sales and performance is provided to let all these people know how they are doing. At formal appraisal meetings, managers and their employees can review progress toward goals and further feedback can be provided.

Linking MBO and Goal-Setting Theory

Goal-setting theory demonstrates that hard goals result in a higher level of individual performance than do easy goals, that specific hard goals result in higher levels of performance than do no goals at all or the generalized goal of "do your best," and that feedback on one's performance leads to higher performance. Compare these findings with MBO.

MBO directly advocates specific goals and feedback. MBO implies, rather than explicitly states, that goals must be perceived as feasible. Consistent with goal setting, MBO would be most effective when the goals are difficult enough to require the person to do some stretching.

The only area of possible disagreement between MBO and goal-setting theory is related to the issue of participation—MBO strongly advocates it, whereas goal-setting theory demonstrates that assigning goals to individuals frequently works just as well. The major benefit to using participation, however, is that it increases the likelihood that individuals will accept more difficult goals.

MBO in Practice

You'll find MBO programs in many business, health care, educational, government, and nonprofit organizations. Most organizations, in fact, make some use of MBO features because managers find that goals give people direction and it doesn't make sense to establish goals and then fail to evaluate whether or not they're being achieved.

MBO's popularity should not be construed to mean that it always works. There are a number of documented cases in which MBO was implemented but failed to meet management's expectations. A close look at those cases, however, indicates that the problems rarely lie with MBO's basic components. Rather, the culprits tend to be factors such as unrealistic expectations regarding results, lack of commitment by top management, and an inability or unwillingness by management to allocate rewards based on goal accomplishment.[2] Nevertheless, MBO provides managers with the vehicle for implementing goal-setting theory.

BEHAVIOR MODIFICATION

A now-classic study took place almost 30 years ago with freight packers at Emery Air Freight (now part of FedEx).[3] Emery's management wanted packers to aggregate shipments into freight containers rather than handling many separate items. Management believed that using containers would save money. When packers were asked what percentage of shipments they put in containers, the standard reply was 90 percent. An analysis by Emery found, however, that the rate of container use was only 45 percent. In order to encourage employees to use containers, management established a program of feedback and positive reinforcements. Each packer was instructed to keep a checklist of his or her daily packings, both in containers and not. At the end of each day, the packer computed his or her rate of container use. Almost unbelievably, container use jumped to more than 90 percent on the first day of the program and held to that level. Emery reported that this simple program of feedback and positive reinforcements saved the company millions of dollars.

This program at Emery Air Freight illustrates the use of behavior modification, or what has become more popularly called **OB Mod**.[4] It represents the application of reinforcement theory to individuals in the work setting.

What Is OB Mod?

The typical OB Mod program, as shown in Exhibit 5-2, follows a five-step problem-solving model: (1) Identify performance-related behaviors; (2) measure the behaviors; (3) identify behavioral contingencies; (4) develop and implement an intervention strategy; and (5) evaluate performance improvement.[5]

Everything an employee does on his or her job is not equally important in terms of performance outcomes. The first step in OB Mod, therefore, is to identify the critical behaviors that have a significant impact on the employee's job performance. These are those 5 to 10 percent of behaviors that may account for up to 70 or 80 percent of each employee's performance. Freight packers at Emery Air Freight using containers whenever possible is an example of a critical behavior.

The second step requires the manager to develop some baseline performance information; that is, the number of times the identified behavior is occurring under present conditions. In our freight-packing example at Emery, this would have been that 45 percent of all shipments were put in containers.

The third step is to perform a functional analysis to identify the behavioral contingencies or consequences of performance. This step tells the manager which cues emit the behavior and the consequences that are currently maintaining it. At Emery Air Freight, social norms and the greater difficulty in packing containers were the cues. Those factors encouraged the practice of packing items separately. Moreover, the consequences for continuing this behavior, before the OB Mod intervention, were social acceptance and escaping more demanding work.

Once the functional analysis is complete, the manager is ready to develop and implement an intervention strategy to strengthen desirable performance behaviors

EXHIBIT 5–2 Steps in OB Mod

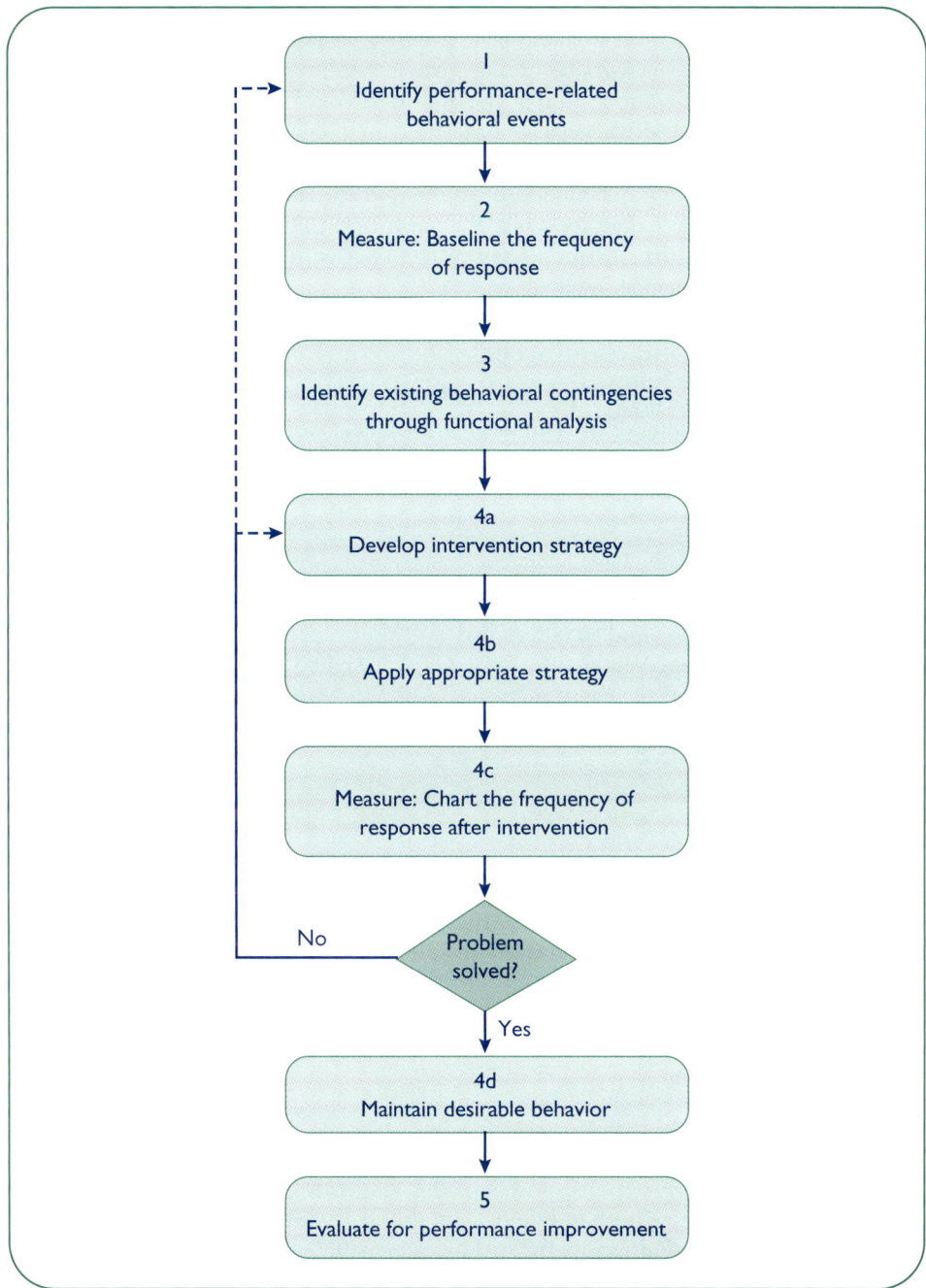

Source: Adapted by permission of the publisher from *Personnel,* July–August 1974. Fred Luthans, American Management Association, New York. All rights reserved.

and weaken undesirable behaviors. The appropriate strategy will entail changing some element of the performance/reward linkage—structure, processes, technology, groups, or the task—with the goal of making high-level performance more rewarding. In the Emery example, the work technology was altered to require keeping a checklist. The checklist plus the computation at the end of the day of the rate of container use acted to reinforce the desired behavior of using containers.

The final step in OB Mod is to evaluate performance improvement. In the Emery intervention, the immediate improvement in the rate of container use demonstrated that behavioral change took place. That it rose to 90 percent and held at that level further indicates that learning took place. That is, the employees underwent a relatively permanent change in behavior.

Linking OB Mod and Reinforcement Theory

Reinforcement theory relies on positive reinforcement, shaping, and recognizing the impact of different schedules of reinforcement on behavior. OB Mod uses these concepts to provide managers with a powerful and proven means for changing employee behavior.

OB Mod in Practice

OB Mod has been used to improve employee productivity and to reduce errors, absenteeism, tardiness, and accident rates.[6] Major companies such as General Electric, General Mills, Weyerhauser, and Xerox have had considerable success using OB Mod. And a general review of numerous OB Mod programs found that, on average, they produced a 17 percent improvement in employee performance.[7]

EMPLOYEE RECOGNITION PROGRAMS

Laura Schendell makes only $7.25 an hour working at her fast-food job in Pensacola, Florida. And the job, itself, isn't very challenging or interesting. Yet Laura talks enthusiastically about her job, her boss, and the company that employs her. "What I like is the fact that Guy [her supervisor] appreciates the effort I make. He compliments me regularly in front of the other people on my shift. And I've been chosen "Employee of the Month" twice in the past 6 months. Did you see my picture on that plaque on the wall?"

Organizations are increasingly recognizing what Laura Schendell is acknowledging: Recognition can be a potent motivator.

What Are Employee Recognition Programs?

Employee recognition programs can take numerous forms. The best ones use multiple sources and recognize both individual and group accomplishments.

Examples of recognition might include personally congratulating an employee in private for a good job; sending a handwritten note or e-mail message acknowledging something positive the employee has done; a write-up in the company magazine; or formal award ceremonies at which trophies and plaques are handed out to individuals or teams. Some organizations—including NASA, Walt Disney Imagineering, BMC Software, and Nissan—actively use their public relations capabilities to widely publicize the outstanding achievements of their technical and design teams.

Linking Recognition Programs and Reinforcement Theory

A few years back, 1,500 employees were surveyed in a variety of work settings to find out what they considered to be the most powerful workplace motivator. Their response? Recognition, recognition, and more recognition![8]

Consistent with reinforcement theory, rewarding a behavior with recognition immediately following that behavior is likely to encourage its repetition. And, as noted previously, that recognition can take many forms. However, to maximize the motivation potential of recognition, it's probably best to publicly communicate who recipients are and why they are being recognized. Prudential Insurance, for instance, has an extensive formal recognition program.[9] Prudential managers are encouraged to carefully tailor recognition and rewards to their departmental objectives; to promote both the nomination and reward process in company newsletters, e-mails, and on Intranet sites; and to publicly provide detailed explanations of winners' accomplishments.

Employee Recognition Programs in Practice

In today's highly competitive global economy, most organizations are under severe cost pressures. That makes recognition programs particularly attractive. In contrast to most other motivators, recognizing an employee's superior performance often costs little or no money. Maybe that's why a survey of 3,000 employers found that two-thirds use or plan to use special recognition awards.[10]

One of the most well-known and widely used recognition devices is the use of suggestion systems. Employees offer suggestions for improving processes or cutting costs and are recognized with small cash awards. The Japanese have been especially effective at making suggestion systems work. For instance, a typical high-performing Japanese plant in the auto components business generates 47 suggestions per employee a year and pays approximately the equivalent of U.S. $35 per suggestion. In contrast, a comparable Western factory generates about one suggestion per employee per year, but pays out $90 per suggestion.[11]

EMPLOYEE INVOLVEMENT PROGRAMS

What do the following examples have in common? At a General Electric aircraft assembly plant in Durham, North Carolina, the 170 employees are organized into nine self-directed teams. They basically have no boss. Decisions such as who does what work; how to balance training, vacations, and overtime against workflow; how to make the manufacturing process more efficient; and how to handle teammates who slack off are all made within the team. At Childress Buick, an automobile dealer in Phoenix, salespeople are allowed to negotiate and finalize deals with customers without any approval from management. Finally, the laws of Germany, France, Denmark, Sweden, and Austria require companies to have elected representatives from their employee groups as members of their board of directors. The common element in these examples is that they all illustrate employee involvement programs.

What Is Employee Involvement?

Employee involvement has become a convenient catchall term to cover a variety of techniques.[12] For instance, it encompasses popular ideas such as employee participation or participative management, workplace democracy, empowerment, and employee ownership. Our position is that, although each of these ideas has some unique characteristics, they all have a common core—that of employee involvement.

So what specifically do we mean by **employee involvement?** We define it as a participative process that uses the entire capacity of employees and is designed to encourage increased commitment to the organization's success.[13] The underlying logic is that involving workers in decisions that will affect them and increasing their autonomy and control over their work lives will make employees more motivated, more committed to the organization, more productive, and more satisfied with their jobs.

Does that mean that *participation* and *employee involvement* are synonyms? No. *Participation* is a more limited term. It's a subset within the larger framework of employee involvement. Each of the employee involvement programs we'll describe include some form of employee participation, but the term *participation*, per se, is too narrow and limiting.

Examples of Employee Involvement Programs

In this section, we'll describe three forms of employee involvement: participative management, representative participation, and employee stock ownership plans.

Participative Management The distinct characteristic common to all **participative management** programs is the use of joint decision making. That is, employees actually share a significant degree of decision-making power with their immediate superiors.

Participative management has, at times, been promoted as a panacea for poor morale and low productivity. One author even argued that participative management is an ethical imperative.[14] But participative management is not appropriate for every organization or every work unit. For it to work, there must be adequate time to participate, the issues in which employees get involved must be relevant to them, employees must have the ability (intelligence, technical knowledge, communication skills) to participate, and the organization's culture must support employee involvement.[15]

Dozens of studies have been conducted on the participation/performance relationship. The findings, however, are mixed.[16] When the research is looked at carefully, it appears that participation typically has only a modest influence on variables such as employee productivity, motivation, and job satisfaction. Of course, that conclusion doesn't mean that the use of participative management can't be beneficial under the right conditions. What it says, however, is that the use of participation is no sure means for improving employee performance.

Representative Participation Almost every country in Western Europe has some type of legislation requiring companies to practice **representative participation**. That is, rather than participate directly in decisions, workers are represented by a small group of employees who actually participate. Representative participation has been called "the most widely legislated form of employee involvement around the world."[17]

The goal of representative participation is to redistribute power within an organization, putting labor on a more equal footing with the interests of management and stockholders.

The two most common forms of representative participation are works councils and board representatives. **Works councils** link employees with management. They are groups of nominated or elected employees who must be consulted when management makes decisions involving personnel. For example, in the Netherlands, if a Dutch company is taken over by another firm, the former's works council must be informed at an early stage, and if the council objects, it has 30 days to seek a court injunction to stop the takeover. **Board representatives** are employees who sit on a company's board of directors and represent the interests of the firm's employees. In some countries, large companies may be legally required to make sure that employee representatives have the same number of board seats as stockholder representatives.

The overall influence of representative participation on working employees seems to be minimal. For instance, the evidence suggests that works councils are dominated by management and have little impact on employees or the organization. And, although this form of employee involvement might increase the motivation and satisfaction of the individuals who are doing the representing, there is little evidence that this effect trickles down to the operating employees whom they represent. Overall, "the greatest value of representative participation is symbolic. If one is interested in changing employee attitudes or in improving organizational performance, representative participation would be a poor choice."[18]

Employee Stock Ownership Plans The final employee involvement approach we'll discuss is **employee stock ownership plans (ESOPs)**. Employee stock ownership plans are company-established benefit plans in which employees acquire stock as part of their benefits. United Airlines, Publix Supermarkets, Graybar Electric, and window manufacturer Andersen Corp. are four examples of companies that are more than 50 percent owned by their employees through ESOPs.[19]

In the typical ESOP, an employee stock ownership trust is created. Companies contribute either stock or cash to buy stock for the trust and allocate the stock to employees. Although employees hold stock in their company, they usually cannot take physical possession of their shares or sell them as long as they're still employed at the company.

The research on ESOPs indicates that they increase employee satisfaction. In addition, they frequently result in improved organizational performance. For instance, one study found that ESOPs averaged nearly 7 percent higher shareholder returns over the 4 years after the ESOP was established than market returns of similar companies without an ESOP.[20]

Linking Employee Involvement Programs and Motivation Theories

Employee involvement draws on several motivation theories discussed in Chapter 4. For instance, Theory Y is consistent with participative management, and Theory X aligns with the more traditional autocratic style of managing people. In terms of the two-factor theory, employee involvement programs could provide employees with intrinsic motivation by increasing opportunities for growth, responsibility, and involvement in the work itself.

Employee Involvement Programs in Practice

Germany, France, the Netherlands, and the Scandinavian countries have firmly established the principle of industrial democracy in Europe, and other nations, including Japan and Israel, have traditionally practiced some form of representative participation for decades. Participative management and representative participation were much slower to gain ground in North American organizations. But nowadays, employee involvement programs that stress participation have become the norm. Some managers continue to resist sharing decision-making power, but the pressure is on managers to give up their autocratic decision-making style in favor of a more participative, supportive, coaching-like role.

What about ESOPs? They are becoming a popular form of employee involvement program. They've grown from just a handful 30 years ago to over 10,000 now, covering more than 10 million employees.[21]

VARIABLE-PAY PROGRAMS

For more than 30 years, Nucor Steel has had an incentive compensation plan in place that pays bonuses of as much as 150 percent of base to employees. Bonuses are calculated on the basis of the company's profitability. Rick Benson, an investment banker with Merrill Lynch, earned $1.4 million in 2001—more than six times his base salary. How did he make so much money? He gets performance bonuses based on the profitability of his department. C. Michael Armstrong, Chairman and CEO of AT&T, saw his annual salary and bonus drop 29 percent (from $4.59 million to $3.26 million) in 2000 because his pay package is closely tied to his company's performance and 2000 was not a good year for AT&T. The common thread in each of these examples is that they all illustrate variable-pay programs.

What Are Variable-Pay Programs?

Piece-rate plans, wage incentives, profit sharing, bonuses, and gainsharing are all forms of **variable-pay programs**. What differentiates these forms of compensation from more traditional programs is that a person is paid not only for time on the job or seniority; a portion of an employee's pay is based on some individual or organizational measure of performance or both. Unlike more traditional base-pay programs, variable pay is not an annuity. There is no guarantee that just because you made $60,000 last year, you'll make the same amount this year. With variable pay, earnings fluctuate with the measure of performance.

It is precisely the fluctuation in variable pay that has made these programs attractive to management. It turns part of an organization's fixed labor costs into a variable cost, thereby reducing expenses when performance declines. In addition, when pay is tied to performance, earnings recognize contribution rather than being a form of entitlement. Low performers find, over time, that their pay stagnates, and high performers enjoy pay increases commensurate with their contributions.

Four of the more widely used of the variable-pay programs are piece-rate wages, bonuses, profit sharing, and gainsharing. Piece-rate wages have been around for nearly a century. They have long been popular as a means for compensating production workers. In **piece-rate pay plans**, workers are paid a fixed sum for each unit of production completed. A system in which an employee gets no base salary and is paid only for what he or she produces is a pure piece-rate plan. People who work ballparks selling peanuts and soda pop frequently are paid this way. They might, for instance, get to keep 50 cents for every bag of peanuts they sell. If they sell 200 bags during a game, they make $100. If they sell only 40 bags, their take is a mere $20. The harder they work and the more peanuts they sell, the more they earn. Many organizations use a modified piece-rate plan, in which employees earn a base hourly wage plus a piece-rate differential. So a zipper installer at a Levi Strauss plant might be paid $8 an hour plus $.10 per zipper. Such modified plans provide a floor under an employee's earnings while still offering a productivity incentive.

Bonuses can be paid exclusively to executives or to all employees. For instance, annual bonuses in the millions of dollars are not uncommon in American corporations. Steve Jobs, CEO at Apple Computer, received a $90 million bonus in 2000 for his success in turning the company's financial fortunes around. Increasingly, bonus plans are taking on a larger net within organizations to include lower-ranking employees. At Eastman Chemical Co., for example, all 18,000 employees have the opportunity to earn a bonus equal to 30 percent of their annual pay, based on how much the company earns on its cost of invested capital.

Profit-sharing plans are organization-wide programs that distribute compensation based on some established formula designed around a company's profitability. These can be direct cash outlays or, particularly in the case of top managers, allocated as stock options. For example, executives such as Michael Eisner, the CEO at Disney, can earn over $200 million in one year. Almost all of it would come from cashing in stock options previously granted on the basis of company profit performance.

The variable-pay program that has gotten the most attention in recent years is undoubtedly **gainsharing**. This is a formula-based group incentive plan. Improvements in group productivity—from one period to another—determine the total amount of money to be allocated. And the division of productivity savings can be split between the company and employees in any number of ways, but 50-50 is pretty typical.

Isn't gainsharing the same thing as profit sharing? They're similar but not the same thing. By focusing on productivity gains rather than on profits, gainsharing rewards specific behaviors that are less influenced by external factors than profits are. Employees in a gainsharing plan can receive incentive awards even when the organization isn't profitable.

Do variable-pay programs work? Do they increase motivation and productivity? The answer is a qualified "yes." Gainsharing, for example, has been found to improve productivity in most cases and often has a positive impact on employee attitudes. One expert says gainsharing boosts employee productivity between 3 and 26 percent.[22] An American Management Association study of 83 companies that used gainsharing also found, on average, that grievances dropped 83 percent, absences fell 84 percent, and lost-time accidents decreased by 69 percent.[23]

Linking Variable-Pay Programs and Expectancy Theory

Variable pay is compatible with expectancy theory predictions. Specifically, individuals should perceive a strong relationship between their performance and the rewards they receive if motivation is to be maximized. If rewards are allocated completely on nonperformance factors such as seniority or job title, employees are likely to reduce their effort.

A strong case nowadays can be made for using group and organization-wide incentives. They reinforce and encourage employees to sublimate personal goals for the best interests of their work unit or the organization. Group-based performance incentives are also a natural extension for organizations that are trying to build a strong team ethic. Linking rewards to team performance encourages employees to make extra efforts to help their team succeed.

Variable-Pay Programs in Practice

Variable pay is a concept that is rapidly replacing the annual cost-of-living raise. One reason, as cited above, is its motivational power—but don't ignore the cost implications. Bonuses, gainsharing, and other variable-reward programs avoid the fixed expense of permanent salary boosts.

Pay-for-performance has been "in" for compensating managers for several decades. The new trend has been expanding this practice to nonmanagerial employees. IBM, Wal-Mart, Pizza Hut, Cigna Corp., and John Deere are just a few examples of companies using variable pay with rank-and-file employees. In the United States, for example, 72 percent of all companies had some form of variable-pay plan for nonexecutives in the year 2000, as compared with 47 percent in 1990 and less than 30 percent in 1985.[24]

Gainsharing's popularity seems to be narrowly focused among large, unionized manufacturing companies.[25] It's being used in about 2,000 companies, including major firms such as Bell & Howell, American Safety Razor, Champion Spark Plug, Cincinnati Milacron, Eaton, Firestone Tire, Hooker Chemical, and Mead Paper.

SKILL-BASED PAY PLANS

Organizations hire people for their skills, then typically put them in jobs and pay them on the basis of their job title or rank. So the director of corporate sales earns $150,000 a year, the regional sales managers make $90,000, and the district sales managers get $70,000. But if organizations hire people because of their competencies, why don't they pay them for those same competencies? Some organizations do.

What Are Skill-Based Pay Plans?

Skill-based pay is an alternative to job-based pay. Rather than having an individual's job title define his or her pay category, **skill-based pay** (sometimes called *competency-based pay*) sets pay levels on the basis of how many skills employees have or how many jobs they can do.[26] For instance, workers at American Steel & Wire can boost their annual salaries by up to $12,480 by acquiring as many as 10 skills, and Frito-Lay ties its compensation for managers to their progress in developing skills in leadership, group process facilitation, and communications.

What's the appeal of skill-based pay plans? From management's perspective: flexibility. Filling staffing needs is easier when employee skills are interchangeable. This is particularly true today, as many organizations cut the size of their workforce. Downsizing requires more generalists and fewer specialists. Skill-based pay encourages employees to acquire a broad range of skills. But there are other benefits to skill-based pay. It facilitates communication throughout the organization because people gain a better understanding of others' jobs. It lessens dysfunctional "protection of territory" behavior. For instance, where skill-based pay exists, you're less likely to hear the phrase, "It's not my job!" Skill-based pay also helps meet the needs of ambitious employees who confront minimal advancement opportunities.

These people can increase their earnings and knowledge without a promotion in job title.

What's the downside of skill-based pay? People can "top out"—learning all the skills the program calls for them to learn. Topping out can frustrate employees after they've become challenged by an environment of learning, growth, and continual pay raises. Skills can also become obsolete. Finally, skill-based plans don't address level of performance, only whether someone can perform the skill. For some skills—such as checking quality or leading a team—level of performance may be equivocal. Although it's possible to assess how well employees perform each of the skills and combine that assessment with a skill-based plan, doing so is not an inherent part of skill-based pay.

Linking Skill-Based Pay Plans to Motivation Theories

Skill-based pay plans are consistent with several motivation theories. Because they encourage employees to learn, expand their skills, and grow, they are consistent with Maslow's hierarchy of needs theory. Among employees whose lower-order needs are substantially satisfied, the opportunity to experience growth can be a motivator.

Paying people to expand their skill levels is also consistent with research on the achievement need. High achievers have a compelling drive to do things better or more efficiently. By learning new skills or improving the skills they already hold, high achievers will find their jobs more challenging.

There is also a link between reinforcement theory and skill-based pay. Skill-based pay encourages employees to develop their flexibility, to continue to learn, to cross-train, to be generalists rather than specialists, and to work cooperatively with others in the organization. To the degree that management wants employees to demonstrate such behaviors, skill-based pay should act as a reinforcer.

Skill-based pay may also have equity implications. When employees make their input:outcome comparisons, skills may provide a fairer input criterion for determining pay than factors such as seniority or education. To the degree that employees perceive skills as the critical variable in job performance, the use of skill-based pay may increase the perception of equity and help optimize employee motivation.

Skill-Based Pay in Practice

A number of studies have investigated the use and effectiveness of skill-based pay. The overall conclusion, based on these studies, is that use of skill-based pay is expanding and that it generally leads to higher employee performance and satisfaction. For instance, approximately 60 percent of *Fortune* 1000 firms are using some form of skill-based pay.[27] And a survey of 27 companies that pay employees for learning extra skills found that 70 to 88 percent reported higher job satisfaction, product quality, or productivity. Some 70 to 75 percent cited lower operating costs or lower turnover.[28]

Skilled-based pay appears to be an idea whose time has come. As one expert noted, "Slowly, but surely, we're becoming a skill-based society where your market value is tied to what you can do and what your skill set is. In this new world where skills and knowledge are what really counts, it doesn't make sense to treat people as jobholders. It makes sense to treat them as people with specific skills and to pay them for those skills."[29]

IMPLICATIONS FOR MANAGERS

Organizations have introduced a number of programs designed to increase employee motivation, productivity, and satisfaction. Importantly, these programs are grounded on basic motivation theories.

It's easy to criticize educators and researchers for their focus on building theories. Students and practitioners often think that these theories are unrealistic or irrelevant to solving real-life problems. This chapter makes a good rebuttal to those critics. It illustrates how tens of thousands of organizations and millions of managers in countries around the globe are using motivation theories to build practical incentive programs.

The six motivation programs we discussed in this chapter are not applicable to every organization or every manager's needs. But an understanding of these programs will help you design internal systems that can increase employee productivity and satisfaction.

CHAPTER 6

Individual Decision Making

After reading this chapter, you should be able to

1. Explain the six-step rational decision-making model and its assumptions
2. Identify the key components in the three-component model of creativity
3. Describe actions of the boundedly rational decision maker
4. Define heuristics and explain how they bias decisions
5. Explain escalation of commitment
6. Identify four decision-making styles
7. Explain the implications of stages of moral development to decision making

Individuals in organizations make decisions. Top managers, for instance, determine their organization's goals, what products or services to offer, how best to organize corporate headquarters, or where to locate a new manufacturing plant. Middle- and lower-level managers determine production schedules, select new employees, and decide how pay raises are to be allocated. The making of decisions, however, is not the sole province of managers. Nonmanagerial employees also make decisions that affect their jobs and the organizations they work for. The more obvious of these decisions might include whether to come to work on any given day, how much effort to put forward once at work, and whether to comply with a request made by the boss.

So all individuals in every organization regularly engage in **decision making**; that is, they make choices from among two or more alternatives. Undoubtedly, many of these choices are almost reflex actions undertaken with little conscious thought. For example, the boss asks you to complete a certain report by the end of the day and you comply, assuming the request is reasonable. In such instances, choices are still being made even though they don't require much thought. But when individuals confront new or important decisions, they can be expected to reason them out thoughtfully. Alternatives will be developed. Pros and cons will be weighed. The result is that what people do on their jobs is influenced by their decision processes.

In this chapter, we focus on two different approaches to understanding decision making. First we describe how decisions *should* be made. Then, we review a large body of evidence to show you how decisions *actually* are made in organizations. We conclude by offering some specific suggestions on how managers can improve their decision-making effectiveness.

HOW SHOULD DECISIONS BE MADE?

Let's begin by describing how individuals should behave in order to maximize a certain outcome. We call this the rational decision-making process.

The Rational Decision-Making Process

The optimizing decision maker is **rational**. That is, he or she makes consistent, value-maximizing choices within specified constraints. These choices are made following a six-step model. Specific assumptions underlie this model.

The Rational Model The six steps in the rational decision-making model are listed in Exhibit 6-1.[1] The model begins by *defining the problem*. A problem exists when there is a discrepancy between an existing and a desired state of affairs. If you calculate your monthly expenses and find you're spending $50 more than you allocated in your budget, you have defined a problem. Many poor decisions can be traced to the decision maker's overlooking a problem or incorrectly defining the problem.

Once a decision maker has defined the problem, he or she needs to *identify the decision criteria* that will be important in solving the problem. In this step, the decision maker is determining what's relevant in making the decision. This step brings the decision maker's interests, values, and personal preferences into the process. Identifying criteria is important because what one person thinks is relevant, another may not. Also keep in mind that any factors not identified in this step are considered as irrelevant to the decision maker.

The criteria identified are rarely all equal in importance. So the third step requires the decision-maker to *weight the previously identified criteria* in order to give them correct priority in the decision.

The fourth step requires the decision maker to *generate possible alternatives* that could succeed in resolving the problem. No attempt is made in this step to appraise these alternatives, only to list them.

Once the alternatives have been generated, the decision maker must critically analyze and evaluate each one. This is done by *rating each alternative on each criterion*.

EXHIBIT 6–1   The Six-Step Rational Decision-Making Model

1. Define the problem
2. Identify decision criteria
3. Weight the criteria
4. Generate alternatives
5. Rate each alternative on each criterion
6. Compute the optimal decision

The strengths and weaknesses of each alternative become evident as they are compared with the criteria and weights established in the second and third steps.

The final step in this model requires *computing the optimal decision*. This is done by evaluating each alternative against the weighted criteria and selecting the alternative with the highest total score.

Assumptions of the Model   The rational decision-making model we just described contains a number of assumptions. Let's briefly outline them.

1. *Problem clarity*. The problem is clear and unambiguous. The decision maker is assumed to have complete information regarding the decision situation.
2. *Known options*. It is assumed that the decision maker can identify all the relevant criteria and can list all the viable alternatives. Further, the decision maker is aware of all the possible consequences of each alternative.
3. *Clear preferences*. Rationality assumes that the criteria and alternatives can be ranked and weighted to reflect their importance.
4. *Constant preferences*. It's assumed that the specific decision criteria are constant and that the weights assigned to them are stable over time.
5. *No time or cost constraints*. The rational decision maker can obtain full information about criteria and alternatives because it's assumed that there are no time or cost constraints.
6. *Maximum payoff*. The rational decision maker will choose the alternative that yields the highest perceived value.

Improving Creativity in Decision Making

The rational decision maker needs **creativity**: that is, the ability to produce novel and useful ideas. These are ideas that are different from what's been done before but that are also appropriate to the problem or opportunity presented. Why is creativity important to decision making? It allows the decision maker to appraise and understand the problem more fully, including seeing problems others can't see. However, creativity's most obvious value is in helping the decision maker identify all viable alternatives.

Creative Potential   Most people have creative potential that they can use when confronted with a decision-making problem. But to unleash that potential, they have to get out of the psychological ruts most of us get into and learn how to think about a problem in divergent ways.

We can start with the obvious. People differ in their inherent creativity. Einstein, Edison, Picasso, and Mozart were individuals of exceptional creativity. Not surprisingly, exceptional creativity is scarce. A study of lifetime creativity of 461 men and women found that fewer than 1 percent were exceptionally creative.[2] But 10 percent were highly creative, and about 60 percent were somewhat creative. This suggests that most of us have creative potential, if we can learn to unleash it.

Three-Component Model of Creativity   Given that most people have the capacity to be at least moderately creative, what can individuals and organizations do to stimulate employee creativity? The best answer to this question lies in the **three-component model of creativity**.[3] Based on an extensive body of research, this model proposes that individual creativity essentially requires expertise, creative-thinking skills, and intrinsic task motivation (see Exhibit 6-2). Studies confirm that the higher the level of each of these three components, the higher the creativity is.

Expertise is the foundation of all creative work. Picasso's understanding of art and Einstein's knowledge of physics were necessary conditions for them to be able to make creative contributions to their fields. And you wouldn't expect someone with a minimal knowledge of programming to be very creative as a software engineer. The potential for creativity is enhanced when individuals have abilities, knowledge, proficiencies, and similar expertise in their fields of endeavor.

The second component is *creative-thinking skills*. This encompasses personality characteristics associated with creativity, the ability to use analogies, as well as the talent to see the familiar in a different light. For instance, the following individual traits have been found to be associated with the development of creative ideas: intelligence, independence, self-confidence, risk-taking, an internal locus of control, tolerance for ambiguity, and perseverance in the face of frustration.[4] The effective use of analogies allows decision makers to apply an idea from one context to another. One of the most famous examples in which analogy resulted in a creative breakthrough was Alexander Graham Bell's observation that it might be possible to take concepts that operate in the ear and apply them to his "talking box." He noticed that the bones in the ear are operated by a delicate, thin membrane. He wondered why, then, a thicker and stronger piece of membrane shouldn't be able to move a piece of steel. Out of that analogy, the telephone was conceived. Of course, some people have developed their skill at being able to see problems a new way. They're able to make the strange familiar and the familiar strange.[5] For instance, most of us think of hens laying eggs. But how many of us have considered that a hen is only an egg's way of making another egg?

The final component in our model is *intrinsic task motivation*. This is the desire to work on something because it's interesting, involving, exciting, satisfying, or per-

EXHIBIT 6–2   The Three Components of Creativity

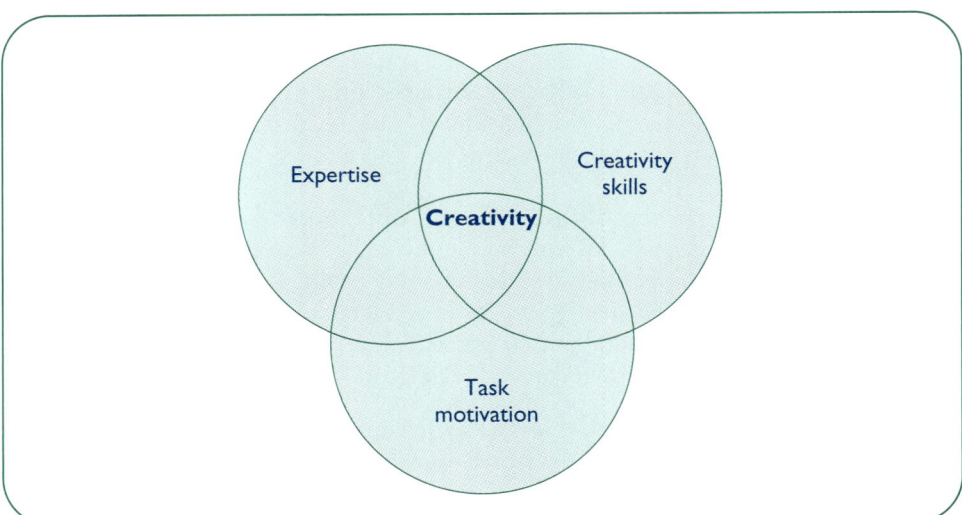

Source: T.M. Amabile, "Motivating Creativity in Organizations," *California Management Review*, Fall 1997, p. 43.

sonally challenging. This motivational component is what turns creativity *potential* into *actual* creative ideas. It determines the extent to which individuals fully engage their expertise and creative skills. So creative people often love their work, to the point of seeming obsessed. Importantly, an individual's work environment can have a significant effect on intrinsic motivation. Specifically, five organizational factors have been found that can impede your creativity: (1) expected evaluation—focusing on how your work is going to be evaluated, (2) surveillance—being watched while you're working, (3) external motivators—emphasizing external, tangible rewards; (4) competition—facing win-lose situations with peers, and (5) constrained choice—being given limits on how you can do your work.[6]

HOW DECISIONS ARE ACTUALLY MADE IN ORGANIZATIONS

Are decision makers in organizations rational? Do they carefully assess problems, identify all relevant criteria, use their creativity to identify all viable alternatives, and painstakingly evaluate every alternative to find the optimal choice? In some situations they do. When decision makers are faced with a simple problem having few alternative courses of action, and when the cost of searching out and evaluating alternatives is low, the rational model provides a fairly accurate description of the decision-making process. But such situations are the exception. Most decisions in the real world don't follow the rational model. For instance, people are usually content to find an acceptable or reasonable solution to their problem rather than the optimal one. Consequently, decision makers generally make limited use of their creativity. Choices tend to be confined to the neighborhood of the problem symptom and to the neighborhood of the current alternative. As one expert in decision making concluded: "Most significant decisions are made by judgment, rather than by a defined prescriptive model."[7] The following section reviews a large body of evidence to provide you with a more accurate description of how most decisions in organizations are actually made.

Bounded Rationality

When you considered which college to attend, did you look at *every* viable alternative? Did you carefully identify all the criteria that were important in your decision? Did you evaluate each alternative against the criteria in order to find the optimal college? I expect the answer to all these questions is *no*. Well, don't feel bad. Few people made their college choice this way. Instead of optimizing, you probably "satisficed."

When faced with a complex problem, most people respond by reducing the problem to a level at which it can be readily understood. The limited information-processing capability of human beings makes it impossible to assimilate and understand all the information necessary to optimize. So people *satisfice*; that is, they seek solutions that are satisfactory and sufficient.

Because the capacity of the human mind for formulating and solving complex problems is far too small to meet the requirements for full rationality, individuals operate within the confines of **bounded rationality**. They construct simplified models that extract the essential features from problems without capturing all of their complexity.[8] Individuals can then behave rationally within the limits of the simple model.

How does bounded rationality work for the typical individual? Once a problem is identified, the search for criteria and alternatives begins. But the list of criteria is likely to be far from exhaustive. The decision maker will identify a limited list made up of the more conspicuous choices. These are the choices that are easy to find and that tend to be highly visible. In most cases, they will represent familiar criteria and previously tried-and-true solutions. Once this limited set of alternatives is identified, the decision maker will begin reviewing them. But the review will not be comprehensive—not all of the alternatives will be carefully evaluated. Instead, the decision maker will begin with alternatives that differ only in a relatively small degree from the choice currently in effect. Following along familiar and well-worn paths, the decision maker proceeds to review alternatives only until he or she identifies an alternative that is "good enough"—one that meets an acceptable level of performance. The first alternative that meets the "good enough" criterion ends the search. So the final solution represents a satisficing choice rather than an optimal one.

One of the more interesting aspects of bounded rationality is that the order in which alternatives are considered is critical in determining which alternative is selected. Remember, in the fully rational optimizing model, all alternatives are eventually listed in a hierarchy of preferred order. Because all alternatives are considered, the initial order in which they are evaluated is irrelevant. Every potential solution gets a full and complete evaluation. But this isn't the case with bounded rationality. If we assume that a problem has more than one potential solution, the satisficing choice will be the first *acceptable* one the decision maker encounters. Decision makers use simple and limited models, so they typically begin by identifying alternatives that are obvious, ones with which they are familiar, and those not too far from the status quo. Solutions that depart least from the status quo and meet the decision criteria are most likely to be selected. A unique and creative alternative may present an optimizing solution to the problem, but it's unlikely to be chosen because an acceptable solution will be identified well before the decision maker is required to search very far beyond the status quo.

Intuition

"Sometimes you've just got to go with your gut feeling," the manager said as he tried to explain how he chose between two qualified job applicants. Was this manager wrong to use his "gut feeling"? Is using gut feelings a sign of being a poor manager? Does it necessarily result in inferior results? The answers to these questions are all *no*. Managers regularly use their intuition, and doing so may actually help improve decision making.[9]

Intuitive decision making is an unconscious process created out of distilled experience. It doesn't necessarily operate independently of rational analysis; rather, the two complement each other. Research on chess playing provides an excellent illustration of how intuition works.[10] Novice chess players and grand masters were shown an actual, but unfamiliar, chess game with about 25 pieces on the board. After 5 or 10 seconds, the pieces were removed and each player was asked to reconstruct the pieces by position. On average, the grand master could put 23 or 24 pieces in their correct squares, but the novice was able to replace only 6. Then the exercise was changed.

This time the pieces were placed randomly on the board. Again, the novice got only about 6 correct, but so did the grand master! The second exercise demonstrated that the grand master didn't have any better memory than the novice. What he did have was the ability, based on the experience of having played thousands of chess games, to recognize patterns and clusters of pieces that occur on chessboards in the course of games. Studies further show that chess professionals can simultaneously play 50 or more games, in which decisions often must be made in only seconds, and exhibit only a moderately lower level of skill than when playing one game under tournament conditions, in which decisions often take half an hour or longer. Experience allows the expert to recognize a situation and draw on previously learned information associated with that situation to arrive quickly at a decision. The result is that the intuitive decision maker can decide rapidly with what appears to be very limited information.

Identifying Problems

Problems don't come with flashing neon lights to identify themselves. And one person's *problem* is another person's *acceptable status quo*. So how do decision makers identify and select problems?

Problems that are visible tend to have a higher probability of being selected than ones that are important.[11] Why? We can offer at least two reasons. First, it's easier to recognize visible problems. They are more likely to catch a decision maker's attention. Second, remember that we're concerned with decision making in organizations. Decision makers want to appear competent and "on top of problems." This desire motivates them to focus on problems that are visible to others.

And don't ignore the decision maker's self-interest. If a decision maker faces a conflict between selecting a problem that is important to the organization and one that is important to the decision maker, self-interest tends to win out.[12] This tendency also is related to the issue of visibility. It's usually in a decision maker's best interest to attack high-profile problems. It conveys to others that things are under control. Moreover, when the decision maker's performance is later reviewed, the evaluator is more likely to give a high rating to someone who has been aggressively attacking visible problems than to someone whose actions have been less obvious.

Developing Alternatives

Since decision makers rarely seek an optimal solution, but rather a satisficing one, we should expect to find a minimal use of creativity in the search for alternatives. And that expectation is generally on target.

Efforts will be made to try to keep the search process simple. It will tend to be confined to the neighborhood of the current alternative. More complex search behavior, which includes the development of creative alternatives, will be resorted to only when a simple search fails to uncover a satisfactory alternative.

Evidence indicates that decision making is incremental rather than comprehensive; that is, decision makers rarely formulate new and unique problem definitions and alternatives and rarely explore unfamiliar territory.[13] They avoid the difficult task of considering all the important factors, weighing their relative merits and drawbacks, and calculating the value for each alternative. Instead, they make successive limited (incremental) comparisons. This branch approach simplifies decision choices by comparing only alternatives that differ in relatively small degree from the choice currently in effect. This approach also makes it unnecessary for the decision maker to thoroughly examine an alternative and its consequences; one need investigate only those aspects in which the proposed alternative and its consequences differ from the status quo.

What emerges from the above description is a decision maker who takes small steps toward an objective. It acknowledges the noncomprehensive nature of choice; in other words, decision makers make successive comparisons because decisions are never made forever and written in stone, but rather they are made and remade endlessly in small comparisons between narrow choices.

Making Choices

In order to avoid information overload, decision makers rely on **heuristics**, or judgmental shortcuts, in decision making.[14] There are two common categories of heuristics—availability and representativeness. Each creates biases in judgment. Another bias that decision makers often make is the tendency to escalate commitment to a failing course of action.

Availability Heuristic   A lot more people suffer from fear of flying than from fear of driving a car. The reason is that many people think flying is more dangerous. It isn't, of course. With apologies ahead of time for this graphic example, if flying on a commercial airline was as dangerous as driving, the equivalent of two 747s, filled to capacity, would have to crash every week, killing all aboard, to match the risk of being killed in a car accident. But the media give a lot more attention to air accidents than to car accidents, so we tend to overstate the risk in flying and understate the risk in driving.

This illustration is an example of the **availability heuristic**, which is the tendency for people to base their judgments on information that is readily available to them. Events that evoke emotions, that are particularly vivid, or that have occurred recently tend to be most available in our memory. As a result, we tend to be prone to overestimating unlikely events such as an airplane crash. The availability heuristic can also explain why managers, when doing annual performance appraisals, tend to give more weight to recent behaviors of an employee than to those of 6 or 9 months ago.

Representative Heuristic   Literally millions of inner-city, African American boys in the United States talk about the goal of playing basketball in the NBA. In reality, they have a better chance of becoming medical doctors than they do of playing in the NBA. But these kids are suffering from a **representative heuristic**. They tend to assess the likelihood of an occurrence by trying to match it with a preexisting category. They hear about some boy from their neighborhood 10 years ago who went on to play professional basketball. Or they watch NBA games on television and think that the players are like them. We all are guilty of using this heuristic at times. Managers, for example, frequently predict the performance of a new product by relating it to a previous product's success. Or they hired three graduates from the same university who turned out to be poor performers, so they predict that a current job applicant from that university won't be a good employee.

Escalation of Commitment   Another bias that creeps into decisions in practice is a tendency to escalate commitment when a decision stream represents a series of decisions.[15] **Escalation of commitment** is an increased commitment to a previous decision in spite of negative information. For example, a friend of mine had been dating a woman for about 4 years. Although he admitted that things weren't going too well in the relationship, he informed me that he was going to marry the woman. A bit surprised by his decision, I asked him why. He responded, "I have a lot invested in the relationship!" Similarly, another friend was explaining why she was working on a doctorate in education, although she disliked teaching and didn't want to continue her career in education. She told me she really wanted to be a software programmer. But then she hit me with her escalation-of-commitment explanation: "I already have a master's in education and I'd have to go back and complete some deficiencies if I changed to work on a degree in software programming now."

It has been well documented that individuals escalate commitment to a failing course of action when they view themselves as responsible for the failure. That is, they "throw good money after bad" to demonstrate that their initial decision wasn't wrong and to avoid having to admit they made a mistake. Escalation of commitment is also congruent with evidence that people try to appear consistent in what they say and do. Increasing commitment to previous actions conveys consistency.

Escalation of commitment has obvious implications for managerial decisions. Many an organization has suffered large losses because a manager was determined to prove that his or her original decision was right by continuing to commit resources to what was a lost cause from the beginning. In addition, consistency is a characteristic often associated with effective leaders. So managers, in an effort to appear effective, may be motivated to be consistent when switching to another course of action may be preferable. In actuality, effective managers are those who are able to differentiate between situations in which persistence will pay off and situations where it won't.

Individual Differences

Put Chad and Sean into the same decision situation and Chad almost always seems to take longer to come to a solution. Chad's final choices aren't necessarily always better than Sean's, he's just slower in processing information. In addition, if there's an obvious risk dimension in the decision, Sean seems consistently to prefer a riskier option than does Chad. What this illustrates is that all of us bring personality and other individual differences to the decisions we make. Two of these individual differences seem particularly relevant to decision making in organizations—decision-making styles and level of moral development.

Decision-Making Styles The decision-styles model identifies four different individual approaches to making decisions.[16] It was designed to be used by managers and aspiring managers, but its general framework can be used with any individual decision maker.

The foundation of the model is the recognition that people differ along two dimensions. The first is their way of *thinking*. Some people are logical and rational. They process information serially. In contrast, some people are intuitive and creative. They perceive things as a whole. Note that these differences are above and beyond the general human characteristics—specifically, bounded rationality—discussed earlier. The other dimension addresses a person's *tolerance for ambiguity*. Some people have a high need to structure information in ways that minimize ambiguity; others are able to process many thoughts at the same time. When these two dimensions are diagrammed, they form four styles of decision making (see Exhibit 6-3). These are: Directive, Analytical, Conceptual, and Behavioral.

EXHIBIT 6–3   Decision-Style Model

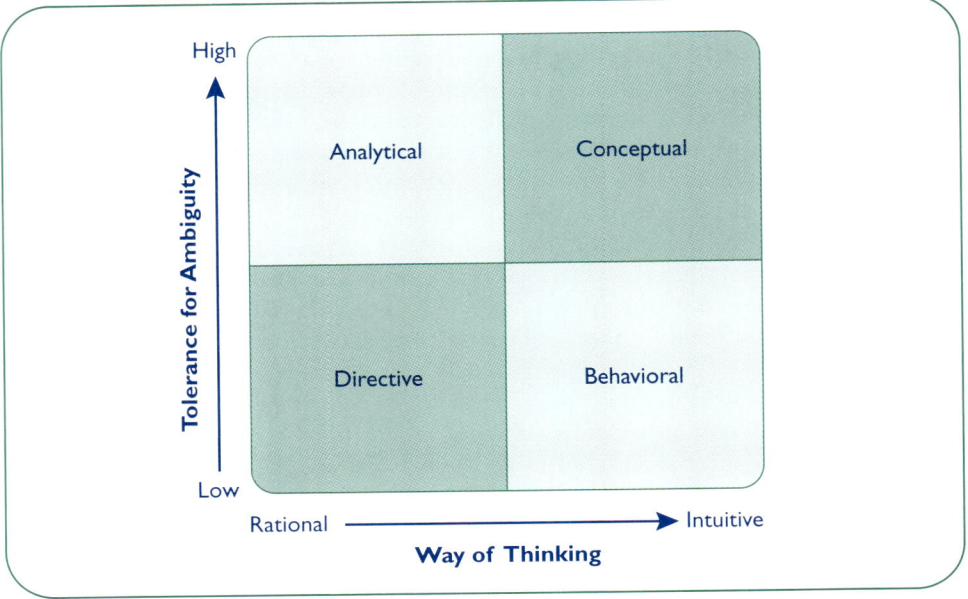

Source: A.J. Rowe and J.D. Boulgarides, *Managerial Decision Making* (Upper Saddle River, NJ: Prentice Hall, 1992), p. 29.

People using the *directive* style have low tolerance for ambiguity and seek rationality. They are efficient and logical. But their concern for efficiency results in their making decisions with minimal information and assessing few alternatives. Directive types make decisions fast, and they focus on the short run.

The *analytical* type has a much greater tolerance for ambiguity than do directive decision makers. They desire more information and consider more alternatives than do directives. Analytical managers would be best characterized as careful decision makers with the ability to adapt or cope with new situations.

Individuals with a *conceptual* style tend to be very broad in their outlook and consider many alternatives. Their focus is long range, and they are very good at finding creative solutions to problems.

The final category—those with a *behavioral* style—characterizes decision makers who work well with others. They're concerned with the achievements of peers and subordinates. They're receptive to suggestions from others and rely heavily on meetings for communicating. This type of manager tries to avoid conflict and seeks acceptance.

Although these four categories are distinct, most managers have characteristics that fall into more than one. So it's probably best to think in terms of a manager's dominant style and his or her backup styles. Some managers rely almost exclusively on their dominant style; more flexible managers can make shifts depending on the situation.

Business students, lower-level managers, and top executives tend to score highest in the analytical style. That's not surprising, given the emphasis that formal education, particularly business education, gives to developing rational thinking. For instance, courses in accounting, statistics, and finance all stress rational analysis.

In addition to providing a framework for looking at individual differences, focusing on decision styles can be useful for helping you understand how two equally intelligent people, with access to the same information, can differ in the ways they approach decisions and the final choices they make.

Level of Moral Development Moral development is relevant in decision making because many decisions have an ethical dimension. An understanding of this concept can help you see how different people impose different ethical standards on their decisions.

A substantial body of research confirms the existence of three levels of moral development, each comprising two stages.[17] At each successive stage, an individual's moral judgment grows less and less dependent on outside influences. The three levels and six stages are described in Exhibit 6-4.

The first level is labeled *preconventional*. At this level, individuals respond to notions of right or wrong only when personal consequences are involved, such as physical punishment, reward, or exchange of favors. Reasoning at the *conventional* level indicates that moral value resides in maintaining the conventional order and the

EXHIBIT 6–4 Levels and Stages of Moral Development

Level	Stage/Description
Principled	6. Following self-chosen ethical principles even if they violate the law
	5. Valuing rights of others; and upholding nonrelative values and rights regardless of the majority's opinion
Conventional	4. Maintaining conventional order by fulfilling obligations to which you have agreed
	3. Living up to what is expected by people close to you
Preconventional	2. Following rules only when it's in your immediate interest
	1. Sticking to rules to avoid physical punishment

Source: Adapted from L. Kohlberg, "Moral Stages and Moralization: The Cognitive-Developmental Approach," in T. Lickona (ed.), *Moral Development and Behavior: Theory, Research, and Social Issues* (New York: Holt, Rinehart & Winston, 1976), pp. 34-35.

expectations of others. In the *principled* level, individuals make a clear effort to define moral principles apart from the authority of the groups to which they belong or society in general.

Research on these stages of moral development allows us to draw several conclusions.[18] First, people proceed through the six stages in a lock-step fashion. They gradually move up a ladder, stage by stage. They don't jump steps. Second, there is no guarantee of continued development. Development can terminate at any stage. Third, most adults are at stage 4. They are limited to obeying the rules and laws of society. Finally, the higher the stage a manager reaches, the more he or she will be predisposed to make ethical decisions. For instance, a stage 3 manager is likely to make decisions that will receive approval by his or her peers; a stage 4 manager will seek to be a "good corporate citizen" by making decisions that respect the organization's rules and procedures; and a stage 5 manager is likely to challenge organizational practices that he or she believes to be wrong.

Organizational Constraints

The organization itself constrains decision makers. Managers, for instance, shape their decisions to reflect the organization's performance evaluation and reward system and organizationally imposed time constraints. Previous organizational decisions also act as precedents to constrain current decisions.

Performance Evaluation Managers are strongly influenced in their decision making by the criteria by which they are evaluated. If a division manager believes that the manufacturing plants under his responsibility are operating best when he hears nothing negative, we shouldn't be surprised to find that his plant managers spend a good part of their time ensuring that negative information doesn't reach the division boss. Similarly, if a college dean believes that an instructor should never fail more than 10 percent of her students—to fail more reflects on the instructor's ability to teach—we should expect that new instructors, who want to receive favorable evaluations, will decide not to fail too many students.

Reward Systems The organization's reward system influences decision makers by suggesting to them what choices are preferable in terms of personal payoff. For example, if the organization rewards risk aversion, managers are likely to make conservative decisions. From the 1930s through the mid-1980s, General Motors consistently gave out promotions and bonuses to managers who kept a low profile, avoided controversy, and were good team players. The result was that GM managers became very adept at dodging tough issues and passing controversial decisions on to committees.

System-Imposed Time Constraints Organizations impose deadlines on decisions. For instance, department budgets need to be completed by next Friday. Or the report on new product development has to be ready for the executive committee to review by the first of the month. A host of decisions have to be made quickly in order to stay ahead of the competition and keep customers satisfied. And almost all important decisions come with explicit deadlines. These conditions create time pressures on decision makers and often make it difficult, if not impossible, to gather all the information they might like before having to make a final choice. The rational model ignores the reality that, in organizations, decisions come with time constraints.

Historical Precedents Rational decision making takes an unrealistic and insulated perspective. It views decisions as independent and discrete events. But that isn't the way it is in the real world! Decisions aren't made in a vacuum. They have a context. In fact, individual decisions are more accurately characterized as points in a *stream of decisions*.

Decisions made in the past are ghosts that continually haunt current choices. For instance, commitments made in the past constrain current options. To use a social situation as an example, the decision you might make after meeting "Mr. (or Ms.) Right" is more complicated if you're married than if you're single. Prior commitments—in this case, having gotten married—constrain your options. In a business context, Eastman Kodak is a good example of a firm that has had to live with its past mistakes.[19] Starting in the early 1970s, Kodak's management concluded that the days of silver halide photography were numbered. They predicted other technologies, such as electronic photography, would soon replace it. But instead of approaching the problem deliberately, Kodak management panicked. They took off in all directions. And today, virtually all of Kodak's problems can be traced to the decisions made and not made since then. Government budget decisions also offer an illustration of our point. It's common knowledge that the largest determining factor of the size of any given year's budget is last year's budget.[20] Choices made today, therefore, are largely a result of choices made over the years.

Cultural Differences

The rational model does not acknowledge cultural differences. But Arabs, for instance, don't necessarily make decisions the same way that Canadians do. Therefore, we need to recognize that the cultural background of the decision maker can have significant influence on his or her selection of problems, depth of analysis, the importance placed on logic and rationality, or whether organizational decisions should be made autocratically by an individual manager or collectively in groups.[21]

Cultures, for example, differ in terms of time orientation, the importance of rationality, their belief in the ability of people to solve problems, and preference for collective decision making. Differences in time orientation help us understand why managers in Egypt will make decisions at a much slower and more deliberate pace than their American counterparts. A North American manager might make an important decision intuitively, but he or she knows that it's important to appear to proceed in a rational fashion because rationality is highly valued in the West. In countries such as Iran, where rationality is not deified, efforts to appear rational are not necessary. Some cultures emphasize solving problems; others focus on accepting situations as they are. The United States falls into the former category; Thailand and Indonesia fall into the latter. Because problem-solving managers believe that they can and should change situations to their benefit, American managers might identify a problem long before their Thai or Indonesian counterparts would choose to recognize it as such. Decision making by Japanese managers is much more group-oriented than in the United States. The Japanese value conformity and cooperation. So before Japanese CEOs make an important decision, they collect a large amount of information, which is then used in consensus-forming group decisions.

ETHICS IN DECISION MAKING

We can't emphasize enough the importance today of considering ethics in decision making. We've already addressed individual differences in our discussion of moral development. We conclude this chapter by presenting three different ways that individuals frame decisions and their implications for managerial decision making.

An individual can use three different criteria in making ethical choices.[22] The first is the *utilitarian* criterion, in which decisions are made solely on the basis of their outcomes or consequences. The goal of **utilitarianism** is to provide the greatest good for the greatest number. This view tends to dominate business decision making. It's consistent with goals such as efficiency, productivity, and high profits. By maximizing profits, for instance, a business executive can argue he is securing the greatest good for the greatest number—as he hands out dismissal notices to 15 percent of his employees.

Another ethical criterion is to focus on *rights*. This calls on individuals to make decisions consistent with fundamental liberties and privileges as set forth in documents such as the Bill of Rights. An emphasis on rights in decision making means respecting and protecting the basic rights of individuals, such as the right to privacy, to free speech, and to due process. For instance, use of this criterion would protect employees who report unethical or illegal practices by their organization to the press or government agencies on the grounds of their right to free speech.

A third criterion is to focus on *justice*. This requires individuals to impose and enforce rules fairly and impartially so there is an equitable distribution of benefits and costs. Union members typically favor this view. It justifies paying people the same wage for a given job, regardless of performance differences, and it uses seniority as the primary determinant in making layoff decisions.

Each of these three criteria has advantages and liabilities. A focus on utilitarianism promotes efficiency and productivity, but it can result in ignoring the rights of some individuals, particularly those with minority representation in the organization. The use of rights as a criterion protects individuals from injury and is consistent with freedom and privacy, but it can create an overly legalistic workplace that hinders productivity and efficiency. A focus on justice protects the interests of the underrepresented and less powerful, but it can encourage a sense of entitlement that reduces risk taking, innovation, and productivity.

Decision makers, particularly in for-profit organizations, tend to feel safe and comfortable when they use utilitarianism. A lot of questionable actions can be justified when framed as being in the best interests of "the organization" and stockholders. But many critics of business decision makers argue that this perspective needs to change. Increased concerns in society about individual rights and social justice suggest the need for managers to develop ethical standards based on nonutilitarian criteria. This presents a solid challenge to today's managers because making decisions using criteria such as individual rights and social justice involves far more ambiguities than using utilitarian criteria such as effects on efficiency and profits. This helps explain why managers are increasingly finding themselves criticized for their actions. Raising prices, selling products with questionable effects on consumer health, closing down manufacturing plants, laying off large numbers of employees, moving production overseas to cut costs, and similar decisions can be justified in utilitarian terms. But that may no longer be the single criterion by which good decisions should be judged.

IMPLICATIONS FOR MANAGERS

Individuals think and reason before they act. Thus, an understanding of how people make decisions can be helpful if we are to explain and predict their behavior.

Under some decision situations, people follow the rational model. But for most people, and most nonroutine decisions, this is probably more the exception than the rule. Few important decisions are simple or unambiguous enough for the rational model's assumptions to apply. So individuals look for solutions that satisfice rather than optimize, inject biases and prejudices into the decision process, and rely on intuition.

Given the evidence we've described on how decisions are actually made in organizations, what can managers do to improve their decision making? We offer five suggestions.

First, analyze the situation. Adjust your decision-making style to the national culture in which you're operating and to criteria your organization evaluates and rewards. For instance, if you're in a country that doesn't value rationality, don't feel compelled to follow the rational decision-making model or even to try to make your decisions appear rational. Similarly, organizations differ in terms of the importance they place on risk, the use of groups, and the like. Adjust your decision style to ensure it's compatible with the organization's culture.

Second, be aware of biases. We all bring biases to the decisions we make. If you understand the biases influencing your judgment, you can begin to change the way you make decisions to reduce those biases.

Third, combine rational analysis with intuition. These are not conflicting approaches to decision making. By using both, you can actually improve your decision effectiveness. As you gain managerial experience, you should feel increasingly confident in imposing your intuitive processes on top of your rational analysis.

Fourth, don't assume that your specific decision style is appropriate for every job. Just as organizations differ, so too do jobs within organizations. And your effectiveness as a decision maker will increase if you match your decision style to the requirements of the job. For instance, if you have a directive style of decision making, you'll be more effective working with people whose jobs require quick action. This style, for example, would match up well with managing stockbrokers. An analytical style, on the other hand, would work well managing accountants, market researchers, or financial analysts.

Finally, try to enhance your creativity. Overtly look for novel solutions to problems, attempt to see problems in new ways, and use analogies. In addition, try to remove work and organizational barriers that might impede your creativity.

PART III: Groups in the Organization

CHAPTER 7

Foundations of Group Behavior

After reading this chapter, you should be able to

1. Differentiate between formal and informal groups
2. Explain why people join groups
3. Describe how role requirements change in different situations
4. Explain the importance of the Hawthorne studies
5. Describe the importance of the Asch studies
6. Identify the implications of social loafing
7. Outline the benefits and disadvantages of cohesive groups
8. Explain the effect of diversity on group performance
9. Contrast groupthink and groupshift

The behavior of individuals in groups is something more than the sum total of each acting in his or her own way. When individuals are in groups they act differently from when they are alone. This chapter introduces basic concepts about groups and demonstrates how an understanding of groups can help explain the larger phenomenon of organizational behavior.

DEFINING AND CLASSIFYING GROUPS

A **group** is defined as two or more individuals, interacting and interdependent, who come together to achieve particular objectives. Groups can be either formal or informal. By formal, we mean defined by the organization's structure, with designated work assignments establishing tasks and work groups. In formal groups, the behaviors that one should engage in are stipulated by and directed toward organizational goals. In contrast, informal groups are alliances that are neither structured nor organizationally determined. In the work environment, these groups form naturally as responses to the need for social contact.

It's possible to further subclassify groups into command, task, interest, or friendship categories. Command and task groups are dictated by the formal organization, whereas interest and friendship groups are informal alliances.

The *command group* is determined by the organizational chart. It is composed of the subordinates who report directly to a given manager. An elementary school principal and her 12 teachers form a command group, as do the director of postal audits and his 5 inspectors.

*Task group*s, also organizationally determined, represent persons working together to complete a job. However, a task group's boundaries are not limited to its immediate hierarchical superior. It can cross command relationships. For instance, if a college student is accused of a campus crime, it may require communication and coordination among the dean of academic affairs, the dean of students, the registrar, the director of security, and the student's adviser. Such a formation would constitute a task group. It should be noted that all command groups are also task groups, but because task groups can cut across the organization, the reverse need not be true.

People who may or may not be aligned into common command or task groups may affiliate to attain a specific objective with which each is concerned. This is an *interest group*. Employees who band together to have their vacation schedule altered, to support a peer who has been fired, or to seek increased fringe benefits represent the formation of a united body to further their common interest.

Groups often develop because the individual members have one or more common characteristics. We call these formations *friendship groups*. Social allegiances, which frequently extend outside the work situation, can be based on, for example, similar age or ethnic heritage, support for Notre Dame football, or holding similar political views, to name just a few such characteristics.

Informal groups provide a very important function by satisfying their members' social needs. Because of interactions that result from the proximity of work stations or tasks, we find workers playing golf together, riding to and from work together, lunching together, and spending their breaks around the water cooler together. We must recognize that these types of interactions among individuals, even though informal, deeply affect their behavior and performance.

There is no single reason why individuals join groups. Because most people belong to a number of groups, it's obvious that different groups provide different benefits to their members. Exhibit 7-1 summarizes the most popular reasons people have for joining groups.

BASIC GROUP CONCEPTS

The following review of basic group concepts builds on the recognition that groups are not unorganized mobs. They have a structure that shapes the behavior of their members.

Roles

Laura Campbell is a buyer with Marks & Spencer, the large British retailer. Her job requires her to play a number of **roles**: that is, to engage in a set of expected behavior patterns that are attributed to occupying a given position in a social unit. For

EXHIBIT 7–1 Why Do People Join Groups?

Reason	Benefit
Security	By joining a group, individuals can reduce the insecurity of "standing alone." People feel stronger, have fewer self-doubts, and are more resistant to threats when they are part of a group.
Status	Inclusion in a group that is viewed as important by others provides recognition and status for its members.
Self-esteem	Groups can provide people with feelings of self-worth. That is, in addition to conveying status to those outside the group, membership can also give increased feelings of worth to the group members themselves.
Affiliation	Groups can fulfill social needs. People enjoy the regular interaction that comes with group membership. For many people, these on-the-job interactions are their primary source for fulfilling their needs for affiliation.
Power	What cannot be achieved individually often becomes possible through group action. There is power in numbers.
Goal achievement	There are times when it takes more than one person to accomplish a particular task—there is a need to pool talents, knowledge, or power in order to get a job completed. In such instances, management will rely on the use of a formal group.

instance, Laura plays the role of a Marks & Spencer employee, a member of the headquarter's buying group, a member of the cost-improvement task force, and an adviser to the committee on diversity. Off the job, Laura Campbell finds herself in still more roles: wife, mother, Methodist, member of the Labor Party, board member at her daughter's school, singer in the St. Andrew's Chapel choir, and a member of the Surrey women's soccer league. Many of these roles are compatible; some create conflicts. For instance, a recent offer of a promotion would require Laura to relocate from London to Manchester, yet her husband and daughter want to remain in London. Can the role demands of her job be reconciled with the demands of her roles as wife and mother?

Like Laura Campbell, we all are required to play a number of roles, and our behavior varies with the role we're playing. The concept of roles can help us explain why Laura's behavior at her soccer league match on Saturday, for instance, is different from her behavior when participating in a meeting of her cost-improvement task force at work—the groups impose different identities and expectations on Laura.

The understanding of role behavior would be dramatically simplified if each of us chose one role and played it out regularly and consistently. Unfortunately, we are required to play diverse roles, both on and off our jobs. Different groups impose different role requirements on people. And we can better understand an individual's behavior in specific situations if we know what role that person is playing.

On the basis of decades of role research, we can make the following conclusions[1]: (1) People play multiple roles. (2) People learn roles from the stimuli around them—friends, books, movies, television. For instance, many current police officers learned their roles from reading Joseph Wambaugh novels, while many of tomorrow's lawyers will be influenced by watching the actions of attorneys in *Ally McBeal* or *The Practice*. (3) People have the ability to shift roles rapidly when they recognize that the situation and its demands clearly require major changes. (4) People often experience role conflict when compliance with one role requirement is at odds with another. An increasing number of people, for instance, are experiencing the stress that Laura Campbell is experiencing as a result of trying to reconcile work and family roles.

So if you're a manager, of what value is a knowledge of roles? When you're dealing with employees, it helps to think in terms of what group they're predominantly identifying with at the time and what behaviors would be expected of them in that role. This perspective can often allow you to more accurately predict the employee's behavior and guide you in determining how best to handle situations with that employee.

Norms

Did you ever notice that golfers don't speak while their partners are putting on the green or that employees don't criticize their bosses in public? This is because of **norms**. That is, there are acceptable standards of behavior within a group that are shared by the group's members.[2]

Each group will establish its own set of norms. For instance, group norms might determine appropriate dress, when it's acceptable to goof off, with whom group members eat lunch, and friendships on and off the job. However, probably the most widespread norms—and the ones with which managers tend to be most concerned—deal with performance-related processes. Work groups typically provide their members with explicit cues on how hard they should work, how to get the job done, their level of output, appropriate communication channels, and the like. These norms are extremely powerful in affecting an individual employee's performance. When agreed to and accepted by the group, norms act as a means of influencing the behavior of group members with a minimum of external controls. In fact, it's not unusual to find cases in which an employee with strong abilities and high personal motivation performs at a very modest level because of the overriding influence of group norms that discourage members from producing at high levels.

A key point to remember about norms is that groups exert pressure on members to bring members' behavior into conformity with the group's standards. If people in the group violate its norms, expect group members to act to correct or even punish the violation. This is just one conclusion directly attributable to findings in the Hawthorne studies.

The Hawthorne Studies It's generally agreed among behavioral scientists that full-scale appreciation of the importance norms play in influencing worker behavior did not occur until the early 1930s. This enlightenment grew out of a series of studies undertaken at Western Electric Company's Hawthorne Works in Chicago between 1924 and 1932.[3] Originally initiated by Western Electric officials and later overseen by Harvard professor Elton Mayo, the Hawthorne studies concluded that a worker's behavior and sentiments were closely related, that group influences were significant in affecting individual behavior, that group standards were highly effective in establishing individual worker output, and that money was less a factor in determining worker output than were group standards, sentiments, and security. Let us briefly review the

Hawthorne investigations and demonstrate the importance of these findings in explaining group behavior.

The Hawthorne researchers began by examining the relation between the physical environment and productivity. Illumination and other working conditions were selected to represent this physical environment. The researchers' initial findings contradicted their anticipated results.

They began with illumination experiments with various groups of workers. The researchers manipulated the intensity of illumination upward and downward, while at the same time noting changes in group output. Results varied, but one thing was clear: In no case was the increase or decrease in output in proportion to the increase or decrease in illumination. So the researchers introduced a control group: An experimental group was presented with varying intensity of illumination, while the controlled unit worked under a constant intensity of illumination. Again, the results were bewildering to the Hawthorne researchers. As the light level was increased in the experimental unit, output rose for both the control and the experimental group. But to the surprise of the researchers, as the light level was dropped in the experimental group, productivity continued to increase in both groups. In fact, a productivity decrease was observed in the experimental group only when the light intensity had been reduced to that of moonlight. The Hawthorne researchers concluded that illumination intensity was only a minor influence among the many that affected an employee's productivity, but they could not explain the behavior they had witnessed.

As a follow-up to the illumination experiments, the researchers began a second set of experiments in the relay assembly test room at Western Electric. A small group of women was isolated from the main work group so that their behavior could be more carefully observed. They went about their job of assembling small telephone relays in a room laid out similarly to their normal department. The only significant difference was the placement in the room of a research assistant who acted as an observer—keeping records of output, rejects, working conditions, and a daily log sheet describing everything that happened. Observations covering a multiyear period found that this small group's output increased steadily. The number of personal absences and those due to sickness were approximately one-third of those recorded by women in the regular production department. What became evident was that this group's performance was significantly influenced by its status of being a "special" group. The women in the test room thought that being in the experimental group was fun, that they were in sort of an elite group, and that management was concerned with their interest by engaging in such experimentation.

A third study in the bank wiring observation room was introduced to ascertain the effect of a sophisticated wage incentive plan. The assumption was that individual workers would maximize their productivity when they saw that it was directly related to economic rewards. The most important finding coming out of this study was that employees did not individually maximize their outputs. Rather, their output became controlled by a group norm that determined what was a proper day's work. Output was not only being restricted, but individual workers were giving erroneous reports. The total for a week would check with the total week's output, but the daily reports showed a steady level of output regardless of actual daily production. What was going on?

Interviews determined that the group was operating well below its capability and was leveling output in order to protect itself. Members were afraid that if they significantly increased their output, the unit incentive rate would be cut, the expected daily output would be increased, layoffs might occur, or slower workers would be reprimanded. So the group established its idea of a fair output—neither too much nor too little. They helped each other out to ensure their reports were nearly level.

The norms the group established included a number of "don'ts." *Don't* be a ratebuster, turning out too much work. *Don't* be a chiseler, turning out too little work. *Don't* be a squealer on any of your peers.

How did the group enforce these norms? Their methods were neither gentle nor subtle. They included sarcasm, name-calling, ridicule, and even physical punches to the upper arm of members who violated the group's norms. Members would also ostracize individuals whose behavior was against the group's interest.

The Hawthorne studies made an important contribution to our understanding of group behavior—particularly the significant place that norms have in determining individual work behavior.

Conformity and the Asch Studies As a member of a group, you desire continued acceptance by the group, so you are susceptible to conforming to the group's norms. There is considerable evidence that groups can place strong pressures on individual members to change their attitudes and behaviors to conform to the group's standard. Group influence was demonstrated in the now-classic studies undertaken by Solomon Asch.[4]

Asch made up groups of seven or eight people who sat in a classroom and were asked to compare two cards held by the experimenter. One card had one line, the other had three lines of varying length. As shown in Exhibit 7-2, one of the lines on the three-line card was identical to the line on the one-line card. Also, as shown in Exhibit 7-2, the difference in line length was quite obvious; under ordinary conditions, subjects made errors less than one percent of the time. The object was to announce aloud which of the three lines matched the single line. But what happens if all the members in the group begin to give incorrect answers? Will the pressures to conform result in the unsuspecting subject (USS) altering his or her answer to align with the others? That was what Asch wanted to know. He arranged the group so that only the USS was unaware that the experiment was "fixed." The seating was prearranged so that the USS was the last to announce his or her decision.

The experiment began with several sets of matching exercises. All the subjects gave the right answers. On the third set, however, the first subject gave an obviously

EXHIBIT 7–2 Examples of Cards Used in Asch Study

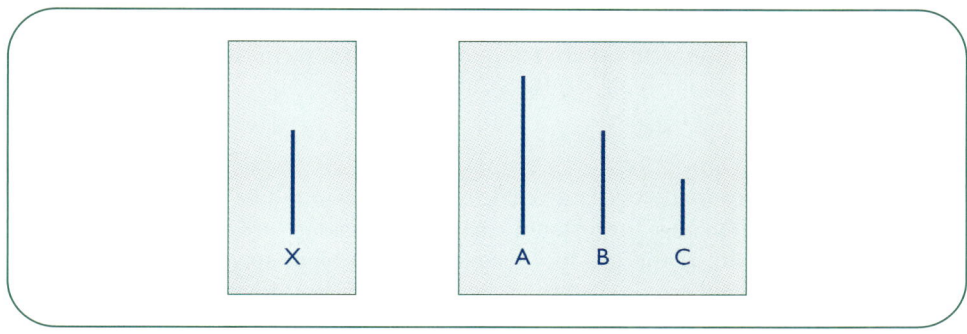

wrong answer—for example, saying "C" in Exhibit 7-2. The next subject gave the same wrong answer, and so did the others until it got to the unsuspecting subject. He knew "B" was the same as "X," yet everyone had said "C." The decision confronting the USS was this: Do you state a perception publicly that differs from the preannounced position of the others? Or do you give an answer that you strongly believe is incorrect in order to have your response agree with that of the other group members?

The results obtained by Asch demonstrated that over many experiments and many trials, subjects conformed in about 35 percent of the trials; that is, the subjects gave answers they knew were wrong but that were consistent with the replies of other group members.

What can we conclude from this study? The results suggest that there are group norms that press us toward conformity. We desire to be one of the group, and we avoid being visibly different. We can generalize further to say that when an individual's opinion of objective data differs significantly from that of others in the group, he or she feels extensive pressure to align his or her opinion to conform with those of the others.

Cohesiveness

Groups differ in their **cohesiveness**; that is, the degree to which members are attracted to each other and are motivated to stay in the group. For instance, some work groups are cohesive because the members have spent a great deal of time together, or the group's small size facilitates higher interaction, or the group has experienced external threats that have brought members closer together. Cohesiveness is important because it's been found to be related to the group's productivity.[5]

Studies consistently show that the relationship of cohesiveness and productivity depends on the performance-related norms established by the group. The more cohesive the group, the more its members will follow its goals. If performance-related norms are high (for example, high output, quality work, cooperation with individuals outside the group), a cohesive group will be more productive than a less cohesive group. But if cohesiveness is high and performance norms are low, productivity will be low. If cohesiveness is low and performance norms are high, productivity increases, but less than in the high cohesiveness–high norms situation. Where cohesiveness and performance-related norms are both low, there will be no significant effect on productivity. These conclusions are summarized in Exhibit 7-3.

As a manager, what can you do to encourage group cohesiveness? You might try one or more of the following [6]: (1) make the group smaller, (2) encourage agreement with group goals, (3) increase the time members spend together, (4) increase the status of the group and the perceived difficulty of attaining membership in the group, (5) stimulate competition with other groups, (6) give rewards to the group rather than to individual members, or (7) physically isolate the group.

Size

Does the size of a group affect the group's overall behavior? The answer is a definite *Yes*.[7] The evidence indicates, for instance, that smaller groups are faster at completing tasks than larger ones. If the group is engaged in problem solving, however, large groups consistently get better marks than their smaller counterparts. Translating these results into specific numbers is a bit hazardous, but we can offer some parameters.

EXHIBIT 7–3 Relationship of Cohesiveness to Productivity

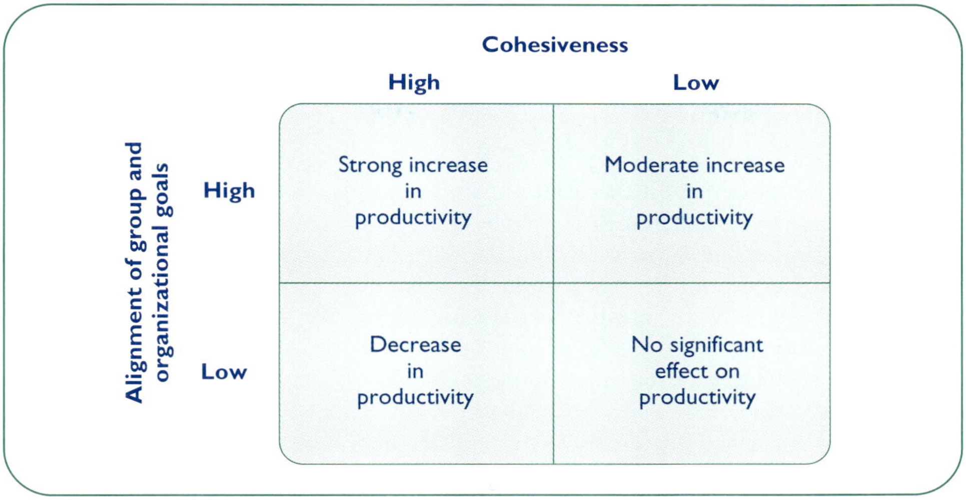

	Cohesiveness	
Alignment of group and organizational goals	**High**	**Low**
High	Strong increase in productivity	Moderate increase in productivity
Low	Decrease in productivity	No significant effect on productivity

Large groups—with a dozen or more members—are good for gaining diverse input. So if the goal of the group is fact-finding, larger groups should be more effective. On the other hand, smaller groups are better at doing something productive with that input. Groups of approximately seven members tend to be more effective for taking action.

One of the most important findings related to the size of a group has been labeled **social loafing**. Social loafing is the tendency for individuals to expend less effort when working collectively than when working individually. It directly challenges the logic that the productivity of the group as a whole should at least equal the sum of the productivity of all the individuals in that group.

A common stereotype about groups is that the sense of team spirit spurs individual effort and enhances the group's overall productivity. In the late 1920s, German psychologist Max Ringelmann compared the results of individual and group performance on a rope-pulling task.[8] He expected that the group's effort would be equal to the sum of the efforts of individuals within the group. That is, three people pulling together should exert three times as much pull on the rope as one person, and eight people should exert eight times as much pull. Ringelmann's results, however, did not confirm his expectations. Groups of three people exerted a force only two-and-a-half times the average individual performance. Groups of eight collectively achieved less than four times the solo rate.

Replications of Ringelmann's research with similar tasks have generally supported his findings.[9] Increases in group size are inversely related to individual performance. More may be better in the sense that the total productivity of a group of four is greater than that of two or three people, but the individual productivity of each group member declines.

What causes this social loafing effect? It may be due to a belief that others in the group are not carrying their fair share. If you see others as lazy or inept, you can reestablish equity by reducing your effort. Another explanation is the dispersion of responsibility. Because the results of the group cannot be attributed to any single person, the relationship between an individual's input and the group's output is clouded. In such situations, individuals may be tempted to become "free riders" and to coast on the group's efforts. In other words, there will be a reduction in efficiency when individuals think that their contribution cannot be measured.

Composition

Most group activities require a variety of skills and knowledge. Given this requirement, it would be reasonable to conclude that heterogeneous groups—those composed of dissimilar individuals—would be more likely to have diverse abilities and information and should be more effective than homogeneous groups. Research studies generally substantiate this conclusion, especially on cognitive, creativity-demanding tasks.[10]

When a group is diverse in terms of personalities, gender, age, education, functional specialization, and experience, there is an increased probability that the group will possess the needed characteristics to complete its tasks effectively.[11] The group may be more conflict-laden and less expedient as varied positions are introduced and assimilated, but the evidence generally supports the conclusion that heterogeneous groups perform more effectively than do those that are homogeneous. Essentially, diversity promotes conflict, which stimulates creativity, which leads to improved decision making.

But what about diversity created by racial or national differences? The evidence indicates that these elements of diversity interfere with group processes, at least in the short term.[12] Cultural diversity seems to be an asset on tasks that call for a variety of viewpoints. But culturally heterogeneous groups have more difficulty in learning to work with each other and solving problems. The good news is that these difficulties seem to dissipate with time. While newly formed culturally diverse groups underperform as compared with newly formed culturally homogeneous groups, the differences disappear after about three months. The reason is that it takes diverse groups a while to learn how to work through disagreements and different approaches to solving problems.

An offshoot of the composition issue has received a great deal of attention by group researchers. This is the degree to which members of a group share a common demographic attribute, such as age, sex, race, educational level, or length of service in the organization, and the impact of this attribute on turnover. We call this variable **group demography**.

Groups and organizations are composed of **cohorts**, which we define as a group of individuals who hold a common attribute. For instance, everyone born in 1960 is of the same age. This means they also have shared common experiences. People born in 1970 have experienced the information revolution, but not the Korean conflict. People born in 1945 shared the Vietnam War, but not the Great Depression. Women in U.S. organizations today who were born before 1945 matured prior to the women's movement and have had substantially different experiences from women born after 1965. Group demography, therefore, suggests that attributes such as age or the date that someone joins a specific work group or organization should help us to predict turnover. Essentially, the logic goes like this: Turnover will be greater among those with dissimilar experiences because communication is more difficult. Conflict and power struggles are more likely, and are more severe when they occur. The increased conflict makes group membership less attractive, so employees are more likely to quit. Similarly, the losers in a power struggle are more apt to leave voluntarily or to be forced out.

A number of studies have sought to test this thesis, and the evidence is quite encouraging.[13] For example, in departments or separate work groups in which a large portion of members entered at the same time, there is considerably more turnover among those outside this cohort. Also, where there are large gaps between cohorts, turnover is higher. People who enter a group or an organization together, or at approximately the same time, are more likely to associate with one another, have a similar perspective on the group or organization, and thus be more likely to stay. On the other hand, discontinuities or bulges in the group's date-of-entry distribution are likely to result in a higher turnover rate within that group.

Status

Status is a prestige grading, position, or rank within a group. It may be formally imposed by a group; that is, organizationally imposed, through titles or amenities such as "the heavyweight champion of the world" or "most congenial." We are all familiar with the trappings associated with high organizational status—large offices with thick carpeting, impressive titles, high pay and fringe benefits, preferred work schedules, and so on. Whether management acknowledges the existence of a status hierarchy, organizations are filled with amenities that are not uniformly available to everyone and, hence, carry status value.

More often, we deal with status in an informal sense. Status may be informally acquired by characteristics such as education, age, gender, skill, or experience. Anything can have status value if others in the group see it as status-conferring. Keep in mind that informal status is not necessarily less important than the formal variety.

Status has been shown to have some interesting effects on the power of norms and pressures to conform. For instance, high-status members of groups often are given more freedom to deviate from norms than are other group members.[14] High-status people also are better able to resist conformity pressures than their lower-status peers. An individual who is highly valued by a group but who doesn't much need or care about social rewards the group provides is particularly able to pay minimal attention to conformity norms.[15]

The previous findings explain why many star athletes, famous actors, top-performing salespeople, and outstanding academics seem oblivious to appearance or to the social norms that constrain their peers. As high-status individuals, they're given a wider range of discretion. But this is true only as long as the high-status person's activities aren't severely detrimental to the achievement of the group's goal.[16]

It's also important for group members to believe that the status hierarchy is equitable. When inequity is perceived, it creates disequilibrium that results in various types of corrective behavior.[17]

The concept of equity presented in Chapter 4 applies also to status. People expect rewards to be proportionate to costs incurred. If Dana and Anne are the two finalists for the head nurse position in a hospital, and it is clear that Dana has more seniority and better preparation for assuming the promotion, Anne will view the selection of Dana to be equitable. However, if Anne is chosen because she is the daughter-in-law of the hospital director, Dana will believe an injustice has been committed.

The trappings that go with formal positions are also important elements in maintaining equity. When we believe there is an inequity between the perceived ranking of an individual and the status accoutrements that person is given by the organization, we are experiencing status incongruence. Examples of this kind of incongruence are the more desirable office location being held by a lower-ranking individual and paid country club membership being provided by the company for division managers but not for vice presidents. Pay incongruence has long been a problem in the insurance industry, where top sales agents often earn two to five times more than senior corporate executives. The result is that it is very hard for insurance companies to entice successful agents into management positions. Our point is that employees expect the things an individual has and receives to be congruent with his or her status.

Groups generally agree within themselves on status criteria and, hence, there is usually high concurrence in group rankings of individuals. However, individuals can find themselves in a conflict situation when they move between groups whose status criteria are different or when they join groups whose members have heterogeneous backgrounds. For instance, business executives may use personal income or the growth rate of their companies as determinants of status. Government bureaucrats may use the size of their budgets. Professional employees may use the degree of autonomy that comes with their job assignment. Blue-collar workers may use years of seniority. In groups made up of heterogeneous individuals or when heterogeneous groups are forced to be interdependent, status differences may initiate conflict as the group attempts to reconcile and align the differing hierarchies. As we'll see in Chapter 8, this can be a particular problem when management creates teams made up of employees from across varied functions within the organization.

GROUP DECISION MAKING

The belief—as embodied by juries—that two heads are better than one has long been accepted as a basic component of North American and many other countries' legal systems. This belief has expanded to the point that, today, many decisions in organizations are made by groups, teams, or committees. In this section, we review group decision making. Let's begin by comparing the strengths of group decisions with those made by individuals.

The Individual versus the Group

A major plus with individual decision making is *speed*. An individual doesn't have to convene a meeting and spend time discussing various alternatives. So when a decision is needed quickly, individuals have the advantage. Individual decisions also have *clear accountability*. You know who made the decision and, therefore, who's responsible for the outcome. Accountability is more ambiguous with group decisions. A third strength of individual decisions is that they tend to convey *consistent values*. Group decisions can suffer from intragroup power struggles. This effect is best illustrated by decisions of the U.S. Congress. Decisions can vary by as much as 180 degrees from one session to the next, reflecting the make-up of members and their ability to influence their peers on any specific issue. Although individuals are not perfectly consistent in their decision making, they do tend to be more consistent than groups.

Now compare the above with the strengths of group decision making. Groups generate *more complete information and knowledge*. By aggregating the resources of several individuals, groups bring more input into the decision process. In addition to more input, groups can bring heterogeneity to the decision process. They offer *increased diversity of views*, so more approaches and alternatives can be considered. The evidence indicates that a group will almost always outperform even the best individual. So groups generate *higher-quality decisions*. Finally, groups lead to *increased acceptance of a solution*. Many decisions fail after the final choice is made because people don't accept the solution. Group members, who participated in making a decision, are more likely to enthusiastically support the decision and encourage others to accept it.

So which is better—individuals or groups? The obvious answer is, "It depends." There are times when decisions are best handled by individuals. For example, evidence indicates that individuals are preferred when the decision is relatively unimportant and doesn't require subordinate commitment to its success. Similarly, individuals should make the decision when they have sufficient information and when subordinates will be committed to the outcome even if they aren't consulted.[18]

Overall, whether individuals or groups should make a decision essentially comes down to weighing effectiveness against efficiency. In terms of effectiveness, groups are superior. They generate more alternatives, are more creative, more accurate, and produce higher-quality decisions than do individuals. But individuals are more efficient than groups. Group efficiency suffers because they consume more time and resources to achieve their solution.

Groupthink and Groupshift

Two byproducts of group decision making have received a considerable amount of attention by researchers in OB. These are the concepts of groupthink and groupshift.

Groupthink Have you ever felt like speaking up in a meeting, classroom, or informal group, but decided against it? One reason may have been shyness. On the other hand, you may have been a victim of **groupthink**, the phenomenon that occurs when group members become so enamored of seeking concurrence that the norm for consensus overrides the realistic appraisal of alternative courses of action and the full expression of deviant, minority, or unpopular views. It describes a deterioration in an individual's mental efficiency, reality testing, and moral judgment as a result of group pressures.[19]

How do you know if a group is showing symptoms of groupthink? It tends to exhibit four characteristics: (1) Group members rationalize any resistance to the assumptions they've made, (2) members pressure any doubters to support the alternative favored by the majority, (3) to give the appearance of group consensus, doubters keep silent about misgivings and even minimize to themselves the importance of their doubts, (4) the group interprets members' silence as a "yes" vote for the majority.

The above symptoms lead to a number of decision-making deficiencies. When groupthink occurs, you'll find one or more of the following: incomplete assessment of the problem, poor information search, selective bias in processing information, limited development of alternatives, incomplete assessment of alternatives, failure to examine risks in preferred choice, and failure to reappraise initially rejected alternatives.

Studies of decision making in U.S. government agencies have found deficient outcomes frequently preceded by symptoms of groupthink. These outcomes included unpreparedness at Pearl Harbor in 1941, the invasion of North Korea in the 1950s, the Bay of Pigs fiasco in the early 1960s, the escalation of the Vietnam War, the failed

Iran hostage rescue in the late 1970s, and the decisions preceding the launch of the ill-fated space shuttle *Challenger*.

Are all groups equally vulnerable to groupthink? The evidence suggests not.[20] Researchers have focused on five variables that seem to influence when groupthink is likely to surface—the group's cohesiveness, its leader's behavior, its insulation from outsiders, time pressures, and failure to follow methodical decision-making procedures. Managers who, when leading a decision-making group, want to minimize the influence of groupthink should keep those variables in mind. First, cohesiveness can be an asset because highly cohesive groups have more discussion and bring out more information than do loose groups. But cohesiveness can also discourage dissent, so managers should be vigilant when working with a cohesive group. Second, managers should strive for an open leadership style. This includes encouraging member participation, refraining from stating one's opinion at the beginning of the meeting, encouraging divergent opinions from all group members, and emphasizing the importance of reaching a wise decision. Third, managers should avoid allowing the group to detach itself from external sources. Insulated groups tend to lose perspective and objectivity. Fourth, managers need to downplay time constraints. When group members feel severe time pressures to reach a decision, they resort to shortcuts that inevitably lead to false or superficial consensus. Finally, managers should encourage the use of methodical decision-making procedures. Following the rational decision-making process described in Chapter 6 will promote constructive criticism and a full analysis of decision options.

Groupshift Comparisons of group decisions with the individual decisions of members within the group suggest that there are differences. In some cases, the group decisions are more cautious than the individual decisions. More often, the shift is toward greater risk.[21]

What appears to happen in groups is that the discussion leads to a significant shift in the positions of members toward a more extreme position in the direction toward which they were already leaning before the discussion. So conservative types become more cautious and the more aggressive types take on more risk. The group discussion tends to exaggerate the initial position of the group.

Groupshift can be viewed as actually a special case of groupthink. The decision of the group reflects the dominant decision-making norm that develops during the group's discussion. Whether the shift in the group's decision is toward greater caution or more risk depends on the dominant prediscussion norm.

The greater occurrence of the shift toward risk has generated several explanations for the phenomenon. For instance, it's been suggested that the discussion creates familiarization among the members. As they become more comfortable with each other, they also become bolder and more daring. Arguably, the most plausible explanation of the shift toward risk seems to be that the group diffuses responsibility. Group decisions free any single member from accountability for the group's final choice. Greater risk can be taken because even if the decision fails, no one member can be held wholly responsible.

So, as a manager, how should you use the findings on groupshift? You should recognize that group decisions exaggerate the initial position of the individual members, that the shift has been shown more often to be toward greater risk, and that whether a group will shift toward greater risk or caution is a function of the members' prediscussion inclinations.

Selecting the Best Group Decision-Making Technique

The most common form of group decision making takes place in face-to-face interacting groups. But as our discussion of groupthink demonstrated, interacting groups often censor themselves and pressure individual members toward conformity of opinion. Brainstorming, the nominal group technique, and electronic meetings have been proposed as ways to reduce many of the problems inherent in the traditional interacting group.

Brainstorming   **Brainstorming** is meant to overcome pressures for conformity in the interacting group that retard the development of creative alternatives. It does so by utilizing an idea-generation process that specifically encourages any and all alternatives, while withholding any criticism of those alternatives.

In a typical brainstorming session, a half-dozen to a dozen people sit around a table. The group leader states the problem in a clear manner so it is understood by all participants. Members then "freewheel" as many alternatives as they can in a given length of time. No criticism is allowed, and all the alternatives are recorded for later discussion and analysis. That one idea stimulates others and that judgments of even the most bizarre suggestions are withheld until later encourage group members to "think the unusual."

Brainstorming, however, is merely a process for generating ideas. The following two techniques go further by offering methods of actually arriving at a preferred solution.

Nominal Group Technique   The nominal group restricts discussion or interpersonal communication during the decision-making process, hence the term **nominal group technique**. Group members are all physically present, as in a traditional committee meeting, but the members are required to operate independently. Specifically, the following steps take place:

1. Members meet as a group, but, before any discussion takes place, each member independently writes down his or her ideas about the problem.
2. This silent period is followed by each member's presenting one idea to the group. Each member takes his or her turn, going around the table, presenting a single idea until all ideas have been presented and recorded (typically on a flip chart or chalkboard). No discussion takes place until all ideas have been recorded.
3. The group then discusses the ideas for clarity and evaluates them.
4. Each group member silently and independently ranks the ideas. The final decision is determined by the idea with the highest aggregate ranking.

The chief advantage of this technique is that it permits the group to meet formally but does not restrict independent thinking, as so often happens in the traditional interacting group.

Electronic Meetings   The most recent approach to group decision making blends the nominal group technique with sophisticated computer technology. It's called the **electronic meeting**.

Once the technology is in place, the concept is simple. Up to 50 people sit around a horseshoe-shaped table, empty except for a series of computer terminals. Issues are presented to participants, and they type their responses onto their computer. Individual comments, as well as aggregate votes, are displayed on a projection screen in the room.

The major advantages of electronic meetings are anonymity, honesty, and speed. Participants can anonymously type any message they want, and it flashes on the screen for all to see at the push of a key on a participant's keyboard. It also allows people to be brutally honest without penalty. And it's fast, because chitchat is eliminated, discussions don't digress, and many participants can "talk" at once without stepping on one another's toes.

IMPLICATIONS FOR MANAGERS

In order to accomplish work tasks, the individuals who make up an organization are typically united into departments, teams, committees, or other forms of work groups. In addition to these formal groups, individuals also create informal groups based on common interests or friendships. It's important for managers to look at employees as members of a group because, in reality, group behavior is not merely the sum of the individual behaviors of its members. The group itself adds an additional dimension to its members' behavior.

How is it relevant to understanding group behavior to know that a Maryland woman, for example, has to reconcile her roles of mother, Methodist, Democrat, councilwoman, and police officer with the city of Baltimore? Knowledge of the role that a person is attempting to enact can make it easier for us to deal with the person, for we have insight into her expected behavior patterns. Also, knowledge of a job incumbent's role makes it easier for others to work with her, for she should behave in ways consistent with others' expectations. In other words, when a person plays out her role as expected, the ability of others to predict her behavior improves.

Norms control group member behavior by establishing standards of right or wrong. Knowing the norms of a given group can help us explain the attitudes and behaviors of its members. Can managers control group norms? Not completely, but they can influence them. By making explicit statements about desirable behaviors, by regularly reinforcing these preferred behaviors, and by linking rewards to the acceptance of preferred norms, managers can exert some degree of influence over group norms.

Should managers seek cohesive groups? The answer is a qualified *Yes*. The qualification lies in the degree of alignment between the group and the organization's goals. Managers should attempt to create work groups whose goals are consistent with those of the organization. If this is achieved, then high group cohesiveness will make a positive contribution to the group's performance.

The implications for managers of the social loafing effect on work groups are significant. When managers use collective work situations to enhance morale and teamwork, they must also provide means by which individual efforts can be identified. If they don't, management must weigh the potential losses in productivity from using groups against any possible gains in worker satisfaction.[22] This conclusion, however, has a Western bias. It's consistent with individualistic cultures, such as the United States and Canada, that are dominated by self-interest. It is not consistent with collective societies in which individuals are motivated by in-group goals. For instance, in studies comparing employees from the United

States with employees from the People's Republic of China and Israel (both collectivist societies), the Chinese and Israelis showed no propensity to engage in social loafing. In fact, the Chinese and Israelis actually performed better in a group than when working alone.[23]

The managerial implications for group composition are related to staffing formal groups and using groups to make decisions. To increase the performance of work groups, you should try to choose as members individuals who can bring a diverse perspective to problems and issues. But don't be surprised if these differences negatively affect the group's performance in the short term. Be patient. As members learn to work with their differences, the group's performance will improve.

Status inequities within a group divert activity away from goal accomplishment and direct it toward resolving the inequities. When inequities exist, managers may find that group members reduce their work effort, attempt to undermine the activities of the members with higher status, or pursue similar dysfunctional behaviors. To the degree that a manager controls status accoutrements, he or she should ensure that they are distributed carefully and consistently with status equity. Inequities are likely to have a negative motivational impact on the group.

Finally, if managers use group decision making, they should particularly try to minimize groupthink. They should encourage member input, especially from those who are less active in the discussion, and avoid expressing their preferred solution early in the group's discussion. Managers might also want to consider one or more of the techniques presented, such as brainstorming or electronic meetings, as a means to lessen pressures to conform.

CHAPTER 8

Understanding Work Teams

After reading this chapter, you should be able to

1. Explain the growing popularity of teams in organizations
2. Contrast teams with groups
3. Identify four types of teams
4. Describe the role of work design in making effective teams
5. Explain composition variables that determine team effectiveness
6. Identify resources and other contextual influences that make teams effective
7. Describe process variables that affect team performance
8. Explain how organizations can create team players

Eaton Corp.'s Aeroquip Global Hose Division, located in the heart of Arkansas' Ozark Mountains, makes hydraulic hose that is used in trucks, tractors, and other heavy equipment. In 1994, to improve quality and productivity, Eaton-Aeroquip's management implemented teams to replace the factory's assembly line. While it took some time for employees to adjust to working in groups, today the plant's 285 workers are organized into more than 50 teams and loving it![1] They're enjoying the freedom to participate in decisions that were once made solely by management—for instance, the teams set their own schedules, select new members, negotiate with suppliers, make calls on customers, and discipline members who create problems. And the move to a team approach has also helped management achieve important company goals. Between 1993 and 1999, response time to customer concerns improved 99 percent; productivity and manufacturing output both increased by more than 50 percent; and accident rates dropped by more than half.

WHY HAVE TEAMS BECOME SO POPULAR?

Thirty years ago, the decision of companies such as Volvo, Toyota, and General Foods to introduce teams into their production processes made news because no one else was doing it. Today, it's just the opposite. It's the organization that *doesn't* use teams that has become newsworthy. Pick up almost any business periodical today and you'll read how teams have become an essential part of the way business is being done in companies such as General Electric, AT&T, Boeing, Hewlett-Packard, Motorola, Apple Computer, Shiseido, FedEx, DaimlerChrysler, 3M Co., John Deere, Australian Airlines, Johnson & Johnson, Shenandoah Life Insurance Co., and Florida Power & Light. Even the world-famous San Diego Zoo has restructured its native habitat zones around cross-departmental teams. The Center for the Study of Work Teams says that 80 percent of *Fortune 500* companies now have half of their employees on teams.[2]

How do we explain the current popularity of teams? The evidence suggests that teams typically outperform individuals when the tasks being done require multiple skills, judgment, and experience.[3] As organizations have restructured themselves to compete more effectively and efficiently, they have turned to teams as a way to better utilize employee talents. Management has found that teams are more flexible and responsive to changing events than are traditional departments or other forms of permanent groupings. Teams have the capability to quickly assemble, deploy, refocus, and disband.

But don't overlook the motivational properties of teams. Consistent with our discussion in Chapter 5 of the role of employee involvement as a motivator, teams facilitate employee participation in operating decisions. For instance, some assembly-line workers at John Deere are part of sales teams that call on customers. These workers know the products better than any traditional salesperson, and by traveling and speaking with farmers, these hourly workers develop new skills and become more involved in their jobs. So another explanation for the popularity of teams is that they are an effective means for management to democratize their organizations and increase employee motivation.

TEAMS VERSUS GROUPS: WHAT'S THE DIFFERENCE?

Groups and teams are not the same thing. In this section, we define and clarify the difference between a work group and a work team. In Chapter 7, we defined a *group* as two or more individuals, interacting and interdependent, who have come together to achieve particular objectives. A **work group** is a group who interact primarily to share information and to make decisions to help one another perform within each member's area of responsibility.

Work groups have no need or opportunity to engage in collective work that requires joint effort. So their performance is merely the sum of all the group members' individual contributions. There is no positive synergy that would create an overall level of performance that is greater than the sum of the inputs.

A **work team** generates positive synergy through coordinated effort. Their individual efforts result in a level of performance that is greater than the sum of those individual inputs. Exhibit 8-1 highlights the differences between work groups and work teams.

These definitions help clarify why so many organizations have restructured work processes around teams. Management is looking for that positive synergy that

EXHIBIT 8–1   Comparing Work Groups and Work Teams

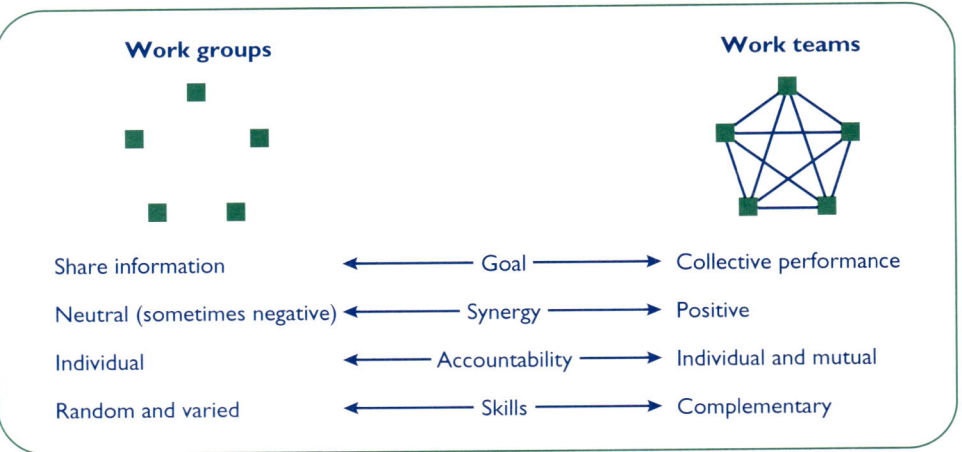

will allow their organizations to increase performance. The extensive use of teams creates the *potential* for an organization to generate greater outputs with no increase in inputs. Notice, however, we said "potential." There is nothing inherently magical in the creation of teams that ensures the achievement of this positive synergy. Merely calling a *group* a *team* doesn't automatically increase its performance. As we'll explain later in this chapter, successful or high-performing teams have certain common characteristics. If management hopes to increase organizational performance through the use of teams, it must ensure that their teams possess these characteristics.

TYPES OF TEAMS

Teams can be classified on the basis of their objective. The four most common forms of teams you're likely to find in an organization are *problem-solving teams*, *self-managed work teams*, *cross-functional teams, and virtual teams* (see Exhibit 8-2).

Problem-Solving Teams

If we look back to the early 1980s, teams were just beginning to grow in popularity. And the form most of these teams took was similar. They typically were composed of five to twelve hourly employees from the same department who met for a few hours

EXHIBIT 8–2   Four Types of Teams

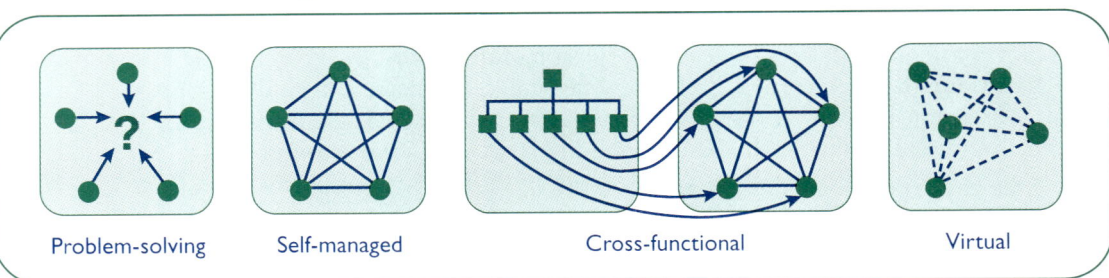

each week to discuss ways of improving quality, efficiency, and the work environment. We call these **problem-solving teams**.

In problem-solving teams, members share ideas or offer suggestions on how work processes and methods can be improved. Rarely, however, are these teams given the authority to unilaterally implement any of their suggested actions.

One of the most widely practiced applications of problem-solving teams during the 1980s was **quality circles**. These are work teams of eight to ten employees and supervisors who have a shared area of responsibility and meet regularly to discuss their quality problems, investigate causes of the problems, and recommend solutions. Management, however, typically retains control over the final decision regarding implementation of the quality circles' recommended solutions. Today, many organizations use problem-solving teams, especially as a means for seeking out ways to improve quality, speed deliveries, eliminate scrap, reduce accident rates, and generally cut costs.

Self-Managed Work Teams

Problem-solving teams were on the right track, but they didn't go far enough in getting employees involved in work-related decisions and processes. This deficiency led to experimentation with truly autonomous teams that could not only solve problems but could also implement solutions and take full responsibility for outcomes.

Self-managed work teams are generally composed of 10 to 15 people who take on the responsibilities of their former supervisors. Typically, these responsibilities include collective control over the pace of work, determination of work assignments, organization of breaks, and collective choice of inspection procedures. Fully self-managed work teams even select their own members and have the members evaluate each other's performance. As a result, supervisory positions take on decreased importance and may even be eliminated. The teams at the Eaton-Aeroquip plant in Arkansas, described at the opening of this chapter, are examples of self-managed work teams.

Xerox, General Motors, Coors Brewing, PepsiCo, Hewlett-Packard, Honeywell, M&M/Mars, and Aetna Life are just a few familiar names that have implemented self-managed work teams. Estimates suggest that about 30 percent of U.S. employers now use this form of team; and among large firms, the number is probably closer to 50 percent.[4]

Recent business periodicals have been chock-full of articles describing successful applications of self-managed teams. For instance, executives at Power-Cable Corp., a manufacturer of high-quality power tools, say self-managed teams are largely responsible for significant improvements in product quality and generating millions of dollars in cost savings.[5] Self-managed teams are given credit for much of the success Industrial Light & Magic has had in dominating the business of visual digitalization.[6] And W.L. Gore & Associates, the people who make Gore-Tex, attributes its continued growth, innovation, and high profitability to organizing its more than 6,200 employees around self-managed teams.[7]

In spite of these impressive stories, a word of caution needs to be offered here. Overall research on the effectiveness of self-managed work teams has not been uniformly positive.[8] For example, individuals on these teams do tend to report higher levels of job satisfaction. But, counter to conventional wisdom, employees on self-managed work teams seem to have higher absenteeism and turnover rates than do employees working in traditional work structures. Additional research is needed to determine the specific reasons for these findings.

Cross-Functional Teams

Custom Research Inc., a Minneapolis-based market-research firm, had been historically organized around functional departments, but senior management concluded that these functional departments weren't meeting the changing needs of the firm's clients. So management reorganized Custom Research's 100 employees into account teams.[9] The idea behind the teams was to have every aspect of a client's work handled within one team rather than by separate departments. The goal was to improve communication and tracking of work, which would lead to increased productivity and more satisfied clients.

Custom Research's reorganization illustrates the use of **cross-functional teams**. These are teams made up of employees from about the same hierarchical level, but from different work areas, who come together to accomplish a task.

Many organizations have used horizontal, boundary-spanning groups for decades. For example, IBM created a large task force in the 1960s—made up of employees from across departments in the company—to develop its highly successful System 360. And a *task force* is really nothing other than a temporary cross-functional team. Similarly, *committees* composed of members from across departmental lines are another example of cross-functional teams. But the popularity of cross-discipline work teams exploded in the late 1980s. For instance, all the major automobile manufacturers—including Toyota, Honda, Nissan, BMW, GM, Ford, and DaimlerChrysler—currently use this form of team to coordinate complex projects. Harley-Davidson relies on specific cross-functional teams to manage each line of its motorcycles. These teams include Harley employees from design, manufacturing, and purchasing, as well as representatives from key outside suppliers.[10] And IBM still makes use of temporary cross-functional teams. Between November 1999 and June 2000, for instance, IBM's senior management pulled together 21 employees from among its 100,000 information technology staff to come up with recommendations on how the company can speed up projects and bring products to market faster.[11] The 21 members were selected because they had one common characteristic—they had all successfully led fast-moving projects. The Speed Team, as they came to be known, spent eight months sharing experiences, examining differences between fast-moving projects and slow-moving ones, and eventually generated recommendations on how to speed up IBM projects.

Cross-functional teams are an effective means for allowing people from diverse areas within an organization (or even between organizations) to exchange information, develop new ideas and solve problems, and coordinate complex projects. Of course, cross-functional teams are no picnic to manage. Their early stages of development are often very time-consuming as members learn to work with diversity and complexity. It takes time to build trust and teamwork, especially among people from different backgrounds, with different experiences and perspectives.

Virtual Teams

The previous types of teams do their work face-to-face. **Virtual teams** use computer technology to tie together physically dispersed members in order to achieve a common goal.[12] They allow people to collaborate, online, regardless of whether they're only a room apart or separated by continents.

Virtual teams can do all the things that other teams do—share information, make decisions, complete tasks. And they can include members all from the same organization or link an organization's members with employees from other organizations (e.g., suppliers and joint partners).

The three primary factors that differentiate virtual teams from face-to-face teams are: (1) the absence of paraverbal and nonverbal cues, (2) limited social context, and (3) the ability to overcome time and space constraints. In face-to-face conversation, people use paraverbal (tone of voice, inflection, voice volume) and nonverbal (eye movement, facial expression, hand gestures, and other body language) cues. These help clarify communication, but aren't available in online interactions. Virtual teams often suffer from less social rapport and less direct interaction among members. They aren't able to duplicate the normal give and take of face-to-face discussion. Especially when members haven't personally met, virtual teams tend to be more task-oriented and exchange less social/emotional information. Not surprisingly, virtual team members report less satisfaction with the group interaction process than do face-to-face teams. Finally, virtual teams are able to do their work even if members are thousands of miles apart and separated by a dozen or more time zones. They allow people to work together who might otherwise never be able to collaborate.

Companies such as Hewlett-Packard, Boeing, Ford, VeriFone, and Royal Dutch/Shell have become heavy users of virtual teams. VeriFone, for instance, is a California-based maker of computerized swipe machines that read credit card information. Yet the use of virtual teams allows its 3,000 employees, who are located all around the globe, to work together on design projects, marketing plans, and making sales presentations. Moreover, VeriFone has found that virtual teams provide strong recruiting inducements. Says a VeriFone vice president, "We don't put relocation requirements on people. If a person enjoys living in Colorado and can do the job in virtual space, we're not intimidated by that."[13]

CREATING EFFECTIVE TEAMS

Recent studies have taken what was once a veritable laundry list of characteristics and organized them into a relatively focused model.[14] Exhibit 8-3 summarizes what we currently know about what makes teams effective. As you'll see, it builds on many of the group concepts introduced in Chapter 7.

The key components making up effective teams can be subsumed into four general categories. The first category is *work design*. The second relates to the team's *composition*. Third are the resources and other *contextual* influences that make teams effective. Finally, *process* variables reflect the things that go on in the team that influence effectiveness.

What does *team effectiveness* mean in this model? Typically this has included objective measures of the team's productivity, managers' ratings of the team's performance, and aggregate measures of member satisfaction.

Work Design

The work-design category includes variables such as freedom and autonomy, the opportunity to utilize different skills and talents, the ability to complete a whole and identifiable task or product, and working on a task or project that has a substantial impact on others. The evidence indicates that these characteristics enhance member motivation and increase team effectiveness.[15] These work-design characteristics motivate because they increase members' sense of responsibility and ownership over the work and because they make the work more interesting to perform.

EXHIBIT 8–3 A Team Effectiveness Model

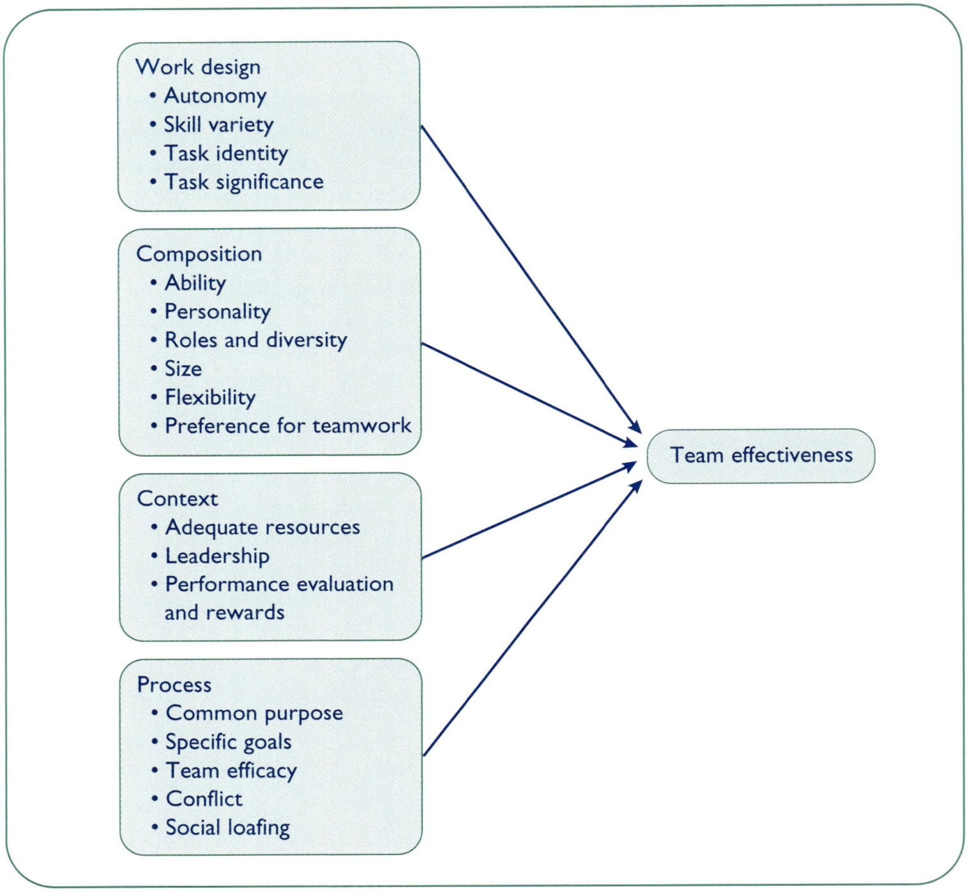

Work design
- Autonomy
- Skill variety
- Task identity
- Task significance

Composition
- Ability
- Personality
- Roles and diversity
- Size
- Flexibility
- Preference for teamwork

Context
- Adequate resources
- Leadership
- Performance evaluation and rewards

Process
- Common purpose
- Specific goals
- Team efficacy
- Conflict
- Social loafing

→ Team effectiveness

Composition

This category includes variables that relate to how teams should be staffed. In this section, we'll address the ability and personality of team members, allocating roles and diversity, size of the team, member flexibility, and members' preference for teamwork.

Abilities of Members To perform effectively, a team requires three different types of skills. First, it needs people with *technical expertise*. Second, it needs people with the *problem-solving and decision-making skills* to be able to identify problems, generate alternatives, evaluate those alternatives, and make competent choices. Finally, teams need people with good listening, feedback, conflict resolution, and other *interpersonal skills*.

No team can achieve its performance potential without developing all three types of skills. The right mix is crucial. Too much of one at the expense of others will result in lower team performance. But teams don't need to have all the complementary skills in place at their beginning. It's not uncommon for one or more members to take responsibility to learn the skills in which the group is deficient, thereby allowing the team to reach its full potential.

Personality We demonstrated in Chapter 3 that personality has a significant influence on individual employee behavior. This can also be extended to team behavior. Many of the dimensions identified in the Big-Five personality model have proved to be relevant to team effectiveness. Specifically, teams that rate higher in mean levels of extroversion, agreeableness, conscientiousness, and emotional stability tend to receive higher managerial ratings for team performance.[16]

Interestingly, the evidence indicates that the variance in personality characteristics may be more important than the mean. So, for example, while a higher mean level of conscientiousness on a team is desirable, mixing both conscientious and not-so-conscientious members tends to lower performance. This may be because members who are highly conscientious not only must perform their own tasks but also perform or redo the tasks of less-conscientious members. It may also be because these differences lead to feelings of contribution inequity. Another interesting finding related to personality is that "one bad apple can spoil the barrel." A single team member who lacks a minimal level of, say, agreeableness, can negatively affect the whole team's performance. So including just one person who is low on agreeableness, conscientiousness, or extroversion can result in strained internal processes and decreased overall performance.

Allocating Roles and Diversity Teams have different needs, and people should be selected for a team to ensure that there is diversity and that all various roles are filled.

We can identify nine potential team roles (see Exhibit 8-4). Successful work teams have people to fill all these roles and have selected people to play these roles based on their skills and preferences.[17] (On many teams, individuals will play multiple roles.) Managers need to understand the individual strengths that each person can bring to a team, select members with their strengths in mind, and allocate work assignments that fit with members' preferred styles. By matching individual preferences with team role demands, managers increase the likelihood that the team members will work well together.

Size of Teams The most effective teams are neither very small (under 4 or 5) or very large (over 12). Very small teams are likely to lack a diversity of views. But when teams have more than about 10 to 12 members, it becomes difficult to get much done. Group members have trouble interacting constructively and agreeing on much; and

EXHIBIT 8–4   Nine Team Roles

Creator-Innovators: Initiate creative ideas
Explorer-Promoters: Champion ideas after they're initiated
Assessor-Developers: Analyze decision options
Thruster-Organizers: Provide structure
Concluder-Producers: Provide direction and follow-through
Controller-Inspectors: Check for details
Upholder-Maintainers: Fight external battles
Reporter-Advisers: Seek full information
Linkers: Coordinate and integrate

Source: C. Margerison and D. McCann, *Margerison-McCann Team Management Systems.* Reproduced by kind permission of TMS Development International Ltd, 2001. For further information, please visit www.tmsdi.com.

large numbers of people usually can't develop the cohesiveness, commitment, and mutual accountability necessary to achieve high performance. So in designing effective teams, managers should keep them in the range of 5 to 12 people. If a natural working unit is larger and you want a team effort, consider breaking the group into subteams.

Member Flexibility   Teams made up of flexible individuals have members who can complete each other's tasks. This is an obvious plus to a team because it greatly improves its adaptability and makes it less reliant on any single member. So selecting members who themselves value flexibility, then cross-training them to do each other's jobs, should lead to higher team performance over time.

Member Preferences   Not every employee is a team player. Given the option, many employees will select themselves *out* of team participation. When people who would prefer to work alone are required to team up, there is a direct threat to the team's morale. This suggests that, when selecting team members, individual preferences should be considered as well as abilities, personalities, and skills. High-performing teams are likely to be composed of people who prefer working as part of a group.

Context

The three contextual factors that appear to be most significantly related to team performance are the presence of adequate resources, effective leadership, and a performance evaluation and reward system that reflects team contributions.

Adequate Resources   Work groups are part of a larger organization system. As such, all work teams rely on resources outside the group to sustain it. And a scarcity of resources directly reduces the ability of the team to perform its job effectively. As one set of researchers concluded, after looking at 13 factors potentially related to group performance, "perhaps one of the most important characteristics of an effective work group is the support the group receives from the organization."[18] This includes support such as timely information, technology, adequate staffing, encouragement, and administrative assistance. Teams must receive the necessary support from management and the larger organization if they are going to succeed in achieving their goals.

Leadership and Structure   Team members must agree on who is to do what and ensure that all members contribute equally in sharing the workload. In addition, the team needs to determine how schedules will be set, what skills need to be developed, how the group will resolve conflicts, and how the group will make and modify decisions. Agreeing on the specifics of work and how they fit together to integrate individual skills requires team leadership and structure. This, incidentally, can be provided directly by management or by the team members themselves as they fulfill promoter, organizer, producer, maintainer, and linker roles (refer back to Exhibit 8-4).

Leadership, of course, isn't always needed. For instance, the evidence indicates that self-managed work teams often perform better than teams with formally appointed leaders.[19] And leaders can obstruct high performance when they interfere with self-managing teams. On self-managed teams, team members absorb many of the duties typically assumed by managers.

Performance Evaluation and Reward Systems   How do you get team members to be both individually and jointly accountable? The traditional, individually oriented evaluation and reward system must be modified to reflect team performance.

Individual performance evaluations, fixed hourly wages, individual incentives, and the like are not consistent with the development of high-performance teams. So in addition to evaluating and rewarding employees for their individual contributions, management should consider group-based appraisals, profit sharing, gainsharing, small-group incentives, and other system modifications that will reinforce team effort and commitment.

Process

The final category related to team effectiveness is process variables. Process variables include member commitment to a common purpose, establishment of specific team goals, team efficacy, a managed level of conflict, and the reduction of social loafing.

A Common Purpose Effective teams have a common and meaningful purpose that provides direction, momentum, and commitment for members. This purpose is a vision. It's broader than specific goals.

Members of successful teams put a tremendous amount of time and effort into discussing, shaping, and agreeing on a purpose that belongs to them both collectively and individually. This common purpose, when accepted by the team, becomes the equivalent of what celestial navigation is to a ship captain—it provides direction and guidance under any and all conditions.

Specific Goals Successful teams translate their common purpose into specific, measurable, and realistic performance goals. Just as we demonstrated in Chapter 4 how goals lead individuals to higher performance, goals also energize teams. These specific goals facilitate clear communication. In addition, they help teams maintain their focus on results.

Also, consistent with the research on individual goals, team goals should be challenging. Difficult goals have been found to raise team performance on those criteria for which they're set. So, for instance, goals for quantity tend to raise quantity, goals for speed tend to raise speed, goals for accuracy raise accuracy, and so on.

Team Efficacy Effective teams have confidence in themselves. They believe they can succeed. We call this *team efficacy*.

Success breeds success. Teams that have been successful raise their beliefs about future success. This, in turn, motivates them to work harder.

What, if anything, can management do to increase team efficacy? Two possible options are helping the team to achieve small successes and skill training. Small successes build team confidence. As a team develops an increasingly stronger performance record, it also increases the collective belief that future efforts will lead to success. In addition, managers should consider providing training to improve members' technical and interpersonal skills. The greater the abilities of team members, the greater the likelihood that the team will develop confidence and the capability to deliver on that confidence.

Conflict Levels Conflict on a team isn't necessarily bad. As we'll elaborate in Chapter 12, teams that are completely void of conflict are likely to become apathetic and stagnant. So conflict can actually improve team effectiveness—but not all types of conflict. Relationship conflicts—those based on interpersonal incompatibilities, tension, and animosity toward others—are almost always dysfunctional. However, on teams performing nonroutine activities, disagreements among members about task content (called task conflicts) is not detrimental. In fact, it's often beneficial because it lessens the likelihood of groupthink. Task conflicts stimulate discussion, promote critical assessment of problems and options, and can lead to better team decisions. So effective teams will be characterized by an appropriate level of conflict.

Social Loafing We learned in Chapter 7 that individuals can hide inside a group. They can engage in social loafing and coast on the group's effort because their individual contributions can't be identified. Effective teams undermine this tendency by holding themselves accountable at both the individual and team levels.

Successful teams make members individually and jointly accountable for the team's purpose, goals, and approach. They are clear on what they are individually responsible for and what they are jointly responsible for.

TURNING INDIVIDUALS INTO TEAM PLAYERS

To this point, we've made a strong case for the value and growing popularity of teams. But many people are not inherently "team players." They're loners or people who want to be recognized for their individual achievements. There are also a great many organizations that have historically nurtured individual accomplishments. They have created competitive work environments in which only the strong survive. If these organizations adopt teams, what do they do about the selfish, "I-have-to-look-out-for-me" employees that they've created? And finally, as we discussed in Chapter 2, countries differ in terms of how they rate on individualism and collectivism. Teams fit well with countries that score high on collectivism. But what if an organization wants to introduce teams into a work population that is made up largely of individuals born and raised in a highly individualistic society? As one writer so aptly put it, in describing the role of teams in the United States: "Americans don't grow up learning how to function in teams. In school we never receive a team report card or learn the names of the team of sailors who traveled with Columbus to America."[20] This limitation would be just as true of Canadians, British, Australians, and others from highly individualistic societies.

The Challenge

The previous points are meant to dramatize that one substantial barrier to using work teams is individual resistance. An employee's success is no longer defined in terms of individual performance. To perform well as team members, individuals must be able to communicate openly and honestly, confront differences and resolve conflicts, and sublimate personal goals for the good of the team. For many employees, this is a difficult—sometimes impossible—task. The challenge of creating team players will be greatest where (1) the national culture is highly individualistic and (2) the teams are being introduced into an established organization that has historically valued individual achievement. These conditions describe, for instance, the situation that faced managers at AT&T, Ford, Motorola, and other large U.S.-based companies. These firms prospered by hiring and rewarding corporate stars, and they bred a competitive climate that encouraged individual achievement and recognition. Employees in these types of firms can be jolted by this sudden shift to the importance of team play. A veteran employee of a large company, who had done very well by working alone, described the experience of joining a team: "I'm learning my lesson. I just had my first negative performance appraisal in 20 years."[21]

On the other hand, the challenge for management is less demanding when teams are introduced where employees have strong collectivist values—such as in Japan or Mexico—or in new organizations that use teams as their initial form for structuring work. For instance, most U.S. dot-com e-businesses—such as Amazon.com, eBay, travelocity.com, and bigwords—make effective use of teams. But they're relatively new companies and were designed around teams from their inception. Everyone in these companies were initially hired with the knowledge that they would be working in teams; and the ability to be a good team player was a basic hiring qualification that all new employees had to meet.

Shaping Team Players

The following summarizes the primary options managers have for trying to turn individuals into team players.

Selection Some people already possess the interpersonal skills to be effective team players. When hiring team members, managers should take care to ensure that candidates can fulfill their team roles as well as having the technical skills required to fill the job.[22]

Many job candidates, especially those socialized around individual contributions, don't have team skills. When faced with such candidates, managers basically have three options. The candidates can undergo training to "make them into team players." If this approach isn't possible or doesn't work, the other two options are to place the candidate in a unit within the organization that doesn't have teams (if one exists) or don't hire the candidate. In established organizations that decide to redesign jobs around teams, it should be expected that some employees will resist being team players and may be untrainable. Unfortunately, such people typically become casualties of the team approach.

Training On a more optimistic note, a large proportion of people raised on the importance of individual accomplishment can be trained to become team players. Training specialists conduct exercises that allow employees to experience the satisfaction that teamwork can provide. They typically offer workshops to help employees improve their problem-solving, communication, negotiation, conflict-management, coaching, and group-development skills. Emerson Electric's Specialty Motor Division in Missouri, for instance, has achieved remarkable success in getting its 650-member workforce not only to accept, but to welcome, team training. Outside consultants were brought in to give workers practical skills for working in teams. After less than a year, employees enthusiastically accepted the value of teamwork.

Rewards The reward system needs to be reworked to encourage cooperative efforts rather than competitive ones. For instance, Lockheed-Martin's Space Launch Systems Company has organized its 1,400 employees into teams. Rewards are structured to return to the team members a percentage increase in the "bottom line" based on the achievement of the team's performance goals.

Promotions, pay raises, and other forms of recognition should be given to individuals for how effective they are as a collaborative team member. This doesn't mean that individual contribution is ignored; rather, it is balanced with selfless contributions to the team. Examples of behaviors that should be rewarded include training new colleagues, sharing information with teammates, helping resolve team conflicts, and mastering new skills that your team needs but in which it's deficient.

Lastly, don't forget the intrinsic rewards that employees can receive from teamwork. Teams provide camaraderie. It's exciting and satisfying to be an integral part of a successful team. The opportunity to engage in personal development and to help teammates grow can be a very satisfying and rewarding experience for employees.

IMPLICATIONS FOR MANAGERS

Few trends have influenced jobs as much as the massive movement to introduce teams into the workplace. The shift from working alone to working on teams requires employees to cooperate with others, share information, confront differences, and sublimate personal interests for the greater good of the team.

Effective teams have been found to have common characteristics. The work that members do should provide freedom and autonomy, the opportunity to utilize different skills and talents, the ability to complete a whole and identifiable task or product, and doing work that has a substantial impact on others. The teams require individuals with technical expertise, as well as problem-solving, decision-making, and interpersonal skills, and high scores on the personality characteristics of extroversion, agreeableness, conscientiousness, and emotional stability. Effective teams are neither too large nor too small—typically they range in size from 5 to 12 people. They have members who fill role demands, are flexible, and who prefer to be part of a group. They also have adequate resources, effective leadership, and a performance evaluation and reward system that reflects team contributions. Finally, effective teams have members committed to a common purpose, specific team goals, members who believe in the team's capabilities, a manageable level of conflict, and a minimal degree of social loafing.

Because individualistic organizations and societies attract and reward individual accomplishment, it is more difficult to create team players in these environments than in collectivistic ones. To make the conversion, management should try to select individuals with the interpersonal skills to be effective team players, provide training to develop teamwork skills, and reward individuals for cooperative efforts.

CHAPTER 9

Communication

After reading this chapter, you should be able to

1. Define communication and list its four functions
2. Describe the communication process
3. Contrast the three common types of small-group networks
4. Identify factors affecting the use of the grapevine
5. Describe common barriers to effective communication
6. List four rules for improving cross-cultural communication
7. Outline behaviors associated with providing effective feedback
8. Identify the behaviors related to effective active listening

Probably the most frequently cited source of interpersonal conflict is poor communication.[1] Because we spend nearly 70 percent of our waking hours communicating—reading, writing, speaking, listening—it seems reasonable to conclude that one of the most inhibiting forces to successful group performance is a lack of effective communication.

No group can exist without communication: the transference of meaning among its members. It is only through transmitting meaning from one person to another that information and ideas can be conveyed. Communication, however, is more than merely imparting meaning. It must also be understood. It's been documented, for instance, that many of the worst aviation disasters in history were directly due to the misunderstanding of instructions between air-traffic controllers and pilots.[2] Keep in mind, therefore, that **communication** must include both the *transference* and *understanding* of meaning.

An idea, no matter how great, is useless until it is transmitted and understood by others. Perfect communication, if there were such a thing, would exist when a thought or idea was transmitted so that the mental picture perceived by the receiver was

113

exactly the same as that envisioned by the sender. Although elementary in theory, perfect communication is never achieved in practice, for reasons we will expand on later. Before making too many generalizations concerning communication and problems in communicating effectively, we need to review briefly the functions that communication performs and describe the communication process.

FUNCTIONS OF COMMUNICATION

Communication serves four major functions within a group or organization: control, motivation, emotional expression, and information. Communication acts to *control* member behavior in several ways. Organizations have authority hierarchies and formal guidelines that employees are required to follow. When employees, for instance, are required to first communicate any job-related grievance to their immediate boss, to follow their job description, or to comply with company policies, communication is performing a control function. But informal communication also controls behavior. When work groups tease or harass a member who produces too much (and makes the rest of the group look bad), they are informally communicating with, and controlling, the member's behavior.

Communication fosters *motivation* by clarifying for employees what is to be done, how well they are doing, and what can be done to improve performance if it's subpar. We saw this aspect of communication operating in our review of goal-setting and reinforcement theories in Chapter 4. The formation of specific goals, feedback on progress toward the goals, and reinforcement of desired behavior all stimulate motivation and require communication.

For many employees, their work group is a primary source for social interaction. The communication that takes place within the group is a fundamental mechanism by which members show their frustrations and feelings of satisfaction. Communication, therefore, provides an avenue for *expression of emotions* and fulfillment of social needs.

The final function that communication performs is related to its role in facilitating decision making. It provides the *information* that individuals and groups need to make decisions by transmitting the data to identify and evaluate choices.

No one of these four functions should be seen as being more important than the others. For groups to perform effectively, they need to maintain some form of control over members, stimulate members to perform, provide a means for emotional expression, and make choices. You can assume that almost every communication interaction that takes place in a group or organization performs one or more of these four functions.

THE COMMUNICATION PROCESS

Before communication can take place, a purpose, expressed as a message to be conveyed, is needed. It passes between a source (the sender) and a receiver. The message is encoded (converted to a symbolic form) and passed by way of some medium (channel) to the receiver, who retranslates (decodes) the message initiated by the sender. The result is a transference of meaning from one person to another.

Exhibit 9-1 depicts this **communication process**. This model is made up of seven parts: (1) the communication source, (2) encoding, (3) the message, (4) the channel, (5) decoding, (6) the receiver, and (7) feedback.

EXHIBIT 9–1   The Communication Process

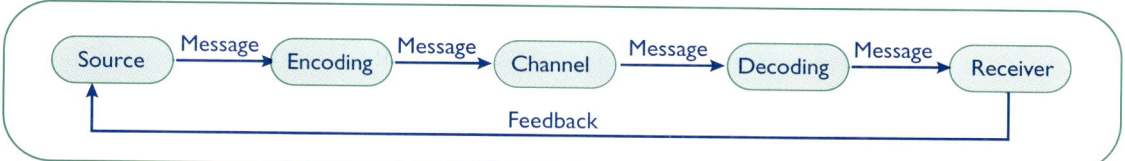

The *source* initiates a message by encoding a thought. The *message* is the actual physical product from the source *encoding*. When we speak, the speech is the message. When we write, the writing is the message. When we gesture, the movements of our arms and the expressions on our faces are the message. The *channel* is the medium through which the message travels. It is selected by the source, who must determine whether to use a formal or informal channel. Formal channels are established by the organization and transmit messages that are related to the professional activities of members. They traditionally follow the authority chain within the organization. Other forms of messages, such as personal or social, follow the informal channels in the organization. The *receiver* is the object to whom the message is directed. But before the message can be received, the symbols in it must be translated into a form that can be understood by the receiver. This step is the *decoding* of the message. The final link in the communication process is a feedback loop. *Feedback* is the check on how successful we have been in transferring our messages as originally intended. It determines whether understanding has been achieved.

DIRECTION OF COMMUNICATION

Communication can flow vertically or laterally. The vertical dimension can be further divided into downward and upward directions.

Downward

Communication that flows from one level of a group or organization to a lower level is a downward communication. When we think of managers communicating with employees, the downward pattern is the one we are usually thinking of. It's used by group leaders and managers to assign goals, provide job instructions, inform employees of policies and procedures, point out problems that need attention, and offer feedback about performance. But downward communication doesn't have to be oral or face-to-face contact. When management sends letters to employees' homes to advise them of the organization's new sick leave policy, it's using downward communication. So is an e-mail from a team leader to the members of her team, reminding them of an upcoming deadline.

Upward

Upward communication flows to a higher level in the group or organization. It's used to provide feedback to higher-ups, to inform them of progress toward goals, and to relay current problems. Upward communication keeps managers aware of how employees feel about their jobs, co-workers, and the organization in general.

Managers also rely on upward communication for ideas on how things can be improved.

Some organizational examples of upward communication are performance reports prepared by lower management for review by middle and top management, suggestion boxes, employee attitude surveys, grievance procedures, superior/subordinate discussions, and informal "gripe" sessions in which employees have the opportunity to identify and discuss problems with their boss or representatives of higher management. For example, FedEx prides itself on its computerized upward communication program. All its employees annually complete climate surveys and reviews of management. This program was cited as a key human resources strength by the Malcolm Baldrige National Quality Award examiners when FedEx won the honor.

Lateral

When communication takes place among members of the same work group, among members of work groups at the same level, among managers at the same level, or among any horizontally equivalent personnel, we describe it as lateral communication.

Why would there be a need for horizontal communications if a group or organization's vertical communications are effective? The answer is that horizontal communications are often necessary to save time and facilitate coordination. In some cases, these lateral relationships are formally sanctioned. More often, they are informally created to short-circuit the vertical hierarchy and expedite action. So lateral communications can, from management's viewpoint, be good or bad. Since strict adherence to the formal vertical structure for all communications can impede the efficient and accurate transfer of information, lateral communications can be beneficial. In such cases, they occur with the knowledge and support of superiors. But they can create dysfunctional conflicts when the formal vertical channels are breached, when members go above or around their superiors to get things done, or when bosses find out that actions have been taken or decisions made without their knowledge.

INTERPERSONAL COMMUNICATION

How do group members transfer meaning between and among each other? There are three basic methods. People essentially rely on oral, written, and nonverbal communication.

Oral Communication

The chief means of conveying messages is oral communication. Speeches, formal one-on-one and group discussions, and the informal rumor mill or grapevine are popular forms of oral communication.

The advantages of oral communication are speed and feedback. A verbal message can be conveyed and a response received in a minimal amount of time. If the receiver is unsure of the message, rapid feedback allows for early detection by the sender and, hence, allows for early correction.

The major disadvantage of oral communication surfaces in organizations or whenever the message has to be passed through a number of people. The more people a message must pass through, the greater the potential distortion. If you ever played the game "telephone" at a party, you know the problem. Each person interprets the message in his or her own way. The message's content, when it reaches its destination, is often very different from that of the original. In an organization, where decisions and other communiqués are verbally passed up and down the authority hierarchy, there are considerable opportunities for messages to become distorted.

Written Communication

Written communications include memos, letters, electronic mail, fax transmissions, organizational periodicals, notices placed on bulletin boards, or any other device that communicates information via written words or symbols.

Why would a sender choose to use written communications? They're tangible and verifiable. Typically, both the sender and receiver have a record of the communication. The message can be stored for an indefinite period of time. If there are questions concerning the content of the message, it is physically available for later reference. This feature is particularly important for complex and lengthy communications. The marketing plan for a new product is likely to contain a number of tasks spread out over several months. By putting it in writing, those who have to initiate the plan can readily refer to it over the life of the plan. A final benefit of written communication comes from the process itself. You're usually more careful with the written word than the oral word. You're forced to think more thoroughly about what you want to convey in a written message than in a spoken one. Thus written communications are more likely to be well thought out, logical, and clear.

Of course, written messages have their drawbacks. They're time-consuming. You could convey far more information to a college instructor in a one-hour oral exam than in a one-hour written exam. In fact, you could probably say the same thing in ten to fifteen minutes that it would take you an hour to write. So, although writing may be more precise, it also consumes a great deal of time. The other major disadvantage is feedback, or lack of it. Oral communication allows the receiver to respond rapidly to what he thinks he hears. Written communication, however, does not have a built-in feedback mechanism. The result is that mailing a memo is no assurance that it has been received, and, if received, there is no guarantee the recipient will interpret it as the sender intended. The latter point is also relevant in oral communiqués, except it's easy in such cases merely to ask the receiver to summarize what you've said. An accurate summary presents feedback evidence that the message has been received and understood.

Nonverbal Communication

Every time we verbally give a message to someone, we also impart a nonverbal message. In some instances, the nonverbal component may stand alone. For example, in a singles bar, a glance, a stare, a smile, a frown, and a provocative body movement all convey meaning. As such, no discussion of communication would be complete without consideration of *nonverbal communication*, which includes body movements, the intonations or emphasis we give to words, facial expressions, and the physical distance between the sender and receiver.

The academic study of body motions has been labeled **kinesics**. It refers to gestures, facial configurations, and other movements of the body. But it is a relatively young field, and it has been subject to far more conjecture and popularizing than the research findings support. Hence, while we acknowledge that body movement is an important segment of the study of communication and behavior, conclusions must, of necessity, be guarded. Recognizing this qualification, let us briefly consider the ways body motions convey meaning.

It can be argued that every *body movement* has a meaning and that no movement is accidental. For example, through body language we say, "Help me, I'm lonely"; "Take me, I'm available"; "Leave me alone, I'm depressed." And rarely do we send our messages consciously. We act out our state of being with nonverbal body language. We lift one eyebrow for disbelief. We rub our noses for puzzlement. We clasp our arms to isolate ourselves or to protect ourselves. We shrug our shoulders for indifference, wink one eye for intimacy, tap our fingers for impatience, slap our forehead for forgetfulness.

We may disagree with the specific meanings of the movements just described, but we can't deny that body language adds to, and often complicates, verbal communication. A body position or movement does not by itself have a precise or universal meaning, but when it is linked with spoken language, it gives fuller meaning to a sender's message.

If you read the verbatim minutes of a meeting, you wouldn't grasp the impact of what was said in the same way you would if you had been there or saw the meeting on video. Why? There is no record of nonverbal communication. The emphasis given to words or phrases is missing. To illustrate how *intonations* can change the meaning of a message, consider the student in class who asks the instructor a question. The instructor replies, "What do you mean by that?" The student's reaction will be different depending on the tone of the instructor's response. A soft, smooth tone creates a different meaning from an intonation that is abrasive with strong emphasis placed on the last word.

The *facial expression* of the instructor in the previous illustration also conveys meaning. A snarling face says something different from a smile. Facial expressions, along with intonations, can show arrogance, aggressiveness, fear, shyness, and other characteristics that would never be communicated if you read a transcript of what had been said.

The way individuals space themselves in terms of *physical distance* also has meaning. What is considered proper spacing is largely dependent on cultural norms. For example, what is considered a businesslike distance in some European countries would be viewed as intimate in many parts of North America. If someone stands closer to you than is considered appropriate, it may indicate aggressiveness or sexual interest; if farther away than usual, it may mean disinterest or displeasure with what is being said.

It's important for the receiver to be alert to these nonverbal aspects of communication. You should look for nonverbal cues as well as listen to the literal meaning of a sender's words. You should particularly be aware of contradictions between the messages. Your boss may say she is free to talk to you about a pressing budget problem, but you may see nonverbal signals suggesting that this is not the time to discuss the subject. Regardless of what is being said, an individual who frequently glances at her wristwatch is giving the message that she would prefer to terminate the conversation. We misinform others when we express one message verbally, such as trust, but nonverbally communicate a contradictory message that reads, "I don't have confidence in you." These contradictions often suggest that "actions speak louder (and more accurately) than words."

ORGANIZATIONAL COMMUNICATION

In this section we move from interpersonal communication to organizational communication. Our focus here will be on formal networks, the grapevine, and computer-aided mechanisms used by organizations to facilitate communication.

Formal Small-Group Networks

Formal organizational networks can be very complicated. They can, for instance, include hundreds of people and a half-dozen or more hierarchical levels. To simplify our discussion, we've condensed these networks into three common small-groups of five people each (see Exhibit 9-2). These three networks are the chain, wheel, and all-channel. Although these three networks have been extremely simplified, they do allow us to describe the unique qualities of each.

The *chain* rigidly follows the formal chain of command. This network approximates the communication channels you might find in a rigid three-level organization. The *wheel* relies on a central figure to act as the conduit for all the group's communication. It simulates the communication network you would find on a team with a strong leader. The *all-channel* network permits all group members to actively communicate with each other. The all-channel network is most often characterized in practice by self-managed teams, in which all group members are free to contribute and no one person takes on a leadership role.

As Exhibit 9-3 demonstrates, the effectiveness of each network depends on the criteria you're concerned about. For instance, the structure of the wheel facilitates the emergence of a leader, the all-channel network is best if you are concerned with having high member satisfaction, and the chain is best if accuracy is most important. Exhibit 9-3 leads us to the conclusion that no single network will be best for all occasions.

The Grapevine

The formal system is not the only communication network in a group or organization. There is also an informal one—the **grapevine**. While the grapevine may be informal, this doesn't mean it's not an important source of information. For instance, a recent

EXHIBIT 9–2   Three Common Small-Group Networks

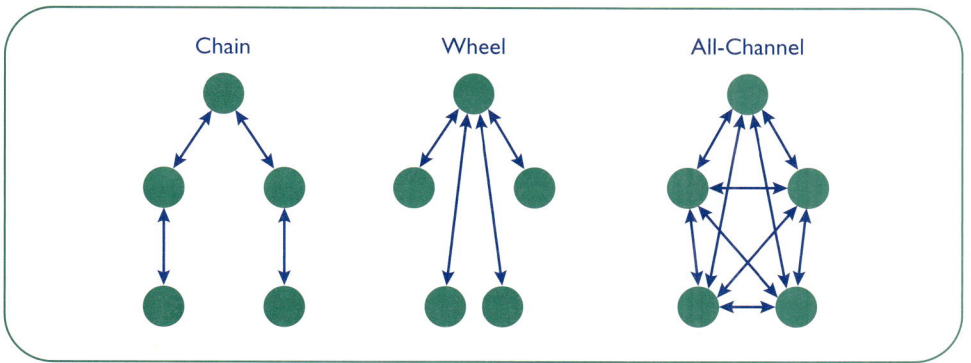

EXHIBIT 9–3 Small-Group Networks and Effectiveness Criteria

	Networks		
Criteria	Chain	Wheel	All Channel
Speed	Moderate	Fast	Fast
Accuracy	High	High	Moderate
Emergence of a leader	Moderate	High	None
Member satisfaction	Moderate	Low	High

survey found that 75 percent of employees hear about matters first through rumors on the grapevine.[3]

The grapevine has three main characteristics. First, it is not controlled by management. Second, it is perceived by most employees as being more believable and reliable than formal communiqués issued by top management. And third, it is largely used to serve the interests of the people within it.

One of the most famous studies of the grapevine investigated the communication pattern among 67 managerial personnel in a small manufacturing firm.[4] The basic approach used was to learn from each communication recipient how he or she first received a given piece of information and then trace it back to its source. It was found that, while the grapevine was an important source of information, only 10 percent of the executives acted as liaison individuals, that is, passed the information on to more than one other person. For example, when one executive decided to resign to enter the insurance business, 81 percent of the executives knew about it, but only 11 percent transmitted this information to others.

Two other conclusions from this study are also worth noting. Information on events of general interest tended to flow between the major functional groups (production, sales) rather than within them. Also, no evidence surfaced to suggest that any one group consistently acted as liaisons; rather, different types of information passed through different liaisons.

An attempt to replicate this study among employees in a small state government office also found that only 10 percent act as liaison individuals.[5] This finding is interesting, because the replication contained a wider spectrum of employees, including operative as well as managerial personnel. But the flow of information in the government office took place within, rather than between, functional groups. It was proposed that this discrepancy might be due to comparing an executive-only sample against one that also included operative workers. Managers, for example, might feel greater pressure to stay informed and thus cultivate others outside their immediate functional group. Also, in contrast to the findings of the original study, the replication found that a consistent group of individuals acted as liaisons by transmitting information in the government office.

Is the information that flows along the grapevine accurate? The evidence indicates that about 75 percent of what is carried is accurate.[6] But what conditions foster an active grapevine? What gets the rumor mill rolling?

It is frequently assumed that rumors start because they make titillating gossip. This is rarely the case. Rumors emerge as a response to situations that are *important* to us, where there is *ambiguity*, and under conditions that arouse *anxiety*. The fact that work situations frequently contain these three elements explains why rumors flourish in organizations. The secrecy and competition that typically prevail in large organizations—around such issues as the appointment of new bosses, the relocation of offices, downsizing decisions, and the realignment of work assignments—create conditions that encourage and sustain rumors on the grapevine. A rumor will persist either until the wants and expectations creating the uncertainty underlying the rumor are fulfilled or until the anxiety is reduced.

What can we conclude from the preceding discussion? Certainly the grapevine is an important part of any group or organization's communication network and is well worth understanding. It identifies for managers confusing issues that employees consider important and that create anxiety. It acts, therefore, as both a filter and a feedback mechanism, picking up the issues that employees consider relevant. For employees, the grapevine is particularly valuable for translating formal communications into their group's own jargon. Maybe more important, again from a managerial perspective, it seems possible to analyze grapevine information and to predict its flow, given that only a small set of individuals (around 10 percent) actively pass on information to more than one other person. By assessing which liaison individuals will consider a given piece of information to be relevant, we can improve our ability to explain and predict the pattern of the grapevine.

Computer-Aided Communication

Communication in today's organizations is enhanced and enriched by computer-aided technologies. These include electronic mail, intranet and extranet links, and videoconferencing. Electronic mail, for instance, has dramatically reduced the number of memos, letters, and phone calls that employees historically used to communicate among themselves and with suppliers, customers, or other outside stakeholders.

E-Mail Electronic mail (or e-mail) uses the Internet to transmit and receive computer-generated text and documents. Its growth has been spectacular. Most white-collar employees now regularly use e-mail. In fact, a recent study found that the average U.S. employee receives 31 e-mail messages a day.[7] And organizations are recognizing the value of e-mail for all workers. Ford Motor Co., for instance, recently made a computer, modem, printer, and e-mail account available for $5 a month to all of its more than 300,000 employees worldwide.[8]

As a communication tool, e-mail has a long list of benefits. E-mail messages can be quickly written, edited, and stored. They can be distributed to one person or thousands with the click of a mouse. They can be read, in their entirety, at the convenience of the recipient. And the cost of sending formal e-mail messages to employees is a fraction of what it would cost to print, duplicate, and distribute a comparable letter or brochure.

E-mail, of course, is not without its drawbacks. At the top of the list is information overload. It's not unusual for employees to get a hundred or more e-mails a day! Reading, absorbing, and responding to such an inflow can literally consume an employee's entire day. In essence, e-mail's ease of use has become its biggest negative. Employees are finding it increasingly difficult to distinguish important e-mails from junk mail and irrelevant messages. Another drawback of e-mails is that they lack emotional content. The nonverbal cues in a face-to-face message or the tone of voice from a phone call convey important information that doesn't come across in e-mail. Finally, e-mail tends to be cold and impersonal. As such, it's not the ideal means to convey information such as layoffs, plant closings, or other messages that might evoke emotional responses and require empathy or social support.

Intranet and Extranet Links   *Intranets* are private, organization-wide information networks that look and act like a Web site but to which only people in an organization have access. Intranets are rapidly becoming the preferred means for employees within companies to communicate with each other. In addition, organizations are creating *extranet* links that connect internal employees with selected suppliers, customers, and strategic partners. The latter, for instance, can allow GM employees to send electronic messages and documents to its steel and rubber suppliers as well as communicate with its dealers. Similarly, all Wal-Mart vendors are linked into its extranet system, allowing Wal-Mart buyers to easily communicate with its suppliers and for suppliers to monitor the inventory status of its products at Wal-Mart stores.

Videoconferencing   *Videoconferencing* is an extension of intranet or extranet systems. It permits employees in an organization to have meetings with people at different locations. Live audio and video images of members allow them to see, hear, and talk with each other. Videoconferencing technology, in effect, allows employees to conduct interactive meetings without the necessity of all physically being in the same location.

In the late 1990s, videoconferencing was basically conducted from special rooms equipped with television cameras, located at company facilities. More recently, cameras and microphones are being attached to individual computers, allowing people to participate in videoconferences without leaving their desks. As the cost of this technology drops, videoconferencing is likely to be increasingly seen as an alternative to expensive and time-consuming travel.

Summary   Computer-aided communications are reshaping the way we communicate in organizations. Specifically, it is no longer necessary for employees to be at their work station or desk to be "available." Pagers, cellular phones, and personal communicators allow employees to be reached when they're in a meeting, during a lunch break, while visiting a customer across town, or during a golf game on Saturday morning. The line between an employee's work and nonwork life is no longer distinct. In the electronic age, all employees can theoretically be "on call" 24 hours a day, 7 days a week.

Organizational boundaries become less relevant as a result of computer-aided communications. Networked computers allow employees to jump vertical levels within the organization, work full-time at home or someplace other than a facility operated by an organization, and conduct ongoing communications with people in other organizations. The market researcher who wants to discuss an issue with the vice president of marketing (who is three levels up in the hierarchy), can bypass the people in between and send an e-mail message directly. And in so doing, the traditional status hierarchy, largely determined by level and access, becomes essentially negated. Or that same market researcher may choose to live in the Cayman Islands and work at home via telecommuting rather than do his or her job in the company's Chicago office. And when an employee's computer is linked to suppliers' and customers' computers, the boundaries separating organizations become further blurred. As a case in point, because Levi Strauss's and Wal-Mart's computers are linked, Levi is able to monitor Wal-Mart's inventory of its jeans and to replace merchandise as needed, clouding the distinction between Levi and Wal-Mart employees.

BARRIERS TO EFFECTIVE COMMUNICATION

A number of barriers can retard or distort effective communication. In this section, we highlight the more important of these barriers.

Filtering

Filtering refers to a sender's purposely manipulating information so it will be seen more favorably by the receiver. For example, when a manager tells his boss what he feels his boss wants to hear, he is filtering information.

The major determinant of filtering is the number of levels in an organization's structure. The more vertical levels in the organization's hierarchy, the more opportunities there are for filtering. But you can expect some filtering to occur wherever there are status differences. Factors such as fear of conveying bad news and the desire to please one's boss often lead employees to tell their superiors what they think those superiors want to hear, thus distorting upward communications.

Selective Perception

We have mentioned selective perception before in this book. It appears again because the receiver, in the communication process, sees and hears things in a selective way, based on his needs, motivations, experience, background, and other personal characteristics. The receiver also projects his interests and expectations into communications as he decodes them. The employment interviewer who expects a female job candidate to put family before career is likely to see that priority in female candidates, regardless of whether the candidates feel that way or not. As we said in Chapter 2, we don't see reality; we interpret what we see and call it reality.

Information Overload

Individuals have a finite capacity for processing data. As noted in our previous discussion of e-mail, when the information we have to work with exceeds our processing capacity, the result is **information overload**. And with e-mails, phone calls, faxes, meetings, and the need to keep current in one's field, more and more managers and professionals are complaining that they're suffering from information overload.

What happens when individuals have more information than they can sort and use? They tend to weed out, ignore, pass over, or forget information. Or they may put off further processing until the overload situation is over. Regardless, the result is lost information and less effective communication.

Gender Styles

Men and women use oral communication for different reasons. Consequently, gender becomes a barrier to effective communication between the sexes.

Research evidence indicates that men use talk to emphasize status, whereas women use it to create connection.[9] That is, men speak and hear a language of status and independence, and women speak and hear a language of connection and intimacy. So, for many men, conversations are primarily a means to preserve independence and maintain status in a hierarchical social order. For many women, conversations are negotiations for closeness, in which people try to seek and give confirmation and support. For example, men frequently complain that women talk on and on about their problems. Women criticize men for not listening. What's happening is that when men hear a problem, they want to assert their desire for independence and control by providing solutions. Women, on the other hand, view relating a problem as a way to promote closeness. Women present the problem to gain support and connection, not to get the men's advice.

Emotions

How the receiver feels at the time of receiving a communication message will influence how he or she interprets it. The same message received when you're angry or distraught is often interpreted differently from when you're happy. Extreme emotions such as jubilation or depression are most likely to hinder effective communication. In such instances, we are most prone to disregard our rational and objective thinking processes and substitute emotional judgments.

Language

Words mean different things to different people. Age, education, and cultural background are three of the more obvious variables that influence the language a person uses and the definitions he or she gives to words.

In an organization, employees usually come from diverse backgrounds. Further, the grouping of employees into departments creates specialists who develop their own jargon or technical language. In large organizations, members are also frequently widely dispersed geographically—even operating in different countries—and individuals in each locale will use terms and phrases that are unique to their area. The existence of vertical levels can also cause language problems. For instance, differences in meaning with regard to words such as *incentives* and *quotas* have been found at different levels in management. Top managers often speak about the need for incentives and quotas, yet these terms imply manipulation and create resentment among many lower managers.

The point is that, although you and I probably speak a common language—English—our usage of that language is far from uniform. If we knew how each of us modified the language, communication difficulties would be minimized. The problem is that members in an organization usually don't know how those with whom they interact have modified the language. Senders tend to assume that the words and terms they use mean the same to the receiver as they do to them. This assumption is often incorrect.

CROSS-CULTURAL COMMUNICATION

Effective communication is difficult under the best of conditions. Cross-cultural factors clearly create the potential for increased communication problems.

The process of encoding and decoding messages into symbols is based on an individual's cultural background and, as a result, is not the same for all people. The greater the differences in backgrounds between sender and receiver, the greater the differences in meanings attached to particular words or behaviors. People from different cultures see, interpret, and evaluate things differently, and consequently act on them differently.

Cultural Context

A better understanding of cultural barriers and their implications for communicating across cultures can be achieved by considering the concepts of high- and low-context cultures.[10]

Cultures tend to differ in the importance to which context influences the meaning that individuals take from what is actually said or written according to whom the other person is. Countries such as China, Vietnam, and Saudi Arabia are **high-context cultures**. They rely heavily on nonverbal and subtle situational cues when communicating with others. What is *not* said may be more significant than what is said. In these cultures, a person's official status, place in society, and reputation carry considerable weight in communications. In contrast, people from Europe and North America reflect their **low-context cultures**. They rely essentially on words to convey meaning. Body language or formal titles are secondary to spoken and written words (see Exhibit 9-4).

What do these contextual differences mean in terms of communication? Actually, quite a lot! Communication in high-context cultures implies considerably more trust by parties. What may appear, to an outsider, to be a casual and insignificant conversation is important because it reflects the desire to build a relationship and create trust. Oral agreements imply strong commitments in high-context cultures. And who you are—your age, seniority, rank in the organization—are highly valued and heavily influence your credibility. But in low-context cultures, enforceable contracts will tend to be in writing, precisely worded, and highly legalistic. Similarly, low-context cultures value directness. Managers are expected to be explicit and precise in conveying intended meaning. It's quite different in high-context cultures, where managers tend to "make suggestions" rather than give orders.

EXHIBIT 9–4   High- vs. Low-Context Cultures

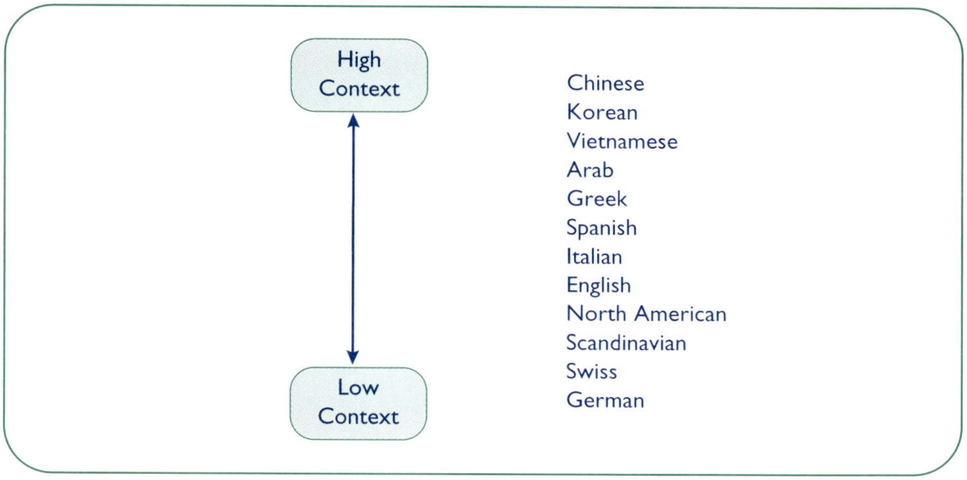

High Context
- Chinese
- Korean
- Vietnamese
- Arab
- Greek
- Spanish
- Italian
- English
- North American
- Scandinavian
- Swiss
- German

Low Context

Source: Based on the work of E.T. Hall from R.E. Dulck, J.S. Fielden, and J.S. Hill, "International Communication: An Executive Primer," *Business Horizons*, January-February 1991, p. 21.

A Cultural Guide

When communicating with people from a different culture, what can you do to reduce misperceptions, misinterpretations, and misevaluations? Following these four rules can be helpful[11]:

1. *Assume differences until similarity is proved.* Most of us assume that others are more similar to us than they actually are. But people from different countries often are very different from us. So you are far less likely to err if you assume that others are different from you rather than assuming similarity until difference is proved.
2. *Emphasize description rather than interpretation or evaluation.* Interpreting or evaluating what someone has said or done, in contrast to description, is based more on the observer's culture and background than on the observed situation. So delay judgment until you've had sufficient time to observe and interpret the situation from the perspectives of all cultures involved.
3. *Practice empathy.* Before sending a message, put yourself in the receiver's shoes. What are his or her values, experiences, and frames of reference? What do you know about his or her education, upbringing, and background that can give you added insight? Try to see the other person as he or she really is.
4. *Treat your interpretation as a working hypothesis.* Once you've developed an explanation for a new situation or think you empathize with someone from a foreign culture, treat your interpretation as a hypothesis that needs further testing rather than as a certainty. Carefully assess the feedback provided by receivers to see if it confirms your hypothesis. For important decisions or communiqués, you can also check with other foreign and home-country colleagues to make sure your interpretations are on target.

ETHICS IN COMMUNICATION: IS IT WRONG TO TELL A LIE?

When we were children, our parents told us, "It's wrong to tell a lie." Yet we all have told lies at one time or another. If most of us agree that telling lies is wrong, how do we justify continuing to do it? The answer is: Most of us differentiate between "real lies" and "little white lies"—the latter being an acceptable, even necessary, part of social interaction. Since lying is so closely intertwined with interpersonal communication, let's look at an issue many managers confront: Does a sound purpose justify intentionally distorting information? Consider the following situation.

An employee who works for you asks you about a rumor she's heard that your department and all its employees will be transferred from New York City to Dallas. You know the rumor is true, but you would rather not let the information out just yet. You're fearful it could hurt departmental morale and lead to premature resignations. What do you say to your employee? Do you lie, evade the question, distort your answer, or tell the truth?

IMPLICATIONS FOR MANAGERS

Given the barriers to communication, what can managers do to minimize problems and attempt to overcome those barriers? The following suggestions should be helpful in making communication more effective.

Use Multiple Channels

When you use multiple channels to convey a message, you improve the likelihood of clarity for two reasons. First, you stimulate a number of the receiver's senses. An e-mail and a phone call, for example, provide sight and sound. Repeating a message by using a different channel acts to reinforce it and decreases the likelihood of distortions. Second, people have different abilities to absorb information. Some understand best when a message is in writing. Others, however, prefer oral communications. The latter tend to rely on nonverbal cues to provide them with enhanced insights that words alone don't convey.

Use Feedback

Many communication problems can be attributed directly to misunderstandings and inaccuracies. These are less likely to occur if the manager ensures that the feedback loop is utilized in the communication process (see Exhibit 9-5). This feedback can be verbal, written, or nonverbal.

If a manager asks a receiver, "Did you understand what I said?", the response represents feedback. But the "yes" or "no" type of feedback can definitely be improved upon. The manager can ask a set of questions relating to a message in order to determine whether the message was received as intended. Better yet, the manager can ask the receiver to restate the message, in his or her own words. If the manager then hears what was intended, understanding and accuracy should be enhanced. Feedback can also be more subtle than the direct

EXHIBIT 9–5   Improving Performance Feedback Skills

The following specific suggestions can help managers to be more effective in providing performance feedback to others:

1. *Focus on specific behaviors.* Feedback should be specific rather than general. For example, instead of saying, "You have a bad attitude," a manager might say, "Bob, I'm concerned with your attitude toward your work. You were a half-hour late to yesterday's staff meeting, and then you told me you hadn't read the preliminary report we were discussing. Today you tell me you're taking off three hours early for a dental appointment." This tells Bob why he is being criticized.
2. *Keep feedback impersonal.* Feedback should be job related. Never criticize someone personally because of an inappropriate action. Telling people they're "stupid," "incompetent," or the like is almost always counterproductive.
3. *Keep feedback goal oriented.* If a manager has to say something negative, he or she should make sure it's directed toward the recipient's goals. A manager should ask whom the feedback is supposed to help. If the answer is essentially that "I've got something I just want to get off my chest," then he or she should not speak.
4. *Make feedback well timed.* Feedback is most meaningful to a recipient when there is a very short interval between his or her behavior and the receipt of feedback about that behavior.
5. *Ensure understanding.* Is the feedback concise and complete enough so the recipient clearly and fully understands the communication? Managers should consider having the recipient rephrase the content of the feedback to see whether it fully captures the intended meaning.
6. *Direct negative feedback toward behavior that is controllable by the recipient.* There's little value in reminding a person of a shortcoming over which he or she has no control. Negative feedback, therefore, should be directed toward behavior the recipient can do something about.

asking of questions or the summarizing of the message by the receiver. General comments can give the manager a sense of a receiver's reaction to a message. In addition, performance appraisals, salary reviews, and promotion decisions represent important, but more subtle, forms of feedback.

Feedback, of course, does not have to be conveyed in words. Actions can speak louder than words. For instance, a sales manager sends out a directive to her staff describing a new monthly sales report that all sales personnel will need to complete. Failure of some of the salespeople to turn in the new report is a type of feedback. It should suggest to her that she needs to clarify further her initial directive. Similarly, when you give a speech to a group of people, you can tell by their eye movements and other nonverbal clues whether group members are getting your message. This benefit of feedback may explain why television performers on situation comedy shows prefer to tape their programs in front of a live audience. Immediate laughter and applause, or their absence, convey to the performers whether they are getting their message across.

Simplify Language

Because language can be a barrier, a manager should seek to structure messages in ways that will make them clear and understandable. Words should be chosen carefully. The manager needs to simplify his or her language and consider the audience to whom a message is directed, so that the language will be compatible with the receiver. Remember, effective communication is achieved when a message is both received and *understood*. Understanding is improved by simplifying the language used in relation to the audience intended. This means, for example, that a hospital administrator should always try to communicate in clear and easily understood terms and that the language used for conveying messages to the surgical staff should be purposely different from that used with employees in the admissions office. Jargon can facilitate understanding when it is used with other group members who speak that language, but it can cause innumerable problems when used outside that group.

Listen Actively

When someone talks, we hear. But, too often, we don't listen. Listening is an active search for meaning, whereas hearing is passive (see Exhibit 9-6). When you listen, two people, the receiver and the sender, are thinking.

Many of us are poor listeners. Why? Because it's difficult and because it's usually more satisfying to talk. Listening, in fact, is often more tiring than talking. It demands intellectual effort. Unlike hearing, active listening demands total concentration. The average person speaks at a rate of about 150 words per minute, whereas we have the capacity to listen at the rate of over 1,000 words per minute. The difference obviously leaves idle brain time and opportunities for the mind to wander.

Active listening is enhanced when the receiver develops empathy with the sender, that is, when the receiver tries to place himself in the sender's position. Because senders differ in attitudes, interests, needs, and expectations, empathy makes it easier to understand the actual content of a message. An empathetic listener reserves judgment on the message's content and carefully listens to what is

EXHIBIT 9–6   Improving Active Listening Skills

> The following specific suggestions can help managers to be more effective active listeners:
>
> 1. *Make eye contact.* We listen with our ears, but people judge whether we're listening by looking at our eyes. Making eye contact with the speaker focuses one's attention, reduces the potential for distractions, and encourages the speaker.
> 2. *Exhibit affirmative head nods and appropriate facial expressions.* The effective listener shows interest in what is being said through nonverbal signals. Affirmative head nods and appropriate facial expressions, when added to good eye contact, convey to the speaker that one is listening.
> 3. *Avoid distracting actions or gestures.* The other side of showing interest is avoiding actions that suggest that the manager's mind is somewhere else. Actions such as looking at one's watch, shuffling papers, or playing with a pencil make the speaker feel the listener is bored or uninterested.
> 4. *Ask questions.* The critical listener analyzes what he or she hears and asks questions. Questioning provides clarification, ensures understanding, and assures the speaker one is listening.
> 5. *Paraphrase.* The effective listener uses phrases such as "What I hear you saying is . . . " or "Do you mean . . . ?" Paraphrasing acts as an excellent control device to check on whether one is listening carefully. It is also a control for accuracy.
> 6. *Avoid interrupting the speaker.* Let the speaker complete his or her thought before responding. Don't try to guess where the speaker's thoughts are going.
> 7. *Don't overtalk.* Most of us would rather voice our own ideas than listen to what someone else says. Too many of us listen only because it's the price we have to pay to get people to let us talk. Talking may be more fun and silence may be uncomfortable, but it's impossible to talk and listen at the same time. The good listener recognizes this fact and doesn't overtalk.

being said. The goal is to improve one's ability to receive the full meaning of a communication, without having it distorted by premature judgments or interpretations.

Constrain Emotions

It would be naive to assume that a manager always communicates in a fully rational manner. Yet we know that emotions can severely cloud and distort the transference of meaning. If we're emotionally upset over an issue, we're likely to misconstrue incoming messages, and we may fail to express clearly and accurately our outgoing messages. What can the manager do? The best approach is to defer further communication until composure is regained.

Use the Grapevine

You can't eliminate the grapevine. What managers should do, therefore, is use it and make it work for them. Managers can use the grapevine to transmit information rapidly, to test the reaction to various decisions before their final consummation, and as a valuable source of feedback when the managers themselves are grapevine members. Of course, the grapevine can carry damaging rumors that reduce the effectiveness of formal communication. To lessen this potentially destructive force, managers should make good use of formal channels by ensuring that they regularly carry the relevant and accurate information that employees seek.

CHAPTER 10

Leadership and Creating Trust

After reading this chapter, you should be able to

1. Summarize the conclusions of trait theories
2. Identify the limitations of behavioral theories
3. Describe Fiedler's contingency model
4. Summarize the path-goal theory
5. List the contingency variables in the leader-participation model
6. Explain gender differences in leadership styles
7. Differentiate *transformational* from *transactional* leadership
8. Identify the skills that visionary leaders exhibit
9. Describe the four specific roles of effective team leaders
10. Summarize how leaders can build trust

It has been accepted as a truism that good leadership is essential to business, to government, and to the countless groups and organizations that shape the way we live, work, and play. If leadership is such an important factor, the critical issue is: What makes a great leader? It's tempting to answer: Great followers! Although there is some truth to this response, the issue is far more complex.

WHAT IS LEADERSHIP?

Leadership is the ability to influence a group toward the achievement of goals. The source of this influence may be formal, such as that provided by the possession of managerial rank in an organization. Because management positions come with some degree of formally designated authority, an individual may assume a leadership role as a result of the position he or she holds in the organization. But not all leaders are managers; nor, for that matter, are all managers leaders. Just because an organization provides its managers with certain rights is no assurance they will be able to lead effectively. Nonsanctioned leadership—that is, the ability to influence that arises outside of the formal structure of the organization—is as important as or more important than formal influence. In other words, leaders can emerge from within a group as well as being formally appointed.

The leadership literature is voluminous, and much of it is confusing and contradictory. In the following pages, we attempt to provide you with some insights into what makes an effective leader.

TRAIT THEORIES

If one were to describe a leader on the basis of the general connotations presented in today's media, one might list qualities such as intelligence, charisma, decisiveness, enthusiasm, strength, bravery, integrity, self-confidence, and so on—possibly eliciting the conclusion that effective leaders must be one part Boy Scout and two parts Jesus Christ. The search for characteristics, such as those listed, that would differentiate leaders from nonleaders occupied the early psychologists who studied leadership.

Is it possible to isolate one or more personality traits in individuals we generally acknowledge as leaders—Winston Churchill, Mother Teresa, Martin Luther King, Jr., John F. Kennedy, Nelson Mandela, Colin Powell—that nonleaders do not possess? We may agree that these individuals meet our definition of a leader, but they represent individuals with utterly different characteristics. If the concept of traits was to be proved valid, specific characteristics had to be found that all leaders possess.

Research efforts at isolating these traits resulted in a number of dead ends. If the search was to identify a set of traits that would always differentiate leaders from followers and effective from ineffective leaders, the search failed. Perhaps it was a bit optimistic to believe that a set of consistent and unique traits could apply across the board to all effective leaders, whether they were in charge of the Mormon Tabernacle Choir, General Electric, Ted's Malibu Surf Shop, the Brazilian national soccer team, or Oxford University.

However, attempts to identify traits consistently associated with leadership have been more successful. Six traits on which leaders differ from nonleaders include (1) drive and ambition, (2) the desire to lead and influence others, (3) honesty and integrity, (4) self-confidence, (5) intelligence, and (6) in-depth technical knowledge related to their area of responsibility.[1]

Yet traits alone are not sufficient for explaining leadership. Their primary failing is that they ignore situational factors. Possessing the appropriate traits only makes it more likely that an individual will be an effective leader. He or she still has to take the right actions. And "the right actions" in one situation are not necessarily right for a different situation.

BEHAVIORAL THEORIES

The inability to strike gold in the "trait mines" led researchers to look at the behaviors that specific leaders exhibited. They wondered if there was something unique in the way effective leaders behave. For example, do they tend to be more democratic than autocratic?

Not only, it was hoped, would the behavioral approach provide more definitive answers about the nature of leadership but, if successful, it would have practical implications quite different from those of the trait approach. If trait research had been successful, it would have provided a basis for selecting the right person to assume a formal position in a group or organization that required leadership. In contrast, if behavioral studies were to turn up critical behavioral determinants of leadership, we could *train* people to be leaders. The difference between trait and behavioral theories, in terms of application, lies in their underlying assumptions. If trait theories were valid, then leaders were basically born: You either had it or you didn't. On the other hand, if there were specific behaviors that identified leaders, then we could teach leadership—we could design programs that implanted these behavioral patterns in individuals who desired to be effective leaders. This was surely a more exciting avenue, for it would mean that the supply of leaders could be expanded. If training worked, we could have an infinite supply of effective leaders.

Ohio State Studies

The most comprehensive and replicated of the behavioral theories resulted from research that began at Ohio State University in the late 1940s.[2] These studies sought to identify independent dimensions of leader behavior. Beginning with over a thousand dimensions, they eventually narrowed the list into two categories that substantially accounted for most of the leadership behavior described by subordinates. They called these two dimensions *initiating structure* and *consideration*.

Initiating structure refers to the extent to which a leader is likely to define and structure his or her role and those of subordinates in the search for goal attainment. It includes behavior that attempts to organize work, work relationships, and goals. The leader characterized as high in initiating structure could be described in terms such as "assigns group members to particular tasks," "expects workers to maintain definite standards of performance," and "emphasizes the meeting of deadlines."

Consideration is described as the extent to which a person is likely to have job relationships characterized by mutual trust, respect for subordinates' ideas, and regard for their feelings. This type of leader shows concern for his followers' comfort, well-being, status, and satisfaction. A leader high in consideration could be described as one who helps subordinates with personal problems, is friendly and approachable, and treats all subordinates as equals.

Extensive research, based on these definitions, found that leaders high in initiating structure *and* consideration (a "high-high" leader) tended to achieve high subordinate performance and satisfaction more frequently than those who rated low either on initiating structure, consideration, or both. But the high-high style did not *always* result in positive consequences. For example, leader behavior characterized as high on initiating structure led to higher rates of grievances, absenteeism, and turnover and lower levels of job satisfaction for workers performing routine tasks. Other studies found that high consideration was negatively related to performance ratings of the leader by his superior. In conclusion, the Ohio State studies suggested that the high-high style generally resulted in positive outcomes, but enough exceptions were found to indicate that situational factors needed to be integrated into the theory.

University of Michigan Studies

Leadership studies undertaken at the University of Michigan's Survey Research Center, at about the same time as those being done at Ohio State, had similar research objectives: To locate behavioral characteristics of leaders that appeared to be related to measures of performance effectiveness.[3] The Michigan group also came up with two dimensions of leadership behavior, which they labeled employee-oriented and production-oriented. Leaders who were *employee-oriented* were described as emphasizing interpersonal relations; they took a personal interest in the needs of their subordinates and accepted individual differences among members. The *production-oriented* leaders, in contrast, tended to emphasize the technical or task aspects of the job—their main concern was accomplishing their group's tasks, and the group members were a means to that end.

The conclusions arrived at by the Michigan researchers strongly favored the leaders who were employee-oriented in their behavior. Employee-oriented leaders were associated with higher group productivity and higher job satisfaction. Production-oriented leaders tended to be associated with low group productivity and low worker satisfaction.

The Managerial Grid

A graphic portrayal of a two-dimensional view of leadership styles was developed by Robert Blake and Jane Mouton.[4] They proposed a **managerial grid** based on the styles of "concern for people" and "concern for production," which essentially represent the Ohio State dimensions of consideration and initiating structure or the Michigan dimensions of employee-oriented and production-oriented.

The grid, depicted in Exhibit 10-1 on page 134, has 9 possible positions along each axis, creating 81 different positions in which the leader's style may fall. The grid does not show results produced but rather the dominating factors in a leader's thinking in regard to getting results.

On the basis of the findings from their research, Blake and Mouton concluded that managers perform best under a 9,9 style, as contrasted, for example, with a 9,1 (task-oriented) or the 1,9 (country-club type) leader. Unfortunately, the grid offers a better framework for conceptualizing leadership style than for presenting any tangible new information in clarifying the leadership quandary, since there is little substantive evidence to support the conclusion that a 9,9 style is most effective in all situations.[5]

Summary of Behavioral Theories

We have described the most popular and important of the attempts to explain leadership in terms of the behavior exhibited by the leader. Unfortunately, there was very little success in identifying consistent relationships between patterns of leadership behavior and group performance. What was missing was consideration of the situational factors that influence success or failure. For example, it seems unlikely that Martin Luther King, Jr., would have been a great civil-rights leader in 1900, yet he was in the 1950s and 1960s. Would Ralph Nader have risen to lead a consumer activist group had he been born in 1834 rather than 1934, or in Costa Rica rather than Connecticut? It seems quite unlikely, yet the behavioral approaches we have described could not clarify these situational factors.

EXHIBIT 10–1   The Managerial Grid

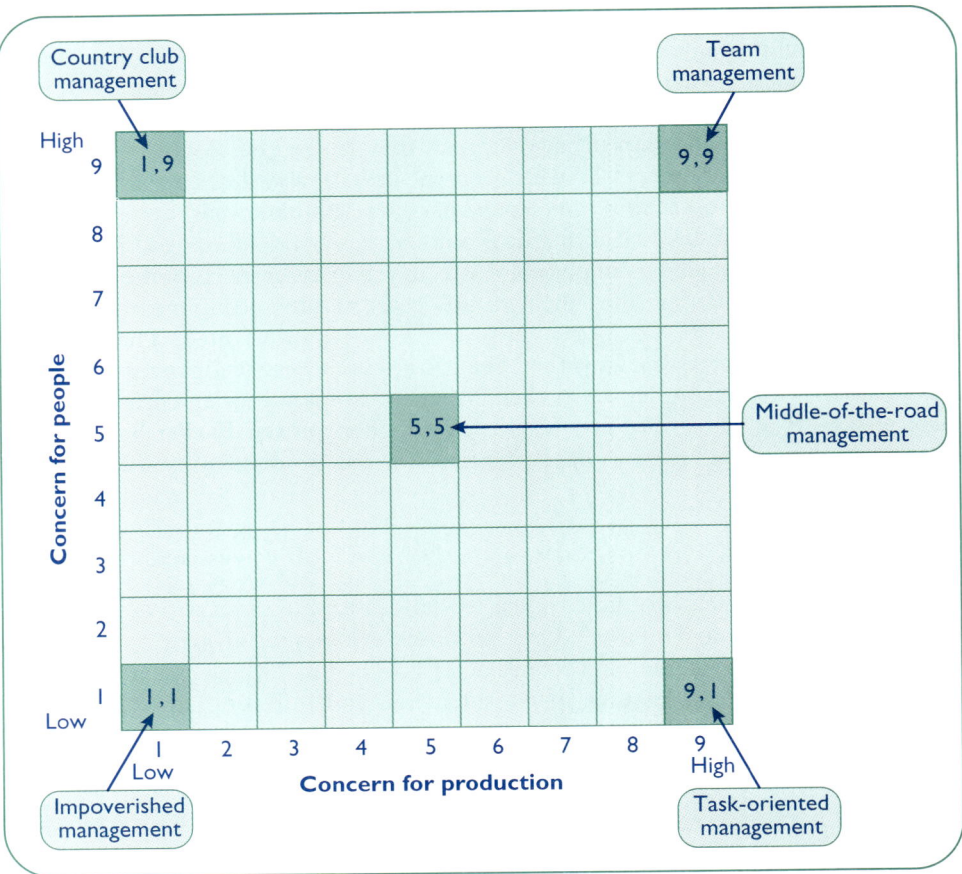

Based on dimensions described in R.R. Blake and J.S. Mouton, *Building a Dynamic Corporation Through Grid Organizational Development* (Reading, MA: Addison Wesley, 1969).

CONTINGENCY THEORIES

It became increasingly clear to those who were studying the leadership phenomenon that predicting leadership success was more complex than isolating a few traits or preferable behaviors. The failure to obtain consistent results led to a new focus on situational influences. The relationship between leadership style and effectiveness suggested that style x would be appropriate under condition a, whereas style y would be more suitable for condition b, and style z for condition c. But what were the conditions a, b, c, and so forth? It was one thing to say that leadership effectiveness was dependent on the situation and another to be able to isolate those situational conditions.

Three contingency theories have received the bulk of attention: Fiedler, path-goal, and leader-participation. We review each in this section. We also take a look at gender as a contingency variable. Although there is no specific contingency theory that directly addresses gender, an expanding body of research compares male and female leadership styles.

The Fiedler Model

The first comprehensive contingency model for leadership was developed by Fred Fiedler.[6] The **Fiedler leadership model** proposes that effective group performance depends on the proper match between the leader's style of interacting with his or her subordinates and the degree to which the situation gives control and influence to the leader.

Fiedler believed that an individual's basic leadership style is a key factor in leadership success. So he began by trying to find out what that basic style was. Fiedler created an instrument, which he called the **least-preferred co-worker (LPC) questionnaire**, for this purpose. It contains 16 contrasting adjectives (such as pleasant/unpleasant, efficient/inefficient, open/guarded, supportive/hostile) and purports to measure whether a person is task-oriented or relationship-oriented. The questionnaire asks the respondent to think of all the co-workers he or she has ever had and to describe the one person he or she *least enjoyed* working with by rating that person on a scale of 1 to 8 for each of the 16 sets of contrasting adjectives. Fiedler believed that what respondents said about others tells more about the respondents than it tells about the persons they're describing. If the least-preferred co-worker was described in relatively positive terms (a high LPC score), then the respondent was primarily interested in good personal relations with co-workers. That is, if you essentially described the person you are least able to work with in favorable terms, Fiedler would label you relationship-oriented. In contrast, if the least-preferred co-worker is seen in relatively unfavorable terms (a low LPC score), the respondent is primarily interested in productivity and thus would be labeled task-oriented. Notice that Fiedler assumed that an individual's leadership style is fixed, that is, either relationship-oriented or task-oriented. As we show below, this assumption is important because it means that if a situation requires a task-oriented leader and the person in that leadership position is relationship-oriented, either the situation has to be modified or the leader replaced if optimal effectiveness is to be achieved.

After an individual's basic leadership style has been assessed through the LPC, it is necessary to match the leader with the situation. The three situational factors or contingency dimensions identified by Fiedler are defined as follows:

1. **Leader-member relations**: The degree of confidence, trust, and respect subordinates have in their leader
2. **Task structure**: The degree to which the job assignments of subordinates are structured or unstructured
3. **Position power**: The degree of influence a leader has over power variables such as hiring, firing, discipline, promotions, and salary increases

The next step in the Fiedler model is to evaluate the situation in terms of these three contingency variables. Leader-member relations are either good or poor, task structure either high or low, and position power either strong or weak. Fiedler stated that the better the leader-member relations, the more highly structured the job, and the stronger the position power, the more control or influence the leader had. For example, a very favorable situation (in which the leader would have a great deal of control) might involve a payroll manager who is well respected and whose subordinates have confidence in him or her (good leader-member relations), where the activities to be done—such as wage computation, check writing, report filing—are specific and clear (high task structure), and the job provides considerable freedom to reward and punish subordinates (strong position power). On the other hand, an unfavorable situation might be the disliked chairman of a voluntary United Way fund-raising team. In this job, the leader has very little control. Altogether, by mixing the three contingency variables, there are potentially eight different situations or categories in which a leader could find himself or herself.

With knowledge of an individual's LPC and an assessment of the three contingency variables, the Fiedler model proposes matching them up to achieve maximum leadership effectiveness. Based on his research, Fiedler concluded that task-oriented leaders tend to perform better in situations that were *very favorable* to them and in situations that were *very unfavorable* (see Exhibit 10-2). So Fiedler would predict that when faced with a category I, II, III, VII, or VIII situation, task-oriented leaders perform better. Relationship-oriented leaders, however, perform better in moderately favorable situations—categories IV through VI. In recent years, Fiedler has condensed these eight situations down to three.[7] He now says that task-oriented leaders perform best in situations with high and low control, while relationship-oriented leaders perform best in moderate control situations.

As a whole, reviews of the major studies that tested the overall validity of the Fiedler model lead to a generally positive conclusion. That is, there is considerable evidence to support at least substantial parts of the model.[8] If predictions from the model use only three categories rather than the original eight, there is ample evidence to support Fiedler's conclusions. But there are problems with the LPC and the practical use of the model that need to be addressed. For instance, the logic underlying the LPC is not well understood, and studies have shown that respondents' LPC scores are

EXHIBIT 10–2 Findings from the Fiedler Model

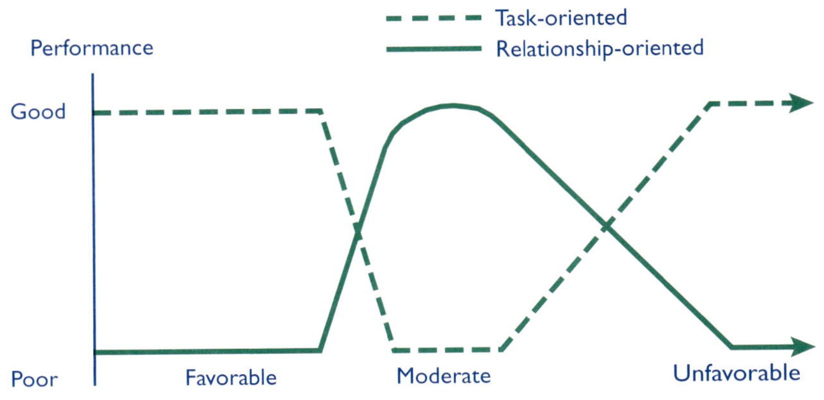

Category	I	II	III	IV	V	VI	VII	VIII
Leader–member relations	Good	Good	Good	Good	Poor	Poor	Poor	Poor
Task structure	High	High	Low	Low	High	High	Low	Low
Position power	Strong	Weak	Strong	Weak	Strong	Weak	Strong	Weak

not stable. Also, the contingency variables are complex and difficult for practitioners to assess. It's often difficult in practice to determine how good the leader-member relations are, how structured the task is, and how much position power the leader has.

Leader-Member Exchange Theory

Have you ever noticed that leaders often act differently toward different people and have favorites? That, in essence, is the foundation of leader-member exchange theory.[9]

The **leader-member exchange (LMX) theory** argues that leaders establish a special relationship with a small group of their followers. These individuals make up the leader's in-group—people whom the leader trusts, who get a disproportionate amount of his or her time, and who are more likely to receive special privileges. Other followers fall into the out-group. They get less of the leader's time, fewer of the preferred rewards that the leader controls, and have leader-follower relations based on formal authority interactions.

The theory proposes that early in the history of the interaction between a leader and a given follower, the leader implicitly categorizes the follower as an "in" or an "out" and that the relationship is relatively stable over time. Just precisely how the leader chooses who falls into each category is unclear, but there is evidence that leaders tend to choose in-group members because they have attitude and personality characteristics that are similar to the leader's or a higher level of competence than out-group members.

Studies confirm several LMX theory predictions: Leaders do differentiate among followers; these disparities are far from random; and followers with in-group status have higher performance ratings, lower turnover intentions, greater satisfaction with their superiors, and higher overall satisfaction than those in the out-group.

Path-Goal Theory

Currently, one of the most respected approaches to leadership is the path-goal theory. Developed by Robert House, **path-goal theory** is a contingency model of leadership that extracts key elements from the Ohio State leadership research on initiating structure and consideration and the expectancy theory of motivation.[10]

The essence of the theory is that it's the leader's job to assist his or her followers in attaining their goals and to provide the direction or support or both needed to ensure that their goals are compatible with the overall objectives of the group or organization. The term *path-goal* is derived from the belief that effective leaders clarify the path to help their followers get from where they are to the achievement of their work goals and make the journey along the path easier by reducing roadblocks and pitfalls.

According to path-goal theory, a leader's behavior is *acceptable* to subordinates to the degree that it is viewed by them as an immediate source of satisfaction or as a means of future satisfaction. A leader's behavior is *motivational* to the degree that it (1) makes subordinate need satisfaction contingent on effective performance and (2) provides the coaching, guidance, support, and rewards that are necessary for effective performance. To test these statements, House identified four leadership behaviors. The *directive leader* lets subordinates know what is expected of them, schedules work to be done, and gives specific guidance on how to accomplish tasks. This dimension closely parallels the Ohio State studies' initiating structure. The *supportive leader* is friendly and shows concern for the needs of subordinates. This dimension is essentially synonymous with the Ohio State studies' consideration. The *participative leader* consults with subordinates and uses their suggestions before making a decision. The *achievement-oriented leader* sets challenging goals and expects subordinates to perform at their highest level. In contrast to Fiedler's view of a leader's behavior, House assumes that leaders are flexible. Path-goal theory implies that the same leader can display any or all of these behaviors depending on the situation.

As Exhibit 10-3 illustrates, path-goal theory proposes two classes of situational, or contingency, variables that moderate the leader behavior–outcome relationship. Those in the *environment* are outside the control of the leader (task structure, formal authority system, and work group). Factors in the second class are part of the personal characteristics of the *subordinate* (locus of control, experience, and perceived ability). Essentially, the theory proposes that leader behaviors should complement these contingency variables. So the leader will be ineffective when his or her behavior is redundant with sources of environmental structure or incongruent with subordinate characteristics.

The following are examples of hypotheses that have evolved out of path-goal theory.

- Directive leadership leads to greater satisfaction when tasks are ambiguous or stressful than when they are highly structured and well laid out.
- Supportive leadership results in high employee performance and satisfaction when subordinates are performing structured tasks. (Leadership complements environment.)
- Directive leadership is likely to be redundant among subordinates with high ability or with considerable experience.
- The clearer and more bureaucratic the formal authority relationships, the more leaders should exhibit supportive behavior and deemphasize directive behavior.
- Directive leadership will lead to higher employee satisfaction when there is substantive conflict within a work group.

EXHIBIT 10–3   The Path-Goal Theory

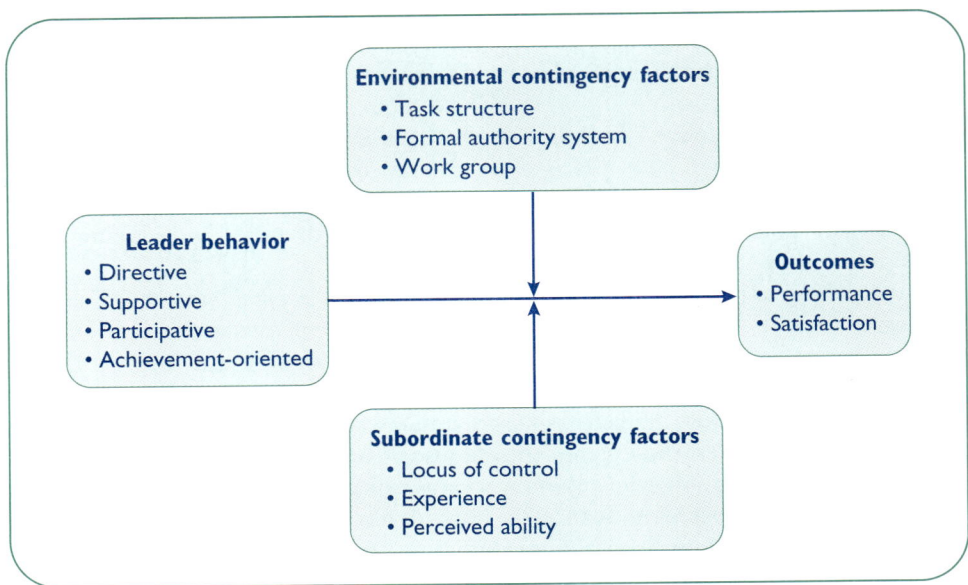

- Subordinates with an internal locus of control (those who believe they control their own destiny) will be most satisfied with a participative style.
- Subordinates with an external locus of control will be most satisfied with a directive style.
- Achievement-oriented leadership will increase subordinates' expectations that effort will lead to high performance when tasks are ambiguously structured.

Research to validate hypotheses such as these is generally encouraging.[11] The evidence supports the logic underlying the theory. That is, employee performance and satisfaction are likely to be positively influenced when the leader compensates for things lacking in either the employee or the work setting. However, the leader who spends time explaining tasks when those tasks are already clear or when the employee has the ability and experience to handle them without interference is likely to be seen as redundant or even insulting.

Leader-Participation Model

In 1973 Victor Vroom and Phillip Yetton developed a **leader-participation model** that related leadership behavior and participation in decision making.[12] Recognizing that task structures have varying demands for routine and nonroutine activities, these researchers argued that leader behavior must adjust to reflect the task structure. Vroom and Yetton's model was normative—it provided a sequential set of rules that should be followed in determining the form and amount of participation in decision making, as determined by different types of situations. The model was a decision tree incorporating seven contingencies (whose relevance could be identified by making "yes" or "no" choices) and five alternative leadership styles.

More recent work by Vroom and Arthur Jago has resulted in a revision of this model.[13] The new model retains the same five alternative leadership styles—from the leader's making the decision completely by himself or herself to sharing the problem with the group and developing a consensus decision—but expands the contingency variables to 12. These are listed in Exhibit 10-4.

Research testing both the original and revised leader-participation models has been encouraging. But, unfortunately, the model is far too complex for the typical manager to use on a regular basis. In fact, Vroom and Jago have developed a computer program to guide managers through all the decision branches in the revised model.

We obviously can't do justice to the model's sophistication in this discussion. What's important, however, is that Vroom and his associates have provided us with some solid, empirically supported insights into contingency variables that you should consider when choosing your leadership style.

[handwritten margin note: CAN YOU CHOOSE YOUR STYLE]

Gender As a Contingency Variable: Do Males and Females Lead Differently?

An extensive review of the literature suggests two conclusions regarding gender and leadership.[14] First, the similarities between men's and women's leadership styles tend to outweigh the differences. Second, what differences there are seem to be that women prefer a democratic leadership style, whereas men feel more comfortable with a directive style.

EXHIBIT 10–4 Contingency Variables in the Revised Leader-Participation Model

1. Importance of the decision
2. Importance of obtaining subordinate commitment to the decision
3. Whether the leader has sufficient information to make a good decision
4. How well structured the problem is
5. Whether an autocratic decision would receive subordinate commitment
6. Whether subordinates "buy into" the organization's goals
7. Whether there is likely to be conflict among subordinates over solution alternatives
8. Whether subordinates have the necessary information to make a good decision
9. Time constraints on the leader that may limit subordinate involvement
10. Whether costs of bringing geographically dispersed subordinates together are justified
11. Importance to the leader of minimizing the time it takes to make the decision
12. Importance of using participation as a tool for developing subordinate decision skills

Source: Based on V.H. Vroom and A.G. Jago, *The New Leadership: Managing Participation in Organizations* (Upper Saddle River, NJ: Prentice Hall, 1988), pp. 111-112; and V.H. Vroom and P.W. Yetton, *Leadership and Decision-Making* (Pittsburgh: University of Pittsburgh Press, 1973), p. 194. Reprinted by permission of the University of Pittsburgh. © 1973 by University of Pittsburgh Press.

The similarities among men and women leaders shouldn't be completely surprising. Almost all the studies looking at this issue have used managerial positions as being synonymous with leadership. As such, gender differences apparent in the general population don't tend to be evident. Why? Because of career self-selection and organization selection. Just as people who choose careers in law enforcement or civil engineering have a lot in common, so do individuals who choose managerial careers. People with traits associated with leadership—such as intelligence, confidence, and sociability—are likely to be perceived as leaders and encouraged to pursue careers in which they can exert leadership. This is true nowadays regardless of gender. Similarly, organizations tend to recruit and promote into leadership positions people who project leadership attributes. The result is that, regardless of gender, those who achieve formal leadership positions in organizations tend to be more alike than different.

Despite the previous conclusion, studies indicate some differences in the inherent leadership styles of women and men. Women encourage participation, share power and information, and attempt to enhance followers' self-worth. They prefer to lead through inclusion and rely on their charisma, expertise, contacts, and interpersonal skills to influence others. Men, on the other hand, are more likely to use a directive command-and-control style. They rely on the formal authority of their position for their influence base. Consistent with our first conclusion, however, these findings need to be qualified. The tendency for female leaders to be more democratic than males declines when women are in male-dominated jobs. Apparently, group norms and masculine stereotypes of leaders override personal preferences so that women abandon their feminine styles in such jobs and act more autocratically.

Given that men have historically held the great majority of leadership positions in organizations, it's tempting to assume that the existence of the noted differences between men and women would automatically work to favor men. It doesn't. In today's organizations, flexibility, teamwork, trust, and information-sharing are replacing rigid structures, competitive individualism, control, and secrecy. The best managers listen to, motivate, and provide support for their people. And many women seem to do those things better than men. As a specific example, the expanded use of cross-functional teams in organizations means that effective managers must become skillful negotiators. The leadership styles women typically use can make them better at negotiating than men, as they are less likely to focus on wins, losses, and competition. They tend to treat negotiations in the context of a continuing relationship—trying hard to make the other party a winner in its own and others' eyes.

TRAIT THEORIES UPDATED: CHARISMATIC LEADERSHIP

Most of the leadership theories discussed in this chapter have involved **transactional leaders**. These people guide or motivate their followers in the direction of established goals by clarifying role and task requirements. There is another type of leader who inspires followers to transcend their own self-interests for the good of the organization and who is capable of having a profound and extraordinary effect on his or her followers. These are charismatic or **transformational leaders**. Jesse Jackson, Winston Churchill, General Douglas MacArthur, and Franklin D. Roosevelt are of this latter type. By the force of their personal abilities they transform their followers by raising the sense of the importance and value of their tasks. "I'd walk through fire if my boss asked me" is the kind of support that charismatic leaders inspire.

What characteristics differentiate **charismatic leaders** from noncharismatic ones? Five attributes seem most important[15]:

Self-confidence: They have complete confidence in their judgment and ability.
A vision: This is an idealized goal that proposes a future better than the status quo. The greater the disparity between this idealized goal and the status quo, the more likely that followers will attribute extraordinary vision to the leader.
Strong convictions in that vision: Charismatic leaders are perceived as being strongly committed. They are perceived as willing to take on high personal risk, incur high costs, and engage in self-sacrifice to achieve their vision.
Extraordinary behavior: Leaders with charisma engage in behavior that is perceived as novel, unconventional, and counter to norms. When successful, these behaviors evoke surprise and admiration in followers.
Image as a change agent: Charismatic leaders are perceived as agents of radical change rather than as caretakers of the status quo.

What can we say about the charismatic leader's impact on his or her followers' attitudes and behavior? One study found that followers of charismatic leaders were more self-assured, experienced more meaningfulness in their work, reported more support from their leaders, worked longer hours, saw their leaders as more dynamic, and had higher performance ratings than the followers of noncharismatic but effective leaders.[16] Another study found that people working under charismatic leaders were more productive and satisfied than those working under leaders who relied on the more traditional transactional behaviors of initiating structure and consideration.[17] Two studies, of course, provide only limited information from which to generalize. We need more research on this subject, but the early evidence is encouraging.

VISIONARY LEADERSHIP

The term *vision* appeared in our previous discussion of charismatic leadership. But visionary leadership goes beyond charisma. In this section, we review recent revelations about the importance of visionary leadership.

Visionary leadership is the ability to create and articulate a realistic, credible, and attractive vision of the future for an organization or organizational unit that grows out of and improves on the present.[18] This vision, if properly selected and implemented, is so energizing that it "in effect jump-starts the future by calling forth the skills, talents, and resources to make it happen."[19]

A vision differs from other forms of direction-setting in several ways: "A vision has clear and compelling imagery that offers an innovative way to improve, which recognizes and draws on traditions, and connects to actions that people can take to realize change. Vision taps people's emotions and energy. Properly articulated, a vision creates the enthusiasm that people have for sporting events and other leisure time activities, bringing the energy and commitment to the workplace."[20]

The key properties of a vision seem to be inspirational possibilities that are value-centered and realizable and have superior imagery and articulation. Visions should be able to create possibilities that are inspirational and unique and offer a new order that can produce organizational distinction. A vision is likely to fail if it doesn't offer a view of the future that is clearly and demonstrably better for the organization and its members. Desirable visions fit the times and circumstances and reflect the uniqueness of the organization. People in the organization must also believe that the vision is attainable. It should be perceived as challenging yet doable. Visions that have clear articulation and powerful imagery are more easily grasped and accepted.

What are some examples of visions? Mary Kay Ash's vision of women as entrepreneurs selling products that improve their self-image gave impetus to her cosmetics company. John Chambers, CEO of Cisco Systems, is creating a vision of how networks can transform business firms. And Steve Case, the CEO of AOL, envisions his firm leading the information revolution by merging AOL with Time Warner.

What skills do visionary leaders exhibit? Once the vision is identified, these leaders appear to have three qualities that are related to effectiveness in their visionary roles.[21] First is the ability to explain the vision to others. The leader needs to make the vision clear in terms of required actions and aims through clear oral and written communication. Second is to be able to express the vision not just verbally but through the leader's behavior. This requires behaving in ways that continually convey and reinforce the vision. The third skill is being able to extend the vision to different leadership contexts. This is the ability to order activities so the vision can be applied in a variety of situations.

TEAM LEADERSHIP

Leadership is increasingly taking place within a team context. Unfortunately, many leaders are not equipped to handle the change to teams. As one prominent consultant noted, "even the most capable managers have trouble making the transition because all the command-and-control type things they were encouraged to do before are no longer appropriate. There's no reason to have any skill or sense of this."[22] This same consultant estimated that "probably 15 percent of managers are natural team leaders;

another 15 percent could never lead a team because it runs counter to their personality. [They're unable to sublimate their dominating style for the good of the team]. Then there's that huge group in the middle: Team leadership doesn't come naturally to them, but they can learn it."[23]

The challenge for most managers, then, is to learn how to become an effective team leader. They have to learn skills such as the patience to share information, to trust others, to give up authority, and understanding when to intervene. Effective leaders have mastered the difficult balancing act of knowing when to leave their teams alone and when to intercede. New team leaders may try to retain too much control at a time when team members need more autonomy, or they may abandon their teams at times when the team needs support and help.

A study of 20 organizations that had reorganized themselves around teams found certain common responsibilities that all leaders had to assume. These included coaching, facilitating, handling disciplinary problems, reviewing team/individual performance, training, and communication.[24] Many of these responsibilities apply to managers in general. A more meaningful way to describe the team leader's job is to focus on two priorities: managing the team's external boundary and facilitating the team process.[25] We've broken these priorities down into four specific roles.

First, team leaders are *liaisons with external constituencies*. These include upper management, other internal teams, customers, and suppliers. The leader represents the team to other constituencies, secures needed resources, clarifies others' expectations of the team, gathers information from the outside, and shares this information with team members.

Second, team leaders are *trouble-shooters*. When the team has problems and asks for assistance, team leaders sit in on meetings and help try to resolve the problems. This rarely relates to technical or operation issues. Why? Because the team members typically know more about the tasks being done than does the team leader. Where the leader is most likely to contribute is by asking penetrating questions, helping the team talk through problems, and by getting needed resources from external constituencies. For instance, when a team in an aerospace firm found itself short-handed, its team leader took responsibility for getting more staff. He presented the team's case to upper management and got the approval through the company's human resources department.

Third, team leaders are *conflict managers*. When disagreements surface, they help process the conflict. What's the source of the conflict? Who is involved? What are the issues? What resolution options are available? What are the advantages and disadvantages of each? By getting team members to address questions such as these, the leader minimizes the disruptive aspects of intrateam conflicts.

Finally, team leaders are *coaches*. They clarify expectations and roles, teach, offer support, cheerlead, and whatever else is necessary to help team members improve their work performance.

IS LEADERSHIP ALWAYS RELEVANT?

Contrary to the emphasis in this chapter, leadership may not always be important! Data from numerous studies collectively demonstrate that, in many situations, whatever behaviors leaders exhibit are irrelevant. Certain individual, job, and organizational variables can act as substitutes for leadership, negating the formal leader's ability to exert either positive or negative influence over subordinates' attitudes and effectiveness.[26]

For instance, characteristics of subordinates such as their experience, training, professional orientation, or need for independence can neutralize the effect of leadership. These characteristics can replace the need for a leader's support or ability to create structure and reduce task ambiguity. Similarly, people in jobs that are inherently unambiguous and routine or that are intrinsically satisfying may have little need for a leader. Finally, organizational characteristics such as explicit formalized goals, rigid rules and procedures, or cohesive work groups can act in the place of formal leadership.

The preceding comments should not be surprising. After all, in Chapter 2 and subsequent chapters, we introduced independent variables that have been documented to have an impact on employee performance and satisfaction. Yet supporters of the leadership concept have tended to place an undue burden on this variable for explaining and predicting behavior. It's too simplistic to consider subordinates as being guided to goal accomplishment solely on the basis of the behavior of their leader. It's important, therefore, to recognize explicitly that leadership is merely another independent variable in explaining organizational behavior. In some situations, it may contribute a lot toward explaining employee productivity, absence, turnover, and satisfaction; but in other situations, it may contribute little toward that end.

Even charismatic leadership may not be the panacea that many in the public and the media think it is. Charismatic leaders may be ideal for pulling a group or organization through a crisis, but they often perform poorly after the crisis subsides and ordinary conditions return. The forceful, confident behavior that was needed during the crisis now becomes a liability. Charismatic managers are often self-possessed, autocratic, and given to thinking that their opinions have a greater degree of certainty than they merit. These behaviors then tend to drive good people away and can lead their organizations down dangerous paths.

TRUST AND LEADERSHIP

Trust, or lack of trust, is an increasingly important issue for today's managers. In the remainder of this chapter, we define what trust is and provide you with some guidelines for helping to build credibility and trust.

What Is Trust?

Trust is a positive expectation that another will not—through words, actions, or decisions—act opportunistically.[27] The two most important elements of our definition is that it implies familiarity and risk.

The phrase *positive expectation* in our definition assumes knowledge and familiarity about the other party. Trust is a history-dependent process based on relevant but limited samples of experience. It takes time to form, building incrementally and accumulating. Most of us find it hard, if not impossible, to trust someone immediately if we don't know anything about them. At the extreme, in the case of total ignorance, we can gamble but we can't trust. But as we get to know someone, and the relationship matures, we gain confidence in our ability to have a positive expectation.

The term *opportunistically* refers to the inherent risk and vulnerability in any trusting relationship. Trust involves making oneself vulnerable as when, for example, we disclose intimate information or rely on another's promises. By its very nature, trust provides the opportunity for disappointment or to be taken advantage of. But trust is not taking risk per se; rather it is a *willingness* to take risk. So when I trust someone, I expect that they will not take advantage of me. This willingness to take risks is common to all trust situations.

What are the key dimensions that underlie the concept of trust? Recent evidence has identified five: integrity, competence, consistency, loyalty, and openness (see Exhibit 10-5).[28]

Integrity refers to honesty and truthfulness. Of all five dimensions, this one seems to be most critical when someone assesses another's trustworthiness. "Without a perception of the other's 'moral character' and 'basic honesty,' other dimensions of trust [are] meaningless."[29]

Competence encompasses an individual's technical and interpersonal knowledge and skills. Does the person know what he or she is talking about? You're unlikely to listen to or depend on someone whose abilities you don't respect. You need to believe that the person has the skills and abilities to carry out what he or she says they will do.

Consistency relates to an individual's reliability, predictability, and good judgment in handling situations. "Inconsistencies between words and action decrease trust."[30] This dimension is particularly relevant for managers. "Nothing is noticed more quickly . . . than a discrepancy between what executives preach and what they expect their associates to practice."[31]

Loyalty is the willingness to protect and save face for another person. Trust requires that you can depend on someone not to act opportunistically.

The final dimension of trust is *openness*. Can you rely on the person to give you the full truth?

EXHIBIT 10–5   Trust Dimensions

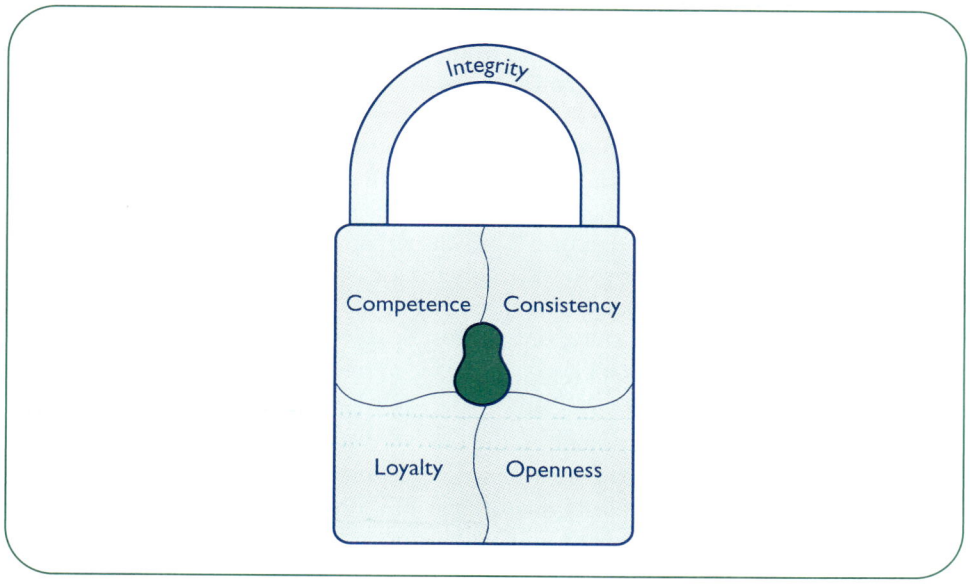

Trust and Leadership

Trust appears to be a primary attribute associated with leadership.[32] When followers trust a leader, they are willing to be vulnerable to the leader's actions—confident that their rights and interests will not be abused. People are unlikely to look up to or follow someone whom they perceive as dishonest or who is likely to take advantage of them. Honesty, for instance, consistently ranks at the top of most people's list of characteristics they admire in their leaders. "Honesty is absolutely essential to leadership. If people are going to follow someone willingly, whether it be into battle or into the boardroom, they first want to assure themselves that the person is worthy of their trust."[33]

Three Types of Trust

There are three types of trust in organizational relationships: *deterrence*-based, *knowledge*-based, and *identification*-based.[34] The following analysis assumes two parties are entering into a new relationship. They have no previous experiences to overcome; they're uncertain about each other; they believe they're vulnerable if they disclose too much too quickly; and they're uncertain about the longevity of the relationship.

Deterrence-Based Trust The most fragile relationships are contained in **deterrence-based trust.** One violation or inconsistency can destroy the relationship. This form of trust is based on fear of reprisal if the trust is violated. Individuals who are in this type of relationship do what they say because they fear the consequences from not following through on their obligations.

Deterrence-based trust will work only to the degree that punishment is possible, consequences are clear, and the punishment is actually imposed if the trust is violated. To be sustained, the potential loss of future interaction with the other party must outweigh the profit potential that comes from violating expectations. Moreover, the potentially harmed party must be willing to introduce harm (for example, I have no qualms about speaking badly of you if you betray my trust) to the person acting distrustingly.

Most new relationships begin on a base of deterrence. Take, as an illustration, a situation in which you're selling your car to a friend of a friend. You don't know the buyer. You might be motivated to refrain from telling this buyer all the problems with the car that you know about. Such behavior would increase your chances of selling the car and securing the highest price. But you don't withhold information. You openly share the car's flaws. Why? Probably because of fear of reprisal. If the buyer later thinks you deceived him, he is likely to share this with your mutual friend. If you knew that the buyer would never say anything to the mutual friend, you might be tempted to take advantage of the opportunity. If it's clear that the buyer would tell and that your mutual friend would think considerably less of you for taking advantage of this buyer-friend, your honesty could be explained in deterrence terms.

Another example of deterrence-based trust is a new manager-employee relationship. As an employee, you typically trust a new boss even though there is little experience to base that trust on. The bond that creates this trust lies in the authority held by the boss and the punishment he or she can impose if you fail to fulfill your job-related obligations.

Knowledge-Based Trust Most organizational relationships are rooted in **knowledge-based trust;** that is, trust is based on the behavioral predictability that comes from a history of interaction. It exists when you have adequate information about someone to understand them well enough to be able to accurately predict their behavior.

Knowledge-based trust relies on information rather than deterrence. Knowledge of the other party and predictability of his or her behavior replaces the contracts, penalties, and legal arrangements more typical of deterrence-based trust. This knowledge develops over time, largely as a function of experience that builds confidence of trustworthiness and predictability. The better you know someone, the more accurately you can predict what he or she will do. Predictability enhances trust—even if the other is predictably untrustworthy—because the ways that the other will violate the trust can be predicted! The more communication and regular interaction you have with someone else, the more this form of trust can be developed and depended on.

Interestingly, at the knowledge-based level, trust is not necessarily broken by inconsistent behavior. If you believe you can adequately explain or understand another's apparent violation, you can accept it, forgive the person, and move on in the relationship. However, the same inconsistency at the deterrence level is likely to irrevocably break the trust.

In an organizational context, most manager-employee relationships are knowledge-based. Both parties have enough experience working with each other that they know what to expect. A long history of consistently open and honest interactions, for instance, is not likely to be permanently destroyed by a single violation.

Identification-Based Trust The highest level of trust is achieved when there is an emotional connection between the parties. It allows one party to act as an agent for the other and substitute for that person in interpersonal transactions. This is called **identification-based trust**. Trust exists because the parties understand each other's intentions and appreciate the other's wants and desires. This mutual understanding is developed to the point that each can effectively act for the other.

Controls are minimal at this level. You don't need to monitor the other party because there exists unquestioned loyalty.

The best example of identification-based trust is a long-term, happily married couple. A husband comes to learn what's important to his wife and anticipates those actions. She, in turn, trusts that he will anticipate what's important to her without having to ask. Increased identification enables each to think like the other, feel like the other, and respond like the other.

You see identification-based trust occasionally in organizations among people who have worked together for long periods of time and have a depth of experience that allows them to know each other inside and out. This is also the type of trust that managers ideally seek in teams. Team members are so comfortable and trusting of each other that they can anticipate each other and freely act in each other's absence.

How Do You Build Trust?

Managers who have learned to build trusting relationships engage in certain common practices. The following summarizes what you can do to emulate these successful managers.[35]

Practice openness. Mistrust comes as much from what people don't know as from what they do know. So keep people informed, make certain the criteria on how decisions are made are overtly clear, explain the rationale for your decisions, be candid about problems, and fully disclose relevant information.

Be fair. Before making decisions or taking actions, consider how others will perceive them in terms of objectivity and fairness. Give credit where it's due, be objective and impartial in performance appraisals, and pay attention to equity perceptions in reward distributions.

Speak your feelings. Managers who convey only hard facts come across as cold and distant. If you share your feelings, others will see you as real and human. They will know who you are and their respect for you will increase.

Tell the truth. If integrity is critical to trust, you must be perceived as someone who tells the truth. People are generally more tolerant of learning something they "don't want to hear" than finding out that their manager lied to them.

Show consistency. People want predictability. Take the time to think about your values and beliefs. Then let them consistently guide your decisions.

Fulfill your promises. Trust requires that people believe that you are dependable. So you need to ensure that you keep your word and commitments. Promises made must be promises kept.

Maintain confidences. People trust those who are discreet and upon whom they can rely. If people make themselves vulnerable by telling you something in confidence, they need to feel assured that you will not discuss it with others or betray that confidence.

Demonstrate competence. Develop the admiration and respect of others by demonstrating technical and professional ability. Pay particular attention to developing and displaying your communication, negotiating, and other interpersonal skills.

IMPLICATIONS FOR MANAGERS

The topic of leadership certainly doesn't lack for theories. But from an overview perspective, what does it all mean? Let's try to identify commonalities among the leadership theories and attempt to determine what, if any, practical value the theories hold for managers.

Careful examination discloses that the concepts of "task" and "people"—often expressed in more elaborate terms that hold substantially the same meaning—permeate most of the theories. The task dimension is called just that by Fiedler, but it goes by the name of "initiating structure" for the Ohio State group, "directive" by path-goal supporters, "production orientation" by the Michigan researchers, and "concern for production" by Blake and Mouton. The people dimension gets similar treatment, going under such aliases as "consideration," "supportive," and "employee-oriented" or "relationship-oriented" leadership. Clearly, leadership behavior can be shrunk down to two dimensions—task and people—but researchers continue to differ as to whether the orientations are two ends of a single continuum (you could be high on one or the other but not on both) or two independent dimensions (you could be high or low on both).

How should we interpret the findings presented in this chapter? Some traits have been shown, over time, to be modest predictors of leadership effectiveness. But the fact that a manager possessed intelligence, drive, self-confidence, or the like would by no means assure us that his or her subordinates would be productive and satisfied employees. The ability of these traits to predict leadership success is just not that strong.

The early task/people approaches (the Ohio State, Michigan, and managerial grid theories) also offer us little substance. The strongest statement one can make on the basis of these theories is that leaders who rate high in people orientation should end up with satisfied employees. The research is too mixed to make predictions regarding employee productivity or the effect of a task orientation on productivity and satisfaction.

A major breakthrough in our understanding of leadership came when we recognized the need to develop contingency theories that included situational factors. At present, the evidence indicates that relevant situational variables would include the task structure of the job, level of group support, and follower characteristics such as personality, experience, and ability.

Finally, we discussed the role that trust plays in leadership. Effective managers today must develop trusting relationships with those they seek to lead. Why? Because as organizations have become less stable and predictable, strong bonds of trust are replacing bureaucratic rules in defining expectations and relationships.

CHAPTER 11

Power and Politics

After reading this chapter, you should be able to

1. Define power
2. Describe the five bases of power
3. Explain what creates dependency in power relationships
4. Describe how power is central to understanding sexual harassment
5. Define political behavior
6. Describe the importance of a political perspective
7. Explain the factors contributing to political behavior in organizations
8. Identify seven techniques for managing the impression you make on others

*P*ower may be the last dirty word. It is easier for most of us to talk about money or even sex than it is to talk about power. People who have it deny it; people who want it try to appear not to be seeking it; and those who are good at getting it are secretive about how they got it.[1]

In this chapter, we show that power determines what goals a group will pursue and how the group's resources will be distributed among its members. Further, we show how group members with good political skills use their power to influence the distribution of resources in their favor.

A DEFINITION OF POWER

Power refers to a capacity that A has to influence the behavior of B so that B does something he or she would not otherwise do. This definition implies (1) a *potential* that need not be actualized to be effective, (2) a *dependence* relationship, and (3) that B has some *discretion* over his or her own behavior. Let's look at each of these points more closely.

Power may exist but not be used. It is, therefore, a capacity or potential. One can have power but not impose it.

Probably the most important aspect of power is that it is a function of dependence. The greater B's dependence on A, the greater is A's power in the relationship. Dependence, in turn, is based on alternatives that B perceives and the importance that B places on the alternatives that A controls. A person can have power over you only if he or she controls something you desire. If you want a university degree, have to pass a certain course to get that degree, and your current instructor is the only faculty member in the university who teaches that course, he or she has power over you. Your alternatives are definitely limited, and you place a high degree of importance on obtaining a passing grade. Similarly, if you're attending university on funds provided entirely by your parents, you probably recognize the power they hold over you. You're dependent on them for financial support. But once you're out of school, have a job, and are making a solid income, your parents' power is reduced significantly. Who among us, though, has not known or heard of the rich relative who is able to control a large number of family members merely through the implicit or explicit threat of writing them out of the will?

For A to get B to do something he or she otherwise would not do means B must have the discretion to make choices. At the extreme, if B's job behavior is so programmed that he is allowed no room to make choices, he obviously is constrained in his ability to do something other than what he is doing. For instance, job descriptions, group norms, organizational rules and regulations, as well as community laws and standards constrain people's choices. As a nurse, you may be dependent on your supervisor for continued employment. But, in spite of this dependence, you're unlikely to comply with her request to perform heart surgery on a patient or steal several thousand dollars from petty cash. Your job description and laws against stealing constrain your ability to make those choices.

CONTRASTING LEADERSHIP AND POWER

A careful comparison of our description of power with our description of leadership in the previous chapter should bring the recognition that the two concepts are closely intertwined. Leaders use power as a way to attain group goals, and power is a means for facilitating their achievement.

What differences are there between leadership and power? One difference is related to goal compatibility. Power does not require goal compatibility, merely dependence. Leadership, on the other hand, requires some congruence between the goals of the leader and those of the led. The other difference deals with the direction that research on the two concepts has taken. Leadership research, for the most part, emphasizes style. It seeks answers to questions such as: How supportive should a leader be? How much decision making should be shared with subordinates? In contrast, the research on power has tended to encompass a broader area and to focus on tactics for gaining compliance. It has gone beyond the individual as exerciser because power can be used by groups as well as by individuals to control other individuals or groups.

BASES OF POWER

Where does power come from? What is it that gives an individual or a group influence over others? The answer to these questions is a five-category classification scheme identified by John French and Bertram Raven.[2] They proposed five types of bases, or sources, of power: coercive, reward, legitimate, expert, and referent (see Exhibit 11-1).

Coercive Power

The **coercive power** base is defined by French and Raven as being dependent on fear. One reacts to this power out of fear of the negative results that might occur if one failed to comply. It rests on the application, or the threat of application, of physical sanctions such as the infliction of pain, the generation of frustration through restriction of movement, or the controlling by force of basic physiological or safety needs.

In the 1930s, when John Dillinger went into a bank, held a gun to a teller's head, and asked for money, he was incredibly successful at getting compliance with his request. His power base was coercive. A loaded gun gives its holder power because others are fearful that they will lose something that they hold dear—their lives.

> Of all the bases of power available . . . , the power to hurt others is possibly most often used, most often condemned, and most difficult to control . . . The state relies on its military and legal resources to intimidate nations, or even its own citizens. Businesses rely upon the control of economic resources. Schools and universities rely upon their rights to deny students formal education, while the church threatens individuals with loss of grace. At the personal level, individuals exercise coercive power through a reliance upon physical strength, verbal facility, or the ability to grant or withhold emotional support from others. These bases provide the individual with the means to physically harm, bully, humiliate, or deny love to others.[3]

At the organizational level, A has coercive power over B if A can dismiss, suspend, or demote B, assuming that B values his or her job. Similarly, if A can assign B

EXHIBIT 11–1   Measuring Bases of Power

Does a person have one or more of the five bases of power? Affirmative responses to the following statements can answer this question:

- The person can make things difficult for people, and you want to avoid getting him or her angry (coercive power)
- The person is able to give special benefits or rewards to people, and you find it advantageous to trade favors with him or her (reward power)
- The person has the right, considering his or her position and your job responsibilities, to expect you to comply with legitimate requests (legitimate power)
- The person has the experience and knowledge to earn your respect, and you defer to his or her judgment in some matters (expert power)
- You like the person and enjoy doing things for him or her (referent power)

Source: G. Yukl and C.M. Falbe, "Importance of Different Power Sources in Downward and Lateral Relations," *Journal of Applied Psychology,* June 1991, p. 417. Copyright ©1991 by the American Psychological Association. Reprinted with permission.

work activities that B finds unpleasant or treat B in a manner that B finds embarrassing, A possesses coercive power over B.

Reward Power

The opposite of coercive power is **reward power**. People comply with the wishes or directives of another because doing so produces positive benefits; therefore, one who can distribute rewards that others view as valuable will have power over them. These rewards can be anything that another person values. In an organizational context, we think of money, favorable performance appraisals, promotions, interesting work assignments, friendly colleagues, important information, and preferred work shifts or sales territories.

Coercive and reward power are actually counterparts. If you can remove something of positive value from another or inflict something of negative value on him or her, you have coercive power over that person. If you can give someone something of positive value or remove something of negative value, you have reward power over that person. As with coercive power, you don't need to be a manager to be able to exert influence through rewards. Rewards such as friendliness, acceptance, and praise are available to everyone in an organization. To the degree that an individual seeks such rewards, your ability to give or withhold them gives you power over that individual.

Legitimate Power

In formal groups and organizations, probably the most frequent access to one or more of the power bases is one's structural position. This is called **legitimate power**. It represents the power a person receives as a result of his or her position in the formal hierarchy of an organization.

Positions of authority include coercive and reward powers. Legitimate power, however, is broader than the powers to coerce and reward. Specifically, it includes acceptance by members of an organization of the authority of a position. When school principals, bank presidents, or army captains speak (assuming that their directives are viewed to be within the authority of their positions), teachers, tellers, and first lieutenants listen and usually comply.

Expert Power

Expert power is influence wielded as a result of expertise, special skill, or knowledge. Expertise has become one of the most powerful sources of influence as the world has become more technologically oriented. As jobs become more specialized, we become increasingly dependent on "experts" to achieve goals. So, just as physicians have expertise and hence expert power—most of us follow the advice our doctor gives us—so too do computer specialists, tax accountants, solar engineers, industrial psychologists, and other specialists.

Referent Power

The last category of influence that French and Raven identified was **referent power**. Its base is identification with a person who has desirable resources or personal traits. If I admire and identify with you, you can exercise power over me because I want to please you.

Referent power develops out of admiration of another person and a desire to be like him or her. In a sense, then, it is a lot like charisma. If you admire someone to the point of modeling your behavior and attitudes after him or her, that person possesses referent power over you. Referent power explains why celebrities are paid millions of dollars to endorse products in commercials. Marketing research shows that people like Bob Dole, Cindy Crawford, and Michael Jordan have the power to influence your choice of pharmaceuticals, health clubs, and athletic shoes. With a little practice, you or I could probably deliver as smooth a sales pitch as these celebrities, but the buying public doesn't identify with you and me. In organizations, if you are articulate, domineering, physically imposing, or charismatic, you hold personal characteristics that may be used to get others to do what you want.

DEPENDENCY: THE KEY TO POWER

Earlier in this chapter we noted the important relationship between power and dependence. In this section, we show how an understanding of dependency is central to furthering our understanding of power itself.

The General Dependency Postulate

Let's begin with a general postulate: *The greater B's dependency on A, the greater power A has over B.* When you possess anything that others require but that you alone control, you make them dependent on you and, therefore, you gain power over them.[4] Dependency, then, is inversely proportional to the alternative sources of supply. If something is plentiful, possession of it will not increase your power. If everyone is intelligent, intelligence gives no special advantage. Similarly, among the super-rich, money is no longer power. But, as the old saying goes, "In the land of the blind, the one-eyed man is king!" If you can create a monopoly by controlling information, prestige, or anything that others crave, they become dependent on you. Conversely, the more you can expand your options, the less power you place in the hands of others. This principle explains, for example, why so many of us aspire to financial independence. Financial independence reduces the power others can have over us.

What Creates Dependency?

Dependency is increased when the resource you control is *important* and *scarce*.[5]

Importance If nobody wants what you've got, it's not going to create dependency. To create dependency, therefore, you must control things that are perceived as important. It's been found, for instance, that organizations seek to avoid uncertainty. We should, therefore, expect that individuals or groups who can absorb an organization's uncertainty will be understood to control an important resource. For instance, a study of industrial organizations found that the marketing departments in these firms were consistently rated as the most powerful. It was concluded by the researcher that the most critical uncertainty facing these firms was selling their products. This fact might suggest that, during a labor strike, the organization's negotiating representatives have increased power or that engineers, as a group, would be more powerful at Intel than at Procter & Gamble. These inferences appear to be generally valid. Labor negotiators do become more powerful within the personnel area and the organization as a whole during periods of labor strife. An organization such as Intel, which is a technology-driven company, is dependent on its engineers to maintain its product quality; therefore, at Intel, engineers are clearly the most powerful group. At Procter & Gamble, marketing is the name of the game, and marketers are the most powerful group. These examples support not only the view that the ability to reduce uncertainty increases a group's importance and, hence, its power but also that what's important is situational. It varies among organizations and undoubtedly also varies over time within any given organization.

Scarcity As noted previously, if something is plentiful, possession of it will not increase your power. A resource needs to be perceived as scarce to create dependency. This relationship can help to explain how low-ranking members in an organization who have important knowledge not available to high-ranking members, can gain power over the high-ranking members. The need to obtain a scarce resource—in this case, important knowledge—makes the high-ranking member dependent on the low-ranking member. The relation of scarcity to dependency also helps make sense of behaviors of low-ranking members that otherwise might seem illogical, such as destroying the procedure manuals that describe how a job is done, refusing to train people in their job or even to show others exactly what they do, creating specialized language and terminology that inhibit others from understanding their jobs, or operating in secrecy so that the activity will appear more complex and difficult than it really is.

The scarcity-dependency relationship can further be seen in the power of occupational categories. Individuals in occupations in which the supply of personnel is low relative to demand can negotiate compensation and benefit packages far more attractive than can those in occupations in which there is an abundance of candidates. University administrators have no problem today finding English instructors. The market for computer-science instructors, in contrast, is extremely tight, with the demand high and the supply limited. The result is that the bargaining power of computer-science faculty allows them to negotiate higher salaries, lighter teaching loads, and other benefits.

POWER IN GROUPS: COALITIONS

Those "out of power" and seeking to be "in" will first try to increase their power individually. Why spread the spoils if one doesn't have to? But if this approach proves ineffective, the alternative is to form a coalition. There *is* strength in numbers.

The natural way to gain influence is to become a powerholder. Therefore, those who want power will attempt to build a personal power base. But, in many instances, doing so may be difficult, risky, costly, or impossible. In such cases, efforts will be made to form a coalition of two or more "outs" who, by joining together, can each better themselves at the expense of those outside the coalition.

Historically, blue-collar workers who were unsuccessful in bargaining on their own behalf with management resorted to labor unions to bargain for them. In recent years, white-collar employees and professionals have increasingly turned to unions after finding it difficult to exert power individually to attain higher wages and greater job security.

What predictions can we make about the formation of coalitions? First, coalitions in organizations often seek to maximize their size. In political science theory, coalitions move the other way—they try to minimize their size. They tend to be just large enough to exert the power necessary to achieve their objectives. But legislatures are different from organizations in that legislators make the policy decisions that are then carried out by separate administrators or managers. Decision making in organizations does not end with merely selecting from among a set of alternatives. The decision must also be implemented. In organizations, the implementation of and commitment to the decision are at least as important as the decision itself. It's necessary, therefore, for coalitions in organizations to seek a broad constituency to support the coalition's objectives, so the coalition must be expanded to encompass as many interests as possible. Coalition expansion to facilitate consensus-building, of course, is more likely to occur in organizational cultures in which cooperation, commitment, and shared decision making are highly valued than in autocratic and hierarchically controlled organizations, where maximizing the coalition's size is less likely to be sought.

Another prediction about coalitions is related to the degree of interdependence within the organization. More coalitions will likely be created where there is a great deal of task and resource interdependence. In contrast, there will be less interdependence among subunits and less coalition formation activity where subunits are largely self-contained or resources are abundant.

Finally, coalition formation will be influenced by the actual tasks that workers perform. The more routine the task of a group, or the work of individual jobs, the greater the likelihood that coalitions will form. In routine situations, group members or workers are substitutable; thus, their dependence is greater than in nonroutine situations. To offset this dependence, they can be expected to resort to a coalition. We see, therefore, that unions appeal more to low-skill and nonprofessional workers than to skilled and professional types. Of course, where the supply of skilled and professional employees is high relative to their demand or where organizations have standardized traditionally unique jobs, we would expect even these incumbents to find unionization attractive.

POWER AND SEXUAL HARASSMENT

The issue of sexual harassment has received increasing attention by corporations and the media because of the growing ranks of female employees, especially in nontraditional work environments.

Legally, **sexual harassment** is defined as unwelcome advances, requests for sexual favors, and other verbal or physical conduct, whether overt or subtle, of a sexual nature. But there is a great deal of disagreement about what specifically constitutes sexual harassment. Organizations have made considerable progress in the past few years toward limiting overt forms of sexual harassment, including unwanted physical touching, recurring requests for dates after a clear refusal, and threats that refusing a sexual proposition will result in losing one's job. The problems today are likely to surface around the more subtle forms of sexual harassment—unwanted looks or comments; sexual artifacts, such as nude calendars, in the workplace; or misinterpretation of where the line between "being friendly" ends and "harassment" begins.

Most studies confirm that the concept of power is central to understanding sexual harassment.[6] This seems to be true whether the harassment comes from a supervisor, a co-worker, or even a subordinate. The supervisor-employee dyad best characterizes an unequal power relationship, in which position power gives the supervisor the capacity to reward and coerce. Supervisors give subordinates their assignments, evaluate their performance, make recommendations for salary adjustments and promotions, and even decide whether an employee retains his or her job. These decisions give a supervisor power. Because subordinates want favorable performance reviews, salary increases, and the like, it's clear that supervisors control resources that most subordinates consider important and scarce. It's also worth noting that individuals who occupy high-status roles (management positions, for example) sometimes believe that sexually harassing subordinates is merely an extension of their right to make demands on lower-status individuals. Because of power inequities, sexual harassment by one's boss creates great difficulty for the person being harassed. If there are no witnesses, it is one person's word against another's. Are there others this boss has harassed and, if so, will they come forward? Because of the supervisor's control over resources, many who are harassed are afraid to speak out for fear of retaliation by the supervisor.

Co-workers don't have position power, but they can have influence and use it to sexually harass peers. In fact, although co-workers appear to engage in somewhat less severe forms of harassment than do supervisors, co-workers are the most frequent perpetrators of sexual harassment in organizations. How do co-workers exercise power? Most often it's by providing or withholding information, cooperation, and support. For example, the effective performance of most jobs requires interaction and support from co-workers, especially nowadays, as work increasingly is assigned to teams. By threatening to withhold or delay providing information that's necessary for the successful achievement of your work goals, co-workers can exert power over you.

Harassment by subordinates doesn't get nearly the attention that harassment by a supervisor does, but it does occur. Persons in positions of power can be subjected to sexual harassment from persons in less powerful positions within the organization. Usually the subordinate will devalue the superior through highlighting traditional gender stereotypes that reflect negatively on the person in power (such as helplessness or passivity if the victim is a woman; impotence or timidity if a man). Why would a subordinate engage in such practices? To gain some power over the higher-ranking person or to minimize power differentials.

The topic of sexual harassment is about power. It's about one individual's controlling or threatening another. It's wrong. It's illegal. But you can understand how sexual harassment surfaces in organizations if you analyze it in terms of power.

POLITICS: POWER IN ACTION

When people get together, power will be exerted. People want to carve out a niche from which to exert influence, earn rewards, and advance their careers. When employees in organizations convert their power into action, they are engaged in politics. Those with good political skills have the ability to use their bases of power effectively.

A Definition of Political Behavior

There have been no shortages of definitions for organizational politics. Essentially, however, they have focused on the use of power to affect decision making in the organization or on behaviors by members that are self-serving and organizationally non-sanctioned.[7] For our purposes, we define **political behavior** in organizations as *those* *activities that are not required as part of one's formal role in the organization, but that influence, or attempt to influence, the distribution of advantages and disadvantages within the organization.*[8]

This definition encompasses key elements of what most people mean when they talk about organizational politics. Political behavior is *outside* one's specified job requirements. The behavior requires some attempt to use one's *power* bases. Our definition encompasses efforts to influence the goals, criteria, or processes used for *decision making* when we state that politics is concerned with the distribution of advantages and disadvantages within the organization. Our definition is broad enough to include such varied political behaviors as withholding key information from decision makers, whistle-blowing, filing of grievances, spreading rumors, leaking confidential information about organizational activities to the media, exchanging favors with others in the organization for mutual benefit, or lobbying for or against a particular individual or decision.

The Importance of a Political Perspective

Those who fail to acknowledge political behavior ignore the reality that organizations are political systems. It would be nice if all organizations or formal groups within organizations could be described as supportive, harmonious, trusting, collaborative, or cooperative. A nonpolitical perspective can lead one to believe that employees will always behave in ways consistent with the interests of the organization. In contrast, a political view can explain much of what may seem to be irrational behavior in organizations. It can help to explain, for instance, why employees withhold information, restrict output, attempt to "build empires," publicize their successes, hide their failures, distort performance figures to make themselves look better, and engage in similar activities that appear to be at odds with the organization's desire for effectiveness and efficiency.

Factors Contributing to Political Behavior

Recent research and observation have identified a number of factors that appear to be associated with political behavior. Some are individual characteristics, derived from the unique qualities of the people whom the organization employs; others are a result of the organization's culture or internal environment.

Individual Factors Researchers have identified certain personality characteristics, needs, and other individual factors that are likely to be related to political behavior. Employees who are authoritarian, have a propensity for high risk, or possess an external locus of control (believe that forces outside themselves control their destiny) act politically with less regard for the consequences to the organization. A high need for power, autonomy, security, or status is also a major contributor to an employee's tendency to engage in political behavior.[9]

Organizational Factors Political activity is probably more a function of the organization's culture than of individual differences. Why? Because most organizations have a large number of employees with the characteristics previously listed, yet the presence of political behavior varies widely.

Although we acknowledge the role that individual differences can play in fostering politicking, the evidence more strongly supports that certain cultures promote politics. Cultures characterized by low trust, role ambiguity, unclear performance evaluation systems, zero-sum reward allocation practices, democratic decision making, high pressures for performance, and self-serving senior managers will create opportunities for political activities to be nurtured.[10]

The less trust there is within the organization, the higher the level of political behavior. So high trust should suppress the level of political behavior.

Role ambiguity means that the prescribed behaviors of the employee are not clear. There are few limits, therefore, to the scope and functions of the employee's political actions. Since political activities are defined as those not required as part of one's formal role, the greater the role ambiguity, the more one can engage in political activity with little chance of its being visible.

Performance evaluation is far from a perfected science. The more that organizations use subjective criteria in the appraisal, emphasize a single outcome measure, or allow significant time to pass between an action and its appraisal, the greater the likelihood an employee can get away with politicking. Subjective performance criteria create ambiguity. The use of a single outcome measure encourages individuals to do whatever is necessary to look good on that measure, but often at the expense of performing well on other important parts of the job that are not being appraised. The amount of time that elapses between an action and its appraisal is also a relevant factor. The longer the time, the more unlikely it is that the employee will be held accountable for political behaviors.

The more an organization's culture emphasizes the zero-sum or win-lose approach to reward allocations, the more employees will be motivated to engage in politicking. The zero-sum approach treats the reward "pie" as fixed so that any gain one person or group achieves has to come at the expense of another person or group. If I win, you must lose! If $20,000 in annual raises is to be distributed among five employees, then any employee who gets more than $4,000 takes money away from one or more of the others. Such a practice encourages making others look bad and increasing the visibility of what you do.

For several decades now, there has been a general move in North America toward making organizations less autocratic. Managers are being asked to behave more democratically. They're told they should allow subordinates to advise them on decisions and they should rely to a greater extent on group input into the decision process. Such moves toward democracy, however, are not necessarily embraced by all individual managers. Many managers sought their positions in order to have legitimate power to make unilateral decisions. They fought hard and often paid high personal costs to achieve their influential positions. Sharing their power with others rubs directly against their desires. The result is that managers may use the required teams, committees, conferences, and group meetings in a superficial way—as arenas for maneuvering and manipulating.

The more pressure that employees feel to perform well, the more likely they are to engage in politicking. Holding people strictly accountable for outcomes puts great pressure on them to "look good." A person who perceives that his or her entire career is riding on next quarter's sales figures or next month's plant productivity report will be highly motivated to do whatever is necessary to make sure the numbers come out favorably.

Finally, when employees see the people on top engaging in political behavior, especially when they do so successfully and are rewarded for it, a climate is created that supports politicking. Politicking by top management, in a sense, gives permission to those lower in the organization to play politics by implying that such behavior is acceptable.

Impression Management

We know that people have an ongoing interest in how others perceive and evaluate them. For example, North Americans spend billions of dollars on diets, health club memberships, cosmetics, and plastic surgery—all intended to make them more attractive to others. Being perceived positively by others should have benefits for people in organizations. It might, for instance, help them initially to get the jobs they want in an organization and, once hired, to get favorable evaluations, superior salary increases, and more rapid promotions. In a political context, it might help sway the distribution of advantages in their favor.

The process by which individuals attempt to control the impression others form of them is called **impression management**.[11] In this section we review impression management (IM) techniques and ascertain whether they actually work in organizations.

Techniques Most of the attention given to IM techniques has centered on seven verbal self-presentation behaviors that individuals use to manipulate information about themselves.[12] Let's briefly define them and give an example of each.

Self-descriptions: Statements made by a person that describe personal characteristics such as traits, abilities, feelings, opinions, and personal lives. An example: Job applicant to interviewer, "I got my Harvard M.B.A. even though I suffer from dyslexia."

Conformity: Agreeing with someone else's opinion in order to gain his or her approval. An example: Manager to boss, "You're absolutely right on your reorganization plan for the western regional office. I couldn't agree with you more."

Accounts: Excuses, justifications, or other explanations of a predicament-creating event aimed at minimizing the apparent severity of the predicament. An example: Sales manager to boss, "We failed to get the ad in the paper on time but no one responds to those ads anyway."

Apologies: Admitting responsibility for an undesirable event and simultaneously seeking to get a pardon for the action. An example: Employee to boss, "I'm sorry I made a mistake on the report. Please forgive me."

Acclaiming: Explanation of favorable events by someone in order to maximize the desirable implications for that person. An example: Salesperson to peer, "The sales in our division have nearly tripled since I was hired."

Flattery: Complimenting others about their virtues in an effort to make oneself appear perceptive and likable. An example: New sales trainee to peer, "You handled that client's complaint so tactfully! I could never have handled that as well as you did."

Favors: Doing something nice for someone to gain that person's approval. An example: Salesperson to prospective client, "I've got two tickets to the theater for tonight that I can't use. Take them. Consider it a thank-you for taking the time to talk with me."

Keep in mind that nothing in IM implies that the impressions people convey are necessarily false (although, of course, they sometimes are). You can, for instance, *actually* believe that ads contribute little to sales in your region or that you *are* the key ingredient in the tripling of your division's sales. But misrepresentation can have a high cost. If the image claimed is false, you may be discredited. If you "cry wolf" once too often, no one is likely to believe you when the wolf really comes. So one must be cautious not to be perceived as insincere or manipulative.

Are individuals more likely to misrepresent themselves or to get away with it in some situations than in others? Yes. Highly uncertain or ambiguous situations provide relatively little information for challenging a fraudulent claim and thus reduce the risks associated with misrepresentation.

Effectiveness Only a limited number of studies have been undertaken to test the effectiveness of IM techniques, and these have been essentially limited to determining whether or not IM behavior is related to job interview success. Employment interviews make a particularly relevant area of study since applicants are clearly attempting to present positive images of themselves and there are relatively objective outcome measures (written assessments and typically a hire–don't hire recommendation).

The evidence is that IM behavior works.[13] In one study, for instance, interviewers felt that the applicants for a position as a customer-service representative who used IM techniques performed better in the interview than those who didn't use IM, and they seemed somewhat more inclined to hire these people.[14] Moreover, the researchers considered applicants' credentials and concluded it was the IM techniques alone that influenced the interviewers. That is, it didn't seem to matter if applicants were well or poorly qualified. If they used IM techniques, they did better in the interview. Of course, it could be argued that since the job for which applicants were being considered—customer-service representative—was a public contact position, self-presentation may be a job-relevant skill and more important than qualifications such as college or university major, grades, or prior work experience. Nevertheless, IM techniques seem to work in interviews.

The Ethics of Behaving Politically

We conclude our discussion of politics by providing some ethical guidelines for political behavior. While there are no clear-cut ways to differentiate ethical from unethical politicking, there are some questions you should consider.[15]

Exhibit 11-2 illustrates a decision tree to guide ethical actions. The first question you need to answer addresses self-interest versus organizational goals. Ethical actions are consistent with the organization's goals. Spreading untrue rumors about the safety of a new product introduced by your company, in order to make that product's design group look bad, is unethical. However, there may be nothing unethical if a department head exchanges favors with her division's purchasing manager in order to get a critical contract processed quickly.

The second question concerns the rights of other parties. If the department head described in the previous paragraph went to the mailroom during her lunch hour and read through the mail directed to the purchasing manager with the intent of "getting something on him" so he would expedite a contract, she would be acting unethically. She would have violated the purchasing manager's right to privacy.

The final question that needs to be addressed is related to whether the political activity conforms to standards of equity and justice. The department head that inflates the performance evaluation of a favored employee and deflates the evaluation of a

EXHIBIT 11–2   Is a Political Action Ethical?

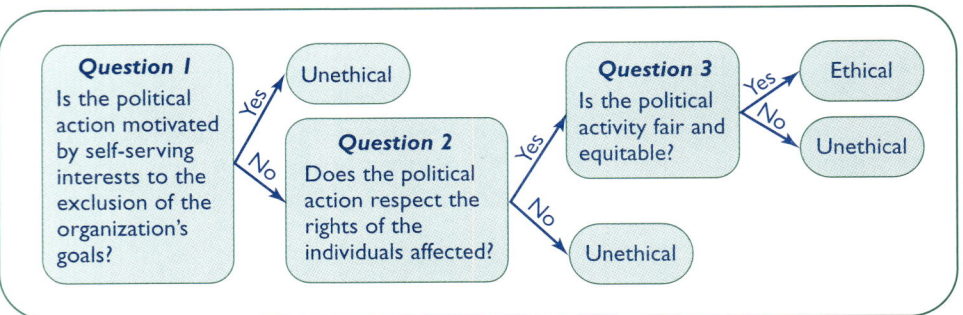

Adapted from G.F. Cavanagh, D. Moberg, and M. Valasquez, "The Ethics of Organizational Politics," *Academy of Management Review*, July 1981, p. 368. Reprinted by permission.

disfavored employee—then uses these evaluations to justify giving the former a big raise and nothing to the latter—has treated the disfavored employee unfairly.

Unfortunately, the answers to the questions in Exhibit 11-2 are often argued in ways to make unethical practices seem ethical. Powerful people, for example, can become very good at explaining self-serving behaviors in terms of the organization's best interests. Similarly, they can persuasively argue that unfair actions are really fair and equitable. Our point is that immoral people can justify almost any behavior. Those who are powerful, articulate, and persuasive are most vulnerable because they are likely to be able to get away with unethical practices successfully. When faced with an ethical dilemma regarding organizational politics, try to answer the questions in Exhibit 11-2 truthfully. And, if you have a strong power base, recognize the ability of power to corrupt. Remember, it's a lot easier for the powerless to act ethically, for no other reason than that they typically have very little political discretion to exploit.

IMPLICATIONS FOR MANAGERS

If you want to get things done in a group or organization, it helps to have power. As a manager who wants to maximize your power, you will want to increase others' dependence on you. You can, for instance, increase your power in relation to your boss by developing knowledge or a skill that he needs and for which he perceives no ready substitute. But power is a two-way street. You will not be alone in attempting to build your power bases. Others, particularly employees and peers, will be seeking to make you dependent on them. The result is a continual battle. While you seek to maximize others' dependence on you, you will be seeking to minimize your dependence on others. And, of course, others you work with will be trying to do the same.

The effective manager accepts the political nature of organizations. By assessing behavior in a political framework, you can better predict the actions of others and use this information to formulate political strategies that will gain advantages for you and your work unit.

CHAPTER 12

Conflict and Negotiation

After reading this chapter, you should be able to

1. Define conflict
2. Differentiate between the traditional, human relations, and interactionist views of conflict
3. Contrast functional and dysfunctional conflict
4. Outline the conflict process
5. Describe the five conflict-handling orientations
6. Contrast distributive and integrative bargaining
7. Identify decision biases that hinder effective negotiation
8. Explain ways for individuals to improve their negotiating skills

It's been said that conflict is a theme that has occupied humans more than any other—with the exception of God and love. But what do we mean by the term *conflict*?

A DEFINITION OF CONFLICT

While there has been no shortage of definitions for *conflict*, several common themes underlie most definitions. First, conflict must be *perceived* by the parties to it. Whether conflict exists is a perception issue. If no one is aware of a conflict, it is generally agreed that no conflict exists. Of course, conflicts perceived may not be real, and, conversely, many situations that otherwise could be described as conflictive are not because the group members involved do not perceive the conflict. In addition, most definitions of conflict include the concepts of *opposition*, *scarcity*, and *blockage* and the assumption there are two or more parties whose interests or goals appear to be *incompatible*. Resources—money, jobs, prestige, and power, for example—are not unlimited, and their scarcity encourages blocking behavior. The parties are therefore in opposition. When one party blocks the means to a goal of another, a state of conflict exists.

Differences between definitions tend to center around *intent* and whether conflict is a term limited only to *overt* acts. The intent issue is a debate over whether blockage behavior must be a determined action or whether it could occur as a result of fortuitous circumstances. As to whether conflict can refer only to overt acts, some definitions, for example, require signs of manifest fighting or open struggle as criteria for the existence of conflict.

Our definition of conflict acknowledges awareness (perception), opposition, scarcity, and blockage. Further, we assume it to be a determined action, which can exist at either the latent or overt level. We define **conflict** as a process in which an effort is purposely made by A to offset the efforts of B by some form of blocking that will result in frustrating B in attaining his or her goals or furthering his or her interests.

TRANSITIONS IN CONFLICT THOUGHT

It is entirely appropriate to say that there has been conflict over the role of conflict in groups and organizations. One school of thought has argued that conflict must be avoided, that it indicates a malfunction within the group. We call this the *traditional view*. Another school of thought, the *human relations view*, argues that conflict is a natural and inevitable outcome in any group. It need not be evil, but rather has the potential to be a positive force in determining group performance. The third, and most recent, perspective proposes not only that conflict can be a positive force in a group, but explicitly argues that some conflict is *absolutely necessary* for a group to perform effectively. We label this third school the *interactionist view*. Let's take a closer look at each of these views.[1]

The Traditional View

The early approach to conflict assumed that conflict was bad. Conflict was viewed negatively, and it was used synonymously with terms such as *violence*, *destruction*, and *irrationality* in order to reinforce its negative connotation. Conflict, then, was to be avoided.

The traditional view was consistent with the attitudes that prevailed about group behavior in the 1930s and 1940s. From findings provided by studies such as those done at Hawthorne, it was argued that conflict was a dysfunctional outcome resulting from poor communication, a lack of openness and trust between people, and the failure of managers to be responsive to the needs and aspirations of their employees.

The view that all conflict is bad certainly offers a simple approach to looking at the behavior of people who create conflict. Since all conflict is to be avoided, we need merely direct our attention to the causes of conflict and correct these malfunctionings in order to improve group and organizational performance. Although studies now provide strong evidence to dispute that this approach to conflict reduction results in high group performance, most of us still evaluate conflict situations on the basis of this outmoded standard.

The Human Relations View

The human relations position argued that conflict was a natural occurrence in all groups and organizations. Since conflict was inevitable, the human relations school advocated acceptance of conflict. They rationalized its existence: It cannot be eliminated, and there are even times when conflict may benefit a group's performance. The human relations view dominated conflict theory from the late 1940s through the mid-1970s.

The Interactionist View

The current view toward conflict is the interactionist perspective. Whereas the human relations approach *accepted* conflict, the interactionist approach *encourages* conflict on the grounds that a harmonious, peaceful, tranquil, and cooperative group is likely to become static, apathetic, and nonresponsive to needs for change and innovation. The major contribution of the interactionist approach, therefore, is encouraging group leaders to maintain an ongoing minimal level of conflict—enough to keep the group alive, self-critical, and creative.

Given the interactionist view, which is the one we take in this chapter, it becomes evident that to say that conflict is all good or all bad is inappropriate and naive. Whether a conflict is good or bad depends on the type of conflict. Specifically, it's necessary to differentiate between functional and dysfunctional conflicts.

DIFFERENTIATING FUNCTIONAL FROM DYSFUNCTIONAL CONFLICTS

The interactionist view does not propose that *all* conflicts are good. Rather, some conflicts support the goals of the group and improve its performance; these are functional, constructive forms of conflict. There are also conflicts that hinder group performance; these are dysfunctional or destructive forms.

What differentiates functional from dysfunctional conflict? The evidence indicates that you need to look at the *type* of conflict.[2] Specifically, there are three types: task, relationship, and process.

Task conflict relates to the content and goals of the work. **Relationship conflict** focuses on interpersonal relationships. **Process conflict** relates to how the work gets done. Studies demonstrate that relationship conflicts are almost always dysfunctional. Why? It appears that the friction and interpersonal hostilities inherent in relationship conflicts increase personality clashes and decrease mutual understanding, thereby hindering the completion of organizational tasks. On the other hand, low levels of process conflict and low-to-moderate levels of task conflict are functional. For process conflict to be productive, it must be kept low. Intense arguments about who should do what become dysfunctional when they create uncertainty about task roles, increase the time to complete tasks, and lead to members working at cross-purposes. A low-to-moderate level of task conflict consistently demonstrates a positive effect on group performance because it stimulates discussion of ideas that help groups perform better.

THE CONFLICT PROCESS

The **conflict process** can be thought of as progressing through four stages: potential opposition, cognition and personalization, behavior, and outcomes. The process is diagrammed in Exhibit 12-1.

Stage I: Potential Opposition

The first step in the conflict process is the presence of conditions that create opportunities for conflict to arise. They *need not* lead directly to conflict, but one of these conditions is necessary if conflict is to arise. For simplicity's sake, these conditions (which also may be looked at as causes or sources of conflict) have been condensed into three general categories: communication, structure, and personal variables.[3]

Communication The communicative source represents opposing forces that arise from semantic difficulties, misunderstandings, and "noise" in the communication channels. Much of this discussion can be related to our comments on communication and communication networks in Chapter 9.

One of the major misconceptions that most of us carry around with us is that poor communication is the reason for conflicts. Such a conclusion is not unreasonable, given the amount of time each of us spends communicating. But, of course, poor communication is certainly not the source of *all* conflicts, though there is considerable evidence to suggest that problems in the communication process act to retard collaboration and stimulate misunderstanding.

EXHIBIT 12–1 The Conflict Process

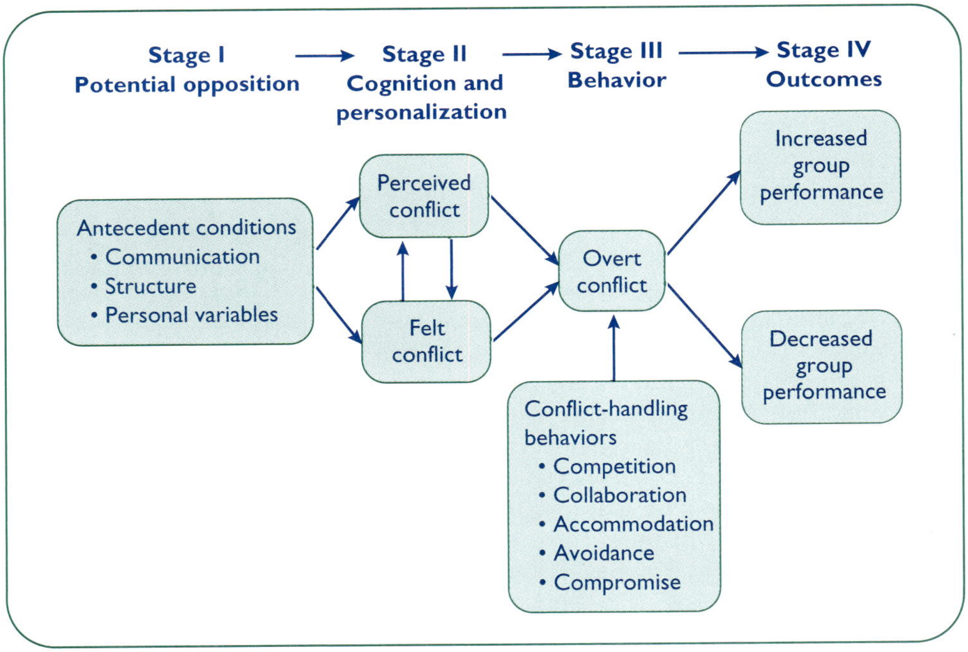

A review of the research suggests that semantic difficulties, insufficient exchange of information, and noise in the communication channel are all barriers to communication and are potential antecedent conditions to conflict. Specifically, evidence demonstrates that semantic difficulties arise as a result of differences in training, selective perception, and inadequate information about others. Research has further demonstrated a surprising finding: The potential for conflict increases when either too little or too much communication takes place. Apparently, an increase in communication is functional up to a point, whereupon it is possible to "overcommunicate," resulting in an increase in the potential for conflict. Too much information as well as too little can lay the foundation for conflict. Further, the channel chosen for communicating can have an influence on stimulating opposition. The filtering process that occurs as information is passed between members and the divergence of communications from formal or previously established channels offer potential opportunities for conflict to arise.

Structure The term *structure* is used, in this context, to include variables such as size; degree of routinization, specialization, and standardization in the tasks assigned to group members; heterogeneity of the group; leadership styles; reward systems; and the degree of dependence between groups. Research indicates that size and specialization act as forces to stimulate conflict. The larger the group and the more specialized its activities, the greater the likelihood of conflict. Tenure and conflict have been found to be inversely related. The potential for conflict tends to be greatest when group members are younger and when turnover is high.

There is some indication that a close style of leadership, that is, tight and continuous observation with restrictive control of the others' behaviors, increases the potential for conflict, but the evidence is not strong. Too much reliance on participation may also stimulate conflict. Research tends to confirm that participation and conflict are highly correlated, apparently because participation encourages the promotion of differences. Reward systems, too, are found to create conflict when one member's gain is at another's expense. Finally, if a group is dependent on another group (in contrast to the two being mutually independent) or if interdependence allows one group to gain at another's expense, opposing forces are stimulated.

Personal Variables The most important personal variables are individual value systems and individual idiosyncrasies and differences. The evidence indicates that certain personality types—for example, individuals who are highly authoritarian, dogmatic, and who demonstrate low self-esteem—lead to potential conflict. Most important, and probably the most overlooked variable in the study of social conflict, is the notion of differing value systems. That is, people differ in the importance they give to values such as freedom, pleasure, hard work, self-respect, honesty, obedience, and equality. Value differences, for example, are the best explanation of such diverse issues as prejudice, disagreements over one's contribution to the group and the rewards one deserves, or assessments of whether this particular book is any good. The fact that John dislikes blacks and Dana thinks that John's position indicates his ignorance, that an employee thinks he is worth $30,000 a year but his boss believes him to be worth $24,000, and that Ann thinks this book is interesting while Jennifer views it as "a crock," are all value judgments. And differences in value systems are important in creating the potential for conflict.

Stage II: Cognition and Personalization

If the conditions cited in stage I generate frustration, then the potential for opposition becomes realized in the second stage. The antecedent conditions can lead to conflict only when one or more of the parties are affected by, and cognizant of, the conflict.

As we noted in our definition of conflict, perception is required. Therefore, one or more of the parties must be aware of the existence of the antecedent conditions. However, because a conflict is perceived does not mean it is personalized. You may be aware that you and a co-worker are in disagreement. But the disagreement may not make you tense or anxious and it may not influence your affection toward this co-worker. It is at the level where conflict is felt, when individuals become emotionally involved, that parties experience anxiety, tension, frustration, or hostility.

Stage III: Behavior

The third stage of the conflict process occurs when a member engages in action that frustrates the attainment of another's goals or prevents the furthering of the other's interests. This action must be intended; that is, there must be a known effort to frustrate another. At this juncture, the conflict is out in the open.

Overt conflict covers a full range of behaviors, from subtle, indirect, and highly controlled forms of interference to direct, aggressive, violent, and uncontrolled struggle. At the low range, this overt behavior is illustrated by the student who raises his or her hand in class and questions a point the instructor has made. At the high range, strikes, riots, and wars come to mind.

Stage III is also where most conflict-handling behaviors are initiated. Once the conflict is overt, the parties will develop a method for dealing with it. Conflict-handling behaviors might be initiated in stage II, but, in most cases, techniques for reducing frustration are used not as preventive measures but only when the conflict has become observable. Five conflict-handling approaches are typically available: competition, collaboration, avoidance, accommodation, and compromise.[4]

Competition When one party seeks to achieve certain goals or to further personal interests, regardless of the impact on the parties to the conflict, he or she competes and dominates. These win-lose struggles, in formal groups or in an organization, frequently utilize the formal authority of a mutual superior as the dominant force, and each of the conflicting parties will use his or her own power base in order to resolve a victory in his or her favor.

Collaboration When each of the parties in conflict desires to satisfy fully the concern of all parties, we have cooperation and the search for a mutually beneficial outcome. In collaboration, the behavior of the parties is aimed at solving the problem and at clarifying the differences rather than accommodating various points of view. The participants consider the full range of alternatives, the similarities and differences in viewpoints become more clearly focused, and the causes or differences become outwardly evident. Because the solution sought is advantageous to all parties, collaboration is often thought of as a win-win approach to resolving conflicts. It is, for example, a tool used frequently by marriage counselors. Behavioral scientists, who value openness, trust, and spontaneity in relationships, are also strong advocates of a collaborative approach to resolving conflicts.

Avoidance   Recognizing that a conflict exists, a party may react by withdrawing from or suppressing it. Indifference or the desire to evade overt demonstration of a disagreement can result in withdrawal: The parties acknowledge physical separation, and each stakes out a territory distinct from the other's. If withdrawal is not possible or desirable, the parties may suppress, that is, withhold their differences. When group members are required to interact because of the interdependence of their tasks, suppression is a more probable outcome than withdrawal.

Accommodation   When the parties seek to appease their opponents, they may be willing to place their opponents' interests above their own. In order to maintain the relationship, one party is willing to be self-sacrificing. We refer to this behavior as accommodation. When husbands and wives have differences, it is not uncommon for one to accommodate the other by placing a spouse's interest above one's own.

Compromise   When each party to the conflict must give up something, sharing occurs, resulting in a compromised outcome. In compromising, there is no clear winner or loser. Rather, there is a rationing of the object of the conflict or, where the object is not divisible, one rewards the other by yielding something of substitute value. The distinguishing characteristic of compromise, therefore, is the requirement that each party give up something. In negotiations between unions and management, compromise is required in order to reach a settlement and agree on a labor contract.

The Impact of National Culture on Conflict Behavior   Your approach to handling conflict will, to some degree, be influenced by your cultural roots. Americans, for example, have a reputation for being open, direct, and competitive. These characteristics are consistent with a society marked by relatively low uncertainty avoidance and high quantity-of-life rankings.

As we discovered in Chapter 2, people in countries low in uncertainty avoidance feel secure and relatively free from threats of uncertainty. Their organizations, therefore, tend to be rather open and flexible. Countries ranked high in quantity of life emphasize assertiveness. The cultural climate of low uncertainty avoidance and high quantity of life tends to shape a society that is open, direct, and competitive. It would also tend to create individuals who favor conflict-handling behaviors such as competition and collaboration.

This premise suggests that uncertainty avoidance and quantity/quality-of-life rankings would be fairly good predictors of which conflict styles are preferred in different countries. It suggests, for instance, that when one is in a Scandinavian country—which tends to rate high on quality of life—avoidance or accommodation behaviors should be emphasized. The same recommendation would apply in Japan, Greece, or other countries that rate high on uncertainty avoidance, because the extensive use of formal rules and employment guarantees tends to minimize conflicts and encourage cooperation.

Stage IV: Outcomes

The interplay between the overt conflict behavior and conflict-handling behaviors results in consequences. As Exhibit 12-1 demonstrates, they may be functional in that the conflict has resulted in an improvement in the group's performance. Conversely, group performance may be hindered and the outcome then would be dysfunctional.

Functional Outcomes How might conflict increase group performance? It is hard to visualize a situation in which open or violent aggression could be functional. But it is possible to envision how low or moderate levels of conflict could improve the effectiveness of a group. Because it is often difficult to think of instances in which conflict can be constructive, let's consider some examples and then look at the research evidence.

Conflict is constructive when it improves the quality of decisions, stimulates creativity and innovation, encourages interest and curiosity among group members, provides the medium through which problems can be aired and tensions released, and fosters an environment of self-evaluation and improvement. The evidence suggests that conflict can enhance the quality of decision making by allowing all points, particularly the ones that are unusual or held by a minority, to be weighed in important decisions. Conflict is an antidote for groupthink. It does not allow the group to rubber-stamp decisions that may be based on weak assumptions, inadequate consideration of relevant alternatives, or other debilities. Conflict challenges the status quo and therefore furthers the creation of new ideas, promotes reassessment of group goals and activities, and increases the probability that the group will respond to change.

For an example of a company that has suffered because it had too little functional conflict, you don't have to look further than automobile behemoth General Motors.[5] Many of GM's problems over the past three decades can be traced to a lack of functional conflict. It hired and promoted individuals who were "yes men," loyal to GM to the point of never questioning company actions. Managers were, for the most part, conservative white Anglo-Saxon males raised in the midwestern United States who resisted change—they preferred looking back to past successes rather than forward to new challenges. They were almost sanctimonious in their belief that what had worked in the past would continue to work in the future. Moreover, by sheltering executives in the company's Detroit offices and encouraging them to socialize with others inside the GM ranks, the company further insulated managers from conflicting perspectives.

Research studies in diverse settings confirm the functionality of conflict. Consider the following findings. A comparison of six major decisions during the administrations of four U.S. presidents found that conflict reduced the chance that groupthink would overpower policy decisions. The comparisons demonstrated that conformity among presidential advisers was related to poor decisions, while an atmosphere of constructive conflict and critical thinking surrounded the well-developed decisions.[6]

There is further evidence that conflict leads to better and more innovative decisions, as well as increased group productivity. It was demonstrated that, among established groups, performance tended to improve more when there was conflict among members than when there was fairly close agreement. The investigators observed that when groups analyzed decisions that had been made by the individual members of that group, the average improvement among the high-conflict groups was 73 percent greater than that of those groups characterized by low-conflict conditions.[7] Other researchers have found similar results: Groups composed of members with different interests tend to produce higher-quality solutions to a variety of problems than do homogeneous groups.[8] The preceding findings suggest that, contrary to the traditional view, conflict in the group might be an indication of strength rather than weakness.

Dysfunctional Conflict The destructive consequences of conflict on a group or organization's performance are generally well known. A reasonable summary might state: Uncontrolled opposition breeds discontent, which acts to dissolve common ties and eventually leads to destruction of the group. And, of course, there is a substantial body of literature to document how the dysfunctional varieties of conflict can reduce group effectiveness. Among the more undesirable consequences are a retarding of communication, reductions in group cohesiveness, and subordination of group goals to the primacy of infighting among members. At the extreme, conflict can bring group functioning to a halt and potentially threaten the group's survival.

The demise of an organization as a result of too much conflict isn't as unusual as it might first appear. For instance, one of New York's best-known law firms, Shea & Gould, closed down solely because the 80 partners just couldn't get along.[9] As one legal consultant, familiar with the organization, said: "This was a firm that had basic and principled differences among the partners that were basically irreconcilable." That same consultant also addressed the partners at their last meeting: "You don't have an economic problem," he said. "You have a personality problem. You hate each other!"

NEGOTIATION

Negotiation permeates the interactions of almost everyone in groups and organizations. There's the obvious: Labor bargains with management. There's the not-so-obvious: Managers negotiate with subordinates, peers, and bosses; salespeople negotiate with customers; purchasing agents negotiate with suppliers. And there's the subtle: A worker agrees to answer a colleague's phone for a few minutes in exchange for some past or future benefit. In today's team-based organizations, where members are increasingly finding themselves having to work with colleagues over whom they have no direct authority and with whom they may not even share a common boss, negotiation skills become critical.

For our purposes, we define **negotiation** as a process in which two or more parties exchange goods or services and attempt to agree on the exchange rate for them.[10] In addition, we use the terms *negotiation* and *bargaining* interchangeably.

Bargaining Strategies

There are two general approaches to negotiation—*distributive bargaining* and *integrative bargaining*.[11] These are compared in Exhibit 12-2.

Distributive Bargaining You see a used car advertised for sale in the newspaper. It appears to be just what you've been looking for. You go out to see the car. It's great and you want it. The owner tells you the asking price. You don't want to pay that much. The two of you then negotiate over the price. The negotiating process you are engaging in is called *distributive bargaining*. Its most identifying feature is that it operates under zero-sum conditions. That is, any gain I make is at your expense, and vice versa. In the used car example, every dollar you can get the seller to cut from the car's price is a dollar you save. Conversely, every dollar more he can get from you comes at your expense. So the essence of **distributive bargaining** is negotiating over who gets what share of a fixed pie.

EXHIBIT 12–2   Distributive versus Integrative Bargaining

Bargaining Characteristic	Distributive Bargaining	Integrative Bargaining
Available amount of resources to be divided	Fixed	Variable
Primary motivations	I win; you lose	I win; you win
Primary interests	Opposed to each other	Convergent or congruent with each other
Focus of relationships	Short term	Long term

Adapted from R.J. Lewicki and J.A. Litterer, *Negotiation* (Homewood, IL: Richard D. Irwin, 1985), p. 280. Copyright © R.J. Lewicki and J.A. Litterer, 1985. Reprinted by permission of Richard D. Irwin, Inc.

Probably the most widely cited example of distributive bargaining is in labor–management negotiations over wages. Typically, labor's representatives come to the bargaining table determined to get as much money as possible out of management. Every cent more that labor negotiates increases management's costs, so each party bargains aggressively and treats the other as an opponent who must be defeated.

Exhibit 12-3 depicts the distributive bargaining strategy. Parties A and B represent the two negotiators. Each has a *target point* that defines what he or she would like to achieve. Each also has a *resistance point*, which marks the lowest outcome that is acceptable—the point below which they would break off negotiations rather than accept a less favorable settlement. The area between their resistance points is the settlement range. As long as there is some overlap in their aspiration ranges, there exists a settlement area where each one's aspirations can be met.

When engaged in distributive bargaining, one's tactics focus on trying to get one's opponent to agree to one's specific target point or to get as close to it as possible. Examples of such tactics are persuading your opponent of the impossibility of getting

EXHIBIT 12–3   Staking Out the Bargaining Zone

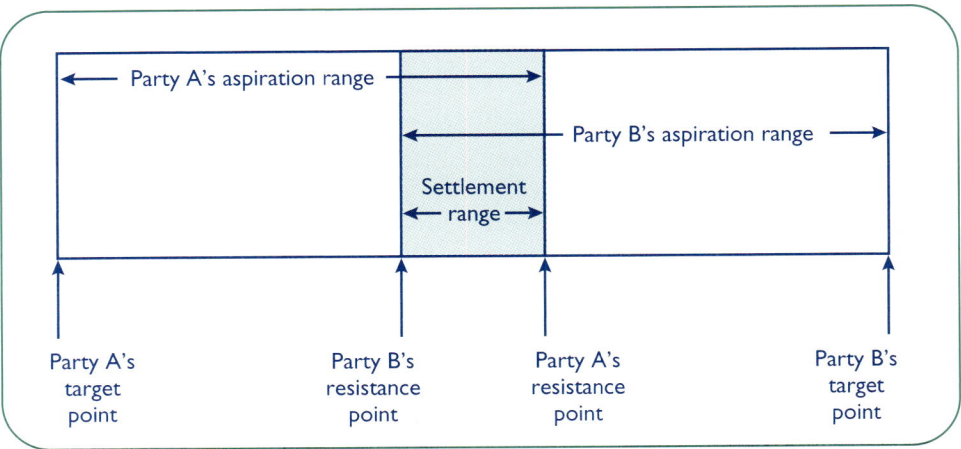

to his or her target point and the advisability of accepting a settlement near yours; arguing that your target is fair, while your opponent's isn't; and attempting to get your opponent to feel emotionally generous toward you and thus accepting an outcome close to your target point.

Integrative Bargaining A sales representative for a women's sportswear manufacturer has just closed a $15,000 order from a small clothing retailer. The sales rep calls in the order to her firm's credit department. She is told the firm can't approve credit to this customer because of a past slow-pay record. The next day, the sales rep and the firm's credit manager meet to discuss the problem. The sales rep doesn't want to lose the business. Neither does the credit manager, but he also doesn't want to get stuck with an uncollectible debt. The two openly review their options. After considerable discussion, they agree on a solution that meets both their needs: The credit manager will approve the sale, but the clothing store's owner will provide a bank guarantee that will ensure payment if the bill isn't paid within 60 days.

This sales-credit negotiation is an example of **integrative bargaining**. In contrast to distributive bargaining, integrative problem solving operates under the assumption that one or more settlements exist that can create a win-win solution.

All things being equal, integrative bargaining is preferable to distributive bargaining. Why? Because the former builds long-term relationships and facilitates working together in the future. It bonds negotiators and allows each to leave the bargaining table feeling that he or she has achieved a victory. Distributive bargaining, on the other hand, leaves one party a loser. It tends to build animosities and deepen divisions when people have to work together on an ongoing basis.

Why, then, don't we see more integrative bargaining in organizations? The answer lies in the conditions necessary for this type of negotiation to succeed. These include parties who are open with information and candid about their concerns; a sensitivity by both parties to the other's needs; the ability to trust one another; and a willingness by both parties to maintain flexibility. Since many organizational cultures and interorganizational relationships are not characterized by openness, trust, and flexibility, it isn't surprising that negotiations often take on a win-at-any-cost dynamic.

Issues in Negotiation

We conclude our discussion of negotiation by reviewing three contemporary issues in negotiation: decision-making biases; the role of personality traits; and the effect of cultural differences on negotiating styles.

Decision-Making Biases That Hinder Effective Negotiation All of us have had negotiating experiences in which the results have been less than we had hoped for. Why? We tend to be blind to opportunities that would allow us to get as much as possible out of a negotiation. The following identifies seven decision-making biases that can blind us.[12]

1. *Irrational escalation of commitment.* People tend to continue a previously selected course of action beyond what rational analysis would recommend. Such misdirected persistence can lead to wasting a great deal of time, energy, and money. Time and money already invested are "sunk costs." They cannot be recovered and should not be considered when selecting future courses of action.

2. *The mythical fixed pie.* Bargainers assume that their gain must come at the expense of the other party. As noted with integrative bargaining, that needn't be the case. There are often win-win solutions. By assuming a zero-sum game, you preclude opportunities to find options that can allow multiple victories.

3. *Anchoring and adjustments.* People often have a tendency to anchor their judgments on irrelevant information, such as an initial offer. Many factors influence the initial positions people take when entering a negotiation. They are often meaningless. Effective negotiators don't let an initial anchor minimize the amount of information and the depth of thinking they use to evaluate a situation, and they don't give too much weight to their opponent's initial offer too early in the negotiation.

4. *Framing negotiations.* People tend to be overly affected by the way information is presented to them. For instance, in a labor-management contract negotiation, assume that your employees are currently making $15 an hour but the union is seeking a $4 raise. You are prepared to go to $17. The union's response is likely to be different if you can successfully frame this as a $2 an hour gain (in comparison to the current wage) rather than a $2 an hour loss (when compared against the union's demand).

5. *Availability of information.* Negotiators often rely too much on readily available information while ignoring more relevant data. Things or events that people have often encountered are usually easy to remember—they're "available" in their memory. It's also easy to remember or imagine vivid events. Information that is easily recalled, because it's familiar or vivid, may be interpreted as being reliable when it's not. Effective negotiators learn to distinguish what's emotionally familiar to them from what is reliable and relevant.

6. *The winner's curse.* A friend went in to a local dealership to buy a new, luxury sports car. The list price was $42,300. My friend estimated that the dealer probably paid around $35,000 for the car. My friend was prepared to go as high as $41,000, but he made an initial offer of $38,000. To his surprise, the dealer accepted his offer. Two hours later he was driving home in his new car. That night he couldn't sleep. In spite of the fact that he had paid $3,000 less than he expected, he felt that he still may have paid too much. He was experiencing "winner's curse," or the regret one feels after closing a negotiation. Because your opponent accepted your offer, you become concerned that you offered too much. This postnegotiation reaction is not unusual. In most negotiations, one side (usually the seller) has much better information than the other. Yet people often tend to act in a negotiation as if their opponent is inactive and ignore the valuable information that can be learned by thinking about the other side's decisions. You can reduce the "curse" by gaining as much information as possible and putting yourself in your opponent's shoes.

7. *Overconfidence.* Many of the previous biases can combine to inflate a person's confidence in his or her judgment and choices. When people hold certain beliefs and expectations, they tend to ignore information that contradicts them. The result is that negotiators tend to be overconfident. Overconfidence, in turn, lessens the incentive to compromise. Considering the suggestions of qualified advisers or seeking objective assessment about your position from a neutral party are two ways to temper this tendency.

The Role of Personality Traits in Negotiation

Can you predict an opponent's negotiating tactics if you know something about his or her personality? It's tempting to answer Yes to that question. For instance, you might assume that high risk takers would be aggressive bargainers who make few concessions. Surprisingly, the evidence doesn't support that assumption.[13]

Overall assessments of the personality-negotiation relationship find that personality traits have no significant direct effect on either the bargaining process or negotiation outcomes. This conclusion is important. It suggests that you should concentrate on the issues and the situational factors in each bargaining episode and not on your opponent and his or her characteristics.

Cultural Differences in Negotiations   Although there appears to be no significant direct relationship between an individual's personality and negotiation style, cultural background does seem to be relevant. Negotiating styles clearly vary among national cultures.[14]

The French like conflict. They frequently gain recognition and develop their reputations by thinking and acting against others. As a result, the French tend to take a long time in negotiating agreements, and they aren't overly concerned about whether their opponents like or dislike them.[15] The Chinese also draw out negotiations, but for a different reason. They believe that negotiations never end. Just when you think you've pinned down every detail and reached a final solution with a Chinese executive, that executive might smile and start the process all over again. Like the Japanese, the Chinese negotiate to develop a relationship and a commitment to work together rather than to tie up every loose end.[16] Americans are known around the world for their impatience and their desire to be liked. Astute negotiators from other countries often turn these characteristics to their advantage by dragging out negotiations and making friendship conditional on the final settlement.

The cultural context of the negotiation significantly influences the amount and type of preparation for bargaining, the relative emphasis on task versus interpersonal relationships, the tactics used, and even where the negotiation should be conducted. To further illustrate some of these differences, let's look at two studies comparing the influence of culture on business negotiations.

The first study compared North Americans, Arabs, and Russians.[17] Among the factors that were looked at were their negotiating style, how they responded to an opponent's arguments, their approach to making concessions, and how they handled negotiating deadlines. North Americans tried to persuade by relying on facts and appealing to logic. They countered opponents' arguments with objective facts. They made small concessions early in the negotiation to establish a relationship and usually reciprocated opponents' concessions. North Americans treated deadlines as very important. The Arabs tried to persuade by appealing to emotion. They countered opponents' arguments with subjective feelings. They made concessions throughout the bargaining process and almost always reciprocated opponents' concessions. Arabs approached deadlines very casually. The Russians based their arguments on asserted ideals. They made few, if any, concessions. Any concession offered by an opponent was viewed as a weakness and was almost never reciprocated. Finally, the Russians tended to ignore deadlines.

The second study looked at verbal and nonverbal negotiation tactics exhibited by North Americans, Japanese, and Brazilians during half-hour bargaining sessions.[18] Some of the differences were particularly interesting. For instance, the Brazilians on average said No eighty-three times, as compared with five times for the Japanese and nine times for the North Americans. The Japanese displayed more than five periods of silence lasting longer than ten seconds during each thirty-minute session. North Americans averaged 3.5 such periods; the Brazilians had none. The Japanese and

North Americans interrupted their opponent about the same number of times, but the Brazilians interrupted two-and-a-half to three times more often than the North Americans and the Japanese. Finally, while the Japanese and the North Americans had no physical contact with their opponents during negotiations except for handshaking, the Brazilians touched each other almost five times every half-hour.

IMPLICATIONS FOR MANAGERS

Managing Conflict

Many people assume that conflict is related to lower group and organizational performance. This chapter has demonstrated that this assumption is often false. Conflict can be either constructive or destructive to the functioning of a group or unit. When it's too high or too low, it hinders performance. An optimal level is one in which there is enough conflict to prevent stagnation, stimulate creativity, allow tensions to be released, and initiate the seeds for change, yet not so much as to be disruptive.

What advice can we give to managers faced with excessive conflict and the need to reduce it? Don't assume that there's one conflict-handling approach that will always be best! You should select the resolution technique appropriate for each situation. Some guidelines follow.[19]

Use *competition* when quick, decisive action is vital (in emergencies); on important issues, when unpopular actions need implementing (in cost cutting, enforcing unpopular rules, discipline); on issues vital to the organization's welfare when you know you're right; and against people who take advantage of noncompetitive behavior.

Use *collaboration* to find an integrative solution when both sets of concerns are too important to be compromised; when your objective is to learn; to merge insights from people with different perspectives; to gain commitment by incorporating concerns into a consensus; and to work through feelings that have interfered with a relationship.

Use *avoidance* when an issue is trivial or when more important issues are pressing; when you perceive no chance of satisfying your concerns; when potential disruption outweighs the benefits of resolution; to let people cool down and regain perspective; when gathering information supersedes immediate decision; when others can resolve the conflict more effectively; and when issues seem tangential or symptomatic of other issues.

Use *accommodation* when you find you are wrong and to allow a better position to be heard, to learn, and to show your reasonableness; when issues are more important to others than to yourself and to satisfy others and maintain cooperation; to build social credits for later issues; to minimize loss when you are outmatched and losing; when harmony and stability are especially important; and to allow employees to grow by learning from mistakes.

Use *compromise* when goals are important but not worth the effort of potential disruption of more assertive approaches; when opponents with equal power are committed to mutually exclusive goals; to achieve temporary settlements for complex issues; to arrive at expedient solutions under time pressure; and as a backup when collaboration or competition is unsuccessful.

Toward Improving Negotiation Skills

The following recommendations should help improve your effectiveness at negotiating.[20]

Research Your Opponent. Acquire as much information as you can about your opponent's interests and goals. What constituencies must he or she appease? What is his or her strategy? This knowledge will help you to better understand your opponent's behavior, predict responses to your offers, and help you to frame solutions in terms of his or her interests.

Begin with a Positive Overture. Research shows that concessions tend to be reciprocated and lead to agreements. As a result, begin bargaining with a positive overture—perhaps a small concession—and then reciprocate your opponent's concessions.

Address the Problem, Not Personalities. Concentrate on the negotiation issues not on the personal characteristics of your opponent. When negotiations get tough, avoid the tendency to attack your opponent. It's your opponent's ideas or position that you disagree with, not him or her personally. Separate the people from the problem, and don't personalize differences.

Pay Little Attention to Initial Offers. Treat initial offers as merely a point of departure. Everyone has to have an initial position. They tend to be extreme and idealistic. Treat them as such.

Emphasize Win-Win Solutions. If conditions are supportive, look for an integrative solution. Frame options in terms of your opponent's interests, and look for solutions that can allow both you and your opponent to declare a victory.

Create an Open and Trusting Climate. Skilled negotiators are good listeners, ask questions, focus their arguments directly, are not defensive, and have learned to avoid words and phrases that can irritate an opponent (e.g., "generous offer," "fair price," "reasonable arrangement"). In other words, they are good at creating the open and trusting climate necessary for reaching an integrative settlement.

PART IV: The Organization System

CHAPTER 13

Foundations of Organization Structure

After reading this chapter, you should be able to

1. Identify the six key elements that define an organization's structure
2. Describe a simple structure
3. Explain the characteristics of a bureaucracy
4. Describe a matrix organization
5. Explain the characteristics of a "virtual" organization
6. Summarize why managers want to create boundaryless organizations
7. List the factors that favor different organization structures
8. Explain the behavioral implications of different organization structures

The theme of this chapter is that organizations have different structures and that these structures have a bearing on employee attitudes and behavior. More specifically, in the following pages, we'll define the key components that make up an organization's structure, present half a dozen or so structural design options, identify the contingency factors that make certain structural designs preferable in different situations, and conclude by considering the different effects that various organization structures have on employee behavior.

WHAT IS ORGANIZATION STRUCTURE?

An **organization structure** defines how job tasks are formally divided, grouped, and coordinated. For instance, Johnson & Johnson has historically grouped activities into semi-autonomous companies organized around products and allowed managers of these companies considerable decision-making latitude.

There are six key elements that managers need to address when they design their organization's structure. These are work specialization, departmentalization, chain of command, span of control, centralization and decentralization, and formalization.[1] Exhibit 13-1 presents each of these elements as answers to an important structural question. The following sections describe these six elements of structure.

Work Specialization

Early in the twentieth century, Henry Ford became rich and famous by building automobiles on an assembly line. Every Ford worker was assigned a specific, repetitive task. For instance, one person would just put on the right front wheel and someone else would install the right front door. By breaking jobs up into small standardized tasks, which could be performed over and over again, Ford was able to produce cars at the rate of one every ten seconds, while using employees who had relatively limited skills.

Ford demonstrated that work can be performed more efficiently if employees are allowed to specialize. Today we use the term **work specialization** or *division of labor* to describe the degree to which tasks in the organization are subdivided into separate jobs.

The essence of work specialization is that, rather than an entire job being done by one individual, it is broken down into steps, each step being completed by a separate individual. In essence, individuals specialize in doing part of an activity rather than the entire activity.

By the late 1940s, most manufacturing jobs in industrialized countries were being done with high work specialization. Management saw this as a means to make the most efficient use of its employees' skills. In most organizations, some tasks require highly developed skills; others can be performed by untrained workers. If all workers were engaged in each step of, say, an organization's manufacturing process, all would have to have the skills necessary to perform both the most demanding and the least demanding jobs. The result would be that, except when performing the most skilled or highly sophisticated tasks, employees would be working below their skill levels. And, since skilled workers are paid more than unskilled workers and their wages tend to reflect their highest level of skill, paying highly skilled workers to do easy tasks represents an inefficient use of organizational resources.

EXHIBIT 13–1 Six Key Questions That Managers Need to Answer in Designing the Proper Organization Structure

The Key Question Is	The Answer Is Provided by
1. To what degree are tasks subdivided into separate jobs?	*Work specialization*
2. On what basis will jobs be grouped together?	*Departmentalization*
3. To whom do individuals and groups report?	*Chain of command*
4. How many individuals can a manager efficiently and effectively direct?	*Span of control*
5. Where does decision-making authority lie?	*Centralization and decentralization*
6. To what degree will there be rules and regulations to direct employees and managers?	*Formalization*

Managers also looked for other efficiencies that could be achieved through work specialization. Employee skills at performing a task successfully increase through repetition. Less time is spent in changing tasks, in putting away one's tools and equipment from a prior step in the work process, and in getting ready for another. Equally important, training for specialization is more efficient from the organization's perspective. It is easier and less costly to find and train workers to do specific and repetitive tasks than to do a broad range of diverse tasks. This is especially true of highly sophisticated and complex operations. For example, could Cessna produce one Citation jet a year if one person had to build the entire plane alone? Not likely! Finally, work specialization increases efficiency and productivity by encouraging the creation of special inventions and machinery.

For much of the first half of the twentieth century, managers viewed work specialization as an unending source of increased productivity. And, up to a point, they were probably right. Because specialization was not widely practiced, its introduction almost always generated higher productivity. But, by the 1960s, there was increasing evidence that a good thing can be carried too far. The point had been reached in some jobs at which the human diseconomies from specialization—which surface as boredom, fatigue, stress, low productivity, poor quality, increased absenteeism, and high turnover—more than offset the economic advantages (see Exhibit 13-2). In such cases, productivity could be increased by enlarging, rather than narrowing, the scope of job activities. In addition, some companies found that by giving employees a variety of activities to do, allowing them to do a whole and complete job, and putting them into teams with interchangeable skills, they often achieved significantly higher output with increased employee satisfaction.

Most managers today see work specialization as neither obsolete nor an unending source of increased productivity. Rather, managers recognize the economies it provides in certain types of jobs and the problems it creates when it's carried too far. You'll find, for example, high work specialization being used by McDonald's to effi-

EXHIBIT 13–2 Economies and Diseconomies of Work Specialization

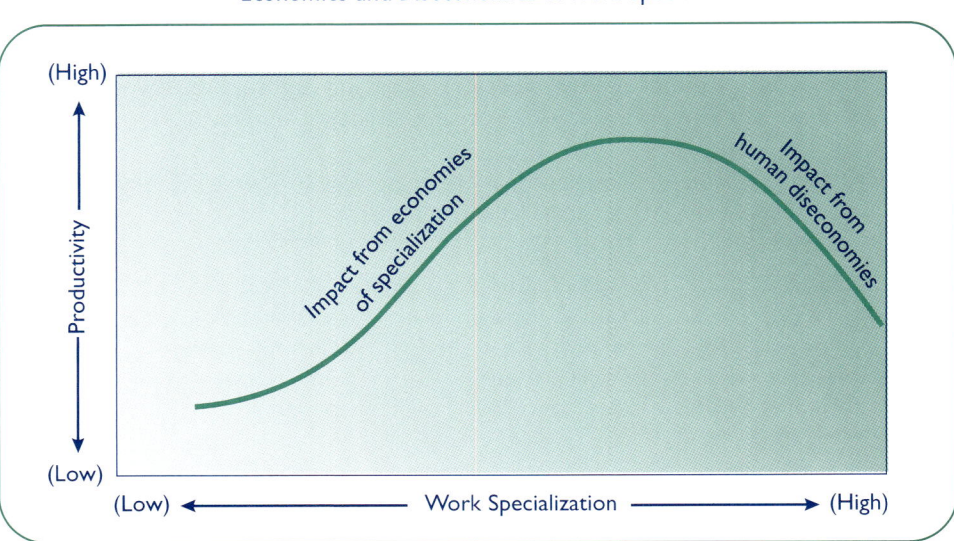

ciently make and sell hamburgers and fries and by medical specialists in most health maintenance organizations. On the other hand, companies such as Saturn Corporation, Xerox, and Unisys have had success by broadening the scope of jobs and reducing specialization.

Departmentalization

Once you've divided up jobs through work specialization, you need to group these jobs together so that common tasks can be coordinated. The basis by which jobs are grouped together is called **departmentalization**.

One of the most popular ways to group activities is by *functions* performed. A manufacturing manager might organize his or her plant by separating engineering, accounting, manufacturing, personnel, and purchasing specialists into common departments. Of course, departmentalization by function can be used in all types of organizations. Only the functions change to reflect the organization's objectives and activities. A hospital might have departments devoted to research, patient care, accounting, and so forth. The major advantage to this type of grouping is obtaining efficiencies from putting like specialists together. Functional departmentalization seeks to achieve economies of scale by placing people with common skills and orientations into common units.

Tasks can also be departmentalized by the type of *product* the organization produces. Procter & Gamble, for instance, recently reorganized along these lines. Each major product—such as Tide, Pampers, Charmin, and Pringles—is now under the authority of an executive who will have complete global responsibility for that product. The major advantage of this type of grouping is increased accountability for product performance, since all activities related to a specific product are under the direction of a single manager. If an organization's activities were service-related rather than product-related, each service would be autonomously grouped. For instance, an accounting firm could have departments for taxes, management consulting, auditing, and the like. Each would offer a common array of services under the direction of a product or service manager.

Another way to departmentalize is on the basis of *geography* or territory. The sales function, for instance, may have western, southern, midwestern, and eastern regions. Each of these regions is, in effect, a department organized around geography. This form of departmentalization can be valuable if an organization's customers are scattered over a large geographical area.

At an Alcoa aluminum tubing plant in upstate New York, production is organized into five departments: casting; pressing; tubing; finishing; and inspecting, packing, and shipping. This is an example of *process* departmentalization because each department specializes in one specific phase in the production of aluminum tubing. The metal is cast in huge furnaces; sent to the press department, where it is extruded into aluminum pipe; transferred to the tube mill, where it is stretched into various sizes and shapes of tubing; moved to finishing, where it is cut and cleaned; and finally arrives in the inspection, packing, and shipping department. Because each process requires different skills, this method offers a basis for the homogeneous categorization of activities.

A final category of departmentalization is to use the particular type of *customer* the organization seeks to reach. The sales activities in an office supply firm, for instance, can be broken down into three departments to service retail, wholesale, and government customers. A large law office can segment its staff on the basis of whether they service corporate or individual clients. The assumption underlying customer departmentalization is that customers in each department have a common set of problems and needs that can best be met by having specialists for each.

Large organizations may use all of the forms of departmentalization that we've described. A major Japanese electronics firm, for instance, organizes each of its divisions along functional lines and its manufacturing units around processes; it departmentalizes sales around seven geographical regions and divides each sales region into four customer groupings. Two general trends, however, seem to be gaining momentum in the past decade. First, customer departmentalization has grown in popularity. In order to better monitor the needs of customers and to be better able to respond to changes in those needs, many organizations have put greater emphasis on customer departmentalization. The second trend is that rigid functional departmentalization is being complemented by teams that cross traditional departmental lines. As we described in Chapter 8, as tasks have become more complex and more diverse skills are needed to accomplish those tasks, management has turned to cross-functional teams.

Chain of Command

In the 1970s, the chain-of-command concept was a basic cornerstone in the design of organizations. As you'll see, it has far less importance today. But contemporary managers should still consider its implications when they decide how best to structure their organizations.

The **chain of command** is an unbroken line of authority that extends from the top of the organization to the lowest echelon and clarifies who reports to whom. It answers questions for employees such as, "Who do I go to if I have a problem?" and "Who am I responsible to?"

You can't discuss the chain of command without discussing two complementary concepts: authority and unity of command. **Authority** refers to the rights inherent in a managerial position to give orders and expect the orders to be obeyed. To facilitate coordination, organizations give each managerial position a place in the chain of command, and each manager is given a degree of authority in order to meet his or her responsibilities. The **unity-of-command principle** helps preserve the concept of an unbroken line of authority. It states that a person should have one and only one superior to whom he or she is directly responsible. If the unity of command is broken, a subordinate might have to cope with conflicting demands or priorities from several superiors.

Times change, and so do the basic tenets of organizational design. The concepts of chain of command, authority, and unity of command have substantially less relevance today because of advancements in computer technology and the trend toward empowering employees. A low-level employee today can access information in seconds that was available only to top managers 20 years ago. Similarly, networked computers increasingly allow employees anywhere in an organization to communicate with anyone else without going through formal channels. Moreover, the concepts of authority and maintaining the chain of command are increasingly less relevant as operating employees are being empowered to make decisions that previously were reserved for management. Add to this trend the popularity of self-managed and cross-functional teams and the creation of new structural designs that include multiple bosses, and the unity-of-command concept takes on less relevance. There are, of course, still many organizations that find they can be most productive by enforcing the chain of command. There just seem to be fewer of them nowadays.

Span of Control

How many subordinates can a manager efficiently and effectively direct? This question of **span of control** is important because, to a large degree, it determines the number of levels and managers an organization has. All things being equal, the wider or larger the span, the more efficient the organization. An example can illustrate the validity of this statement.

Assume that we have two organizations, both of which have approximately 4,100 operative-level employees. As Exhibit 13-3 illustrates, if one has a uniform span of four and the other a span of eight, the wider span would have two fewer levels and approximately 800 fewer managers. If the average manager made $50,000 a year, the wider span would save $40 million a year in management salaries! Obviously, wider spans are more efficient in terms of cost. But at some point wider spans reduce effectiveness. That is, when the span becomes too large, employee performance suffers because supervisors no longer have the time to provide the necessary leadership and support.

Small spans have their advocates. By keeping the span of control to five or six employees, a manager can maintain close control. But small spans have three major drawbacks. First, as already described, they're expensive because they add levels of management. Second, they make vertical communication in the organization more

EXHIBIT 13–3   Contrasting Spans of Control

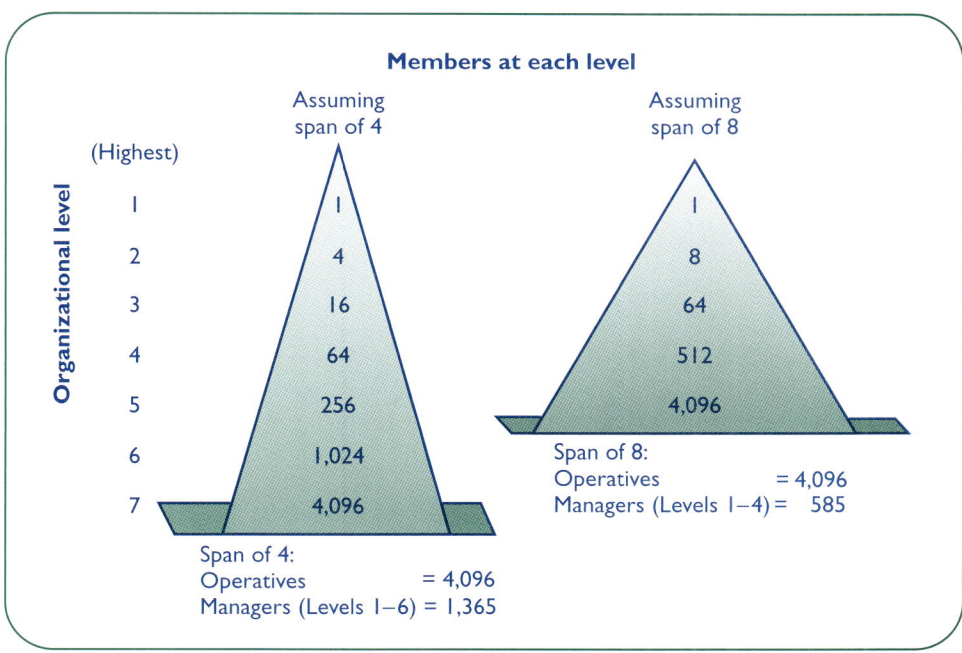

complex. The added levels of hierarchy slow down decision making and tend to isolate upper management. Third, small spans of control encourage overly tight supervision and discourage employee autonomy.

The trend in recent years has been toward larger spans of control. Wide spans are consistent with recent efforts by companies to reduce costs, cut overhead, speed up decision making, increase flexibility, get closer to customers, and empower employees. However, to ensure that performance doesn't suffer because of these wider spans, organizations have been investing heavily in employee training. Managers recognize that they can handle a wider span when employees know their jobs inside and out or can turn to their co-workers when they have questions.

Centralization and Decentralization

In some organizations, top managers make all the decisions. Lower-level managers merely carry out top management's directives. At the other extreme are organizations in which decision making is pushed down to the managers who are closest to "the action." The former organizations are highly centralized; the latter are decentralized.

The term **centralization** refers to the degree to which decision making is concentrated at a single point in the organization. The concept includes only formal authority; that is, the rights inherent in one's position. Typically, it's said that if top management makes the organization's key decisions with little or no input from lower-level personnel, then the organization is centralized. In contrast, the more that lower-level personnel provide input or are actually given the discretion to make decisions, the more *decentralization* there is.

An organization characterized by centralization is an inherently different animal structurally from one that is decentralized. In a decentralized organization, action can be taken more quickly to solve problems, more people provide input into decisions, and employees are less likely to feel alienated from those who make the decisions that affect their work lives.

Consistent with recent management efforts to make organizations more flexible and responsive, there has been a marked trend toward decentralizing decision making. In large companies, lower-level managers are closer to the action and typically have more detailed knowledge about problems than do top managers. Big retailers such as Sears and J.C. Penney have given their store managers considerably more discretion in choosing what merchandise to stock so that their stores can compete more effectively against local merchants. Similarly, Illinois Tool Works is producing $6 billion a year in sales from more than 400 separate business units.[2] The management of Illinois Tool—which makes everything from welding equipment to nails to molded plastic parts—has found that creating these hundreds of separate units, each with its own general manager, allows each business to focus on its customer set with laser-like intensity. The fact that Illinois Tool has had average annual earnings growth of 17 percent over the past ten years indicates that its highly decentralized structure works.

Formalization

Formalization refers to the degree to which jobs within an organization are standardized. If a job is highly formalized, then the job incumbent has a minimum amount of discretion over what is to be done, when it is to be done, and how he or she should do it. Employees can be expected always to handle the same input in exactly the same way, resulting in a consistent and uniform output. There are explicit job descriptions, lots of organizational rules, and clearly defined procedures covering work processes in organizations that have a high degree of formalization. Where formalization is low, job behaviors are relatively nonprogrammed and employees have a great deal of freedom to exercise discretion in their work. An individual's discretion on the job is inversely related to the amount of behavior in that job that is preprogrammed by the organization; therefore, the greater the standardization, the less input the employee has into how his or her work is to be done. Standardization not only eliminates the possibility of employees' engaging in alternative behaviors, but it removes the need for employees even to consider alternatives.

The degree of formalization can vary widely among organizations and within organizations. Certain jobs, for instance, are well known to have little formalization. College book travelers—the representatives of publishers who call on professors to inform them of their company's new publications—have a great deal of freedom in their jobs. They have no standard sales "spiel," and the extent of rules and procedures governing their behavior may be little more than the requirement that they submit a weekly sales report and some suggestions on what to emphasize for the various new titles. At the other extreme, employees in clerical and editorial positions in the same publishing houses are required to "clock in" at their workstations by 8:00 A.M. or be docked a half-hour of pay and, once at that workstation, to follow a set of precise procedures dictated by management.

COMMON ORGANIZATIONAL DESIGNS

We now turn to describing three of the more common organizational designs in use: the *simple structure*, the *bureaucracy*, and the *matrix structure*.

The Simple Structure

What do a small retail store, an electronics firm run by a hard-driving entrepreneur, a new Planned Parenthood office, and an airline in the midst of a companywide pilot's strike have in common? They probably all have a simple structure.

The **simple structure** is characterized most by what it is not rather than what it is. The simple structure is not elaborate.[3] It has a low degree of departmentalization, wide spans of control, and little formalization. The simple structure is a "flat" organization; it usually has only two or three vertical levels, a loose body of employees, and one individual in whom the decision-making authority is centralized. It's most widely practiced in small businesses in which the manager and the owner are one and the same. But it is also the preferred structure in a time of temporary crisis because it centralizes control.

The strength of the simple structure lies in its simplicity. It's fast, flexible, and inexpensive to maintain, and accountability is clear. One major weakness is that it's difficult to maintain in anything other than small organizations. It becomes increasingly inadequate as an organization grows because its low formalization and high centralization tend to create information overload at the top. As size increases, decision making typically becomes slower and can eventually come to a standstill as the single executive tries to continue making all the decisions. This outcome proves to be the undoing of many small businesses. When an organization begins to employ fifty or a hundred people, it's very difficult for the owner-manager to make all the choices. If the structure isn't changed and made more elaborate, the firm often loses momentum and can eventually fail. The simple structure's other weakness is that it's risky—everything depends on one person. One heart attack can literally destroy the organization's information and decision-making center.

The Bureaucracy

Standardization! That's the key concept that underlies all bureaucracies. Take a look at the bank where you keep your checking account; the department store where you buy your clothes; or the government offices that collect your taxes, enforce health regulations, or provide local fire protection. They all rely on standardized work processes for coordination and control.

The **bureaucracy** is characterized by highly routine operating tasks achieved through specialization, very formalized rules and regulations, tasks that are grouped into functional departments, centralized authority, narrow spans of control, and decision making that follows the chain of command.

The primary strength of the bureaucracy lies in its ability to perform standardized activities in a highly efficient manner. Putting like specialties together in functional departments results in economies of scale, minimum duplication of personnel and equipment, and employees who have the opportunity to talk "the same language" among their peers. Further, bureaucracies can get by nicely with less talented—and, hence, less costly—middle- and lower-level managers. The pervasiveness of rules and regulations substitutes for managerial discretion. Standardized operations, coupled with high formalization, allow decision making to be centralized. There is little need, therefore, for innovative and experienced decision makers below the level of senior executives.

One of the major weaknesses of bureaucracy is that specialization creates subunit conflicts. Functional unit goals can override the overall goals of the organization. The other major weakness of bureaucracy is something we've all experienced at one time or another when having to deal with people who work in these organizations: obsessive concern with following the rules. When cases arise that don't precisely fit the rules, there is no room for modification. The bureaucracy is efficient only as long as employees confront problems that they have previously encountered and for which programmed decision rules have already been established.

The peak of bureaucracy's popularity was probably in the 1950s and 1960s. At that time, for instance, just about every major corporation in the world—firms such as IBM, General Electric, Volkswagen, Matsushita, and Royal Dutch Shell—was organized as a bureaucracy. Although the bureaucracy is out of fashion today—largely because it has difficulty responding rapidly to change—the majority of large organizations still take on basic bureaucratic characteristics, particularly specialization and high formalization. However, spans of control have generally been widened, authority has become more decentralized, and functional departments have been supplemented with an increased use of teams. Another trend is toward breaking bureaucracies up into smaller, though fully functioning, minibureaucracies. Each of these smaller versions, with 150 to 250 people, has its own mission and profit goals. It's been estimated that about fifteen percent of large corporations have taken this direction.[4] For instance, Eastman Kodak has transformed over 100 production units into separate businesses. And as we saw earlier, Illinois Tool Works has structured its entire organization into small, independent businesses.

The Matrix Structure

Another popular organizational design option is the **matrix structure**. It is used in advertising agencies, aerospace firms, research and development laboratories, construction companies, hospitals, government agencies, universities, management consulting firms, and entertainment companies. Essentially, the matrix combines two forms of departmentalization—functional and product.

The strength of functional departmentalization lies in putting like specialists together. Grouping specialists minimizes the number necessary while allowing specialized resources to be pooled and shared across products. Its major weakness is that it is difficult to coordinate the specialists' tasks so that their diverse projects are completed on time and within budget. Product departmentalization, on the other hand, has exactly the opposite strengths and weaknesses. It facilitates coordination of specialists so that they can meet deadlines and budget targets, and further, it provides clear responsibility for all activities related to a product. But activities and costs are duplicated. The matrix attempts to gain the strengths of each while avoiding their weaknesses.

The most obvious structural characteristic of the matrix is that it breaks the unity-of-command concept. Employees in the matrix have two bosses—their functional department managers and their product managers. Therefore, the matrix has a dual chain of command.

Exhibit 13-4 shows the matrix form as used in a college of business administration. The academic departments of accounting, administrative studies, marketing, and

EXHIBIT 13–4 Matrix Structure for a College of Business Administration

Academic Departments \ Programs	Undergraduate	Master's	Ph.D.	Research	Executive Development	Community Service
Accounting						
Administrative Studies						
Finance						
Information and Decision Sciences						
Marketing						
Organizational Behavior						
Quantitative Methods						

so forth are functional units. In addition, specific programs (that is, products) are overlaid on the functions. In this way, members in a matrix structure have a dual assignment—to their functional department and to their product groups. For instance, a professor of accounting teaching an undergraduate course reports to the director of undergraduate programs as well as to the chairperson of the accounting department.

The strength of the matrix lies in its ability to facilitate coordination when the organization has multiple complex and interdependent activities. As an organization gets larger, its information-processing capacity can become overloaded. In a bureaucracy, complexity results in increased formalization. The direct and frequent contact between different specialties in the matrix can make for better communication and more flexibility. Information permeates the organization and more quickly reaches the people who need to take account of it. Further, the matrix reduces bureau-pathologies. The dual lines of authority reduce tendencies of departmental members to become so busy protecting their little worlds that the organization's overall goals become secondary.

There is also another advantage to the matrix. It facilitates the efficient allocation of specialists. When individuals with highly specialized skills are lodged in one functional department or product group, their talents are monopolized and underutilized. The matrix achieves the advantages of economies of scale by providing the organization with both the best resources and an effective way of ensuring their efficient deployment.

The major disadvantages of the matrix lie in the confusion it creates, its propensity to foster power struggles, and the stress it places on individuals. When you dispense with the unity-of-command concept, ambiguity is significantly increased, and ambiguity often leads to conflict. For example, it's frequently unclear who reports to whom, and it is not unusual for product managers to fight over getting the best specialists assigned to their products. Confusion and ambiguity also create the seeds of power struggles. Bureaucracy reduces the potential for power grabs by defining the rules of the game. When those rules are "up for grabs," power struggles between functional and product managers result. For individuals who desire security and absence of ambiguity, this work climate can produce stress. Reporting to more than one boss introduces role conflict, and unclear expectations introduce role ambiguity. The comfort of bureaucracy's predictability is replaced by insecurity and stress.

NEW OPTIONS

In recent years, senior managers in a number of organizations have been working to develop new structural options that can better help their firms compete effectively. In this section, we'll describe three such structural designs: the team structure, the virtual organization, and the boundaryless organization.

The Team Structure

As described in Chapter 8, teams have become an extremely popular means around which to organize work activities. An organization that uses teams as its central coordination device has a team structure. The primary characteristics of the team structure are that it breaks down departmental barriers and decentralizes decision making to the level of the work team.

In smaller companies, the team structure can define the entire organization. For instance, Radius, an upscale restaurant in Boston that employs 30 people, is organized completely around teams.[5] There are teams at every station in the kitchen—meat, fish, pastry—and each has full responsibility for their part of the meal. Even a few large companies are using teams throughout. For example, although Gore-tex maker W. L. Gore & Associates employs 6,200 people, the company's plants are kept to 200 employees or less and everyone is part of a self-managed team.[6]

More often, particularly among larger organizations, the team structure complements what is typically a bureaucracy. The organization is thus able to achieve the efficiency of bureaucracy's standardization while gaining the flexibility that teams provide.

The Virtual Organization

Why own when you can rent? That's the essence of the **virtual organization**—a small, core organization that outsources major business functions. In structural terms, the virtual organization is highly centralized, with little or no departmentalization.

Companies such as Nike, Reebok, Liz Claiborne, and Cisco Systems are just a few of the thousands of companies that have found that they can do hundreds of millions of dollars in business without owning manufacturing facilities. Nike, for instance, owns no plants. It designs shoes and then outsources their manufacturing. Most of Cisco System's computer networks are made and assembled by outside firms. National Steel Corp. contracts out its mailroom operations. AT&T farms out its credit-card processing. ExxonMobil Corp. has turned over maintenance of its refineries to another firm.

What's going on here? A quest for maximum flexibility. These "virtual" organizations have created networks of relationships that allow them to contract out manufacturing, distribution, marketing, or any other business function that management feels can be done better or cheaper by others.[7]

The virtual organization stands in sharp contrast to the typical bureaucracy, which has many vertical levels of management and where control is sought through ownership. In such organizations, research and development are done in-house, production occurs in company-owned plants, and sales and marketing are performed by the company's own employees. To support all these levels, management has to employ extra personnel, including accountants, human resource specialists, and lawyers. The virtual organization, however, outsources many of these functions and concentrates on what it does best.

Exhibit 13-5 shows a virtual organization in which management outsources all of the primary functions of the business. The core of the organization is a small group of executives. Their job is to oversee directly any activities that are done in-house and to coordinate relationships with the other organizations that manufacture, distribute, and perform other crucial functions for the virtual organization. The dotted lines in Exhibit 13-5 represent those relationships, typically maintained under contracts. In essence, managers in virtual structures spend most of their time coordinating and controlling external relations, typically by way of computer-network links.

The major advantage to the virtual organization is its flexibility. The primary drawback to this structure is that it reduces management's control over key parts of its business.

EXHIBIT 13–5   Structure of a Virtual Organization

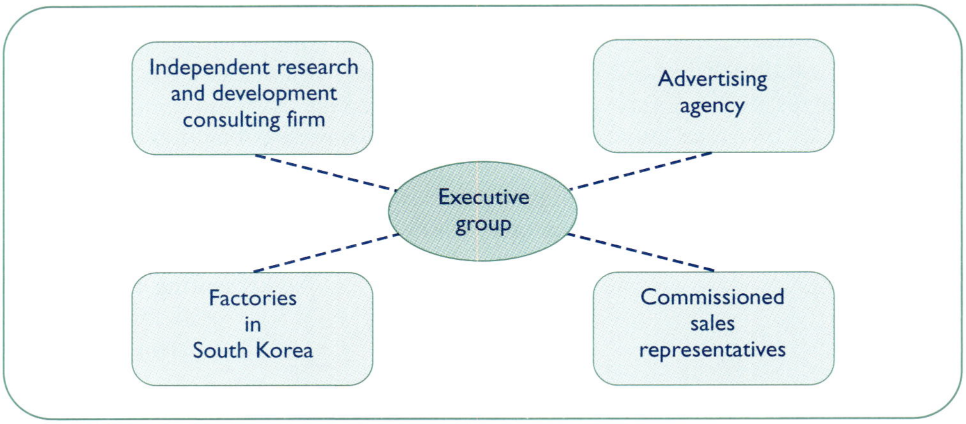

```
Independent research
and development          Advertising
consulting firm          agency

         Executive
          group

Factories                Commissioned
   in                    sales
South Korea              representatives
```

The Boundaryless Organization

General Electric's now former chairman, Jack Welch, coined the term **boundaryless organization** to describe his idea of what he wanted GE to become. Welch wanted to turn his company into a "$60 billion family grocery store."[8] That is, in spite of its monstrous size, he wanted to eliminate *vertical* and *horizontal* boundaries within GE and to break down *external* barriers between the company and its customers and suppliers. The boundaryless organization seeks to eliminate the chain of command, have limitless spans of control, and replace departments with empowered teams.

GE hasn't yet achieved this boundaryless state—and probably never will—but it has made significant progress. So have other companies, such as Hewlett-Packard, AT&T, and Motorola. Let's take a look at what a boundaryless organization would look like and what some firms are doing to make it a reality.

By removing *vertical* boundaries, management flattens the hierarchy. Status and rank are minimized. And the organization looks more like a silo than a pyramid. Cross-hierarchical teams (which include top executives, middle managers, supervisors, and operative employees), participative decision-making practices, and the use of 360-degree performance appraisals (peers and others above and below the employee evaluate his or her performance) are examples of what GE is doing to break down vertical boundaries.

Functional departments create *horizontal* boundaries. The way to reduce these barriers is to replace functional departments with cross-functional teams and to organize activities around processes. For instance, some AT&T units are now doing annual budgets based not on functions or departments but on processes such as the maintenance of a worldwide telecommunications network. Another way management can cut through horizontal barriers is to use lateral transfers and rotate people into and out of different functional areas. This approach turns specialists into generalists.

When fully operational, the boundaryless organization also breaks down barriers to *external* constituencies and barriers created by geography. Globalization, strategic alliances, customer-organization linkages, and telecommuting are all examples of practices that reduce external boundaries. For instance, firms such as NEC Corp., Boeing, and Apple Computer each have strategic alliances or joint partnerships with dozens of companies. These alliances blur the distinction between one organization and another as employees work jointly on projects.

The one common technological thread that makes the boundaryless organization possible is networked computers. These allow people to communicate across intraorganizational and interorganizational boundaries.

WHY DO STRUCTURES DIFFER?

The organization structures described so far ranged from the highly structured and standardized bureaucracy to the loose and amorphous boundaryless organization. Exhibit 13-6 reconceptualizes the preceding discussions by presenting two extreme models of organization structure. One extreme we'll call the **mechanistic model**. It is generally synonymous with the bureaucracy in that it has extensive departmentalization, high formalization, a limited information network (mostly downward communication), and little participation by low-level members in decision making. At the other extreme is the **organic model**. This model looks a lot like the boundaryless organization. It is flat, uses cross-hierarchical and cross-functional teams, has low formalization, possesses a comprehensive information network (using lateral and upward communication as well as downward), and involves high participation in decision making.

What are the forces that determine whether an organization will be structured after the mechanistic model or the organic model? With these two models in mind, we're now prepared to address that question.[9]

Strategy

An organization's structure is a means to help management achieve its objectives. Since objectives are derived from the organization's overall strategy, it is only logical that strategy and structure should be closely linked. More specifically, structure

EXHIBIT 13–6 Mechanistic versus Organic Structures

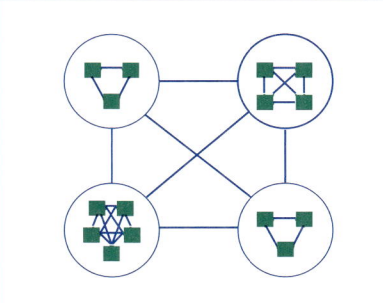

Mechanistic structure
- High horizontal differentiation
- Rigid hierarchical relationships
- Fixed duties
- High formalization
- Formalized communication channels
- Centralized decision authority

Organic structure
- Low horizontal differentiation
- Collaboration (both vertical and horizontal)
- Adaptable duties
- Low formalization
- Informal communication
- Decentralized decision authority

should follow strategy. If management makes a significant change in its organization's strategy, the structure will need to be modified to accommodate and support that change.

Most current strategy frameworks focus on three strategy dimensions—innovation, cost minimization, and imitation—and the structural design that works best with each.[10] To what degree does an organization introduce major new products or services? An **innovation strategy** does not mean a strategy merely for simple or cosmetic changes from previous offerings but rather one for meaningful and unique innovations. Obviously, not all firms pursue innovation. This strategy may appropriately characterize 3M Co., but it's not a strategy pursued by the conservative British retailer Marks & Spencer.

An organization that is pursuing a **cost-minimization strategy** tightly controls costs, refrains from incurring unnecessary innovation or marketing expenses, and cuts prices in selling a basic product. This would describe the strategy pursued by Wal-Mart or the sellers of generic grocery products.

Organizations following an **imitation strategy** try to capitalize on the best of both of the previous strategies. They seek to minimize risk and maximize the opportunity for profit. Their strategy is to move into new products or new markets only after their viability has been proved by innovators. They take the successful ideas of innovators and copy them. Manufacturers of mass-marketed fashion goods that are rip-offs of designer styles follow the imitation strategy. This label also probably characterizes well-known firms such as IBM and Caterpillar. They essentially follow their smaller and more innovative competitors with superior products, but only after their competitors have demonstrated that the market is there.

So how do we link strategy and structure? Innovators need the flexibility of the organic structure, while cost minimizers seek the efficiency and stability of the mechanistic structure. Imitators combine the two structures. They use a mechanistic structure in order to maintain tight controls and low costs in their current activities, while at the same time they create organic subunits in which to pursue new undertakings.

Organization Size

There is considerable evidence to support the notion that an organization's size significantly affects its structure.[11] For instance, large organizations—typically those employing 2,000 or more people—tend to have more specialization, more departmentalization, more vertical levels, and more rules and regulations than do small organizations. But the relationship isn't linear. Rather, size affects structure at a decreasing rate. The impact of size becomes less important as an organization expands. Why? Essentially, once an organization has around 2,000 employees, it's already fairly mechanistic. An additional 500 employees will not have much impact. On the other hand, adding 500 employees to an organization that has only 300 members is likely to result in a shift toward a more mechanistic structure.

Technology

The term *technology* refers to how an organization transfers its inputs into outputs. Every organization has at least one technology for converting financial, human, and physical resources into products or services. The Ford Motor Co., for instance, predominantly uses an assembly-line process to make its products. On the other hand, universities may use a number of instruction technologies—the ever-popular formal lecture method, the case analysis method, the experiential exercise method, the programmed learning method, and so forth. In this section we show that organization structures adapt to their technology.

Numerous studies have been carried out on the technology-structure relationship.[12] The details of those studies are quite complex, so we'll go straight to "the bottom line" and summarize what we know. The common theme that differentiates technologies is their *degree of routineness*. By this term we mean that technologies tend toward either routine or nonroutine activities. The former are characterized by automated and standardized operations. Nonroutine activities are customized. They include such varied operations as furniture restoring, custom shoemaking, and genetic research.

What relationships have been found between technology and structure? Although the relationship is not overwhelmingly strong, we find that routine tasks are associated with taller and more departmentalized structures. The relationship between technology and formalization, however, is stronger. Studies consistently show routineness to be associated with the presence of rule manuals, job descriptions, and other formalized documentation.

Environmental Uncertainty

An organization's environment is composed of institutions or forces that are outside the organization and potentially affect the organization's performance. The environment has acquired a large following as a key determinant of structure.

Why should an organization's structure be affected by its environment? Because of environmental uncertainty. Some organizations face relatively static environments; other organizations face very dynamic environments. Static environments create significantly less uncertainty for managers than do dynamic ones. And, since uncertainty is a threat to an organization's effectiveness, management will try to minimize it. One way to reduce environmental uncertainty is through adjustments to the organization's structure.[13]

There is substantial evidence that relates the degree of environmental uncertainty to different structural arrangements. Essentially, the more dynamic and uncertain the environment, the greater the need for flexibility. Hence, the organic structure will lead to higher organizational effectiveness. Conversely, in stable and predictable environments, the mechanistic form will be the structure of choice.

ORGANIZATION STRUCTURE AND EMPLOYEE BEHAVIOR

We opened this chapter by implying that an organization's structure can have profound effects on its members. In this section, we directly assess just what those effects might be.

A review of the evidence linking organization structures to employee performance and satisfaction leads to a pretty clear conclusion—you can't generalize! Not everyone prefers the freedom and flexibility of organic structures. Some people are most productive and satisfied when work tasks are standardized and ambiguity is minimized—that is, in mechanistic structures. So any discussion of the effect of organizational design on employee behavior has to address individual differences. To illustrate this point, let's consider employee preferences for work specialization, span of control, and centralization.[14]

The evidence generally indicates that *work specialization* contributes to higher employee productivity but at the price of reduced job satisfaction. However, this statement ignores individual differences and the type of job tasks people do.

As we noted previously, work specialization is not an unending source of higher productivity. Problems start to surface, and productivity begins to suffer, when the human diseconomies of doing repetitive and narrow tasks overtake the economies of specialization. As the workforce has become more highly educated and desirous of jobs that are intrinsically rewarding, the point at which productivity begins to decline seems to be reached more quickly than in decades past.

Undoubtedly people today are less tolerant of overly specialized jobs than were their parents or grandparents, but it would be naive to ignore the reality that there is still a segment of the workforce that prefers the routine and repetitiveness of highly specialized jobs. Some individuals want work that makes minimal intellectual demands and provides the security of routine. For these people, high work specialization is a source of job satisfaction. The empirical question, of course, is whether this group represents two percent of the workforce or fifty-two percent. Given that there is some self-selection operating in the choice of careers, we might conclude that negative behavioral outcomes from high specialization are most likely to surface in professional jobs occupied by individuals with high needs for personal growth and diversity.

A review of the research indicates that it is probably safe to say there is no evidence to support a relationship between *span of control* and employee performance. It is intuitively attractive to argue that large spans lead to higher employee performance because they provide more distant supervision and more opportunity for personal initiative, but the research fails to support this notion. At this point, it is impossible to state that any particular span of control is best for producing high performance or high satisfaction among subordinates. The reason is, again, probably individual differences. Some people like to be left alone, whereas others prefer the security of a boss who is quickly available at all times. Several of the contingency theories of leadership discussed in Chapter 10 would lead us to expect factors such as employees' experience and abilities and the degree of structure in their tasks to explain when wide or narrow spans of control are likely to contribute to their performance and job satisfaction.

We find fairly strong evidence linking *centralization* and job satisfaction. In general, organizations that are less centralized have a greater amount of participative decision making. And the evidence suggests that participative decision making is positively related to job satisfaction. But, again, individual differences surface. The relationship between decentralization and satisfaction is strongest with employees who have low self-esteem. Because such individuals have little confidence in their abilities, they place a fairly high value on shared decision making, which means that they're not held solely responsible for decision outcomes.

Our overall conclusion: To maximize employee performance and satisfaction, individual differences—such as experience, personality, and the work task—should be taken into account.

IMPLICATIONS FOR MANAGERS

An organization's internal structure contributes to explaining and predicting employee behavior. That is, in addition to individual and group factors, the structural relationships in which people work have an important bearing on their attitudes and behavior.

What's the basis for the argument that structure has an impact on both attitudes and behavior? Because an organization's structure reduces ambiguity and clarifies relationships, it shapes employees' attitudes and facilitates and motivates them to higher levels of performance.

Of course, structure also constrains employees to the extent that it limits and controls what they do. For example, organizations structured around high levels of formalization and specialization, strict adherence to the chain of command, limited delegation of authority, and narrow spans of control give employees little autonomy. Controls in such organizations are tight, and behavior will tend to vary within a narrow range. In contrast, organizations that are structured around limited specialization, low formalization, wide spans of control, and the like provide employees greater freedom and, thus, will be characterized by greater behavioral diversity.

CHAPTER 14

Technology and Work Design

After studying this chapter, you should be able to

1. Explain the three key elements in process reengineering
2. Contrast mass production and mass customization
3. Identify the challenges to motivating employees in e-organizations
4. Explain how e-organizations are rewriting the rules of communication
5. Describe the job characteristics model
6. Contrast the social information-processing model with the job characteristics model
7. Describe how a job can be enriched
8. Compare the advantages and disadvantages of flextime
9. Describe why telecommuting has grown in popularity

Technology is completely changing most organizations. In this chapter, we focus on how technologies of operations and information are influencing management and work processes, and how managers can design jobs and work schedules to maximize employee performance.

TECHNOLOGY IN THE WORKPLACE

We introduced the term *technology* in the previous chapter's discussion of why structures differ. We said it was how an organization transfers its inputs into outputs. In recent years, the term has become widely used by economists, managers, consultants, and business analysts to describe machinery and equipment that use sophisticated electronics and computers to produce those outputs.

The common theme among new technologies in the workplace is that they substitute machinery for human labor in transforming inputs into outputs. This substitution of capital for labor has been going on essentially nonstop since the Industrial Revolution in the mid-1800s. For instance, the introduction of electricity allowed textile factories to introduce mechanical looms that could produce cloth far more quickly and more cheaply than was possible when the looms were powered by individuals. But it has been the computerization of equipment and machinery in the past quarter-century that has been the prime mover in reshaping today's workplace. Automated teller machines, for example, have replaced tens of thousands of human tellers in banks. Ninety-eight percent of the spot welds on new Ford Tauruses are performed by robots, not by people. Many cars now come equipped with on-board computers that take only seconds to diagnose problems that used to take mechanics hours to diagnose. IBM has built a plant in Austin, Texas, that can produce laptop computers without the help of a single worker. Everything from the time parts arrive at the IBM plant to the final packing of finished products is completely automated.

This book is concerned with the behavior of people at work. No coverage of this topic, today, would be complete without discussing how recent advances in technology are changing the workplace and affecting the work lives of employees. In this section, we'll look at three specific issues related to technology and work. These are continuous improvement processes, process reengineering, and mass customization.

Continuous Improvement Processes

In Chapter 1, we described quality management as seeking the constant attainment of customer satisfaction through the continuous improvement of all organizational processes. This search for continuous improvement recognizes that *good* isn't *good enough* and that even excellent performance can, and should, be improved upon. For instance, a 99.9 percent error-free performance sounds like a high standard of excellence. However it doesn't sound so great when you realize that this standard would result in the U.S. Post Office losing 2,000 pieces of mail an hour, U.S. doctors performing 500 incorrect surgical procedures each week, or two plane crashes a day at O'Hare Airport in Chicago![1]

Quality management programs seek to achieve continuous process improvements so that variability is constantly reduced. When you eliminate variations, you increase the uniformity of the product or service. Increasing uniformity, in turn, results in lower costs and higher quality. For instance, Advanced Filtration Systems Inc., of Champaign, Illinois, cut the number of product defects—as determined by a customer quality audit—from 26.5 per 1,000 units to 0 over a 4-year period. During that same period, monthly unit production tripled and the number of workers declined by 20 percent.

As tens of thousands of organizations introduce continuous process improvement, how will employees be affected? They will no longer be able to rest on their previous accomplishments and successes. So some people may experience increased stress from a work climate that no longer accepts complacency with the status quo. A race with no finish line can never be won—a situation that creates constant tension. This tension may be positive for the organization (remember *functional conflict* from Chapter 12?), but the pressures from an unrelenting search for process improvements can create anxiety and stress in some employees. Probably the most significant implication for employees is that management will look to them as the prime source for improvement ideas. Employee involvement programs, therefore, are part and parcel of continuous improvement. Empowered work teams who have hands-on involvement in process improvement, for instance, are widely used in organizations that have introduced quality programs.

Process Reengineering

We also introduced process reengineering in Chapter 1. We described it as considering how you would do things if you could start from scratch. The term *reengineering* comes from the process of taking apart an electronic product and designing a better version. Michael Hammer applied the term to organizations. When he found companies using computers simply to automate outdated processes, rather than finding fundamentally better ways of doing things, he realized that the principles of reengineering could be applied to business. So, as applied to organizations, process reengineering means that management should start with a clean sheet of paper—rethinking and redesigning those processes by which the organization creates value and does work and ridding itself of operations that have become antiquated.[2]

Key Elements Three key elements of process reengineering are identifying an organization's distinctive competencies, assessing core processes, and reorganizing horizontally by process. An organization's distinctive competencies define what it is that the organization does better than its competition. Examples might include better store locations, a more efficient distribution system, higher-quality products, more-knowledgeable sales personnel, or superior technical support. Dell Computer, for instance, differentiates itself from its competitors by emphasizing high-quality hardware, comprehensive service and technical support, and low prices. Why is identifying distinctive competencies so important? Because it guides decisions regarding what activities are crucial to the organization's success.

Management also needs to assess the core processes that clearly add value to the organization's distinctive competencies. These are the processes that transform materials, capital, information, and labor into products and services that the customer values. When the organization is viewed as a series of processes, ranging from strategic planning to after-sales customer support, management can determine to what degree each adds value. Not surprisingly, this process-value analysis typically uncovers a lot of activities that add little or nothing of value and whose only justification is "we've always done it this way."

Process reengineering requires management to reorganize around horizontal processes. This means using cross-functional and self-managed teams. It means focusing on processes rather than functions. So, for instance, the vice president of marketing might become the "process owner of finding and keeping customers."[3] It also means cutting out levels of middle management. As Hammer points out, "Managers are not value-added. A customer never buys a product because of the caliber of management. Management is, by definition, indirect. So if possible, less is better. One of the goals of reengineering is to minimize the necessary amount of management."[4]

Implications for Employees Process reengineering has been popular since the early 1990s. Almost all major companies in the United States, Asia, and Europe have reengineered at least some of their processes. The result has been that lots of people have lost their jobs. Staff support jobs, especially middle managers, have been particularly vulnerable to process reengineering efforts. So, too, have clerical jobs in service industries.

Employees who keep their jobs after process reengineering have typically found that they aren't the same jobs. These new jobs typically require a wider range of skills, including more interaction with customers and suppliers, greater challenge, increased responsibilities, and higher pay. However, the three- to five-year period it takes to implement process reengineering is usually tough on employees. They suffer from uncertainty and anxiety associated with taking on new tasks and having to discard long-established work practices and formal social networks.

Mass Customization

The Tom Clancy or Stephen King paperbacks you find on bookstore shelves are printed on huge offset presses, then stored in hangar-size warehouses, and finally shipped to bookstores in fleets of trucks. The novels are mass-produced, with initial printings of several-hundred thousand copies. Book publishers require these large print runs to keep production costs down.

New technology is completely changing this process.[5] This new technology, called Print on Demand, allows books to be produced and sold in small quantities—even one at a time—almost instantly. Publishers have only to digitize a book's contents and store it in a centralized computer. Then, when ordered by a customer, a single high-tech printing-and-binding machine goes into action, creating a slick, high-quality paperback. These high-tech machines can be located in bookstores, allowing a store to custom-print a book for a customer in sixty seconds or less.

From the days of Henry Ford through the late 1990s, production efficiencies demanded **mass production**. Firms used division of labor, standardization, and automated processes to manufacture products in large quantities. Economies of scale favored large quantities because that reduced costs. Industry after industry relied on mass-production systems to minimize costs. Ford's Model T, McDonald's, and Levittown stand as icons to mass production.

New technologies such as computer-aided design and manufacturing (CAD/CAM), however, are undermining the economies of mass production. And they're making possible **mass customization** like Print On Demand. Mass customization encompasses production processes that are flexible enough to create products and services that are individually tailored to individual customers. The future of production manufacturing is one of mass customization. Some products, such as packaged foods, will probably continue to be made using traditional mass-production methods. But for products for which customers want custom features, firms will be converting to "build to order" systems. And it seems that customers are increasingly seeking products that have been configured for their particular needs.[6] The Case Corp. and Levi Strauss are two examples of firms that have successfully embraced mass customization.

Case is a huge farm and construction equipment manufacturer that has converted all its products to mass customization. For instance, its $85,000 MX-series Magnum farm tractors are now made exclusively to order. Under its old system, farmers had to select from the models and options that a dealer had in stock. Or they had to wait 6 months to get the one they wanted. Now buyers can make up to 28 choices on options such as engine, tires, and power train. And Case can deliver the customized tractor in 5 to 6 weeks.

Levi makes 130 styles of jeans. Still, many customers can't find a pair that is exactly what they're looking for. No problem! Levi can provide them with a custom-fitted pair, choosing from 3 basic models, 10 fabrics, 5 leg styles, and 2 types of fly. While these "made to order" jeans cost a bit more (about $55), Levi uses computer technology to standardize options and cut costs.

Mass customization offers advantages to both customers and manufacturers. Customers don't have to compromise. They can have the products they want, tailored to their individual tastes and needs. For manufacturers, they create more satisfied customers while, at the same time, increasing production efficiency. Mass customization results in little or no work-in-progress or finished-goods inventories and no obsolete products gathering dust on shelves or in showrooms, and it requires less working capital. Case says, for instance, that merely by reducing inventories of its finished tractors by more than half, it's saving between $1,500 and $2,000 per machine.

The downside of mass customization is that it creates increased coordination demands on management. And it typically requires employees to go through significant retraining. Mass customization usually requires reengineering of processes, and reorganizing work around teams to increase flexibility.

ORGANIZATIONAL BEHAVIOR IN AN E-WORLD

No area of technology is changing organizations more than electronic technology. For instance, terms like *e-commerce* and *e-business* have become a standard part of the current lexicon. In this section, we'll define an e-organization and the affect it is having on both individual and group behavior in the workplace.

What's an E-Organization?

E-commerce refers to the sales side of electronic business. When you read about the tremendous number of people who are shopping on the Internet; and how businesses can set up Web sites where they sell goods, conduct transactions, get paid, and fulfill orders, you're hearing about e-commerce. In contrast, **e-business** is the full breadth of activities included in a successful Internet-based enterprise. It includes developing strategies for running Internet-based companies; improving communication between employees, suppliers, and customers; and collaborating with partners to electronically coordinate design and production. As such, e-commerce is really a subset of e-business. And the term **e-organization** (e-orgs) merely refers to applications of e-business concepts to all organizations. E-orgs include not only business firms, but also hospitals, schools, museums, government agencies, and the military. For instance, the Internal Revenue Service is an e-organization because it now provides access to taxpayers over the Internet.

The best way to understand the e-organization concept is to look at its three underlying components—the Internet, intranets, and extranets. The **Internet** is a worldwide network of interconnected computers; **intranets** are an organization's private Internet; and **extranets** are extended intranets, accessible only to selected employees and authorized outsiders. As Exhibit 14-1 illustrates, an e-org is defined by the degree to which it uses global (Internet) and private (intranet and extranet) network linkages. Type A's are traditional organizations such as small retailers and service firms. Most organizations today fall into this category. Type B's are contemporary organizations with heavy reliance on intranets and extranets. Type C's are most small e-commerce firms. And finally, Type D's are full e-orgs. They've com-

EXHIBIT 14–1 What Defines an E-Organization?

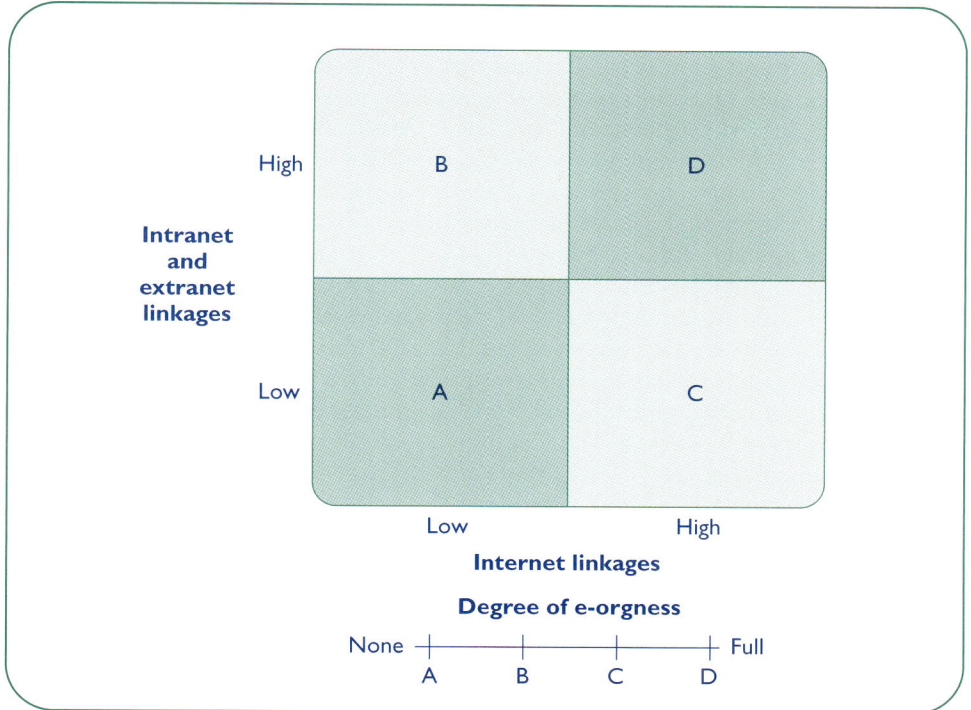

pletely integrated global and private networks. Type D's would include such firms as eBay, Cisco Systems, Amazon.com, and Wal-Mart. Note that as an organization moves from a Type A toward a Type D, it increases the degree to which it takes on e-org properties.

The following discussion looks at how e-organizations affect employee behavior. But since e-orgs, in actuality, encompass a range of electronic technology applications, our observations and predictions need to be qualified: The more an organization uses global and private network linkages, the more our comments about e-orgs will be applicable to its employees.

Selected Implications for Individual Behavior

We could develop a full chapter or more of detailed discussions on how e-orgs will affect individual behavior. Given our space limitations, let's look at just two selected individual topics—motivation and ethics.

Motivation Are there unique challenges to motivating employees in e-organizations? The answer appears to be "yes." Employees in e-orgs, for instance, are more susceptible to distractions that can undermine their work effort and reduce their productivity. In addition, technical and professional employees in e-orgs often have skills that make them very marketable, and many realize their employers' dependence on these skills. As a result, employees in e-organizations frequently have different compensation expectations than do their peers in more traditional organizations.

Employees have always been susceptible to distractions at work such as interruptions by colleagues or personal phone calls. The Internet, however, has significantly broadened these distractions to include surfing the Net, playing online games, stock trading, shopping at work, conducting "cyberaffairs," and searching for other jobs online. Some of the most visited sites people access from work, for instance, are the Weather Channel, Amazon.com, and eBay.[7]

The average U.S. employee with Net access is spending 90 minutes each day visiting sites unrelated to his or her job![8] Recent estimates indicate that 30 to 40 percent of lost worker productivity is due solely to cyberloafing; and this cyberloafing is costing U.S. employers alone $54 billion a year.[9]

If the work itself isn't interesting or creates excessive stress, employees are likely to be motivated to do something else. If they have easy access to the Internet, that "something else" is increasingly using the Net as a diversion. The solution to this problem includes making jobs more interesting to employees, providing formal breaks to overcome monotony, and establishing clear guidelines so employees know what online behaviors are expected. Many employers are also installing Web-monitoring software, although there is evidence that such efforts can undermine trust in the organization and adversely affect employee morale.[10]

Etensity, a Virginia-based Web-consulting and services firm, has a motivated and committed workforce.[11] Its turnover rate is only 5 percent a year, about 15 points below the industry average. And what is Etensity doing to stimulate and keep its people? Quite a lot actually. The company's Hot Wheels program, for instance, give employees up to $400 a month to pay for a new car; and another program, called Raise the Roof, gives employees $10,000 toward a new home.

It's difficult for e-organizations to find and keep technical and professional employees. So many have implemented an extensive list of attractive incentives and benefits rarely seen by nonmanagerial employees in typical organizations: for instance, signing bonuses, stock options, cars, free health-club memberships, full-time onsite concierges, and cell phone bill subsidies.

These incentives and benefits may benefit their recipients but there are downsides. One is the effect these rewards have on those who don't get them. The other is the increasing problem created by stock options. Specifically, while they look very good when a firm is growing and the stock market looks favorably on the company's future, stock options can demotivate employees when conditions reverse.

The potential for perceived inequities is very high among employees in Internet-based organizations. There are often glaring discrepancies between the rewards provided to hard-to-hire employees—particularly software designers and engineers—and other employees. This creates the potential for demotivating those who feel they're being inequitably treated. In addition, there is the problem of interfirm comparisons. How would you feel if you were making $50,000 a year but saw someone with similar experience, age, and qualifications making $10 million because she just happened to join a firm that gave out stock options and now her company has gone public, making those options incredibly valuable? The creation of interfirm inequities has tended to create a wanderlust mentality among many e-org employees, continually chasing the next wealth-creating opportunity.

The implosion of dot-com stocks in 2000 and 2001 illustrates that the use of stock options as motivators is a two-way street. Many e-organizations encouraged hard-to-hire employees to give up a large salary in exchange for stock options. This worked fine when stock options seemed to go only up. But when stock prices drop, many stock options become worthless.[12] For individuals who joined and stayed with firms mainly for the possibility of getting rich through stock options, a declining market can be a powerful demotivator.

Ethics Electronic surveillance of employees by employers is an issue that pits an organization's desire for control against an employee's right to privacy. The development of increasingly sophisticated surveillance software only adds to the ethical dilemma of how far an organization should go in monitoring the behavior of employees who do their work on computers.[13]

For instance, the Web activity of every one of Xerox's 92,000 employees—in countries around the world—is routinely monitored by the company. In October 1999 Xerox fired 40 of its employees because they were caught in the act of surfing forbidden Web sites. The company's monitoring software recorded the unauthorized visits to shopping and pornography sites, and every minute they had spent at those sites.[14]

Is Xerox unique? No. A recent survey by the American Management Association found that more than 50 percent of employers monitored their employees' phone calls, computer files, or e-mail messages.[15]

Employers argue that they need surveillance controls. These controls allow them to make sure employees are working and not goofing off and that employees are not distributing organization secrets and to protect the organization against employees who might create a hostile environment for women or members of minority groups.

The surveillance dilemma is exacerbated by the blurring of workplace parameters. There seems to be little dispute that employers have the right to monitor employees at work, when using the organization's equipment, and when employees know they are being watched. But as home life and work life are increasingly intermingled—for instance, employees doing job-related work at home rather than at the office—the ethics and legality of surveillance is less clear.

Selected Implications for Group Behavior

In this section, we will show how issues such as decision making, communication, leadership, and organizational politics take on a different look and importance in e-organizations.

Decision Making The traditional approach taken in OB when discussing decision making needs to be modified for e-organizations. Exactly what those modifications should be are not yet fully clear. However, we offer two projections.

First, individual decision-making models are likely to become increasingly obsolete. E-organizations are typically team-based communities. So group decision-making models will offer greater relevance.

Second, the thoughtful, rational models of decision making—which dominate the management literature (see pages 70–73)—will be replaced by action models. There are no proven business models for e-organizations.[16] Success goes to firms that value experimentation—those that utilize trial and error and are able to gather data quickly and assimilate it and that can accept failure and learn from it.

E-organizations don't have the luxury of trying to fine-tune decisions in search of perfection. E-organizations make decisions with often very limited information and, as a result, don't fear making mistakes. Decisions in e-organizations are in a continual flux, with past choices being continually modified and even discarded. And routine decision programs are essentially useless because few of the decisions that need to be made have been encountered before. So not only do decisions in e-orgs need to be made fast, they have to be made based on little previous experience. This, of course, increases the probability of errors and the need to be able to recover quickly from mistakes and move on.

Communication E-organizations are rewriting the rules of communication. Because they're designed around comprehensive, integrated information networks, traditional hierarchical levels no longer constrain communication. E-organizations allow, even encourage, individuals to communicate directly without going through channels. Employees can communicate instantly anytime, with anyone, anywhere. These open communication systems break down historical status hierarchies. They make obsolete or revise interpersonal communication concepts such as the distinction between formal and informal networks, nonverbal communication, and filtering. They also redefine how activities such as meetings, negotiations, supervision, and "water cooler" talk are conducted. For instance, virtual meetings allow people in geographically dispersed locations to meet regularly. Moreover, it's now easier for employees in San Francisco and Singapore to share company gossip than those offline employees who work two cubicles apart. And employees in a number of industries even have Web sites that are becoming electronic grapevines.[17] Young lawyers are going to www.greedyassociates.com to gripe about working conditions and pay; truckers are comparing rigs and routes on www.truckinlife.com, and flight attendants share gossip at www.insidetheweb.com.

The downside of this open communication network is communication overload. A recent poll found that the average U.S. worker receives five phone calls, 36 e-mails, 18 pieces of mail, and 18 in-house memos daily.[18] He or she also reads 13 Post-It messages, 14 faxes, and listens to 23 voice mail or cell phone messages. These frequent incoming communication interruptions cost employees valuable time, erode their ability to concentrate, and can negatively effect their work productivity.

Leadership Is leadership in an e-organization different from that in a traditional organization? Business executives who've worked in both think there is. They tend to focus on three differences: the speed at which they have to make decisions, the importance of maintaining flexibility, and need to create a vision of the future.

Managers in all organizations never have all the data they want when making decisions. But the problem is much worse in e-organizations. The world is moving quickly and the competition is intense. Meg Whitman, the president and CEO at eBay says, "We're growing at 40 percent to 50 percent per quarter. That pace absolutely changes the leadership challenge: Every three months we become a different company. In one year we went from 30 employees to 140, and from 100,000 registered users to 2.2 million. At Hasbro [where she previously had been an executive], we would set a yearlong strategy, and then we would simply execute against it. At eBay, we constantly revisit the strategy—and revise the tactics."[19]

Leaders in e-orgs see themselves as sprinters and their contemporaries in offline businesses as long-distance runners. They frequently inject the term *Internet time*—a reference to a rapidly speeded up working environment. "Every [e-business] leader today has to unlearn one lesson that was drilled into each one of them: You gather data so that you can make considered decisions. You can't do that on Internet time."[20]

In addition to speed, leaders in e-orgs need high flexibility. They have to be able to roll with the ups and downs. They need to be able to redirect their group or organization when they find that something doesn't work. They have to encourage experimentation. Mark Cuban, cofounder of Broadcast.com, amplifies on this point: "When we started, we thought advertising would be the core of our business. We were wrong. We thought that the way to define our network was to distribute servers all over the country. We were wrong. We've had to recalibrate again and again—and we'll have to keep doing it in the future."[21]

The founder of PriceLine.com says, "Forget about today's problems: You've got to focus constantly on the next generation of problems."[22] This requires visionary leadership and a deep understanding of how technology is going to change the leader's business. "The best leaders carry a mental map of the industry, of opportunities, and of discontinuities—and they check that map constantly."[23]

Visionary leadership is undoubtedly important in every organization. But in a hyperkinetic environment, people require more from their leaders. The rules, policies, and regulations that characterize more traditional organizations provide direction and reduce uncertainty for employees. Such formalized guidelines don't typically exist in e-orgs, and it falls on e-leaders to provide direction through their vision.

Politics and Networking OB recognizes the political nature of organizations, the role that politics play in decision making, and the importance of networking in developing contacts both within and outside an organization. But preliminary indicators suggest that effective politicking and networking are different in e-orgs than in the more traditional offline organization.

In traditional organizations, effective politicians keep themselves visible, utilize impression management techniques, and participate in activities that will put them in close contact with influential people. But these are essentially face-to-face activities that aren't likely to be as effective in e-organizations. E-politicians are likely to rely much more on cyber-schmoozing via the electronic grapevine. Internet chat rooms and message boards, for instance, open up opportunities to meet and talk with people who can help employees be more effective in their jobs and their careers.

Cyber-schmoozing isn't likely to replace the water cooler, cocktail party, university alumni get-togethers, or trade shows as places to make contacts and build political allies. But online networking will become increasingly popular and effective as a supplement to more traditional political channels.

Will E-Orgs Redefine Interpersonal Relationships?

Electronic technology has redefined workplace possibilities. Employees in e-organizations are no longer constrained by time or place in doing their work. But what are the implications of these e-orgs to interpersonal relationships?

There is substantive evidence that people generally are spending more time online today than just a few years ago. For instance, in 1997 the mean time people spent online was 4.4 hours per week. In 1999 it was 7.6 hours. In 2000 it was predicted to be 8.2 hours.[24] There is also preliminary evidence from a Stanford University study indicating that the more time people spend online, the less time they spend in real-life relationships with friends and family.[25] About one-quarter of regular Web users report that they now are spending less time attending social activities and talking on the phone to friends and family; and 13 percent reported reduced face-to-face social interactions.[26] One of the Stanford study's co-authors, in fact, expressed concern that the Internet could become the ultimate isolating technology, promoting individual behavior over community involvement.

It's far too early in the development of the digital age to conclude that the Internet will undermine a sense of social community. But it clearly creates new ways to interact with work colleagues. Employees will increasingly be working on teams with people they've never met and may never meet. They'll develop "office" friendships with people thousands of miles away. And "good interpersonal skills" may increasingly mean not only the ability to interact effectively with people face to face, but may include the skills to communicate warmth, emotion, trust, and leadership through written words on a computer screen.

WORK DESIGN

The way that tasks are combined to create individual jobs has a direct influence on employee performance and satisfaction. In this section, we'll look at task characteristics theories, work redesign, and work schedule options.

Task Characteristics Theories

Most of us acknowledge these two facts: (1) Jobs are different, and (2) some are more interesting and challenging than others. These facts have not gone unnoticed by OB researchers. They have responded by developing task characteristics theories that seek to identify task characteristics of jobs, how these characteristics are combined to form different jobs, and the relationship of these task characteristics to employee motivation, satisfaction, and performance. In this section we'll review the two most important theories—the job characteristics model and the social information-processing model.

The Job Characteristics Model The dominant framework today for defining task characteristics and understanding their relationship to employee motivation, performance, and satisfaction is J. Richard Hackman and Greg Oldham's **job characteristics model** (JCM).[27]

According to the JCM, any job can be described in terms of five core job dimensions, defined as follows:

1. *Skill variety*: The degree to which the job requires a variety of different activities so the worker can use a number of different skills and talent
2. *Task identity*: The degree to which the job requires completion of a whole and identifiable piece of work
3. *Task significance*: The degree to which the job has a substantial impact on the lives or work of other people
4. *Autonomy*: The degree to which the job provides substantial freedom, independence, and discretion to the individual in scheduling the work and in determining the procedures to be used in carrying it out
5. *Feedback*: The degree to which carrying out the work activities required by the job results in the individual's obtaining direct and clear information about the effectiveness of his or her performance

Exhibit 14-2 offers examples of job activities that rate high and low for each characteristic.

Exhibit 14-3 presents the job characteristics model. Notice how the first three dimensions—skill variety, task identity, and task significance—combine to create meaningful work. That is, if these three characteristics exist in a job, we can predict that the incumbent will view the job as being important, valuable, and worthwhile. Notice, too, that jobs that possess autonomy give the job incumbent a feeling of personal responsibility for the results and that, if a job provides feedback, the employee will know how effectively he or she is performing. From a motivational standpoint, the model says that internal rewards are obtained by an individual when she learns (knowledge of results) that she personally (experienced responsibility) has performed well on a task that she cares about (experienced meaningfulness).[28] The more that these three psychological states are present, the greater will be the employee's motivation, performance, and satisfaction and the lower his or her absenteeism and likelihood of leaving the organization. As Exhibit 14-3 shows, the links between the job dimensions and the outcomes are moderated or adjusted by the strength of the individual's growth need: that is, by the employee's desire for self-esteem and self-actualization. This means that individuals with a high growth need are more likely to experience the psychological states when their jobs are enriched than are their counterparts with a low growth need.

EXHIBIT 14–2 Examples of High and Low Job Characteristics

Characteristic	Example
Skill variety	
High variety	The owner-operator of a garage who does electrical repair, rebuilds engines, does body work, and interacts with customers
Low variety	A bodyshop worker who sprays paint 8 hours a day
Task identity	
High identity	A cabinetmaker who designs a piece of furniture, selects the wood, builds the object, and finishes it to perfection
Low identity	A worker in a furniture factory who operates a lathe solely to make table legs
Task significance	
High significance	Nursing the sick in a hospital intensive care unit
Low significance	Sweeping hospital floors
Autonomy	
High autonomy	A telephone installer who schedules his or her own work for the day, makes visits without supervision, and decides on the most effective techniques for a particular installation
Low autonomy	A telephone operator who must handle calls as they come according to a routine, highly specified procedure
Feedback	
High feedback	An electronics factory worker who assembles a modem and then tests it to determine if it operates properly
Low feedback	An electronics factory worker who assembles a modem and then routes it to a quality control inspector who tests it for proper operation and makes needed adjustments

Adapted from G. Johns, *Organizational Behavior: Understanding and Managing Life at Work*, 4th ed. Copyright ©1996 by HarperCollins Publishers. Reprinted by permission of Addison-Wesley Educational Publishers, Inc.

EXHIBIT 14–3   The Job Characteristics Model

Core job dimensions	Critical psychological states	Personal and work outcomes
Skill variety Task identity Task significance	Experienced meaningfulness of the work	High internal work motivation
Autonomy	Experienced responsibility for outcomes of the work	High-quality work performance High satisfaction with the work
Feedback	Knowledge of the actual results of the work activities	Low absenteeism and turnover

Employee growth need strength

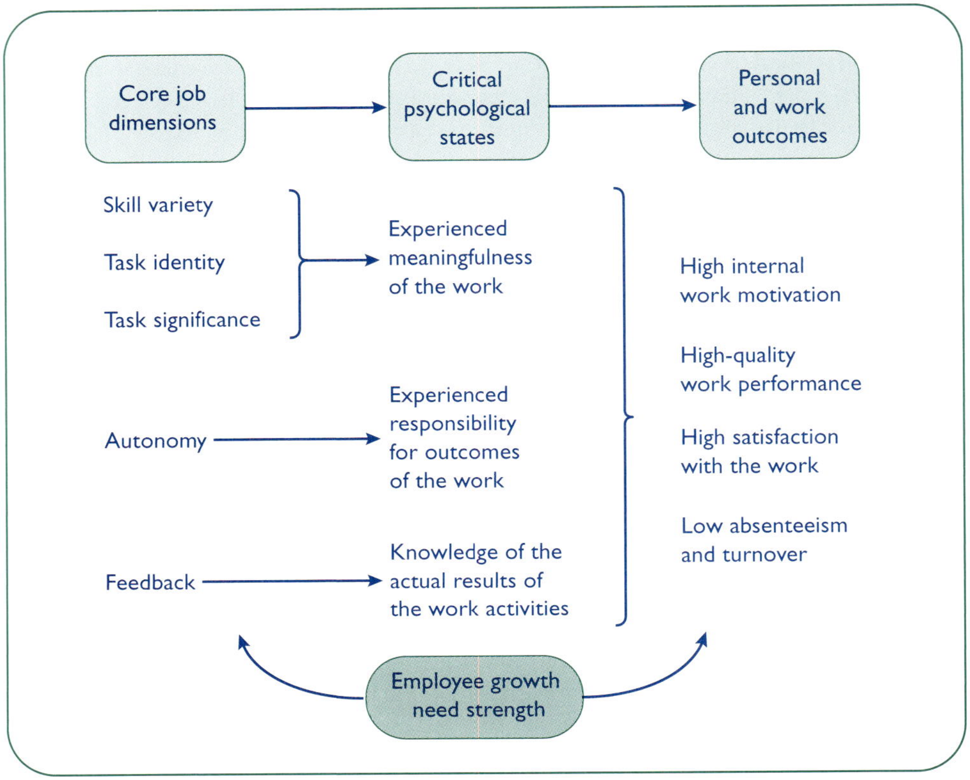

Source: J.R. Hackman and J.L. Suttle, eds., *Improving Life at Work* (Glenview, IL: Scott, Foresman, 1977), p. 29.

Moreover, they will respond more positively to the psychological states when they are present than will individuals with a low growth need.

The job characteristics model has been well researched. Most of the evidence supports the general framework of the theory—that is, there is a set of job characteristics, and these characteristics affect behavioral outcomes.[29] But there is still considerable debate about the five specific core dimensions in the JCM and the validity of growth need strength as a moderating variable.

Where does this leave us? Given the current state of evidence, we can make the following statements with relative confidence: (1) People who work on jobs with high-core job dimensions are generally more motivated, satisfied, and productive than are those who do not; and (2) job dimensions operate through the psychological states in influencing personal and work outcome variables rather than influencing the outcomes directly.[30]

Social Information-Processing Model Would it surprise you to know that two people can have the same job yet view it differently? Probably not! As made clear in our discussion of perception in Chapter 2, people respond to their jobs *as they perceive them* rather than to the *objective* jobs themselves. This is the central thesis in our second task characteristics theory. It's called the **social information-processing (SIP) model**.[31]

The SIP model argues that employees adopt attitudes and behaviors in response to the social cues provided by others with whom they have contact. These others can be co-workers, supervisors, friends, family members, or customers. For instance, Gary Ling got a summer job working in a British Columbia sawmill. Since jobs were scarce and this one paid particularly well, Gary arrived on his first day of work highly motivated. Two weeks later, however, his motivation was quite low. What had happened was that his co-workers consistently bad-mouthed their jobs. They said the work was boring, that having to clock in and out proved management didn't trust them, and that supervisors never listened to their opinions. The objective characteristics of Gary's job had not changed in the two-week period; rather, Gary had reconstructed reality on the basis of messages he had received from others.

A number of studies generally confirm the validity of the SIP model.[32] For instance, it has been shown that employee motivation and satisfaction can be manipulated by subtle actions such as a co-worker or boss commenting on the existence or absence of job features such as difficulty, challenge, and autonomy. So managers should give as much (or more) attention to employees' perceptions of their jobs as they give to the actual characteristics of those jobs. They might, for example, spend more time telling employees how interesting and important their jobs are. And managers should also not be surprised that newly hired employees and people transferred or promoted to a new position are more likely to be receptive to social information than are those with greater seniority.

Work Redesign

What are some of the options managers have at their disposal if they want to redesign jobs to make them more interesting and motivating for employees? The following discusses four of those options: job rotation, job enlargement, job enrichment, and team-based work designs.

Job Rotation If employees suffer from overroutinization of their work, one alternative is to use **job rotation** (or what many now call *cross-training*). With this technique, when an activity is no longer challenging, the employee is rotated to another job, at the same level, that has similar skill requirements. For instance, America West Airlines cross-trains all their customer service representatives. The company says that this gives employees more job variety and challenge. And for employees who are interested in upward mobility, cross-training exposes them to about sixteen different areas of the company versus only one they would be exposed to if jobs were specialized.[33]

The strengths of job rotation are that it reduces boredom and increases motivation through diversifying the employee's activities. Of course, it can also have indirect benefits for the organization since employees with a wider range of skills give management more flexibility in scheduling work, adapting to changes, and filling vacancies. On the other hand, job rotation has its drawbacks. Training costs are increased, and productivity is reduced by moving a worker into a new position just when his or her efficiency at the prior job was creating organizational economies. Job rotation also creates disruptions. Members of the work group have to adjust to the new employee. The supervisor may also have to spend more time answering questions and monitoring the work of the recently rotated employee. Finally, job rotation can demotivate intelligent and ambitious trainees who seek specific responsibilities in their chosen specialty.

Job Enlargement More than 30 years ago, the idea of expanding jobs horizontally, or what we call **job enlargement**, grew in popularity. Increasing the number and variety of tasks that an individual performed resulted in jobs with more diversity. Instead of only sorting the incoming mail by department, for instance, a mail sorter's job could be enlarged to include physically delivering the mail to the various departments or running outgoing letters through the postage meter.

Efforts at job enlargement met with less than enthusiastic results.[34] As one employee who experienced such a redesign of his job remarked, "Before I had one lousy job. Now, through enlargement, I have three!"

Although job enlargement attacked the lack of diversity in overly specialized jobs, it did little to instill challenge or meaningfulness to a worker's activities. Job enrichment was introduced to deal with the shortcomings of enlargement.

Job Enrichment **Job enrichment** refers to the vertical expansion of jobs. It increases the degree to which the worker controls the planning, execution, and evaluation of his or her work. An enriched job organizes tasks so as to allow the worker to do a complete activity, increases the employee's freedom and independence, increases responsibility, and provides feedback, so an individual will be able to assess and correct his or her own performance.

How does management enrich an employee's job? The following suggestions, based on the job characteristics model, specify the types of changes in jobs that are most likely to lead to improving their motivating potential (see Exhibit 14-4).

1. *Combine tasks.* Managers should seek to take existing and fractionalized tasks and put them back together to form a new and larger module of work. This measure increases skill variety and task identity.
2. *Create natural work units.* The creation of natural work units means that the tasks an employee does form an identifiable and meaningful whole. This measure increases employee "ownership" of the work and improves the likelihood that employees will view their work as meaningful and important rather than as irrelevant and boring.

EXHIBIT 14–4   Guidelines for Enriching a Job

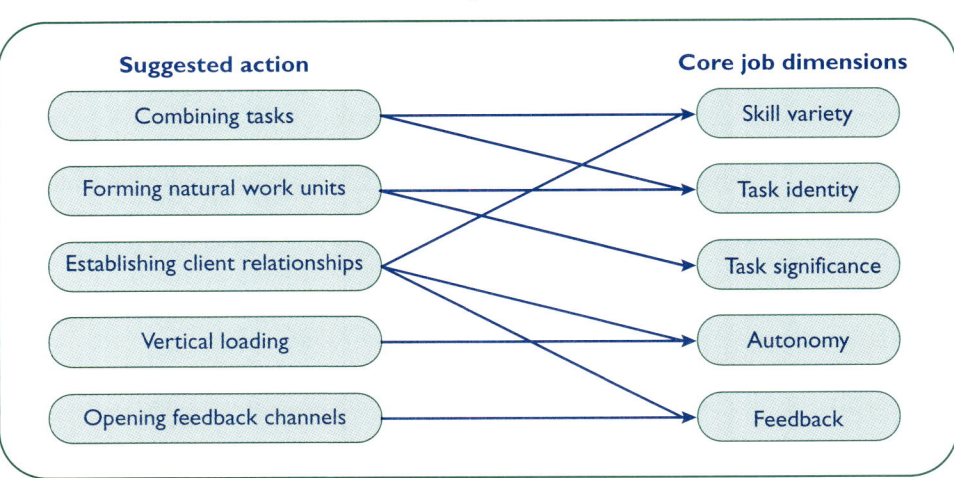

Source: J.R. Hackman and J.L. Suttle, eds., *Improving Life at Work* (Glenview, IL: Scott, Foresman, 1977), p. 138.

3. *Establish client relationships.* The client is the user of the product or service that the employee works on (and may be an internal customer as well as someone outside the organization). Wherever possible, managers should try to establish direct relationships between workers and their clients to increase skill variety, autonomy, and feedback for the employee.
4. *Expand jobs vertically.* Vertical expansion gives employees responsibilities and control that were formerly reserved for management. It seeks to partially close the gap between the "doing" and the "controlling" aspects of the job, and it increases employee autonomy.
5. *Open feedback channels.* Feedback lets employees know not only how well they are performing their jobs but also whether their performance is improving, deteriorating, or remaining at a constant level. Ideally, feedback about performance should be received directly as the employee does the job, rather than from management on an occasional basis.[35]

In general the overall evidence shows that job enrichment reduces absenteeism and turnover costs and increases satisfaction; but on the critical issue of productivity the evidence is inconclusive.[36] In some situations, job enrichment increases productivity; in others, it decreases it. Even when productivity goes down, however, there does seem to be consistently more conscientious use of resources and a higher quality of product or service.

Team-Based Work Designs Revisited Increasingly, people are doing work in groups and teams. What, if anything, can we say about the design of group-based work to try to improve employee performance in those groups? We know a lot more about individual-based work design than we do about design at the group level, mostly because the wide popularity of teams—specifically assigning tasks to a group of individuals instead of to a single person—is a relatively recent phenomenon. That said, the best work in this area offers two sets of suggestions.[37]

First, the JCM recommendations noted above seem to be as valid at the group level as they are at the individual level. Managers should expect a group to perform at a high level when (1) the group task requires members to use a variety of relatively high level skills; (2) the group task is a whole and meaningful piece of work, with a visible outcome; (3) the outcomes of the group's work on the task have significant consequences for other people; (4) the task provides group members with substantial autonomy for deciding how they do the work; and (5) work on the task generates regular, trustworthy feedback about how well the group is performing.

Second, group composition is critical to the success of the work group. Consistent with findings described in Chapter 8, managers should try to ensure that the following four conditions are met: (1) Individual members have the necessary task-relevant expertise to do their work; (2) the group is large enough to perform the work; (3) members possess interpersonal as well as task skills; and (4) membership is moderately diverse in terms of talents and perspectives.

Popular Work Schedule Options

In a work world where employees are increasingly complaining about being pressed for time and the difficulty of balancing personal and work lives, work schedule options such as flextime and telecommuting can be a way to improve employee motivation, productivity, and satisfaction.

Flextime Flextime is short for "flexible work hours." It's a scheduling option that allows employees some discretion over when they arrive at and leave work. Employees have to work a specific number of hours a week, but they are free to vary the hours of work within certain limits. As shown in Exhibit 14-5, each day consists of a common core, usually six hours, with a flexibility band surrounding the core. For example, exclusive of a one-hour lunch break, the core may be 9 A.M. to 3 P.M., with the office actually opening at 6 A.M. and closing at 6 P.M. All employees are required to be at their jobs during the common core period, but they are allowed to accumulate their other two hours before and/or after the core time. Some flextime programs allow extra hours to be accumulated and turned into a free day off each month.

Flextime has become an extremely popular scheduling option. The proportion of full-time U.S. employees on flextime almost doubled from 1991 to 1997. Approximately 25 million employees, or nearly 28 percent of the U.S. full-time workforce, now have flexibility in their daily arrival and departure times.[38] But flextime isn't available to all employees equally. While 42.4 percent of managers enjoy the freedom of flextime, only 23.3 percent of manufacturing workers are offered a flexible schedule.[39]

The benefits claimed for flextime are numerous. They include reduced absenteeism, increased productivity, reduced overtime expenses, a lessening in hostility toward management, reduced traffic congestion around work sites, elimination of tardiness, and increased autonomy and responsibility for employees that may increase employee job satisfaction.[40] But beyond the claims, what's flextime's record?

Most of the performance evidence stacks up favorably. Flextime tends to reduce absenteeism and frequently improves worker productivity,[41] probably for several reasons. Employees can schedule their work hours to align with personal demands, thus reducing tardiness and absences, and employees can adjust their work activities to those hours in which they are individually more productive.

Flextime's major drawback is that it's not applicable to every job. It works well with clerical tasks for which an employee's interaction with people outside his or her department is limited. It is not a viable option for receptionists, sales personnel in retail stores, or similar jobs in which comprehensive service demands that people be at their work stations at predetermined times.

Telecommuting It might be close to the ideal job for many people. No commuting, flexible hours, freedom to dress as you please, and little or no interruptions from colleagues. It's called **telecommuting** and refers to employees who do their work at home at least two days a week on a computer that is linked to their office. (A closely related term—*the virtual office*—is being increasingly used to describe employees who work out of their home on a relatively permanent basis). Currently, about 21 million

EXHIBIT 14–5 Example of a Flextime Schedule

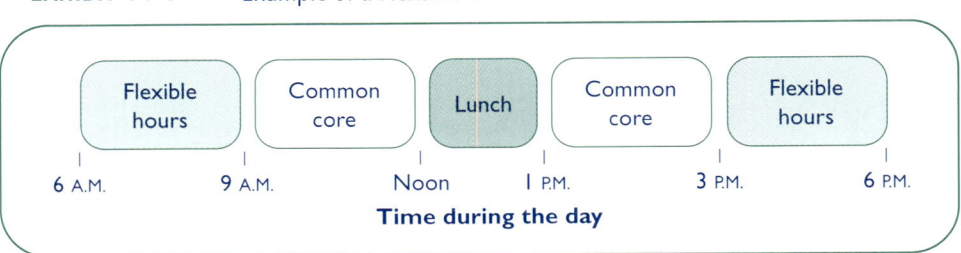

people in the United States telecommute.[42] For instance, 20 percent or more of the employees at PeopleSoft, Erie Insurance, American Management Systems, Great Plains Software, Patagonia, and Xerox are telecommuting.[43]

What kinds of jobs lend themselves to telecommuting? Three categories have been identified as most appropriate: routine information-handling tasks, mobile activities, and professional and other knowledge-related tasks.[44] Writers, attorneys, analysts, and employees who spend the majority of their time on computers or the telephone are natural candidates for telecommuting. For instance, telemarketers, customer-service representatives, reservation agents, and product-support specialists spend most of their time on the phone. As telecommuters, they can access information on their computer screens at home as easily as on the company computer in any office.

There are numerous stories of telecommuting's success.[45] AT&T has 35,000 telecommuters and claims that it has saved the company as much as $500 million. And 75 percent of these AT&T telecommuters said they were more satisfied with their personal and family lives than before they started working at home. Cisco Systems claims that telecommuting has increased productivity 25 percent, has helped retain key employees who might otherwise have left, and saved the company about $1 million in overhead. As the cost of traditional office space has escalated and the cost of telecommunications equipment has plummeted, managers are increasingly motivated to introduce the virtual office as a way to increase employee flexibility and productivity, improve employee morale, and cut costs.

The long-term future of telecommuting depends on some questions for which we don't yet have definitive answers. For instance, will employees who do their work at home be at a disadvantage in office politics? Might they be less likely to be considered for salary increases and promotions? Is being out of sight equivalent to being out of mind? Will non-work-related distractions such as children, neighbors, and the close proximity of the refrigerator significantly reduce productivity for those without superior willpower and discipline?

IMPLICATIONS FOR MANAGERS

Technology is changing people's jobs and their work behavior. Quality management and its emphasis on continuous process improvement can increase employee stress as individuals find that performance expectations are constantly being increased. Process reengineering is completely reshaping the jobs of millions of employees. And mass customization is making it possible for organizations to efficiently tailor products to individual customer's tastes, but typically requires employees to go through significant retraining.

The e-organization applies Internet, intranet, and extranet technologies to the full breadth of its activities. It is creating a number of new challenges for managers. For instance, employees in e-orgs have more distractions that can undermine their work productivity; the availability of employee monitoring software creates ethical dilemmas for managers regarding employee privacy; decisions must be made more quickly and often with little prior precedent; open communications increase the potential for communication overload and further distractions from work tasks; effective leaders in e-orgs must be able to make decisions quickly, maintain high flexibility, and create visions; and employees in e-orgs will likely use electronic networks as a tool for building political allies.

An understanding of work design can help managers design jobs that positively affect employee motivation. For instance, jobs that score high on the JCM increase an employee's control over key elements in his or her work. Therefore, jobs that offer autonomy, feedback, and similar enriching task characteristics help to satisfy the individual goals of employees who desire greater control over their work. Of course, consistent with the social information-processing model, the perception that task characteristics are enriching is probably more important in influencing an employee's motivation than are the objective task characteristics themselves. The key, then, is to provide employees with cues that suggest that their jobs score high on factors such as skill variety, task identity, autonomy, and feedback.

In an effort to help employees cope with work/life conflicts, managers should consider implementing work scheduling options such as flextime and telecommuting where applicable.

CHAPTER 15

Human Resource Policies and Practices

After reading this chapter, you should be able to

1. Describe jobs for which interviews are effective selection devices
2. List the advantages of performance-simulation tests over written tests
3. Identify four types of employee training
4. Identify the advantages of using behaviors rather than traits in appraising performance
5. Explain the most popular performance appraisal criteria
6. Identify who, in addition to a boss, can do performance appraisals
7. Explain actions that can improve the performance appraisal process
8. Describe approaches for managing workforce diversity

The quality of an organization's workforce is largely a result of the people it hires. If a firm hires new employees with inadequate skills, for instance, the work performance of these employees is likely to suffer regardless of management's efforts to provide motivation and leadership, create effective groups, or design challenging jobs.

The message of this chapter is that human resource policies and practices—such as employee selection, training, and performance appraisal systems—influence an organization's effectiveness.[1] We begin our discussion with the subject of hiring.

EMPLOYEE SELECTION

What do application forms, interviews, employment tests, background checks, and personal letters of recommendation have in common? Each is a device for obtaining information about a job applicant that can help the organization determine whether or not the applicant's skills, knowledge, and abilities are appropriate for the job in question. In this section, we review the more important of these selection devices—interviews, written tests, and performance-simulation tests.

Interviews

In South Korea, Japan, and many other Asian countries, employee interviews traditionally have not been part of the selection process. Decisions were made almost entirely on the basis of exam scores, scholastic accomplishments, and letters of recommendation. This is not the case, however, throughout most of the world. It's probably correct to say that most of us don't know many people who have gotten a full-time job without at least one interview. Of all the selection devices that organizations use to differentiate job candidates, the interview continues to be the one most frequently used.[2] Even companies in Asian countries have begun to rely on employee interviews as a screening device.[3]

Not only is the interview widely used, it also seems to carry a great deal of weight. That is, the results tend to have a disproportionate amount of influence on the selection decision. The candidate who performs poorly in the employment interview is likely to be cut from the applicant pool, regardless of his or her experience, test scores, or letters of recommendation. Conversely, "all too often, the person most polished in job-seeking techniques, particularly those used in the interview process, is the one hired, even though he or she may not be the best candidate for the position."[4]

These findings are important because of the unstructured manner in which the selection interview is frequently conducted. The unstructured interview—short in duration, causal, and made up of random questions—has been proven to be an ineffective selection device.[5] The data gathered from such interviews are typically biased and often unrelated to future job performance. Without structure, a number of biases can distort results. These biases include interviewers tending to favor applicants who share their attitudes, giving unduly high weight to negative information, and allowing the order in which applicants are interviewed to influence evaluations.[6] By having interviewers use a standardized set of questions, providing interviewers with a uniform method of recording information, and standardizing the rating of the applicant's qualifications, the variability in results across applicants is reduced and the validity of the interview as a selection device is greatly enhanced.

The evidence indicates that interviews are most valuable for assessing an applicant's intelligence, level of motivation, and interpersonal skills.[7] When these qualities are related to job performance, the validity of the interview as a selection device is increased. For example, these qualities have demonstrated relevance for performance in upper managerial positions. This may explain why applicants for senior management positions typically undergo dozens of interviews with executive recruiters, board members, and other company executives before a final decision is made. It can also explain why organizations that design work around teams may similarly put applicants through an unusually large number of interviews.

In practice, most organizations use interviews for more than a "prediction-of-performance" device.[8] Companies as diverse as Southwest Airlines, Disney, Microsoft, and Procter & Gamble use the interview to assess applicant-organization fit. So in addition to specific, job-relevant skills, organizations are looking at candidates' personality characteristics, personal values, and the like to find individuals that fit with the organization's culture and image.

Written Tests

Typical written tests assess intelligence, aptitude, ability, interests, and integrity. Long popular as selection devices, they have generally declined in use since the late 1960s, especially in the United States. The reason is that such tests have frequently been characterized as discriminating, and many organizations have not validated, or cannot validate, such tests as being job-related.

Tests of intellectual ability, spatial and mechanical ability, perceptual accuracy, and motor ability have been shown to be moderately valid predictors for many semi-skilled and unskilled operative jobs in industrial organizations.[9] Intelligence tests have proven to be particularly good predictors for jobs that require cognitive complexity.[10] Japanese auto makers, when staffing plants in the United States, have relied heavily on written tests to predict which candidates will be high performers.[11] Getting a job with Toyota, for instance, can take up to three days of testing and interviewing. Written tests typically focus on skills such as reading, mathematics, mechanical dexterity, and ability to work with others.

As ethical problems have increased in organizations, integrity tests have gained popularity. These are paper-and-pencil tests that measure factors such as dependability, carefulness, responsibility, and honesty. The evidence is impressive that these tests are powerful in predicting supervisory ratings of job performance and counterproductive employee behavior on the job such as theft, discipline problems, and excessive absenteeism.[12]

Performance-Simulation Tests

What better way is there to find out if an applicant can do a job than having him or her do it? That's precisely the logic of performance-simulation tests.

Performance-simulation tests have increased in popularity during the past two decades. Undoubtedly the enthusiasm for these tests comes from the fact that they more easily meet the requirement of job relatedness than do most written tests.

The two best-known performance-simulation tests are work sampling and assessment centers. The former is suited to routine jobs, whereas the latter is relevant for the selection of managerial personnel.

Work sampling tests are hands-on simulations of part or all of the job that must be performed by applicants. By carefully devising work samples based on a detailed description of the tasks involved in a job, management determines the knowledge, skills, and abilities needed for each job. Then each work sample element is matched with a corresponding job performance element. Work samples are widely used in the hiring of skilled workers, such as welders, machinists, carpenters, and electricians. For instance, candidates for production jobs at BMW's factory in South Carolina are given work sample tests.[13] They're given 90 minutes to perform a variety of typical work tasks on a specially built simulated assembly line.

The results from work sample experiments are impressive. Studies almost consistently demonstrate that work samples yield validities superior to written aptitude and personality tests.[14]

A more elaborate set of performance-simulation tests, specifically designed to evaluate a candidate's managerial potential, is administered in **assessment centers**. In assessment centers, line executives, supervisors, and/or trained psychologists evaluate candidates as they go through one to several days of exercises that simulate real problems that they would confront on the job.[15] Based on a list of descriptive dimensions that the actual job incumbent has to meet, activities might include interviews, in-basket problem-solving exercises, leaderless group discussions, and business decision games. For instance, a candidate might be required to play the role of a manager who must decide how to respond to 10 memos in his or her in-basket within a two-hour period.

How valid is the assessment center as a selection device? The evidence on the effectiveness of assessment centers is impressive. They have consistently demonstrated results that predict later job performance in managerial positions.[16]

TRAINING PROGRAMS

Competent employees don't remain competent forever. Skills deteriorate and can become obsolete. That's why organizations spend billions of dollars each year on formal training. For instance, it was reported that U.S. corporations with 100 or more employees spent $54 billion in one recent year on formal training for 50 million workers.[17] Xerox, as a case in point, spends more than $300 million each year on training and retraining its employees.[18]

Types of Training

Training can include everything from teaching employees basic reading skills to advanced courses in executive leadership. The following summarizes four general skill categories—basic literacy, technical, interpersonal, and problem solving. In addition, we briefly discuss diversity and ethics training.

Basic Literacy Skills Ninety million American adults have limited literacy skills and about 40 million can read little or not at all; this literacy problem is costing U.S. companies $60 billion annually in lost productivity![19] Most workplace demands require a 10th- or 11th-grade reading level, but about 20 percent of Americans between the ages of 21 and 25 can't read at even an 8th-grade level.[20] In 1998, 36 percent of U.S. job applicants failed some version of a basic skills test.[21] In many Third World countries, few workers can read or have gone beyond the equivalent of the third grade.

Organizations are increasingly having to provide basic reading and math skills for their employees. As long as job demands continue to require that individuals have solid skills in the 3Rs, and many job applicants continue to be deficient in these skills, employers will need to take positive action to close the skills gap. Many business firms, for instance, are hiring instructors and offering classes in English and mathematics for employees at the workplace and during work hours.

Technical Skills Most training is directed at upgrading and improving an employee's technical skills. Technical training has become increasingly important today for two reasons—new technology and new structural designs.

Jobs change as a result of new technologies and improved methods. For instance, many auto repair personnel have had to undergo extensive training to fix and maintain recent models with computer-monitored engines, electronic stabilizing equipment, satellite navigation systems, and other innovations. Similarly, computer-controlled equipment has required millions of production employees to learn a whole new set of skills.

In addition, technical training has become increasingly important because of changes in organization design. As organizations flatten their structures, expand their use of teams, and break down traditional departmental barriers, employees need to learn a wider variety of tasks.

Interpersonal Skills Most employees belong to a work unit. To some degree, their work performance depends on their ability to interact effectively with their co-workers and their boss. Some employees have excellent interpersonal skills, but others require training to improve theirs. This includes learning how to be a better listener, how to communicate ideas more clearly, and how to be a more effective team player.

Problem-Solving Skills Managers, as well as many employees who perform nonroutine tasks, have to solve problems on the job. When people require these skills but are deficient in them, they can participate in problem-solving training. This would include activities to sharpen their logic, reasoning, and problem-defining skills, as well as their abilities to assess causation, develop alternatives, analyze alternatives, and select solutions. Problem-solving training has become a basic part of almost every organizational effort to introduce self-managed teams or implement quality-management programs.

What About Diversity Training? The centerpiece of most diversity programs is training. For instance, a recent survey found that, among companies with diversity initiatives, 93 percent used training as part of their programs.[22] Diversity training programs are generally intended to provide a vehicle for increasing awareness and examining stereotypes. Participants learn to value individual differences, increase their cross-cultural understanding, and confront stereotypes.[23]

The typical program lasts from half a day to three days and includes role-playing exercises, lectures, discussions, and group experiences. For example, a training exercise at Hartford Insurance that sought to increase sensitivity to aging asked participants to respond to the following four questions: (1) If you didn't know how old you are, how old would you guess you are? In other words, how old do you feel inside? (2) When I was 18, I thought middle age began at age __. (3) Today, I think middle age begins at age __. (4) What would be your first reaction if someone called you "an older worker"?[24] Answers to these questions were then used to analyze age-related stereotypes. In another program designed to raise awareness of the power of stereotypes, each participant was asked to write an anonymous paper detailing all groups—women, born-again Christians, blacks, gays, Hispanics, men—to which they had attached stereotypes.[25] They were also asked to explain why they'd had trouble working with certain groups in the past. Based on responses, guest speakers were brought into the class to shatter the stereotypes directed at each group. This was followed by extensive discussion.

What About Ethics Training? A survey found that about 75 percent of employees working in the 1,000 largest U.S. corporations receive ethics training.[26] But the evidence on whether you can teach ethics is not clear.

Critics argue that ethics are based on values, and value systems are fixed at an early age. By the time employers hire people, their ethical values have already been established. The critics also claim that ethics cannot be formally "taught," but must be learned by example.

Supporters of ethics training argue that values can be learned and changed after early childhood. And even if they couldn't, ethics training would be effective because it helps employees to recognize ethical dilemmas, become more aware of the ethical issues underlying their actions, and reaffirms an organization's expectations that members will act ethically.

Training Methods

Training methods are most readily classified as formal or informal and on-the-job or off-the-job.

Historically, training meant *formal training*. It's planned in advance and has a structured format. However, evidence has indicated that organizations are increasingly relying on *informal training*—unstructured, unplanned, and easily adapted to situations and individuals—for teaching skills and keeping employees current.[27] In reality, most informal training is nothing more than employees helping each other out. They share information and solve work-related problems with one another. Maybe the most important outcome of this trend is that many managers are now supportive of what used to be considered "idle chatter." At a Siemens plant in North Carolina, for instance, management now recognizes that people needn't be on the production line to be working.[28] Discussions around the water cooler or in the cafeteria weren't, as managers thought, about nonwork topics such as sports or politics. They largely focused on solving work-related problems. So now Siemens' management encourages such casual meetings.

On-the-job training includes job rotation, apprenticeships, understudy assignments, and formal mentoring programs. But the primary drawback of these on-the-job training methods is that they often disrupt the workplace. So organizations invest in *off-the-job training*. The $54 billion figure we cited earlier for training costs was largely spent on the formal, off-the-job variety. What types of training might this include? The most popular is live classroom lectures. But it also encompasses videotapes, public seminars, self-study programs, Internet courses, satellite-beamed television classes, and group activities that use role-playing and case studies. One of the most famous off-the-job training programs is the two-week course offered at McDonald's Hamburger University.[29] Ham U's curriculum combines operations enhancement, equipment management, and interpersonal skills training for restaurant managers and franchisees. And it's all done in a protected environment that maximizes learning while minimizing frustration on real customers. Most of us have experienced that "slow burn" when we have to deal with a clerk, cashier, or other service employee who is undergoing training on the job. They take up our valuable time while a supervisor tries to explain or show an employee how particular tasks are to be done.

PERFORMANCE APPRAISAL

Why are performance appraisals important? How do organizations appraise the performance of their employees? What potential problems can arise to subvert the intentions of objective appraisals, and how can managers overcome these problems? These are the key questions addressed in this section.

Performance Appraisal and Motivation

In Chapter 4, considerable attention was given to the expectancy model of motivation. We argued that this model currently offers the best explanation of what affects the amount of effort an individual will exert on his or her job. A vital component of this model is performance, specifically the effort-performance and performance-reward linkages. Do people see effort as leading to performance, and performance to the rewards that they value? Clearly, people have to know what is expected of them. They need to know how their performance will be measured. Further, they must feel confident that if they exert an effort within their capabilities, it will result in a satisfactory performance as defined by the criteria by which they are being measured. Finally, they must feel confident that if they perform as they are being asked, they will achieve the rewards they value.

In brief, if the objectives that employees are seeking are unclear, if the criteria for measuring those objectives are vague, and if the employees lack confidence that their efforts will lead to a satisfactory appraisal of their performance, or believe there will be an unsatisfactory payoff by the organization when their performance objectives are achieved, we can expect individuals to work considerably below their potential. Hence, performance appraisal plays an important role in influencing an employee's motivation.

What Do We Evaluate?

The criteria or criterion that management chooses to evaluate when appraising employee performance will have a major influence on what employees do. Two examples illustrate this point.

In a public employment agency, which served workers seeking employment and employers seeking workers, employment interviewers were appraised by the number of interviews they conducted. The interviewers' actions were consistent with the thesis that the evaluating criteria influence behavior. Interviewers were more concerned with the number of interviews they conducted than with the number of clients they placed in jobs.[30]

A management consultant specializing in police research noticed that in one community officers would come on duty for their shift, get into their police cars, drive to the highway that cut through the town, and speed back and forth along this highway for their entire shift. Clearly this fast cruising had little to do with good police work, but this behavior made sense once the consultant learned that the community's City Council used mileage on police vehicles as an evaluative measure of police effectiveness.[31]

These examples demonstrate the importance of criteria in performance appraisal, but what *should* management evaluate? The three most popular sets of criteria are individual task outcomes, behaviors, and traits.

Individual Task Outcomes If ends count, rather than means, then management should evaluate an employee's task outcomes. Using task outcomes, a plant manager could be judged on criteria such as quantity produced, scrap generated, and cost per unit of production. Similarly, a salesperson could be assessed on overall sales volume in his or her territory, dollar increase in sales, and number of new accounts established.

Behaviors   In many cases, it's difficult to identify specific outcomes that can be directly attributable to an employee's actions. This is particularly true of employees in staff positions and individuals whose work assignments are intrinsically part of a team effort. In the latter case, the team's performance may be readily evaluated, but the contribution of each team member may be difficult or impossible to identify clearly. In such instances, it is not unusual for management to evaluate the employee's behavior. Using the previous examples, behaviors of a plant manager that could be used for performance appraisal purposes might include promptness in submitting his or her monthly reports or the leadership style that the manager exhibits. Pertinent salesperson behaviors could be average number of contact calls made per day or sick days used per year.

Traits   The weakest set of criteria, yet one that is still widely used by organizations, is individual traits. We say they are weaker than either task outcomes or behaviors because they are furthest removed from the actual performance of the job itself. Traits such as having "a good attitude," showing "confidence," being "dependable" or "cooperative," "looking busy," or possessing "a wealth of experience" may or may not be highly correlated with positive task outcomes, but only the naive would ignore the reality that such traits are frequently used in organizations as criteria for assessing an employee's level of performance.

Who Should Do the Evaluating?

Who should evaluate an employee's performance? The obvious answer would seem to be his or her immediate boss. By tradition, a manager's authority typically has included appraising subordinates' performance. The logic behind this tradition seems to be that since managers are held responsible for their subordinates' performance, it only makes sense that these managers should evaluate that performance. But that logic may be flawed. Others may actually be able to do the job better.

Immediate Superior   About 95 percent of all performance appraisals at the lower and middle levels of the organization are conducted by the employee's immediate boss.[32] Yet a number of organizations are recognizing the drawbacks to using this source of evaluation. For instance, many bosses feel unqualified to evaluate the unique contributions of each of their subordinates. Others resent being asked to "play God" with their employees' careers. In addition, with many of today's organizations using self-managed teams, telecommuting, and other organizing devices that distance bosses from their employees, an employee's immediate superior may not be a reliable judge of that employee's performance.

Peers   Peer evaluations are one of the most reliable sources of appraisal data. Why? First, peers are close to the action. Daily interactions provide them with a comprehensive view of an employee's job performance. Second, using peers as raters results in several independent judgments, whereas a boss can offer only a single evaluation. And the average of several ratings is often more reliable than a single evaluation. On the down side, peer evaluations can suffer from co-workers' unwillingness to evaluate one another and from biases of friendship or animosity.

Self-Evaluation   Having employees evaluate their own performance is consistent with values such as self-management and empowerment. Self-evaluations get high marks from employees themselves; they tend to lessen employees' defensiveness about the appraisal process; and they make excellent vehicles for stimulating job-performance discussions between employees and their superiors. As you might guess, however, they suffer from overinflated assessment and self-serving bias. Moreover, self-evaluations often have low agreement with superiors' ratings.[33] Because of these serious drawbacks, self-evaluations are probably better suited for developmental uses than evaluative purposes.

Immediate Subordinates A fourth judgment source is an employee's immediate subordinates. These evaluations can provide accurate and detailed information about a manager's behavior because the evaluators typically have frequent contact with the manager. They are also consistent with many organizations' efforts to create cultures that value honesty, openness, and employee empowerment. The obvious problem with this form of rating is fear of reprisal from bosses given unfavorable appraisals. Therefore, respondent anonymity is crucial if these evaluations are to be accurate.

The Comprehensive Approach: The 360-Degree Appraisal The latest approach to performance appraisal is the use of **360-degree appraisals**.[34] It provides for performance feedback from the full circle of daily contacts that an employee might have, ranging from mailroom personnel to customers to bosses to peers. The number of appraisals can be as few as 3 or 4 evaluations or as many as 25, with most organizations collecting 8 to 12 per employee.

A survey of 232 companies found that more than 65 percent were using 360-degree appraisals.[35] Companies currently using this approach include Alcoa, DuPont, Levi Strauss, UPS, Sprint, AT&T, and W.L. Gore & Associates.

What's the appeal of 360-degree appraisals? They fit well into organizations that have introduced teams, employee involvement, and quality-management programs. By relying on feedback from co-workers, customers, and subordinates, these organizations are hoping to give everyone a sense of participation in the review process and to gain more accurate readings on employee performance.

Performance Appraisal Methods

Obviously, performance appraisals are important. But how do you evaluate an employee's performance? That is, what are the specific techniques for appraisal? The following reviews the major performance appraisal methods.

Written Essays Probably the simplest method of appraisal is to write a narrative describing an employee's strengths, weaknesses, past performance, potential, and suggestions for improvement. The written essay requires no complex forms or extensive training to complete. But the results often reflect the ability of the writer. A good or bad appraisal may be determined as much by the evaluator's writing skill as by the employee's actual level of performance.

Critical Incidents Critical incidents focus the evaluator's attention on behaviors that are key in making the difference between executing a job effectively or ineffectively. That is, the appraiser writes down anecdotes that describe what the employee did that was especially effective or ineffective. The key here is that only specific behaviors, and not vaguely defined personality traits, are cited. A list of critical incidents provides a rich set of examples from which the employee can be shown the behaviors that are desirable and those that call for improvement.

Graphic Rating Scales   One of the oldest and most popular methods of appraisal is the use of **graphic rating scales**. In this method, a set of performance factors, such as quantity and quality of work, depth of knowledge, cooperation, loyalty, attendance, honesty, and initiative, are listed. The evaluator then goes down the list and rates each on incremental scales. The scales typically specify five points, so a factor such as *job knowledge* might be rated 1 ("poorly informed about work duties") to five ("has complete mastery of all phases of the job").

Why are graphic rating scales so popular? Though they don't provide the depth of information that essays or critical incidents do, they are less time-consuming to develop and administer. They also allow for quantitative analysis and comparison.

Behaviorally Anchored Rating Scales   Behaviorally anchored rating scales combine major elements from the critical incident and graphic rating scale approaches: The appraiser rates the employees on the basis of items along a continuum, but the points are examples of actual behavior on the given job rather than general descriptions or traits.

Behaviorally anchored rating scales specify definite, observable, and measurable job behavior. Examples of job-related behavior and performance dimensions are found by asking participants to give specific illustrations of effective and ineffective behavior regarding each performance dimension. These behavioral examples are then translated into a set of performance dimensions, each dimension having varying levels of performance. The results of this process are behavioral descriptions, such as anticipates, plans, executes, solves immediate problems, carries out orders, and handles emergency situations.

Multiperson Comparisons   Multiperson comparisons evaluate one individual's performance against that of one or more others. It is a relative rather than an absolute measuring device. The three most popular comparisons are group order ranking, individual ranking, and paired comparisons.

The *group order ranking* requires the evaluator to place employees into a particular classification, such as top one-fifth or second one-fifth. This method is often used in recommending students to graduate schools. Evaluators are asked to rank the student in the top 5 percent, the next 5 percent, the next 15 percent, and so forth. But when used by managers to appraise employees, managers deal with all their subordinates. Therefore, if a rater has 20 subordinates, only 4 can be in the top fifth and, of course, 4 must also be relegated to the bottom fifth.

The *individual ranking* approach rank orders employees from best to worst. If the manager is required to appraise 30 subordinates, this approach assumes that the difference between the first and second employee is the same as that between the twenty-first and twenty-second. Even though some of the employees may be closely grouped, this approach allows for no ties. The result is a clear ordering of employees, from the highest performer down to the lowest.

The *paired comparison* approach compares each employee with every other employee and rates each as either the superior or the weaker member of the pair. After all paired comparisons are made, each employee is assigned a summary ranking based on the number of superior scores he or she achieved. This approach ensures that each employee is compared against every other, but it can obviously become unwieldy when many employees are being compared.

Multiperson comparisons can be combined with one of the other methods to blend the best from both absolute and relative standards. For example, a university might use the graphic rating scale and the individual ranking method to provide more accurate information about its students' performance. A student's relative rank in the class could be noted next to an absolute grade of A, B, C, D, or F. A prospective employer or graduate school could then look at two students who each got a B in their different financial accounting courses and draw considerably different conclusions about each where next to one grade it says "ranked fourth out of twenty-six," while the other says "ranked fourteenth out of thirty." Obviously, the latter instructor gives out a lot more high grades!

Suggestions for Improving Performance Appraisals

The performance appraisal process is a potential minefield of problems. For instance, evaluators can make leniency, halo, and similarity errors, or use the process for political purposes. They can unconsciously inflate evaluations (positive leniency), understate performance (negative leniency), or allow the assessment of one characteristic to unduly influence the assessment of other characteristics (the halo error). Some appraisers bias their evaluations by unconsciously favoring people who have qualities and traits similar to themselves (the similarity error). And, of course, some evaluators see the appraisal process as a political opportunity to overtly reward or punish employees they like or dislike. While there are no protections that will *guarantee* accurate performance appraisals, the following suggestions can significantly help to make the process more objective and fair.

Emphasize Behaviors Rather Than Traits Many traits often considered to be related to good performance may, in fact, have little or no relation to performance. For example, traits such as loyalty, initiative, courage, reliability, and self-expression are intuitively appealing as desirable characteristics in employees. But the relevant question is: Are individuals who are evaluated as high on those traits higher performers than those who rate low? We can't answer this question easily. We know that there are employees who rate high on these characteristics and are poor performers. We can find others who are excellent performers but do not score well on traits such as these. Our conclusion is that traits such as loyalty and initiative may be prized by managers, but there is no evidence to support that certain traits will be adequate synonyms for performance in a large section of jobs.

Another weakness of trait evaluation is the judgment itself. What is "loyalty"? When is an employee "reliable"? What you consider "loyalty," I may not. So traits suffer from weak interrater agreement.

Document Performance Behaviors in a Diary Diaries help evaluators to better organize information in their memory. The evidence indicates that by keeping a diary of specific critical incidents for each employee, appraisals tend to be more accurate and less prone to rating errors.[36] Diaries, for instance, tend to reduce leniency and halo errors because they encourage the evaluator to focus on performance-related behaviors rather than traits.

Use Multiple Evaluators As the number of evaluators increases, the probability of attaining more accurate information increases. If rater error tends to follow a normal curve, an increase in the number of appraisers will tend to find the majority congregating about the middle. You see this approach being used in athletic competitions in sports such as diving and gymnastics. A set of evaluators judges a performance, the highest and lowest scores are dropped, and the final performance appraisal is made up from the cumulative scores of those remaining. The logic of multiple evaluators applies to organizations as well.

If an employee has had 10 supervisors, 9 having rated her as excellent and 1 as poor, we can discount the value of the 1 poor appraisal. Therefore, by moving employees about within the organization so as to gain a number of evaluations or by using multiple assessors (as provided in 360-degree appraisals), we increase the probability of achieving more valid and reliable evaluations.

Evaluate Selectively Appraisers should evaluate only in areas in which they have some expertise.[37] If raters make evaluations only on dimensions for which they are in a good position to rate, we increase the interrater agreement and make the appraisal a more valid process. This approach also recognizes that different organizational levels often have different orientations toward those being rated and observe them in different settings. In general, therefore, we would recommend that evaluators should be as close as possible, in terms of organizational level, to the individual being appraised. Conversely, the more levels that separate the evaluator and the person being evaluated, the less opportunity the evaluator has to observe the individual's behavior and, not surprisingly, the greater the possibility for inaccuracies.

Train Evaluators If you can't *find* good evaluators, the alternative is to *make* good evaluators. There is substantial evidence that training evaluators can make them more accurate raters.[38]

Common errors such as halo and leniency have been minimized or eliminated in workshops in which managers practice observing and rating behaviors. These workshops typically run from one to three days, but allocating many hours to training may not always be necessary. One case has been cited in which both halo and leniency errors were decreased immediately after exposing evaluators to explanatory training sessions lasting only five minutes.[39] But the effects of training do appear to diminish over time.[40] This suggests the need for regular refresher sessions.

Provide Employees with Due Process The concept of *due process* can be applied to appraisals to increase the perception that employees are treated fairly.[41] Three features characterize due process systems: (1) individuals are provided with adequate notice of what is expected of them; (2) all relevant evidence to a proposed violation is aired in a fair hearing so individuals affected can respond; and (3) the final decision is based on the evidence and free from bias.

There is considerable evidence that appraisal systems often violate employees' due process by providing them with infrequent and relatively general performance feedback, allowing them little input into the appraisal process, and knowingly introducing bias into performance ratings. However, when due process has been part of the appraisal system, employees report positive reactions to the appraisal process, perceive the evaluation results as more accurate, and express increased intent to remain with the organization.

Don't Forget Performance Feedback!

For many managers, few activities are more unpleasant than providing performance feedback to employees.[42] In fact, unless pressured by organizational policies and controls, managers are likely to ignore this responsibility.[43]

Why the reluctance to give performance feedback? There seem to be at least three reasons. First, managers are often uncomfortable discussing performance weaknesses directly with employees. Given that almost every employee could stand to improve in some areas, managers fear a confrontation when presenting negative feedback. This apparently applies even when people give negative feedback to a computer! Bill Gates reports that Microsoft conducted a project that required users to rate their experience with a computer. "When we had the computer the users had worked with ask for an evaluation of its performance, the responses tended to be positive. But when we had a second computer ask the same people to evaluate their encounters with the first machine, the people were significantly more critical. Their reluctance to criticize the first computer 'to its face' suggested that they didn't want to hurt its feelings, even though they knew it was only a machine."[44] Second, many employees tend to become defensive when their weaknesses are pointed out. Instead of accepting the feedback as constructive and a basis for improving performance, some employees challenge the evaluation by criticizing the manager or redirecting blame to someone else. A survey of 151 area managers in Philadelphia, for instance, found that 98 percent of these managers encountered some type of aggression after giving employees negative appraisals.[45] Finally, employees tend to have an inflated assessment of their own performance. Statistically speaking, half of all employees must be below-average performers. But the evidence indicates that the average employee's estimate of his or her own performance level generally falls around the 75th percentile.[46] So even when managers are providing good news, employees are likely to perceive it as not good enough!

The solution to the performance feedback problem is not to ignore it, but to train managers in how to conduct constructive feedback sessions. An effective review—one in which the employee perceives the appraisal as fair, the manager as sincere, and the climate as constructive—can result in the employee leaving the interview in an upbeat mood, informed about the performance areas in which he or she needs to improve, and determined to correct the deficiencies.[47] In addition, the performance review should be designed more as a counseling activity than a judgment process. This can best be accomplished by allowing the review to evolve out of the employee's own self-evaluation.

What About Team Performance Appraisals?

Performance appraisal concepts have been almost exclusively developed with only individual employees in mind. This fact reflects the belief that individuals are the core building block around which organizations are built. But as we've described throughout this book, more and more organizations are restructuring themselves around teams. How should those organizations using teams evaluate performance? Four suggestions have been offered for designing a system that supports and improves the performance of teams.[48]

1. *Tie the team's results to the organization's goals*. It's important to find measurements that apply to important goals that the team is supposed to accomplish.
2. *Begin with the team's customers and the work process the team follows to satisfy their needs*. The final product the customer receives can be evaluated in terms of the customer's requirements. The transactions between teams can be evaluated on the basis of delivery and quality. And the process steps can be evaluated on the basis of waste and cycle time.

3. *Measure both team and individual performance.* Define the roles of each team member in terms of accomplishments that support the team's work process. Then assess each member's contribution and the team's overall performance.
4. *Train the team to create its own measures.* Having the team define its objectives and those of each member ensures that everyone understands his or her role on the team and helps the team develop into a more cohesive unit.

Performance Appraisal in a Global Context

We previously examined the role that performance appraisal plays in motivation and in affecting behavior. Caution must be used, however, in generalizing across cultures. Why? Because many cultures are not particularly concerned with performance appraisal, or, if they are, they don't look at it in the same way as do managers in the United States or Canada.

To illustrate these points, let's look at three elements of culture: a person's relationship to the environment, time orientation, and focus of responsibility.

U.S. and Canadian organizations hold people responsible for their actions because people in these countries believe they can dominate their environment. In Middle Eastern countries, on the other hand, performance appraisals aren't likely to be widely used, because managers in these countries tend to see people as subjugated to their environment.

Some countries, such as the United States, have a short-term time orientation. Performance appraisals are likely to be frequent in such a culture, conducted at least once a year. In Japan, however, where people hold a long-term time frame, performance appraisals may occur only at five- or ten-year intervals.

Israel's culture values group activities much more than do the cultures of the United States and Canada. So North American managers focus on the individual in performance appraisals, and their counterparts in Israel are likely to emphasize group contributions and performance.

IMPLICATIONS FOR MANAGERS

Managers control the selection process, decisions regarding employee training, and how employees are evaluated. Because these managerial decisions affect the quality of an organization's workforce and the behavior of employees, care needs to be taken to ensure that the organization's selection process, training programs, and appraisal system support high employee performance.

An organization's selection practices will determine who gets hired. If properly designed, they will identify competent candidates and accurately match them to the job and the organization. The use of the proper selection devices will increase the probability that the right person will be chosen to fill a slot.

While employee selection is far from a science, some organizations fail to design their selection systems so as to maximize the likelihood that the right person–job fit will be achieved. When errors are made, the chosen candidate's performance may be less than satisfactory. Training may be necessary to improve the candidate's skills. At worst, the candidate will prove unacceptable and a replacement will need to be found. Similarly, when the selection process results in hiring less qualified candidates or individuals who don't fit into the organization, those chosen are likely to feel anxious, tense, and uncomfortable. This, in turn, is likely to increase dissatisfaction with the job.

The most obvious effect of training programs on work behavior is directly improving the skills necessary for the employee to successfully complete his or her job. An increase in ability improves the employee's potential to perform at a higher level. Of course, whether that potential becomes realized is largely an issue of motivation.

A major goal of performance appraisal is to assess accurately an individual's performance contribution as a basis for making reward allocation decisions. If the performance appraisal process emphasizes the wrong criteria or inaccurately appraises actual job performance, employees will be over- or underrewarded. As demonstrated in Chapter 4, in our discussion of equity theory, this can lead to negative consequences such as reduced effort, increases in absenteeism, or search for alternative job opportunities.

CHAPTER 16

Organizational Culture

After reading this chapter, you should be able to

1. Define the common characteristics that make up organizational culture
2. Contrast strong and weak cultures
3. Identify the functional and dysfunctional effects of organizational culture on people
4. List the factors that maintain an organization's culture
5. Clarify how culture is transmitted to employees
6. Describe spirituality and characteristics of a spiritual culture
7. Contrast organizational culture with national culture
8. Explain the paradox of diversity

Just as individuals have personalities, so, too, do organizations. In Chapter 3, we found that individuals have relatively enduring and stable traits that help us predict their attitudes and behaviors. In this chapter, we propose that organizations, like people, can be characterized as, for example, rigid, friendly, warm, innovative, or conservative. These traits, in turn, can then be used to predict the attitudes and behaviors of the people within these organizations.

The theme of this chapter is that there is a systems variable in organizations that, although hard to define or describe precisely, nevertheless exists and that employees generally describe in common terms. We call this variable *organizational culture*. Just as tribal cultures have totems and taboos that dictate how each member will act toward fellow members and outsiders, organizations have cultures that govern how members behave. Just what organizational culture is, how it has an impact on employee attitudes and behavior, where it comes from, and whether it can be managed are discussed in the following pages.

DEFINING ORGANIZATIONAL CULTURE

There seems to be wide agreement that **organizational culture** refers to a system of shared meaning held by members that distinguishes the organization from other organizations.[1] This system of shared meaning is, on closer examination, a set of key characteristics that the organization values. Research has suggested that seven primary characteristics, in aggregate, capture the essence of an organization's culture.[2]

1. *Innovation and risk taking*—The degree to which employees are encouraged to be innovative and take risks
2. *Attention to detail*—The degree to which employees are expected to exhibit precision, analysis, and attention to detail
3. *Outcome orientation*—The degree to which management focuses on results or outcomes rather than on the techniques and processes used to achieve those outcomes
4. *People orientation*—The degree to which management decisions take into consideration the effect of outcomes on people within the organization
5. *Team orientation*—The degree to which work activities are organized around teams rather than individuals
6. *Aggressiveness*—The degree to which people are aggressive and competitive rather than easygoing
7. *Stability*—The degree to which organizational activities emphasize maintaining the status quo in contrast to growth

Each of these characteristics exists on a continuum from low to high. Appraising the organization on these seven characteristics, then, gives a composite picture of the organization's culture. This picture becomes the basis for feelings of shared understanding that members have about the organization, how things are done in it, and the way members are supposed to behave. Exhibit 16-1 demonstrates how these characteristics can be mixed to create highly diverse organizations.

Culture Is a Descriptive Term

Organizational culture is concerned with how employees perceive the seven characteristics, not whether they like them. That is, it is a descriptive term. This point is important because it differentiates the concept of organizational culture from that of job satisfaction.

Research on organizational culture has sought to measure how employees see their organization: Are there clear objectives and performance expectations? Does the organization reward innovation? Does it encourage competitiveness?

In contrast, research on job satisfaction seeks to measure affective responses to the work environment. It is concerned with how employees feel about the organization's expectations, reward practices, methods for handling conflict, and the like. Although the two terms undoubtedly have characteristics that overlap, keep in mind that the term *organizational culture* is descriptive, whereas *job satisfaction* is evaluative.

Do Organizations Have Uniform Cultures?

Organizational culture represents a common perception held by the organization's members. This feature was made explicit when we defined culture as a system of *shared* meaning. We should expect, therefore, that individuals with different backgrounds or

> **EXHIBIT 16–1** Contrasting Organizational Cultures
>
> **Organization A**
>
> This organization is a manufacturing firm. Managers are expected to fully document all decisions, and "good managers" are those who can provide detailed data to support their recommendations. Creative decisions that incur significant change or risk are not encouraged. Because managers of failed projects are openly criticized and penalized, managers try not to implement ideas that deviate much from the status quo. One lower-level manager quoted an often-used phrase in the company: "If it ain't broke, don't fix it."
>
> Employees in this firm are required to follow numerous rules and regulations. Managers supervise employees closely to ensure there are no deviations. Management is concerned with high productivity regardless of the impact on employee morale or turnover.
>
> Work activities are designed around individuals. There are distinct departments and lines of authority, and employees are expected to minimize formal contact with other employees outside their functional area or line of command. Performance evaluations and rewards emphasize individual effort, although seniority tends to be the primary factor in the determination of pay raises and promotions.
>
> **Organization B**
>
> This organization is also a manufacturing firm. Here, however, management encourages and rewards risk taking and change. Decisions based on intuition are valued as much as those that are well rationalized. Management prides itself on its history of experimenting with new technologies and its success in regularly introducing innovative products. Managers or employees who have a good idea are encouraged to "run with it," and failures are treated as "learning experiences." The company prides itself on being market driven and rapidly responsive to the changing needs of its customers.
>
> There are few rules and regulations for employees to follow, and supervision is loose because management believes that its employees are hardworking and trustworthy. Management is concerned with high productivity but believes that this comes through treating its people right. The company is proud of its reputation as being a good place to work.
>
> Job activities are designed around work teams, and team members are encouraged to interact with people across functions and authority levels. Employees talk positively about the competition between teams. Individuals and teams have goals, and bonuses are based on achievement of those outcomes. Employees are given considerable autonomy in choosing the means by which the goals are attained.

at different levels in the organization will tend to describe the organization's culture in similar terms.

However, acknowledgment that organizational culture has common properties doesn't mean that there can't be subcultures within any given culture. Most large organizations have a dominant culture and numerous sets of subcultures. A *dominant culture* expresses the core values that are shared by a majority of the organization's members. When we talk about an *organization's* culture, we are referring to its dominant culture. It is this macro view of culture that gives an organization its distinct personality. *Subcultures* tend to develop in large organizations to reflect common problems, situations, or experiences faced by members. These subcultures are likely to be defined by department designations and geographical separation. The accounting department, for example, can have a subculture that is uniquely shared by members of that department. It will include the core values of the dominant culture plus additional values unique to members of the accounting department. Similarly, an office or unit of the organization that is physically separated from the organization's main operations may take on a different personality. Again, the core values are essentially retained but modified to reflect the separated unit's distinct situation.

If organizations had no dominant culture and were composed only of numerous subcultures, the value of organizational culture as an independent variable would be significantly lessened. Why? Because there would be no uniform interpretation of what represented appropriate or inappropriate behavior. It is the shared meaning aspect of culture that makes it such a potent device for guiding and shaping behavior.

Strong versus Weak Cultures

It has become increasingly popular to differentiate between strong and weak cultures. The argument is that strong cultures have a greater impact on employee behavior and are more directly related to reduced turnover.

A **strong culture** is characterized by the organization's core values being both intensely held and widely shared.[3] The more members who accept the core values and the greater their commitment to those values, the stronger the culture is. Consistent with this definition, a strong culture will have a greater influence on the behavior of its members because the high degree of sharedness and intensity creates an internal climate of high behavioral control. For example, Seattle-based Nordstrom has developed one of the strongest service cultures in the retailing industry. Nordstrom employees know in no uncertain terms what is expected of them and these expectations go a long way in shaping their behavior.

One specific result of a strong culture should be low employee turnover. A strong culture demonstrates high agreement among members about what the organization stands for. Such unanimity of purpose builds cohesiveness, loyalty, and organizational commitment. These qualities, in turn, lessen employees' propensity to leave the organization.

WHAT DOES CULTURE DO?

We've alluded to organizational culture's impact on behavior. We've also explicitly argued that a strong culture should be associated with reduced turnover. In this section, we more carefully review the functions that culture performs and assess whether culture can be a liability for an organization.

Culture's Functions

Culture performs several functions within an organization. First, it has a boundary-defining role; that is, it creates distinctions between one organization and others. Second, it conveys a sense of identity for organization members. Third, culture facilitates the generation of commitment to something larger than one's individual self-interest. Fourth, it enhances social system stability. Culture is the social glue that helps hold the organization together by providing appropriate standards for what employees should say and do. Finally, culture serves as a sense-making and control mechanism that guides and shapes the attitudes and behavior of employees. This last function is of particular interest to us. As the following quotation makes clear, culture defines the rules of the game:

> Culture by definition is elusive, intangible, implicit, and taken for granted. But every organization develops a core set of assumptions, understandings, and implicit rules that govern day-to-day behavior in the workplace. . . . Until newcomers learn

the rules, they are not accepted as full-fledged members of the organization. Transgressions of the rules on the part of high-level executives or front-line employees result in universal disapproval and powerful penalties. Conformity to the rules becomes the primary basis for reward and upward mobility.[4]

As we show later in this chapter, who is offered a job, who is appraised as a high performer, and who gets a promotion are strongly influenced by the individual-organization fit, that is, whether the applicant's or employee's attitudes and behavior are compatible with the culture. It is not a coincidence that employees at Disneyland and Walt Disney World appear to be almost universally attractive, clean, and wholesome, with bright smiles. That's the image Disney seeks. The company selects employees who will maintain that image. And both the informal norms and formal rules and regulations ensure that Disney employees, once on the job, will act in a relatively uniform and predictable way.

Culture As a Liability

We are treating culture in a nonjudgmental manner. We haven't said that it's good or bad, only that it exists. Many of its functions, as outlined, are valuable for both the organization and the employee. Culture enhances organizational commitment and increases the consistency of employee behavior. These clearly are benefits to an organization. From an employee's standpoint, culture is valuable because it reduces ambiguity. It tells employees how things are done and what's important. But we shouldn't ignore the potentially dysfunctional aspects of culture, especially of a strong culture.

Culture is a liability when the shared values do not agree with those that will further the organization's effectiveness. This situation is most likely to occur when the organization's environment is dynamic. When the environment is undergoing rapid change, the organization's entrenched culture may no longer be appropriate. Consistency of behavior is an asset to an organization in a stable environment. It may, however, burden the organization and hinder its ability to respond to changes in the environment.

CREATING AND SUSTAINING CULTURE

An organization's culture doesn't pop out of thin air. Once established, it rarely fades away. What forces influence the creation of a culture? What reinforces and sustains those forces once they are in place?

How a Culture Begins

An organization's current customs, traditions, and general way of doing things are largely due to what it has done before and the degree of success it had with those endeavors. So the ultimate source of an organization's culture is its founders.[5]

The founders of an organization traditionally have a major impact in establishing the early culture. They have a vision of what the organization should be. They are unconstrained by previous customs for doing things or ideologies. The small size that typically characterizes any new organization further facilitates the founders' imposing their vision on all organizational members. Because the founders have the original idea, they also typically have biases on how to get the idea fulfilled. The organization's culture results from the interaction between the founders' biases and assumptions and what the original members learn subsequently from their own experiences.

Microsoft's culture is largely a reflection of co-founder and current chairman, Bill Gates. Gates himself is aggressive, competitive, and highly disciplined. Those are the same adjectives often used to describe Microsoft. Other contemporary examples of founders who have had an immeasurable impact on their organization's culture are Akio Morita at Sony, Fred Smith at Federal Express, Mary Kay at Mary Kay Cosmetics, and Richard Branson at the Virgin Group.

Keeping a Culture Alive

Once a culture is in place, practices within the organization act to maintain it by exposing employees to a set of similar experiences.[6] For example, many of an organization's human resource practices reinforce its culture. The selection process, performance appraisal criteria, reward practices, training and career development activities, and promotion procedures ensure that those hired fit in with the culture, reward those who support it, and penalize (and even expel) those who challenge it. Three forces play a particularly important part in sustaining a culture—selection practices, the actions of top management, and socialization methods. Let's take a closer look at each.

Selection The explicit goal of the selection process is to identify and hire individuals who have the knowledge, skills, and abilities to perform the jobs within the organization successfully. But, typically, more than one candidate will meet any given job's requirements. The final decision about who is hired will be significantly influenced by the decision maker's judgment of how well the candidates will fit into the organization. It would be naive to ignore this subjective aspect of the decision to hire. This attempt to ensure a proper match, whether purposely or inadvertently, results in the hiring of people who have common values (ones essentially consistent with those of the organization) or at least a good portion of those values. The selection process also gives applicants information about the organization. Candidates who perceive a conflict between their values and those of the organization can self-select themselves out of the applicant pool. Selection, therefore, becomes a two-way street, allowing either employer or applicant to abrogate a marriage if there appears to be a mismatch. In this way, the selection process sustains an organization's culture by selecting out those individuals who might attack or undermine its core values.

For instance, W. R. Gore & Associates, the maker of Gore-tex fabric used in outerwear, prides itself on its democratic culture and teamwork. There are no job titles at Gore; there are no bosses or chains of command. All employees are called "associates" and have equal authority. The company's 40 plants are also kept small so everything can be done in teams. In Gore's selection process, teams of employees put job applicants through extensive interviews to ensure that candidates who can't deal with the level of uncertainty, flexibility, and teamwork that employees have to deal with in Gore plants are selected out.[7]

Top Management The actions of top management also have a major impact on an organization's culture. Through what they say and how they behave, senior executives establish norms that filter down through the organization as to whether risk taking is desirable, how much freedom managers should give their subordinates, what is appropriate dress, what actions will pay off in terms of pay raises, promotions, and other rewards, and the like.

For example, look at Xerox Corp.[8] Its chief executive from 1961 to 1968 was Joseph C. Wilson. An aggressive, entrepreneurial type, he oversaw Xerox's staggering growth on the basis of its 914 copier, one of the most successful products in American history. Under Wilson, Xerox had an entrepreneurial environment, with an informal, high-camaraderie, innovative, bold, risk-taking culture. Wilson's replacement as CEO was C. Peter McColough, a Harvard MBA with a formal management style. He instituted bureaucratic controls and a major change in Xerox's culture. By the time McColough stepped down in 1982, Xerox had become stodgy and formal, with lots of politics and turf battles and layers of watchdog managers. His replacement was David T. Kearns, who believed that the culture he had inherited hindered Xerox's ability to compete. To increase the company's competitiveness, Kearns trimmed Xerox down by cutting 15,000 jobs, delegated decision making downward, and refocused the organization's culture around a simple theme: Boost the quality of Xerox products and services. By his actions and those of his senior managerial cadre, Kearns conveyed to everyone at Xerox that the company valued and rewarded quality and efficiency. When Kearns retired in 1990, Xerox still had its problems. The copier business was mature and Xerox had fared badly in developing computerized office systems. The next CEO, Paul Allaire, again sought to reshape Xerox's culture. Specifically, he reorganized the corporation around a worldwide marketing department, unified product development and manufacturing divisions, and replaced half of the company's top management team with outsiders. Allaire sought to reshape Xerox's culture to focus on innovative thinking and outhustling the competition. In the spring of 1999, Allaire was replaced by Rick Thoman, a former IBM executive. While Thoman lasted only 13 months, he refocused Xerox on technology. He envisioned reshaping Xerox into a fast-moving provider of high-tech services all built around digital documents. Although Thoman is gone, Xerox's current top management team continues trying to fulfill his vision.

Socialization   No matter how good a job the organization does in recruiting and selection, new employees are not fully indoctrinated in the organization's culture. Because they are least familiar with the organization's culture, new employees are potentially the most likely to disturb the beliefs and customs that are in place. The organization will, therefore, want to help new employees adapt to its culture. This adaptation process is called **socialization**.

All Marines must go through boot camp, where they prove their commitment. Of course, at the same time, the Marine trainers are indoctrinating new recruits in the "Marine way." Viant, a rapidly growing Boston-based consulting firm, puts every new employee through a three-week program in which they bond, acquire team skills, and learn about the firm's history and key personnel. New Disneyland employees spend their first two full days of work watching films and listening to lectures on how Disney employees are expected to look and act.

As we discuss socialization, keep in mind that the most critical socialization stage is at the time of entry into the organization. This is when the organization seeks to mold the outsider into an employee in "good standing." Employees who fail to learn the essential or pivotal role behaviors risk being labeled nonconformists or rebels and, ultimately being expelled. But the organization will be socializing every employee, though maybe not explicitly, throughout his or her career in the organization. This continual process further contributes to sustaining the culture.

Socialization can be conceptualized as a process made up of three stages: prearrival, encounter, and metamorphosis. The first stage encompasses all the learning that occurs before a new member joins the organization. In the second stage, the new employee sees what the organization is really like and confronts the likelihood that expectations and reality may diverge. In the third stage, the relatively long-lasting changes take place. The new employee masters the skills required for his or her job, successfully performs his or her new roles, and makes the adjustments to his or her work group's values and norms. This three-stage process has an impact on the new employee's work productivity, commitment to the organization's objectives, and his or her decision to stay with the organization. Exhibit 16-2 depicts this process.

The *prearrival stage* occurs before the employee joins the organization, so that he or she arrives with an established set of values, attitudes, and expectations. These cover both the work to be done and the organization. For instance, in many jobs, particularly professional work, new members will have undergone a considerable degree of prior socialization in training and in school. One major purpose of a business school, for example, is to socialize business students into the attitudes and behaviors that business firms want. If business executives believe that successful employees value the profit ethic, are loyal, will work hard, want to achieve, and work well in teams, they can hire individuals out of business schools who have been premolded in this pattern. But prearrival socialization goes beyond the specific job. The selection process itself is used in most organizations to inform prospective employees about the organization as a whole and to ensure the inclusion of the right type—those who will fit in. "Indeed, the ability of the individual to present the appropriate face during the selection process determines his ability to move into the organization in the first place. Thus, success depends on the degree to which the aspiring member has correctly anticipated the expectations and desires of those in the organization in charge of selection."[9]

Entry into the organization begins the *encounter stage*. Now the individuals confront the possible dichotomy between their expectations—about their job, co-workers, boss, and the organization in general—and reality. If expectations prove to have been more or less accurate, the encounter stage merely provides a reaffirmation of the perceptions gained earlier. But this is often not the case. Where expectations and reality differ, new employees must undergo socialization that will detach them from previous assumptions and replace those assumptions with another set that the organization deems desirable. At the extreme, new members may become totally disillusioned with the actualities of their job and resign. Proper selection should significantly reduce the probability of the latter occurrence.

Finally, new members must work out any problems discovered during the encounter stage. To do so, they may have to go through changes; hence, we call this the *metamorphosis stage*. The choices presented in Exhibit 16-3 are alternatives

EXHIBIT 16–2   A Socialization Model

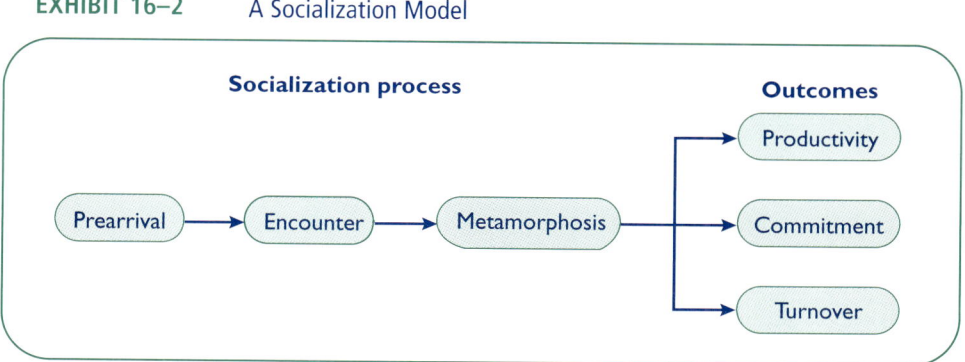

EXHIBIT 16–3 Entry Socialization Options

Formal vs. Informal: The more a new employee is segregated from the ongoing work setting and differentiated in some way to make explicit his or her newcomer's role, the more formal socialization is. Specific orientation and training programs are examples. Informal socialization puts the new employee directly into his or her job, with little or no special attention.

Individual vs. Collective: New members can be socialized individually. Many professional offices socialize new employees in this way. New members can also be grouped together and processed through an identical set of experiences, as in military boot camp.

Fixed vs. Variable: The time schedule in which newcomers make the transition from outsider to insider can be fixed or variable. A fixed schedule establishes standardized stages of transition, such as those used in rotational training programs. It also includes probationary periods, such as the six-year "tenure or out" procedure commonly used with new assistant professors in universities. Variable schedules give no advanced notice of their transition timetable. For example, this describes the typical promotion system, where one is not advanced to the next stage until he or she is "ready."

Serial vs. Random: Serial socialization is characterized by the use of role models who train and encourage the newcomer. Apprenticeship and mentoring programs are examples. In random socialization, role models are deliberately withheld. The new employee is left on his or her own to figure things out.

Investiture vs. Divestiture: Investiture socialization assumes that the newcomer's qualities and qualifications are the necessary ingredients for job success, so those qualities and qualifications are confirmed and supported. Divestiture socialization tries to strip away certain characteristics of the recruit. Fraternity and sorority "pledges" go through divestiture socialization to shape them into the proper role.

Source: Based on J. Van Maanen, "People Processing: Strategies of Organizational Socialization," *Organizational Dynamics*, Summer 1978, pp. 19-36; and E.H. Schein, "Organizational Culture," *American Psychologist*, February 1990, p. 116.

organizations can use to bring about the desired metamorphosis. But what is a desirable metamorphosis? We can say that metamorphosis and the entry socialization process are complete when new members have become comfortable with the organization and their job. They have internalized the norms of the organization and their work group, and they understand and accept those norms. New members feel accepted by their peers as trusted and valued individuals. They are self-confident that they have the competence to complete the job successfully. They understand the system—not only their own tasks, but the rules, procedures, and informally accepted practices as well. Finally, they know how they will be evaluated, that is, what criteria will be used to measure and appraise their work. They know what is expected of them and what constitutes a job well done. As Exhibit 16-2 showed, successful metamorphosis should have a positive impact on the new employees' productivity and their commitment to the organization and reduce their propensity to leave.

Summary: How Cultures Form

Exhibit 16-4 summarizes how an organization's culture is established and sustained. The original culture is derived from the founder's philosophy. This, in turn, strongly influences the criteria used in hiring. The actions of the current top management set the general climate of what is acceptable behavior and what is not. How employees are to be socialized will depend on the degree of success achieved in matching new employees' values to those of the organization in the selection process and top management's preference for socialization methods.

EXHIBIT 16–4   How Organizational Cultures Form

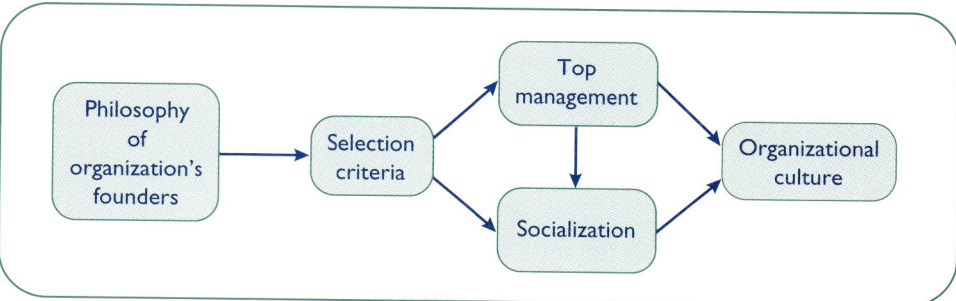

HOW EMPLOYEES LEARN CULTURE

Culture is transmitted to employees in a number of forms, the most potent being stories, rituals, material symbols, and language.

Stories

During the days when Henry Ford II was chairman of the Ford Motor Co., one would have been hard-pressed to find a manager who hadn't heard the story about Mr. Ford's reminding his executives, when they got too arrogant, that "It's *my* name that's on the building." The message was clear: Henry Ford II ran the company.

Nike has a number of senior executives who spend much of their time serving as corporate storytellers. And the stories they tell are meant to convey what Nike is about.[10] When they tell the story of how co-founder (and Oregon track coach) Bill Bowerman went to his workshop and poured rubber into his wife's waffle iron to create a better running shoe, they're talking about Nike's spirit of innovation. When new hires hear tales of Oregon running star Steve Prefontaine's battles to make running a professional sport and to attain better-performing equipment, they learn of Nike's commitment to helping athletes.

Nordstrom employees are fond of the following story. It strongly conveys the company's policy toward customer returns: When this specialty retail chain was in its infancy, a customer came in and wanted to return a set of automobile tires. The salesclerk was not sure how to handle the problem. As the customer and salesclerk spoke, Mr. Nordstrom walked by and overheard the conversation. He immediately interceded, asking the customer how much he had paid for the tires. Mr. Nordstrom then instructed the clerk to take the tires back and provide a full cash refund. After the customer had received his refund and left, the perplexed clerk looked at the boss. "But, Mr. Nordstrom, we don't sell tires!" "I know," replied the boss, "but we do whatever we need to do to make the customer happy. I mean it when I say we have a no-questions-asked return policy." Nordstrom then picked up the telephone and called a friend in the auto parts business to see how much he could get for the tires.

Stories such as these circulate through many organizations. They typically contain a narrative of events about the organization's founders, rule breaking, rags-to-riches successes, reductions in the workforce, relocation of employees, reactions to past mistakes, and organizational coping. These stories anchor the present in the past and provide explanations and legitimacy for current practices.

Rituals

Rituals are repetitive sequences of activities that express and reinforce the key values of the organization, what goals are most important, which people are important, and which are expendable. University faculty members undergo a lengthy ritual in their quest for permanent employment—tenure. Typically, the faculty member is on probation for six years. At the end of that period, the member's colleagues must make one of two choices: extend a tenured appointment or issue a one-year terminal contract. What does it take to obtain tenure? It usually requires satisfactory teaching performance, service to the department and university, and scholarly activity. But, of course, what satisfies the requirements for tenure in one department at one university may be appraised as inadequate in another. The key is that the tenure decision, in essence, asks those who are tenured to assess whether the candidate has demonstrated, in six years of performance, that he or she fits in. Colleagues who have been socialized properly will have proved themselves worthy of being granted tenure. Every year, hundreds of faculty members at colleges and universities are denied tenure. In some cases, this action is a result of poor performance across the board. More often, however, the decision can be traced to the faculty member's not doing well in the areas the tenured faculty believe are important. The instructor who spends dozens of hours each week preparing for class and achieves outstanding evaluations by students but neglects his or her research and publication activities may be passed over for tenure. What has happened, simply, is that the instructor has failed to adapt to the norms set by the department. The astute faculty member will assess early on in the probationary period what attitudes and behaviors his or her colleagues want and will then proceed to give them what they want. And, of course, by demanding certain attitudes and behaviors, the tenured faculty will have made significant strides toward standardizing tenure candidates.

One of the best-known corporate rituals is Mary Kay Cosmetics' annual award meeting. Looking like a cross between a circus and a Miss America pageant, the meeting takes place over a couple of days in a large auditorium, on a stage in front of a large, cheering audience, with all the participants dressed in glamorous evening clothes. Saleswomen are rewarded with an array of flashy gifts—gold and diamond pins, fur stoles, pink Cadillacs—based on success in achieving sales quotas. This "show" acts as a motivator by publicly recognizing outstanding sales performance. In addition, the ritual aspect reinforces Mary Kay's personal determination and optimism, which enabled her to overcome personal hardships, to found her own company, and to achieve material success. It conveys to her salespeople that reaching their sales quota is important and that through hard work and encouragement they too can achieve success.

Material Symbols

Fullers and Lampreia are two of Seattle's most highly rated and expensive restaurants. But, although they're less than 10 blocks apart, the two restaurants convey a very different feel. Fullers is formal to the point of being "stuffy." It has a museum-level decor. The staff is formally attired, serious, focused, and stiff. In contrast, Lampreia is casual and low-key. It has a stylish but minimalist decor. The staff's casual dress and style are consistent with the decor.

Both Fullers and Lampreia consistently receive honors for their food and service; require reservations days, and sometimes weeks, ahead of time; and cost at least

$80 for dinner for two. Yet the restaurants have two different cultures as reflected in things such as the decor and the employees' attire. Moreover, these material symbols convey messages to new employees. At Fullers, the message is that we're serious, formal, and conservative. The message at Lampreia, on the other hand, is that we're relaxed and open.

Messages can also be conveyed by material symbols bestowed on executives. Some corporations provide their top executives with chauffeur-driven limousines and unlimited use of the corporate jet. Executives at other firms may get a car and jet transportation paid for by the company, but the car is a Chevrolet (with no driver) and the plane seat is in the economy section of a commercial airliner.

Other examples of material symbols include the size of offices, the elegance of furnishings, executive perks, the existence of employee lounges or on-site dining facilities, and the presence of reserved parking spaces for certain employees. These material symbols convey to employees who is important, the degree of egalitarianism desired by top management, and the kinds of behavior (for example, risk-taking, conservative, authoritarian, participative, individualistic, social) that are appropriate.

Language

Many organizations and units within organizations use language as a way to identify members of a culture or subculture. By learning this language, members attest to their acceptance of the culture and, in so doing, help to preserve it.

The following are examples of terminology used by employees at Knight-Ridder Information, a California-based data redistributor: *accession number* (a number assigned each individual record in a data base); *KWIC* (a set of key-words-in-context); and *relational operator* (searching a data base for names or key terms in some order). Librarians are a rich source of terminology foreign to people outside their profession. They sprinkle their conversations liberally with acronyms such as ARL (Association for Research Libraries), OCLC (a center in Ohio that does cooperative cataloging), and OPAC (for online patron accessing catalog). If you're a new employee at Boeing, you'll find yourself learning a unique vocabulary of acronyms, including BOLD (Boeing online data); CATIA (computer-graphics-aided, three-dimensional interactive application); MAIDS (manufacturing assembly and installation data system); POP (purchased outside production); and SLO (service-level objectives).[11]

Organizations, over time, often develop unique terms to describe equipment, offices, key personnel, suppliers, customers, or products that are related to its business. New employees are frequently overwhelmed with acronyms and jargon that, after six months on the job, have become fully part of their language. Once assimilated, this terminology acts as a common denominator that unites members of a given culture or subculture.

MANAGING CULTURAL CHANGE

Because an organization's culture is made up of relatively stable characteristics, it's difficult to change. An organization's culture develops over many years and is rooted in deeply held values to which employees are strongly committed. In addition, there are a number of forces continually operating to maintain a given culture. These include written statements about the organization's mission and philosophy, the design of physical spaces and buildings, the dominant leadership style, historical selection criteria, past promotion practices, entrenched rituals, popular stories about key people and events, the organization's past performance evaluation criteria, and the organization's formal structure.

Although changing an organization's culture is difficult, it isn't impossible. For cultural change to be effective, it helps if certain conditions are prevalent. The evidence suggests cultural change is most likely to take when most or all of the following four conditions exist: [12]

A dramatic crisis exists or is created. This is the shock that undermines the status quo and calls into question the relevance of the current culture. Examples of these crises might be a surprising financial setback, the loss of a major customer, or a dramatic technological breakthrough by a competitor. It is not unheard of for some executives to purposely create a crisis in order to stimulate cultural change.

Turnover in leadership. New top leadership, which can provide an alternative set of key values, is usually needed to make cultural change work. They are more likely to be perceived as capable of responding to the crisis. This leadership would definitely include the organization's chief executive but also might need to encompass all senior management positions. Bringing in a new CEO from outside the organization is likely to increase the chances that new cultural values will be introduced. An outside CEO, in contrast to promoting someone from within the organization, also conveys a message to employees that change is in the wind.

Young and small organization. Cultural change is more likely to take if the organization is both young and small. Cultures in younger organizations are less entrenched. And it's easier for management to communicate its new values when the organization is small. This, incidentally, helps explain the difficulty that multibillion-dollar corporations often experience when trying to change their culture.

Weak culture. The more widely held a culture is and the higher the agreement among members on its values, the more difficult it will be to change. Conversely, weak cultures are more amenable to change than strong ones.

Even when the above conditions are favorable, managers shouldn't look for immediate or dramatic shifts in their organization's culture. Cultural change is a lengthy process—which should be measured in years rather than months.

CREATING AN ETHICAL ORGANIZATIONAL CULTURE

The content and strength of a culture influences an organization's ethical climate and the ethical behavior of its members.[13]

An organizational culture most likely to shape high ethical standards is one that's high in risk tolerance, low-to-moderate in aggressiveness, and focuses on means as well as outcomes. Managers in such a culture are supported for taking risks and being innovative, are discouraged from engaging in unbridled competition, and will pay attention to *how* goals are achieved as well as *what* goals are achieved.

A strong organizational culture will exert more influence on employees than a weak one. If the culture is strong and supports high ethical standards, it should have a very powerful and positive influence on employee behavior. Johnson & Johnson, for example, has a strong culture that has long stressed corporate obligations to customers, employees, the community, and shareholders, in that order. When poisoned Tylenol (a J&J product) was found on store shelves, employees at J&J across the

United States independently pulled the product from these stores before management had even issued a statement concerning the tamperings. No one had to tell these individuals what was morally right; they knew what J&J would expect them to do.

What can management do to create a more ethical culture? We suggest a combination of the following practices:

Be a visible role model. Employees will look to top-management behavior as a benchmark for defining appropriate behavior. When senior-management is seen as taking the ethical high road, it provides a positive message for all employees.

Communicate ethical expectations. Ethical ambiguities can be minimized by creating and disseminating an organizational code of ethics. It should state the organization's primary values and the ethical rules that employees are expected to follow.

Provide ethical training. Set up seminars, workshops, and similar ethical training programs. Use these training sessions to reinforce the organization's standards of conduct; to clarify what practices are and are not permissible; and to address possible ethical dilemmas.

Visibly reward ethical acts and punish unethical ones. Performance appraisals of managers should include a point-by-point evaluation of how his or her decisions measured against the organization's code of ethics. Appraisals must include the means taken to achieve goals as well as the ends themselves. People who act ethically should be visibly rewarded for their behavior. Just as importantly, unethical acts should be conspicuously punished.

Provide protective mechanisms. The organization needs to provide formal mechanisms so that employees can discuss ethical dilemmas and report unethical behavior without fear of reprimand. This might include creation of ethical counselors, ombudsmen, or ethical officers.

SPIRITUALITY AND ORGANIZATIONAL CULTURE

What do Southwest Airlines, Ben & Jerry's Homemade, Hewlett-Packard, Wetherill Associates, and Tom's of Maine have in common? They're among a growing number of organizations that have embraced workplace spirituality.

What Is Spirituality?

Workplace spirituality is *not* about organized religious practices. It's not about God or theology. **Workplace spirituality** recognizes that people have an inner life that nourishes and is nourished by meaningful work that takes place in the context of community.[14] Organizations that promote a spiritual culture recognize that people have both a mind and a spirit, seek to find meaning and purpose in their work, and desire to connect with other human beings and be part of a community.

Why Spirituality Now?

Historical models of management and organizational behavior had no room for spirituality. As we noted in our discussion of emotions in Chapter 3, the myth of rationality assumed that the well-run organization eliminated feelings. Similarly, concern about an employee's inner life had no role in the perfectly rational model. But just as we've now come to realize that the study of emotions improves our understanding of organizational behavior, an awareness of spirituality can help you to better understand employee behavior in the twenty-first century.

Of course, employees have always had an inner life. So why has the search for meaning and purposefulness in work surfaced now? There are a number of reasons. We summarize them in Exhibit 16-5.

Characteristics of a Spiritual Organization

The concept of workplace spirituality draws on our previous discussions of topics such as values, ethics, motivation, leadership, and work/life balance. As you'll see, for instance, spiritual organizations are concerned with helping people develop and reach their full potential. This is analogous to Maslow's description of self-actualization that we discussed in relation to motivation. Similarly, organizations that are concerned with spirituality are more likely to directly address problems created by work/life conflicts.

What differentiates spiritual organizations from their nonspiritual counterparts? Although research on this question is only preliminary, our review identified five cultural characteristics that tend to be evident in spiritual organizations.[15]

Strong Sense of Purpose Spiritual organizations build their cultures around a meaningful purpose. While profits may be important, they're not the primary values of the organization. Southwest Airlines, for instance, is strongly committed to providing the lowest-cost airfares, on-time service, and a pleasant experience for customers. Ben & Jerry's Homemade has closely intermeshed socially responsible behavior into its producing and selling of ice cream. Tom's of Maine strives to sell personal care household products that are made from natural ingredients and are environmentally friendly.

Focus on Individual Development Spiritual organizations recognize the worth and value of people. They aren't just providing jobs. They seek to create cultures in which employees can continually learn and grow. Recognizing the importance of people, they also try to provide employment security. Hewlett-Packard, for instance, goes to extremes to try to minimize the effect of economic downturns on its staff. The

EXHIBIT 16–5 Reasons for the Growing Interest in Spirituality

- As a counterbalance to the pressures and stress of a turbulent pace of life. Contemporary lifestyles—single-parent families, geographic mobility, the temporary nature of jobs, new technologies that create distance between people—underscore the lack of community many people feel and increases the need for involvement and connection.
- Aging baby-boomers, reaching mid-life, are looking for something in their life.
- Formalized religion hasn't worked for many people and they continue to look for anchors to replace lack of faith and to fill a growing feeling of emptiness.
- Job demands have made the workplace dominant in many people's lives yet they continue to question the meaning of work.
- The desire to integrate personal life values with one's professional life.
- In times of economic prosperity, more people have the luxury to engage in a search to reach their full potential.

company tries to handle temporary downturns through voluntary attrition and shortened workweeks (shared by all); and longer-term declines through early retirements and buyouts.

Trust and Openness Spiritual organizations are characterized by mutual trust, honesty, and openness. Managers aren't afraid to admit mistakes. And they tend to be extremely upfront with their employees, customers, and suppliers. The president of Wetherill Associates, a highly successful auto parts distribution firm, says: "We don't tell lies here, and everyone knows it. We are specific and honest about quality and suitability of the product for our customers' needs, even if we know they might not be able to detect any problem."[16]

Employee Empowerment The high-trust climate in spiritual organizations, when combined with the desire to promote employee learning and growth, leads to management empowering employees to make most work-related decisions. Managers in spiritually based organizations are comfortable delegating authority to individual employees and teams. They trust their employees to make thoughtful and conscientious decisions. As a case in point, Southwest Airline employees—including flight attendants, customer service representatives, and baggage handlers—are encouraged to take whatever action they deem necessary to meet customer needs or help fellow workers, even if it means breaking company policies.

Toleration of Employee Expression The final characteristic that differentiates spiritually based organizations is that they don't stifle employee emotions. They allow people to be themselves—to express their moods and feelings without guilt or fear of reprimand. Employees at Southwest Air, for instance, are encouraged to express their sense of humor on the job, to act spontaneously, and to make their work fun.

Criticisms of Spirituality

Critics of the spirituality movement in organizations have focused on two issues. First is the question of legitimacy. Specifically, do organizations have the right to impose spiritual values on their employees? Second is the question of economics. Are spirituality and profits compatible?

On the first question, there is clearly the potential for an emphasis on spirituality to make some employees uneasy. Critics might argue that secular institutions, especially business firms, have no business imposing spiritual values on employees. This criticism is undoubtedly valid when spirituality is defined as bringing religion and God into the workplace.[17] However, the criticism seems less stinging when the goal is limited to helping employees find meaning in their work lives. If the concerns listed in Exhibit 16-5 truly characterize a growing segment of the workforce, then maybe the time is right for organizations to help employees find meaning and purpose in their work and to use the workplace as a source of community.

The issue of whether spirituality and profits are compatible objectives is certainly relevant for managers and investors in business. The evidence, although limited, indicates that the two objectives may be very compatible. A research study by a major consulting firm found that companies that introduced spiritually based techniques improved productivity and significantly reduced turnover.[18] Another study found that organizations that provide their employees with opportunities for spiritual development outperformed those that didn't.[19] Other studies also report that spirituality in organizations was positively related to creativity, employee satisfaction, team performance, and organizational commitment.[20] And if you're looking for a single case to make the argument for spirituality, it's hard to beat Southwest Air. Southwest employees have one of the lowest turnover rates in the airline industry; it consistently has the lowest labor costs per miles flown of any major airline; it regularly outpaces its competitors for achieving on-time arrivals and fewest customer complaints; and it has proven itself to be the most consistently profitable airline in the United States.[21]

ORGANIZATIONAL CULTURE VERSUS NATIONAL CULTURE

In places throughout this book we've argued that national differences—that is, national culture—must be taken into account if accurate predictions are to be made about organizational behavior in different countries. But does national culture override an organization's culture? Is an IBM facility in Germany, for example, more likely to reflect German ethnicity or IBM's corporate culture?

The research indicates that national culture has a greater impact on employees than does their organization's culture.[22] German employees at an IBM facility in Munich, therefore, will be influenced more by German culture than by IBM's culture. Organizational culture does have a great influence on the behavior of people at work, but national culture has even more.

The preceding conclusion has to be qualified to reflect the self-selection that goes on at the hiring stage. A British multinational corporation, for example, is likely to be less concerned with hiring the "typical Italian" for its Italian operations than in hiring an Italian who fits with the corporation's way of doing things. We should expect, therefore, that the employee selection process will be used by multinationals to find and hire job applicants who are a good fit with their organization's dominant culture, even if such applicants are somewhat atypical for members of their country.

ORGANIZATIONAL CULTURE AND THE PARADOX OF DIVERSITY

We briefly mention here a contemporary challenge for managers. Socializing new employees who, because of race, gender, ethnic, or other differences, are not like the majority of the organization's members creates what we call *the paradox of diversity*.[23] Management wants new employees to accept the organization's core cultural values. Otherwise, these employees are unlikely to fit in or be accepted. But at the same time, management wants to openly acknowledge and demonstrate support for the differences that these employees bring to the workplace.

Strong cultures put considerable pressure on employees to conform. They limit the range of values and styles that are acceptable. Obviously, this creates a dilemma. Organizations hire diverse individuals because of the alternative strengths these people bring to the workplace, yet these diverse behaviors and strengths are likely to diminish in strong cultures as people attempt to fit in.

Management's challenge in this paradox of diversity is to balance two conflicting goals: Get employees to accept the organization's dominant values and encourage the acceptance of differences. Too much attention to investiture rites is likely to create employees who are misfits. On the other hand, too much emphasis on divestiture rites may eliminate the unique strengths that people of different backgrounds bring to the organization.

IMPLICATIONS FOR MANAGERS

There seems to be little doubt that culture has a strong influence on employee behavior. But what can management do to design a culture that molds employees in the way management wants?

When an organization is just being established, management has a great deal of influence. There are no established traditions. The organization is small. There are few, if any, subcultures. Everyone knows the founder and is directly touched by his or her vision of what the organization is. Not surprisingly, under these conditions management has the opportunity to create a culture that will best facilitate the achievement of the organization's goals. However, when the organization is well established, so too is its dominant culture. Given that this culture is made up of relatively stable and permanent characteristics, it becomes very resistant to change. It took time to form, and once established, it tends to become entrenched. Strong cultures are particularly resistant to change because employees become so committed to them. So, if a given culture, over time, becomes inappropriate to an organization and a handicap to management, there may be little management can do to change it, especially in the short run. Under the most favorable conditions, cultural changes have to be measured in years, not weeks or months. The "favorable conditions" that increase the probability that cultural change can be successfully implemented are the existence of a dramatic crisis, turnover in the organization's top leadership, an organization that is both young and small, and a dominant culture that is weak.

CHAPTER 17

Organizational Change and Development

After reading this chapter, you should be able to

1. Describe forces that act as stimulants to change
2. Define *planned change*
3. Summarize Lewin's three-step change model
4. Explain sources of resistance to change
5. Describe techniques for overcoming resistance to change
6. Explain the values underlying most organizational development (OD) efforts
7. Describe a *learning organization*
8. Identify symptoms of work stress
9. Summarize sources of innovation
10. Define *knowledge management* and explain its importance

This chapter is about organizational change. We describe environmental forces that are requiring managers to implement comprehensive change programs. We compare two views on change. We also consider why people and organizations often resist change and how this resistance can be overcome. Finally, we present the concept of organizational development as a systemwide approach to change and introduce several contemporary issues in organizational change.

FORCES FOR CHANGE

More and more organizations today face a dynamic and changing environment that requires organizations to adapt. Exhibit 17-1 summarizes six specific forces that are acting as stimulants for change.

EXHIBIT 17–1   Forces for Change

Force	Examples
Nature of the workforce	More cultural diversity Increase in professionals Many new entrants with inadequate skills
Technology	Faster and cheaper computers New mobile communication devices Process reengineering programs
Economic shocks	Changes in oil prices Rise and fall of dot-com stocks Decline in the value of the Euro
Competition	Global competitors Mergers and consolidations Growth of e-commerce
Social trends	Internet chat rooms Piercings and tattoos among teenagers Increased interest in urban living
World politics	Black rule of South Africa Opening of markets in China The war on terrorism following 9/11/01

Throughout this book, we've discussed the changing *nature of the workforce*. For instance, almost every organization is having to adjust to a multicultural environment. Human resource policies and practices have to change in order to attract and keep this more diverse workforce. And many companies are having to spend large amounts of money on training to upgrade reading, math, computer, and other skills of employees.

As noted in Chapter 14, *technology* is changing jobs and organizations. For instance, computers are now commonplace in almost every organization; cell phones are being increasingly perceived as necessities by a large segment of the population; and process reengineering programs are eliminating wasteful and redundant job tasks.

We live in an "age of discontinuity." In the 1950s and 1960s, the past was a pretty good indication of the future. Tomorrow was essentially an extended trend line from yesterday. That's no longer true. Beginning in the early 1970s, with the overnight quadrupling of world oil prices, *economic shocks* have continued to impose changes on organizations. In recent years, for instance, oil prices have again significantly increased; new dot-com businesses have been created, turned tens-of-thousands of investors into overnight millionaires, and then crashed; and the Euro has declined 30 percent against other major world currencies.

Competition is changing. In today's global economy, competitors are as likely to come from across the ocean as from across town. Heightened competition also makes it necessary for established organizations to defend themselves against both traditional competitors who develop new products and services and small, entrepreneurial firms with innovative offerings. Successful organizations will be the ones that can change in response to the competition. They'll be fast on their feet, capable of developing new products rapidly and getting them to market quickly. They'll rely on short production runs, short product cycles, and an ongoing stream of new products. In other words, they'll be flexible. They'll require an equally flexible and responsive workforce that can adapt to rapidly and even radically changing conditions.

Social trends don't remain static. For instance, in contrast to just 10 years ago, people are meeting and sharing information in Internet chat rooms; teenagers are increasingly ornamenting their bodies with piercings and tattoos; and many baby boomers and Generation Xers are leaving the suburbs and moving to the cities.

We have argued strongly, throughout this book, for the importance of seeing organizational behavior (OB) in a global context. Business schools have been preaching a global perspective since the early 1980s, but no one—not even the strongest proponents of globalization—could have imagined how *world politics* would change in recent years. A few examples make the point: the fall of the Berlin Wall, the reunification of Germany, Iraq's invasion of Kuwait, and the breakup of the Soviet Union. In just the past decade, changes in world politics have increased business opportunities in South Africa, China, and both South and North Korea.

MANAGING PLANNED CHANGE

A group of housekeeping employees who work for a small hotel confronted the owner: "It's very hard for most of us to maintain rigid 8-to-5 work hours," said their spokeswoman. "Each of us has significant family and personal responsibilities. And rigid hours don't work for us. We're going to begin looking for someplace else to work if you don't set up flexible work hours." The owner listened thoughtfully to the group's ultimatum and agreed to its request. The next day the owner introduced a flextime plan for these employees.

A major automobile manufacturer spent several billion dollars to install state-of-the-art robotics. One area that would receive the new equipment was quality control. Sophisticated computer-controlled equipment would be put in place to significantly improve the company's ability to find and correct defects. Since the new equipment would dramatically change the jobs of the people working in the quality control area, and since management anticipated considerable employee resistance to the new equipment, executives were developing a program to help people become familiar with the equipment and to deal with any anxieties they might be feeling.

Both of the previous scenarios are examples of **change**. That is, both were concerned with making things different. However, only the second scenario described a *planned change*. Many changes in organizations are like the one that occurred at the hotel—they just happen. Some organizations treat all change as an accidental occurrence. We're concerned with change activities that are proactive and purposeful. In this chapter, we address change as an intentional, goal-oriented activity.

What are the goals of **planned change**? Essentially there are two. First, it seeks to improve the ability of the organization to adapt to changes in its environment. Second, it seeks to change employee behavior.

If an organization is to survive, it must respond to changes in its environment. When competitors introduce new products or services, government agencies enact new laws, important sources of supply go out of business, or similar environmental changes take place, the organization needs to adapt. Efforts to stimulate innovation, empower employees, and introduce work teams are examples of planned change activities directed at responding to changes in the environment.

Since an organization's success or failure is essentially due to the things that employees do or fail to do, planned change also is concerned with changing the behavior of individuals and groups within the organization. Later in this chapter, we review techniques that organizations can use to get people to behave differently in the tasks they perform and in their interaction with others.

Who in organizations is responsible for managing change activities? The answer is **change agents.** Change agents can be managers or nonmanagers, employees of the organization, or outside consultants. For major change efforts, internal management often will hire the services of outside consultants to provide advice and assistance. Because they are from the outside, these individuals can offer an objective perspective often unavailable to insiders. Outside consultants, however, are disadvantaged because they usually have an inadequate understanding of the organization's history, culture, operating procedures, and personnel. Outside consultants also may be prone to initiating more drastic changes—which can be a benefit or a disadvantage—because they don't have to live with the repercussions after the change is implemented. In contrast, internal staff specialists or managers, when acting as change agents, may be more thoughtful (and possibly more cautious) because they have to live with the consequences of their actions.

TWO VIEWS OF CHANGE

Simile 1 The organization is like a large ship traveling across the calm Mediterranean Sea to a specific port. The ship's captain has made this exact trip hundreds of times before with the same crew. Every once in a while, however, a storm will appear, and the crew has to respond. The captain will make the appropriate adjustment—that is, implement changes—and, having maneuvered through the storm, will return to calm waters. Implementing change in organizations should therefore be seen as a response to a break in the status quo and needed only in occasional situations.

Simile 2 The organization is more akin to a 40-foot raft than to a large ship. Rather than sailing a calm sea, this raft must traverse a raging river made up of an uninterrupted flow of permanent white-water rapids. To make things worse, the raft is manned by 10 people who have never worked together, none have traveled the river before, much of the trip is in the dark, the river is dotted by unexpected turns and obstacles, the exact destination of the raft is not clear, and at irregular frequencies the raft needs to pull to shore, where new crew members are added and others leave. Change is a natural state and managing change is a continual process.

These two similes present very different approaches to understanding and responding to change. Let's take a closer look at each one.[1]

The "Calm Waters" Simile

Until very recently, the "calm waters" simile dominated the thinking of practicing managers and academics. It's best illustrated in Kurt Lewin's three-step description of the change process.[2] (See Exhibit 17-2.) According to Lewin, successful change requires *unfreezing* the status quo, *changing* to a new state, and *refreezing* the new change to make

EXHIBIT 17–2 Lewin's Description of the Change Process

it permanent. The status quo can be considered an equilibrium state. Moving from this equilibrium requires unfreezing, which can be achieved in one of three ways:

1. The *driving forces*, which direct behavior away from the status quo, can be increased.
2. The *restraining forces*, which hinder movement from the existing equilibrium, can be decreased.
3. The two approaches can be *combined*.

Once unfreezing has been accomplished, the change itself can be implemented. However, the mere introduction of change does not ensure that it will take hold. The new situation therefore needs to be *refrozen* so it can be sustained over time. Unless this last step is attended to, there is a very strong chance the change will be short-lived and employees will revert to the previous equilibrium state. The objective of refreezing, then, is to stabilize the new situation by balancing the driving and restraining forces.

Note how Lewin's three-step process treats change as a break in the organization's equilibrium state. The status quo has been disturbed, and change is necessary to establish a new equilibrium state. This view might have been appropriate to the relatively calm environment that most organizations faced in the 1950s, 1960s, and early 1970s. But one can argue that "calm waters" no longer describe the kind of seas that managers currently have to negotiate.

The "White-Water Rapids" Simile

The "white-water rapids" simile is consistent with the discussion in Chapter 13 of uncertain and dynamic environments. It is also consistent with the dynamics associated with going from an industrial society to a world dominated by information and ideas.

To get a feeling for what managing change might be like when you have to continually maneuver in uninterrupted rapids, consider attending a university that has the following curriculum. Courses vary in length. Unfortunately, when you sign up, you don't know how long a course will last. It might go for 2 weeks or 30 weeks. Furthermore, the instructor can end a course any time he or she wants, with no prior warning. If that isn't bad enough, the length of the class changes each time it meets—sometimes it lasts 20 minutes, other times it runs for 3 hours—and determination of when the next class meeting will take place is set by the instructor during this class. Oh yes, there's one more thing. The exams are all unannounced, so you have to be ready for a test at any time.

To succeed in this university, you'd have to be incredibly flexible and able to respond quickly to every changing condition. Students who were overstructured, rigid, or slow on their feet wouldn't survive.

A growing number of managers are coming to accept that their job is much like what a student would face in such a university. Stability and predictability don't exist. Nor are disruptions in the status quo only occasional and temporary, followed by a return to calm waters. Many of today's managers never get out of the rapids. They face constant change, bordering on chaos. These managers are being forced to play a game they've never played before, governed by rules that are created as the game progresses.

Putting the Two Views in Perspective

Does *every* manager face a world of constant and chaotic change? No, but the set of managers who don't is dwindling rapidly.

Managers in businesses such as women's high-fashion clothing have long confronted a world that looks like white-water rapids. They used to look with envy at their counterparts in industries such as auto manufacturing, oil exploration, banking, fast-food restaurants, office equipment, publishing, telecommunications, and air transportation because these managers historically faced a stable and predictable environment. That might have been true 30 or 40 years ago, but it's not true now.

Few organizations today can treat change as the occasional disturbance in an otherwise peaceful world. Even these few do so at great risk. Too much is changing too fast for any organization or its managers to be complacent. Most competitive advantages last less than 18 months. A firm such as People Express was described in business periodicals as the model "new look" firm, then went bankrupt a short time later. As Tom Peters aptly noted, the old saw "If it ain't broke, don't fix it" no longer applies. In its place, he suggests "If it ain't broke, you just haven't looked hard enough. Fix it anyway."[3]

RESISTANCE TO CHANGE

One of the most well-documented findings from studies of individual and organizational behavior is that organizations and their members resist change. In a sense, this resistance is positive. It provides a degree of stability and predictability to behavior. If there weren't some resistance, organizational behavior would take on characteristics of chaotic randomness. Resistance to change can also be a source of functional conflict. For example, resistance to a reorganization plan or a change in a product line can stimulate a healthy debate over the merits of the idea and result in a better decision. But there is a definite down side to resistance to change. It hinders adaptation and progress.

Resistance to change doesn't necessarily surface in standardized ways. Resistance can be overt, implicit, immediate, or deferred. It is easiest for management to deal with resistance when it is overt and immediate. For instance, a change is proposed and employees quickly respond by voicing complaints, engaging in a work slowdown, threatening to go on strike, or the like. The greater challenge is managing resistance that is implicit or deferred. Implicit resistance efforts are subtle—loss of loyalty to the organization, loss of motivation to work, increased errors or mistakes, increased absenteeism due to "sickness"—and hence difficult to recognize. Similarly, deferred actions cloud the link between the source of the resistance and the reaction to it. A change may produce what appears to be only a minimal reaction at the time it is initiated but surfaces weeks, months, or even years later. Or a single change, in and of itself, has little impact. But it becomes the straw that breaks the camel's back. Reactions to change can build up and then explode in some response that seems totally out of proportion to the change action it follows. The resistance, of course, has merely been deferred and stockpiled. What surfaces is a response to an accumulation of changes.

Let's look at the sources of resistance. For analytical purposes, we've categorized them by individual and organizational sources. In the real world, the sources often overlap.

Individual Resistance

Individual sources of resistance to change reside in basic human characteristics such as perceptions, personalities, and needs. The following summarizes five reasons why individuals may resist change.

Habit Every day, when you go to work or school, do you continually use the same route and streets? Probably. If you're like most people, you find a single route and you use it regularly.

As human beings, we're creatures of habit. Life is complex enough; we don't need to consider the full range of options for the hundreds of decisions we have to make every day. To cope with this complexity, we all rely on habits, or programmed responses. When we are confronted with change, this tendency to respond in our accustomed ways becomes a source of resistance. So when your department is moved to a new office building across town, it means you're likely to have to change many habits: waking up 10 minutes earlier, taking a new set of streets to work, finding a new parking place, adjusting to the new office layout, developing a new lunchtime routine, and so on.

Security People who have a high need for security are likely to resist change because it threatens their feeling of safety. When Boeing announces it's laying off 30,000 people or Ford introduces new robotic equipment, many employees at these firms may fear that their jobs are in jeopardy.

Economic Factors Another source of individual resistance is concern that changes will lower one's income. Changes in job tasks or established work routines also can arouse economic fears if people are concerned they won't be able to perform the new tasks or routines to their previous standards, especially when pay is closely tied to productivity.

Fear of the Unknown Changes substitute ambiguity and uncertainty for the known. And people in general don't like the unknown. The same applies to employees. If, for example, the introduction of a quality management program requires that production workers learn statistical process control techniques, some may fear they'll be unable to do so. They may, therefore, develop a negative attitude toward quality management or behave dysfunctionally if required to use statistical techniques.

Selective Information Processing As we learned in Chapter 2, individuals shape their world through their perceptions. Once they have created this world, they resist changing it. So individuals are guilty of selectively processing information in order to keep their perceptions intact. They hear what they want to hear. They ignore information that challenges the world they've created. The production workers who are faced with the introduction of quality management may ignore the arguments their bosses make in explaining why a knowledge of statistics is necessary or the potential benefits the change will provide them.

Organizational Resistance

Organizations, by their very nature, are conservative. They actively resist change. You don't have to look far to see evidence of this phenomenon. Government agencies want to continue doing what they have been doing for years, whether the need for their service changes or remains the same. Organized religions are deeply entrenched in their history. Changing church doctrine requires great persistence and patience. Educational institutions, which exist to open minds and challenge established doctrine, are themselves extremely resistant to change. Most school systems are using essentially the same teaching technologies today as they were 50 years ago. Most business firms, too, appear highly resistant to change. Six major sources of organizational resistance have been identified.[4]

Structural Inertia Organizations have built-in mechanisms to produce stability. For example, the selection process systematically selects certain people in and certain people out. Training and other socialization techniques reinforce specific role requirements and skills. Formalization provides job descriptions, rules, and procedures for employees to follow.

The people who are hired into an organization are chosen for fit; they are then shaped and directed to behave in certain ways. When an organization is confronted with change, this structural inertia acts as a counterbalance to sustain stability.

Limited Focus of Changes Organizations are made up of interdependent subsystems. You can't change one without affecting the others. For example, if management changes the technological processes without simultaneously modifying the organization's structure to match, the change in technology is not likely to be accepted. So limited changes in subsystems tend to be nullified by the larger system.

Group Inertia Even if individuals want to change their behavior, group norms may act as a constraint. An individual union member, for instance, may be willing to accept the changes in his job suggested by management. But if union norms dictate resisting any unilateral change made by management, he's likely to resist.

Threat to Expertise Changes in organizational patterns may threaten the expertise of specialized groups. The recent move by some companies to outsource many of their human resource activities—such as training, development of pay plans, and benefits administration—has been resisted by many human resource departments. Why? Because this outsourcing is a threat to the specialized skills held by people in HR departments.

Threat to Established Power Relationships Any redistribution of decision-making authority can threaten long-established power relationships within the organization. The introduction of participative decision making or self-managed work teams are examples of changes that often are seen as threats to the power of supervisors and middle managers.

Threat to Established Resource Allocations Groups in the organization that control sizable resources often see change as a threat. They tend to be content with the way things are. Will the change, for instance, mean a reduction in their budgets or a cut in their staff size? Those who most benefit from the current allocation of resources are often threatened by changes that may affect future allocations.

Overcoming Resistance to Change

While there are numerous forces that act to resist change, there are actions that change agents can take to lessen this resistance. The following briefly highlights five of them.

Communication Resistance can be reduced through communicating with employees to help them see the logic of a change. This tactic basically assumes that the source of resistance lies in misinformation or poor communication: If employees receive the full facts and any misunderstandings are cleared up, resistance will subside. Does this approach work? It does, provided that the source of resistance is inadequate communication and that management-employee relations are characterized by mutual trust and credibility. If those conditions do not exist, the change is unlikely to succeed.

Participation People who participate in making a decision are typically more strongly committed to the final outcome than those who weren't involved. And it's difficult for individuals to resist a change decision in which they participated. So before a change is made, those opposed can be brought into the decision process. If the participants have the expertise to make a meaningful contribution, their involvement can reduce resistance, obtain commitment, and increase the quality of the change decision.

Provide Support Change agents can offer a range of supportive efforts to reduce resistance: for instance, showing concern and empathy by practicing active listening, offering employee counseling and therapy, or providing new skills training.

Reward Acceptance of Change As we discovered in Chapters 2 and 5, in our discussion of learning and behavior modification, rewards are a powerful force in shaping behavior. Change agents should, therefore, provide employees with attractive rewards that are contingent on acceptance of change. These rewards can range from praise and recognition to pay increases or promotions.

Create a Learning Organization Resistance is less in an organization that has been intentionally designed with the capacity to continuously adapt and change. We call this a **learning organization**.[5] As shown in Exhibit 17-3, learning organizations have five basic characteristics. People put aside their old ways of thinking, learn to be open with each other, understand how their organization really works, form a plan or vision that everyone can agree upon, and then work together to achieve that vision. Some examples of learning organizations would include FedEx, Ford, General Electric, Motorola, and Wal-Mart.

What can management do to make their firms learning organizations? First, it needs to make explicit its commitment to change, innovation, and continuous improvement. This commitment becomes part of the organization's strategy and vision. Second, the organization's structure needs to be redesigned to reduce boundaries between people and to increase interdependence. This can be achieved by flattening the structure, eliminating or combining departments, and increasing the use of cross-functional teams. Finally, the organization's culture needs to be reshaped to support continual learning. Risk-taking, openness, and growth should become basic values. That means rewarding people who take chances and make mistakes. And management needs to create a climate that brings paradoxes and differences out into the open. This requires encouraging and supporting functional conflict.

EXHIBIT 17–3 Characteristics of a Learning Organization

1. There exists a shared vision which everyone agrees on
2. People discard their old ways of thinking and the standard routines they use for solving problems or doing their jobs
3. Members think of all organizational processes, activities, functions and interactions with the environment as part of a system of interrelationships
4. People openly communicate with each other (across vertical and horizontal boundaries) without fear of criticism or punishment
5. People sublimate their personal self-interest and fragmented departmental interests to work together to achieve the organization's shared vision

Source: P.M. Senge, *The Fifth Discipline* (New York: Doubleday, 1990).

MANAGING CHANGE THROUGH ORGANIZATIONAL DEVELOPMENT

No discussion of managing change would be complete without including organizational development. **Organizational development (OD)** is not an easily defined single concept. Rather, it's a term used to encompass a collection of planned-change interventions built on humanistic-democratic values that seek to improve organizational effectiveness and employee well-being.[6]

The OD paradigm values human and organizational growth, collaborative and participative processes, and a spirit of inquiry.[7] The change agent may be directive in OD; however, there is a strong emphasis on collaboration. Concepts such as power, authority, control, conflict, and coercion are held in relatively low esteem among OD change agents. The following briefly identifies the underlying values in most OD efforts.

1. *Respect for people.* Individuals are perceived as being responsible, conscientious, and caring. They should be treated with dignity and respect.
2. *Trust and support.* The effective and healthy organization is characterized by trust, authenticity, openness, and a supportive climate.
3. *Power equalization.* Effective organizations deemphasize hierarchical authority and control.
4. *Confrontation.* Problems shouldn't be swept under the rug. They should be openly confronted.
5. *Participation.* The more that people who will be affected by a change are involved in the decisions surrounding that change, the more they will be committed to implementing those decisions.

What are some of the OD techniques or interventions for bringing about change? In the following pages, we present five interventions that change agents might consider using.

Sensitivity Training

It can go by a variety of names—laboratory training, **sensitivity training**, encounter groups, or T-groups (training groups)—but all refer to a method of changing behavior through unstructured group interaction.[8] Members are brought together in a free and open environment in which participants discuss themselves and their interactive processes, loosely directed by a professional behavioral scientist. The group is process oriented, which means that individuals learn through observing and participating rather than being told. The professional creates the opportunity for participants to express their ideas, beliefs, and attitudes. He or she does not accept—in fact, overtly rejects—any leadership role.

The objectives of T-groups are to provide the subjects with increased awareness of their own behavior and how others perceive them, greater sensitivity to the behavior of others, and increased understanding of group processes. Specific results sought include increased ability to empathize with others, improved listening skills, greater openness, increased tolerance of individual differences, and improved conflict-resolution skills.

If individuals lack awareness of how others perceive them, then the successful T-group can effect more realistic self-perceptions, greater group cohesiveness, and a reduction in dysfunctional interpersonal conflicts. Furthermore, it can ideally result in a better integration between the individual and the organization. In practice, however, T-groups have been declining in popularity over the past decade or two. Why? One reason is probably the intrusive nature of the process. Many managers are uncomfortable with a process that asks participants to disclose information about themselves and that can threaten an employee's self-image. Second, OD efforts in recent years have moved away from emphasizing individual feelings and focused more on issues related to improving work processes and group performance.

Survey Feedback

One tool for assessing attitudes held by organizational members, identifying discrepancies among member perceptions, and solving these differences is the **survey feedback** approach.[9]

Everyone in an organization can participate in survey feedback, but of key importance is the organizational family—the manager of any given unit and those employees who report directly to him or her. A questionnaire is usually completed by all members in the organization or unit. Organization members may be asked to suggest questions or may be interviewed to determine what issues are relevant. The questionnaire typically asks members for their perceptions and attitudes on a broad range of topics, including decision-making practices; communication effectiveness; coordination between units; and satisfaction with the organization, job, peers, and their immediate supervisor.

The data from this questionnaire are tabulated with data pertaining to an individual's specific "family" and to the entire organization and distributed to employees. These data then become the springboard for identifying problems and clarifying issues that may be creating difficulties for people. Particular attention is given to the importance of encouraging discussion and ensuring that discussions focus on issues and ideas and not on attacking individuals.

Finally, group discussion in the survey feedback approach should result in members identifying possible implications of the questionnaire's findings. Are people listening? Are new ideas being generated? Can decision making, interpersonal relations, or job assignments be improved? Answers to questions like these, it is hoped, will result in the group agreeing on commitments to various actions that will remedy the problems that are identified.

Process Consultation

No organization operates perfectly. Managers often sense that their unit's performance can be improved, but they're unable to identify what can be improved and how it can be improved. The purpose of **process consultation** is for an outside consultant to assist a client, usually a manager, to perceive, understand, and act on process events with which he or she must deal.[10] These might include work flow, informal relationships among unit members, and formal communication channels.

Process consultation (PC) is similar to sensitivity training in its assumption that organizational effectiveness can be improved by dealing with interpersonal problems and in its emphasis on involvement. But PC is more task-directed than sensitivity training.

Consultants in PC are there to give the client 'insight' into what is going on around him, within him, and between him and other people.[11] They do not solve the organization's problems. Rather, the consultant is a guide or coach who advises on the process to help the client solve his or her own problems.

The consultant works with the client in *jointly* diagnosing what processes need improvement. The emphasis is on "jointly" because the client develops a skill at analyzing processes within his or her unit that can be continually called on long after the consultant is gone. In addition, by having the client actively participate in both the diagnosis and the development of alternatives, there will be greater understanding of the process and the remedy and less resistance to the action plan chosen.

Importantly, the process consultant need not be an expert in solving the particular problem that is identified. The consultant's expertise lies in diagnosis and in developing a helping relationship. If the specific problem uncovered requires technical knowledge outside the client's and consultant's expertise, the consultant helps the client to locate such an expert and then instructs the client in how to get the most out of this expert resource.

Team Building

As we've noted in numerous places throughout this book, organizations are increasingly relying on teams to accomplish work tasks. **Team building** utilizes high-interaction group activities to increase trust and openness among team members.[12]

Team building can be applied within groups or at the intergroup level where activities are interdependent. For our discussion, we emphasize the intragroup level and leave intergroup development to the next section. As a result, our interest concerns applications to organizational families (command groups), as well as to committees, project teams, self-managed teams, and task groups.

Not all group activity has interdependence of functions. To illustrate, consider a football team and a track team:

> Although members on both teams are concerned with the team's total output they function differently. The football team's output depends synergistically on how well each player does his particular job in concert with his teammates. The quarterback's performance depends on the performance of his linemen and receivers, and ends on how well the quarterback throws the ball, and so on. On the other hand, a track team's performance is determined largely by the mere addition of the performances of the individual members.[13]

Team building is applicable to the case of interdependence, such as in football. The objective is to improve coordinative efforts of members, which will result in increasing the team's performance.

The activities considered in team building typically include goal setting, development of interpersonal relations among team members, role analysis to clarify each member's role and responsibilities, and team process analysis. Of course, team building may emphasize or exclude certain activities depending on the purpose of the development effort and the specific problems with which the team is confronted. Basically, however, team building attempts to use high interaction among members to increase trust and openness.

It may be beneficial to begin by having members attempt to define the goals and priorities of the team. This will bring to the surface different perceptions of what the team's purpose may be. Following this, members can evaluate the team's performance—how effective is the team in structuring priorities and achieving its goals?

This should identify potential problem areas. This self-critique discussion of means and ends can be done with members of the total team present or, when large size impinges on a free interchange of views, may initially take place in smaller groups followed up by the sharing of their findings with the total team.

Team building can also address each member's role on the team; each role can be identified and clarified. Previous ambiguities can be brought to the surface. For some individuals, it may offer one of the few opportunities they have had to think through thoroughly what their job is all about and what specific tasks they are expected to carry out if the team is to optimize its effectiveness.

Still another team-building activity can be similar to that performed by the process consultant—that is, to analyze key processes that go on within the team to identify the way work is performed and how these processes might be improved to make the team more effective.

Intergroup Development

A major area of concern in OD is the dysfunctional conflict that exists between groups. As a result, this has been a subject to which change efforts have been directed.

Intergroup development seeks to change the attitudes, stereotypes, and perceptions that groups have of each other. For example, in one company, the engineers saw the accounting department as composed of shy and conservative types, and the human resources department as having a bunch of "ultra-liberals who are more concerned that some protected group of employees might get their feelings hurt than with the company making a profit." Such stereotypes can have an obvious negative impact on the coordinative efforts between the departments.

Although there are several approaches for improving intergroup relations, one of the more popular methods emphasizes problem solving.[14] In this method, each group meets independently to develop lists of its perception of itself, the other group, and how it believes the other group perceives it. The groups then share their lists, after which similarities and differences are discussed. Differences are clearly articulated, and the groups look for the causes of the disparities.

Are the groups' goals at odds? Were perceptions distorted? On what basis were stereotypes formulated? Have some differences been caused by misunderstandings of intentions? Have words and concepts been defined differently by each group? Answers to questions like these clarify the exact nature of the conflict. Once the causes of the difficulty have been identified, the groups can move to the integration phase—working to develop solutions that will improve relations between the groups.

Subgroups, with members from each of the conflicting groups, can now be created for further diagnosis and to begin to formulate possible alternative actions that will improve relations.

CONTEMPORARY ISSUES IN ORGANIZATIONAL CHANGE

For many employees, change creates stress. As a result, many managers are asking, *How do I reduce stress among my work staff?* "Innovate or die" is another popular phrase in management circles. *What can managers do to help their organizations become more innovative?* And as organizations have become increasingly concerned with optimizing their intellectual assets, managers are seeking answers to the question: *How do we create a knowledge-management system that can help people do their jobs better?* In the following pages, we address these three questions.

Work Stress

Stress is a dynamic condition in which an individual is confronted with an opportunity, constraint, or demand related to what he or she desires and for which the outcome is perceived to be both uncertain and important.[15] Stress is not necessarily bad in and of itself. Although stress is often discussed in a negative context, it also has a positive value, particularly when it offers a potential gain. For example, it often helps athletes or stage performers achieve a superior performance in a critical situation. However, stress is more often associated with constraints and demands. A constraint prevents you from doing what you desire; demands refer to the loss of something desired. When you take a test at school or you undergo your annual performance review at work, you feel stress because you confront opportunity, constraints, and demands. A good performance review may lead to a promotion, greater responsibilities, and a higher salary. But a poor review may prevent you from getting the promotion. An extremely poor review might cause you to be fired.

Employees today are increasingly complaining about higher stress levels brought on by pressures at work and at home.[16] And managers are paying attention if, for no other reason, it's affecting the bottom line. For instance, job stress is estimated to cost U.S. industry between $200 and $300 billion a year in absenteeism, diminished productivity, employee turnover, accidents, workers' compensation costs, and direct medical, legal, and insurance fees.[17]

Symptoms of Stress What signs indicate that an employee's stress level might be too high? Stress shows itself in a number of ways. For instance, an employee who is experiencing a high level of stress may develop high blood pressure, ulcers, irritability, difficulty in making routine decisions, loss of appetite, accident proneness, and the like. These symptoms can be subsumed under three general categories: physiological, psychological, and behavioral.

Most of the early concern with stress was directed at physiological symptoms, primarily because the topic was researched by specialists in the health and medical sciences. This research led to the conclusion that stress could create changes in metabolism, increase heart and breathing rates, increase blood pressure, bring on headaches, and induce heart attacks. The link between stress and particular physiological symptoms is not clear. There are few, if any, consistent relationships. This inability to pair stress with particular symptoms is attributed to the complexity of the symptoms and the difficulty in measuring them objectively. But physiological symptoms have the least direct relevance to managers.

Of greater importance are the psychological symptoms. Stress can cause dissatisfaction; and job-related stress can cause job-related dissatisfaction. Job dissatisfaction, in fact, is the simplest and most obvious psychological effect of stress. But stress shows itself in other psychological states—for instance, tension, anxiety, irritability, boredom, and procrastination. Behavioral stress symptoms include changes in productivity, absence, and turnover, as well as changes in eating habits, increased smoking or consumption of alcohol, rapid speech, fidgeting, and sleep disorders.[18]

Reducing Stress Not all stress is dysfunctional. Moreover, realistically, stress can never be totally eliminated from a person's life, either off the job or on. As we review stress-reduction techniques, keep in mind that our concern is with reducing the part of stress that is dysfunctional.

In terms of organizational factors, any attempt to lower stress levels has to begin with employee *selection*. Management needs to make sure that an employee's abilities match the requirements of the job. When employees are in over their heads, their stress levels will typically be high. An objective job preview during the selection process will also lessen stress by reducing ambiguity. Improved *organizational communications* will keep ambiguity-induced stress to a minimum. Similarly, a *goal-setting* program will clarify job responsibilities and provide clear performance objectives. *Job redesign* is also a way to reduce stress. If stress can be traced directly to boredom or work overload, jobs should be redesigned to increase challenge or reduce the work load. Redesigns that increase opportunities for employees to participate in decisions and to gain social support have also been found to lessen stress.

Stress that arises from an employee's personal life creates two problems. First, it's difficult for the manager to directly control. Second, there are ethical considerations. Specifically, does the manager have any right to intrude—even in the most subtle ways—in the employee's personal life? If a manager believes it is ethical and the employee is receptive, there are a few approaches the manager can consider. Employee *counseling* can provide stress relief. Employees often want to talk to someone about their problems; and the organization—through its managers, in-house personnel counselors, or free or low-cost outside professional help—can meet that need. For employees whose personal lives suffer from a lack of planning and organization that, in turn, creates stress, the offering of a *time-management program* may prove beneficial in helping them sort out their priorities. Still another approach is organizationally sponsored *physical activity programs*. Some large corporations employ physical fitness specialists who provide employees with exercise advice, teach relaxation techniques, and show individual employees physical activities they can use to keep their stress levels down.

Stimulating Innovation

How can an organization become more innovative? The standard toward which many organizations strive is that achieved by 3M Co.[19] The maker of Scotch Tape and Post-It-Notes has built a reputation as one of the most innovative organizations in the world by consistently developing new products over a very long period of time. 3M has a stated objective that 30 percent of its sales are to come from products less than 4 years old. In one recent year alone, 3M launched more than 500 new products.

What's the secret of 3M's success? What can other organizations do to duplicate 3M's track record for innovation? There is no guaranteed formula, but certain characteristics surface again and again when researchers study innovative organizations. We group them into structural, cultural, and human resource categories. Our message to change agents is that they should consider introducing these characteristics into their organization if they want to create an innovative climate.

Structural Variables Structural variables have been the most studied potential source of innovation. Findings on the structure-innovation relationship lead to the following conclusions[20]: First, organic structures positively influence innovation.

Because they're lower in vertical differentiation, formalization, and centralization, organic organizations facilitate the flexibility, adaptation, and cross-fertilization that make the adoption of innovations easier. Second, long tenure in management is associated with innovation. Managerial tenure apparently provides legitimacy and knowledge of how to accomplish tasks and obtain desired outcomes. Third, innovation is nurtured where there are slack resources. Having an abundance of resources allows an organization to afford to purchase innovations, bear the cost of instituting innovations, and absorb failures. Finally, interunit communication is high in innovative organizations. These organizations are high users of committees, task forces, cross-functional teams, and other mechanisms that facilitate interaction across departmental lines.

Cultural Variables   Innovative organizations tend to have similar cultures. They encourage experimentation. They reward both successes and failures. They celebrate mistakes. Unfortunately, in too many organizations, people are rewarded for the absence of failures rather than for the presence of successes. Such cultures extinguish risk taking and innovation. People will suggest and try new ideas only when they feel that such behaviors exact no penalties.

Human Resource Variables   Innovative organizations actively train and develop their members to keep them current. They offer high job security so that employees won't fear getting fired for making mistakes, and they encourage individuals to become champions of change. Once a new idea is developed, champions of change actively and enthusiastically promote the idea, build support, overcome resistance, and ensure that the innovation is implemented.

Summary   Given the status of 3M as a premier product innovator, we would expect it to have most or all of the properties we've identified. And it does. The company is so highly decentralized that it has many of the characteristics of small organic organizations. All of 3M's scientists and managers are challenged to "keep current." Idea champions are created and encouraged by allowing scientists and engineers to spend up to 15 percent of their time on projects of their own choosing. The company encourages its employees to take risks—and it rewards the failures as well as the successes. Finally, 3M is a model of corporate stability. The average tenure for company officers is 32 years, overall annual employee turnover is a minuscule 3 percent, and the company still prides itself on being an employer for life. Financial analysts, in fact, have recently criticized the company for being *too* stable. In particular, they take issue with management's unwillingness to cut costs through employee layoffs. Management's response is that it's this stability that underpins its innovative culture and allows it to keep its brightest scientists.

Knowledge Management

Siemens, the global telecommunications giant, recently won a $460,000 contract in Switzerland to build a telecommunications network for two hospitals in spite of the fact that its bid was 30 percent higher than the competition. The secret to Siemens's success was its knowledge management system.[21] This system allowed Siemens people in the Netherlands to draw on their experience and provide the Swiss sales reps with technical data that proved the Siemens' network would be substantially more reliable than the competition's.

Siemens is one of a growing number of companies—including Cisco Systems, Ford Motor Co., Johnson & Johnson, Whirlpool, Intel, Volkswagen, Hewlett-Packard, and Royal Bank of Canada—that have realized the value of knowledge management (KM).

What is **knowledge management**? It's a process of organizing and distributing an organization's collective wisdom so the right information gets to the right people at the right time.[22] When done properly, KM provides an organization with both a competitive edge and improved organizational performance because it makes its employees smarter.

Knowledge management is increasingly important today for at least three reasons.[23] First, in many organizations, intellectual assets are now as important as physical or financial assets. Organizations that can quickly and efficiently tap into their employees' collective experience and wisdom are more likely to "outsmart" their competition. Second, as baby boomers begin to leave the workforce, there's an increasing awareness that they represent a wealth of knowledge that will be lost if there are no attempts to capture it. And third, a well-designed KM system will reduce redundancy and make the organization more efficient. For instance, when employees in a large organization undertake a new project, they needn't start from scratch. A knowledge-management system can allow access to what previous employees have learned and cut wasteful time retracing a path that has already been traveled.

How does an organization record the knowledge and expertise of its employees and make that information easily accessible? It needs to develop computer databases of pertinent information that employees can readily access; it needs to create a culture that supports and rewards sharing; and it has to develop mechanisms that allow employees that have developed valuable expertise and insights to share them with others.

KM begins by identifying what knowledge matters to the organization.[24] As with process reengineering, management needs to review processes to identify those that provide the most value. Then it can develop computer networks and databases that can make that information readily available to the people who most need it. But KM won't work unless the culture supports the sharing of information.[25] Remember, as noted in Chapter 11, information that is important and scarce can be a potent source of power. And people who hold that power are often reluctant to share it with others. So KM requires an organizational culture that promotes, values, and rewards sharing knowledge. Finally, KM must provide the mechanisms and the motivation for employees to share knowledge that employees find useful on the job and enables them to achieve better performance.[26] *More* knowledge isn't necessarily *better* knowledge. Information overload needs to be avoided by designing the system to capture only pertinent information and then organizing it so it can be quickly accessed by people whom it can help. Royal Bank of Canada, for instance, has created a KM system with customized e-mail distribution lists carefully broken down by employees' specialty, title, and area of interest; set aside a dedicated site on the company's intranet that serves as a central information repository; and created separate in-house Web sites featuring "lessons learned" summaries where employees with various expertise can share new information with others.[27]

IMPLICATIONS FOR MANAGERS

The need for change encompasses almost all of the concepts within organizational behavior. Think about attitudes, perceptions, teams, leadership, motivation, organizational design, and the like. It's impossible to think about these concepts without inquiring about change.

If environments were perfectly static, if employees' skills and abilities were always up-to-date and incapable of deteriorating, and if tomorrow was always exactly the same as today, organizational change would have little or no relevance to managers. But the real world is turbulent, requiring organizations and their members to undergo dynamic change if they are to perform at competitive levels.

In the past, managers could treat change as an occasional disturbance in their otherwise peaceful and predictable world. Such a world no longer exists for most managers. Today's managers are increasingly finding that their world is one of constant and chaotic change. In this world, managers must continually act as change agents.

Epilogue

The end of a book typically has the same meaning to an author that it has to the reader: It generates feelings of both accomplishment and relief. As both of us rejoice at having completed our tour of the essential concepts in organizational behavior, this is a good time to examine where we've been and what it all means.

The underlying theme of this book has been that the behavior of people at work is not a random phenomenon. Employees are complex entities, but their attitudes and behaviors can nevertheless be explained and predicted with a reasonable degree of accuracy. Our approach has been to look at organizational behavior at three levels: the individual, the group, and the organization system.

We started with the individual and reviewed the major psychological contributions to understanding why individuals act as they do. We found that many of the individual differences among employees can be systematically labeled and categorized, and therefore generalizations can be made. For example, we know that individuals with a conventional type of personality are better matched to certain jobs in corporate management than are people with investigative personalities. So placing people into jobs that are compatible with their personality types should result in higher-performing and more-satisfied employees.

Next, our analysis moved to the group level. We argued that the understanding of group behavior is more complex than merely multiplying what we know about individuals by the number of members in the group, because people act differently when in a group than when alone. We demonstrated how roles, norms, leadership styles, power relationships, and other similar group factors affect the behavior of employees.

Finally, we overlaid systemwide variables on our knowledge of individual and group behavior to further improve our understanding of organizational behavior. Major emphasis was given to showing how an organization's structure, technological processes, work design, human resource policies and practices, and culture affect both the attitudes and behaviors of employees.

It may be tempting to criticize the stress this book placed on theoretical concepts. But as noted psychologist Kurt Lewin is purported to have said, "There is nothing so practical as a good theory." Of course, it's also true that there is nothing so impractical as a good theory that leads nowhere. To avoid presenting theories that led nowhere, this book included a wealth of examples and illustrations. And we regularly stopped to inquire about the implications of theory for the practice of management. The result has been the presentation of numerous concepts that, individually, offer some insights into behavior, but which, when taken together, provide a complex system to help you explain, predict, and control organizational behavior.

Endnotes

CHAPTER 1

1. See P. Addesso, *Management Would Be Easy . . . If It Weren't for the People* (New York: AMACOM, 1996); J. Pfeffer and J.F. Veiga, "Putting People First for Organizational Success," *Academy of Management Executive*, May 1999, pp. 37–48; and R.A. Baron and G.D. Markman, "Beyond Social Capital: How Social Skills Enhance Entrepreneurs' Success," *Academy of Management Executive*, February 2000, pp. 106–16.

2. D. Dorsey, "Change Factory," *Fast Company*, June 2000, pp. 215–24.

3. See, for instance, D.H. Besterfield, et al. (eds.), *Total Quality Management*, 2nd ed. (Upper Saddle River, NJ: Prentice Hall, 1999); and W.J. Kolarik, *Creating Quality: Process Design for Results* (New York: McGraw Hill, 2000).

4. See, for instance, V. Sethi and W.R. King (eds.), *Organizational Transformation Through Business Process Reengineering* (Upper Saddle River, NJ: Prentice Hall, 1998); and C.M. Khoong, *Reengineering in Action* (London: Imperial College Press, 1999).

5. A. Wellner, "How Do You Spell Diversity?" *Training*, April 2000, pp. 34–38.

6. O.C. Richard, "Racial Diversity, Business Strategy, and Firm Performance: A Resource-Based View," *Academy of Management Journal*, April 2000, pp. 164–77.

7. U.S. Department of Labor, Women's Bureau, 2001; and U.S. Census Bureau, 2001.

8. See, for instance, E.E. Kossek and S.A. Lobel (eds.), *Managing Diversity* (Cambridge, MA: Blackwell, 1996); "Building a Competitive Workforce: Diversity—The Bottom Line," *Forbes*, April 3, 2000, pp. 181–94; and O.C. Richard, "Racial Diversity, Business Strategy, and Firm Performance: A Resource-Based View," *Academy of Management Journal*, April 2000, pp. 164–77.

9. S.P. Robbins, *Managing Today!* 2nd ed. (Upper Saddle River, NJ: Prentice Hall, 2000), p. 36.

10. See, for instance, P. Cappelli, J. Constantine, and C. Chadwick, "It Pays to Value Family: Work and Family Tradeoffs Reconsidered," *Industrial Relations*, April 2000, pp. 175–98; M.A. Verespej, "Balancing Act," *Industry Week*, May 15, 2000, pp. 81–85; and R.C. Barnett and D.T. Hall, "How to Use Reduced Hours to Win the War for Talent," *Organizational Dynamics*, vol. 29, no. 3, 2001, pp. 192–210.

11. Cited in J. Lardner, "World-Class Workaholics," *U.S. News & World Report*, December 20, 1999, p. 42.

12. M. Conlin, "9 to 5 Isn't Working Anymore," *Business Week*, September 20, 1999, p. 94; and "The New World of Work: Flexibility Is the Watchword," *Business Week*, January 10, 2000, p. 36.

13. S. Shellenbarger, "What Job Candidates Really Want to Know: Will I Have a Life?" *Wall Street Journal*, November 17, 1999, p. B1; and : "U.S. Employers Polish Image to Woo a Demanding New Generation," *Manpower Argus*, February 2000, p. 2.

14. See, for instance, T.A. Stewart, "Gray Flannel Suit?" *Fortune*, March 16, 1998, pp. 76–82.

CHAPTER 2

1. M. Rokeach, *The Nature of Human Values* (New York: Free Press, 1973), p. 5.

2. Ibid., p. 6.

3. J.M. Munson and B.Z. Posner, "The Factorial Validity of a Modified Rokeach Value Survey for Four Diverse Samples," *Educational and Psychological Measurement*, Winter 1980, pp. 1073–79; and W.C. Frederick and J. Weber, "The Values of Corporate Managers and Their Critics: An Empirical Description and Normative Implications," in W.C. Frederick and L.E. Preston (eds.), *Business Ethics: Research Issues and Empirical Studies* (Greenwich, CT: JAI Press, 1990), pp. 123–44.

4. Frederick and Weber, "The Values of Corporate Managers and Their Critics."

5. Ibid., p. 132.

6. See, for example, R. Zemke, C. Raines, and B. Filipczak, *Generations at Work: Managing the Clash of Veterans, Boomers, Xers, and Nexters in Your Workplace* (New York: AMACOM, 1999); C.Y. Chen, "Chasing the Net Generation," *Fortune*, September 4, 2000, pp. 295–98; C. Penttila, "Generational Gyrations," *Entrepreneur*, April 2001, pp. 102–05; R. Zemke, "Here Come the Millennials," *Training*, July 2001, pp. 44–9; and N. Neusner and P. Basso, "The Boomers' Kids Get a Job," *U.S. News & World Report*, September 3, 2001, pp. 28–30.

7. R.E. Hattwick, Y. Kathawala, M. Monipullil, and L. Wall, "On the Alleged Decline in Business Ethics," *Journal of Behavioral Economics*, Summer 1989, pp. 129–43.

8. B.Z. Posner and W.H. Schmidt, "Values and the American Manager: An Update Updated," *California Management Review*, Spring 1992, p. 86.

9. See, for instance, D.A. Ralston, D.H. Holt, R.H. Terpstra, and Y. Kai-cheng, "The Impact of Culture and Ideology on Managerial Work Values: A Study of the United States, Russia, Japan, and China," in D.P. Moore (ed.), *Academy of Management Best Paper Proceedings*

(Vancouver, BC Academy of Management Conference, August 1995), pp. 187–91.

10. G. Hofstede, *Culture's Consequences: International Differences in Work Related Values* (Beverly Hills, CA: Sage, 1980); G. Hofstede, *Cultures and Organizations: Software of the Mind* (London: McGraw-Hill, 1991); G. Hofstede, "Cultural Constraints in Management Theories," *Academy of Management Executive*, February 1993, pp. 81–94; and G. Hofstede and M.F. Peterson, "National Values and Organizational Practices," in N.M. Ashkanasy, C.P.M. Wilderom, and M.F. Peterson (eds.), *Handbook of Organizational Culture and Climate* (Thousand Oaks, CA: Sage, 2000), pp. 401–16.

11. Hofstede called this dimension *masculinity* versus *femininity*, but we've changed his terms because of their strong sexist connotation.

12. N.J. Adler, "Cross-Cultural Management Research: The Ostrich and the Trend," *Academy of Management Review*, April 1983, pp. 226–32.

13. L. Godkin, C.E. Braye, and C.L. Caunch, "U.S.-Based Cross Cultural Management Research in the Eighties," *Journal of Business and Economic Perspectives*, vol. 15 (1989), pp. 37-45; and T.K. Peng, M.F. Peterson, and Y.P. Shyi, "Quantitative Methods in Cross-National Management Research: Trends and Equivalence Issues," *Journal of Organizational Behavior*, vol. 12 (1991), pp. 87–107.

14. E.A. Locke, "The Nature and Causes of Job Satisfaction," pp. 1319–28, in *Handbook of Industrial and Organizational Psychology* (Chicago: Rand McNally, 1976).

15. See, for instance, A.H. Brayfield and W.H. Crockett, "Employee Attitudes and Employee Performance," *Psychological Bulletin*, September 1955, pp. 396–428; V. H. Vroom, *Work and Motivation* (New York: Wiley, 1964); M.M. Petty, G.W. McGee, and J.W. Cavender, "A Meta-Analysis of the Relationship between Individual Job Satisfaction and Individual Performance," *Academy of Management Review*, October 1984, pp. 712–21; and S. Shellenbarger, "Companies Are Finding Real Payoffs in Aiding Employee Satisfaction," *Wall Street Journal*, October 11, 2000, p. B1.

16. P.E. Spector, *Job Satisfaction: Application, Assessment, Causes and Consequences* (Thousand Oaks, CA: Sage, 1997), pp. 57–8; P.M. Podsakoff, S.B. MacKenzie, J.B. Paine, and D.G. Bachrach, "Organizational Citizenship Behaviors: A Critical Review of the Theoretical and Empirical Literature and Suggestions for Future Research," *Journal of Management*, vol. 26, no. 3, 2000, pp. 526–30; and L.A. Bettencourt, K.P. Gwinner, and M.L. Meuter, "A Comparison of Attitude, Personality, and Knowledge Predictors of Service-Oriented Organizational Citizenship Behaviors," *Journal of Applied Psychology*, February 2001, pp. 29–41.

17. See T.S. Bateman and D.W. Organ, "Job Satisfaction and the Good Soldier: The Relationship Between Affect and Employee 'Citizenship,'" *Academy of Management Journal*, December 1983, pp. 587–95; C.A. Smith, D.W. Organ, and J.P. Near, "Organizational Citizenship Behavior: Its Nature and Antecedents," *Journal of Applied Psychology*, October 1983, pp. 653–63; A.P. Brief, *Attitudes in and Around Organizations* (Thousand Oaks, CA: Sage, 1998), pp. 44–45; and P.M. Podsakoff, S.B. MacKenzie, J.B. Paine, and D.G. Bachrach, "Organizational Citizenship Behaviors: A Critical Review of the Theoretical and Empirical Literature and Suggestions for Future Research," *Journal of Management*, vol. 26, no. 3, 2000, pp. 513–63.

18. D.W. Organ and K. Ryan, "A Meta-Analytic Review of Attitudinal and Dispositional Predictors of Organizational Citizenship Behavior," *Personnel Psychology*, Winter 1995, p. 791.

19. J. Fahr, P.M. Podsakoff, and D.W. Organ, "Accounting for Organizational Citizenship Behavior: Leader Fairness and Task Scope Versus Satisfaction," *Journal of Management*, December 1990, pp. 705–22; R.H. Moorman, "Relationship Between Organization Justice and Organizational Citizenship Behaviors: Do Fairness Perceptions Influence Employee Citizenship?" *Journal of Applied Psychology*, December 1991, pp. 845–55; and M.A. Konovsky and D.W. Organ, "Dispositional and Contextual Determinants of Organizational Citizenship Behavior," *Journal of Organizational Behavior*, May 1996, pp. 253–66.

20. D.W. Organ, "Personality and Organizational Citizenship Behavior," *Journal of Management*, Summer 1994, p. 466.

21. L. Festinger, *Theory of Cognitive Dissonance* (Stanford, CA: Stanford University Press, 1957).

22. A.W. Wicker, "Attitude Versus Action: The Relationship of Verbal and Overt Behavioral Responses to Attitude Objects," *Journal of Social Issues*, Autumn 1969, pp. 41–78.

23. H.H. Kelley, "Attribution in Social Interaction," pp. 1–26 in E. Jones et al. (eds.), *Attribution: Perceiving the Causes of Behavior* (Morristown, NJ: General Learning Press, 1972).

24. See L. Ross, "The Intuitive Psychologist and His Shortcomings," in L. Berkowitz (ed.), *Advances in the Experimental Social Psychology*, vol. 10 (Orlando, FL: Academic Press, 1977), pp. 174–220; A.G. Miller and T. Lawson, "The Effect of an Informational Option on the Fundamental Attribution Error," *Personality and Social Psychology Bulletin*, June 1989, pp. 194–204; and N. Epley and D. Dunning, "Feeling 'Holier Than Thou': Are Self-Serving Assessments Produced by Errors in Self- or Social Prediction," *Journal of Personality and Social Psychology*, December 2000, pp. 861–75.

25. E.L. Thorndike, *Educational Psychology: The Psychology of Learning* (New York: Columbia University Press, 1913); and B.F. Skinner, *Beyond Freedom and Dignity* (New York: Knopf, 1971).

CHAPTER 3

1. See R.R. McCrae and P.T. Costa Jr., "Reinterpreting the Myers/Briggs Type Indicator from the Perspective of

the Five-Factor Model of Personality," *Journal of Personality*, March 1989, pp. 17–40; and C. Fitzgerald and L.K. Kirby (eds.), *Developing Leaders: Research and Applications in Psychological Type and Leadership Development* (Palo Alto, CA: Davies-Black Publishing, 1997).

2. G.N. Landrum, *Profiles of Genius* (New York: Prometheus, 1993).

3. J.M. Digman, "Personality Structure: Emergence of the Five–Factor Model," in M.R. Rosenzweig and L.W. Porter (eds.), *Annual Review of Psychology*, vol. 41, (Palo Alto, CA: Annual Reviews, 1990), pp. 417–440; P.H. Raymark, M.J. Schmit, and R.M. Guion, "Identifying Potentially Useful Personality Constructs for Employee Selection," *Personnel Psychology*, Autumn 1997, pp. 723–36; and G.M. Hurtz and J.J. Donovan, "Personality and Job Performance: The Big Five Revisited," *Journal of Applied Psychology*, December 2000, pp. 869–79.

4. See, for instance, M.R. Barrick and M.K. Mount, "The Big Five Personality Dimensions and Job Performance: A Meta-Analysis," *Personnel Psychology* 44 (1991), pp. 1–26; T.A. Judge, J.J. Martocchio, and C.J. Thoresen, "Five-Factor Model of Personality and Employee Absence," *Journal of Applied Psychology*, October 1997, pp. 745–55; O. Behling, "Employee Selection: Will Intelligence and Conscientiousness Do the Job?" *Academy of Management Executive*, February 1998, pp. 77–86; and F.S. Switzer III and P.L. Roth, "A Meta-Analytic Review of Predictors of Job Performance for Salespeople," *Journal of Applied Psychology*, August 1998, pp. 586–97.

5. J.F. Salgado, "The Five Factor Model of Personality and Job Performance in the European Community," *Journal of Applied Psychology*, February 1997, pp. 30-43.

6. F. Kluckhohn and F.L. Strodtbeck, *Variations in Value Orientations* (Evanston, IL: Row Peterson, 1961).

7. M. Friedman and R.H. Rosenman, *Type A Behavior and Your Heart* (New York: Alfred A. Knopf, 1974), p. 86.

8. J.L. Holland, *Making Vocational Choices: A Theory of Vocational Personalities and Work Environments*, 2nd ed. (Upper Saddle River, NJ: Prentice Hall, 1985); A.R. Spokane, "A Review of Research on Person-Environment Congruence in Holland's Theory of Careers," *Journal of Vocational Behavior*, June 1985, pp. 306–43; and T.J. Tracey and J. Rounds, "Evaluating Holland's and Gati's Vocational-Interest Models: A Structural Meta-Analysis," *Psychological Bulletin*, March 1993, pp. 229–46.

9. See, for example, L.L. Putnam and D.K. Mumby, "Organizations, Emotion and the Myth of Rationality," in S. Fineman (ed.), *Emotion in Organizations* (Thousand Oaks: Sage, 1993), pp. 36–57; and T.A. Domagalski, "Emotion in Organizations: Main Currents," *Human Relations*, June 1999, pp. 833–52.

10. B.E. Ashforth and R.H. Humphrey, "Emotion in the Workplace: A Reappraisal," *Human Relations*, February 1995, pp. 97–125.

11. J.M. George, "Trait and State Affect," in K.R. Murphy (ed.), *Individual Differences and Behavior in Organizations* (San Francisco: Jossey-Bass, 1996), p. 145.

12. See N.H. Frijda, "Moods, Emotion Episodes and Emotions," in M. Lewis and J.M. Haviland (eds.), *Handbook of Emotions* (New York: Guilford Press, 1993), pp. 381-403.

13. H.M. Weiss and R. Cropanzano, "Affective Events Theory," in B.M. Staw and L.L. Cummings (eds.), *Research in Organizational Behavior*, vol. 18 (Greenwich, CT: JAI Press, 1996), pp. 17–19.

14. N.H. Frijda, "Moods, Emotion Episodes and Emotions," p. 381.

15. See J.A. Morris and D.C. Feldman, "The Dimensions, Antecedents, and Consequences of Emotional Labor," *Academy of Management Review*, October 1996, pp. 986–1010; and S.M. Kruml and D. Geddes, "Catching Fire Without Burning Out: Is There an Ideal Way to Perform Emotion Labor?" in N.M. Ashkanasy, C.E.J. Hartel, and W.J. Zerbe (eds.), *Emotions in the Workplace: Research, Theory, and Practice* (Westport, CT: Quorum Books, 2000), pp. 177–88.

16. A.R. Hochschild, "Emotion Work, Feeling Rules, and Social Structure," *American Journal of Sociology*, November 1979, pp. 555–75.

17. B.M. DePaulo, "Nonverbal Behavior and Self-Presentation," *Psychological Bulletin*, March 1992, pp. 203–43.

18. C.S. Hunt, "Although I Might Be Laughing Loud and Hearty, Deep Inside I'm Blue: Individual Perceptions Regarding Feeling and Displaying Emotions at Work"; paper presented at the Academy of Management National Conference, Cincinnati, August 1996, p. 3.

19. H.M. Weiss and R. Cropanzano, "Affective Events Theory," pp. 20–22.

20. R.D. Woodworth, *Experimental Psychology* (New York, Holt, 1938).

21. K. Deaux, "Sex Differences," in M.R. Rosenzweig and L.W. Porter (eds.), *Annual Review of Psychology*, vol. 26 (Palo Alto, CA: Annual Reviews, 1985), pp. 48–82; M. LaFrance and M. Banaji, "Toward a Reconsideration of the Gender-Emotion Relationship," in M. Clark (ed.), *Review of Personality and Social Psychology*, vol. 14 (Newbury Park, CA: Sage, 1992), pp. 178–97; and A.M. Kring and A.H. Gordon, "Sex Differences in Emotion: Expression, Experience, and Physiology," *Journal of Personality and Social Psychology*, March 1998, pp. 686–703.

22. L.R. Brody and J.A. Hall, "Gender and Emotion," in M. Lewis and J.M. Haviland (eds.), *Handbook of Emotions* (New York: Guilford Press, 1993), pp. 447–60; and M. Grossman and W. Wood, "Sex Differences in Intensity of Emotional Experience: A Social Role Interpretation," *Journal of Personality and Social Psychology*, November 1993, pp. 1010–22.

23. J.A. Hall, *Nonverbal Sex Differences: Communication Accuracy and Expressive Style* (Baltimore: Johns Hopkins University Press, 1984).

24. N. James, "Emotional Labour: Skill and Work in the Social Regulations of Feelings," *Sociological Review*, February 1989, pp. 15–42; A. Hochschild, *The Second Shift* (New York: Viking, 1989); and F.M. Deutsch, "Status, Sex, and Smiling: The Effect of Role on Smiling in Men and Women," *Personality and Social Psychology Bulletin*, September 1990, pp. 531–40.

25. A. Rafaeli, "When Clerks Meet Customers: A Test of Variables Related to Emotional Expression on the Job," *Journal of Applied Psychology*, June 1989, pp. 385–93; and M. LaFrance and M. Banaji, "Toward a Reconsideration of the Gender-Emotion Relationship."

26. L.W. Hoffman, "Early Childhood Experiences and Women's Achievement Motives," *Journal of Social Issues*, vol. 28, no. 2, 1972, pp. 128–55.

27. A. Rafaeli and R.I. Sutton, "The Expression of Emotion in Organizational Life," in L.L. Cummings and B.M. Staw (eds.), *Research in Organizational Behavior*, vol. 11 (Greenwich, CT: JAI Press, 1989), p. 8.

28. A. Rafaeli, "When Cashiers Meet Customers: An Analysis of Supermarket Cashiers," *Academy of Management Journal*, June 1989, pp. 245–73.

29. Ibid.

30. Described in S. Emmons, "Emotions at Face Value," *Los Angeles Times*, January 9, 1998, p. E1.

31. R.I. Levy, *Tahitians: Mind and Experience in the Society Islands* (Chicago: University of Chicago Press, 1973).

32. This section is based on D. Goleman, *Emotional Intelligence* (New York: Bantam, 1995); R.K. Cooper, "Applying Emotional Intelligence in the Workplace," *Training & Development*, December 1997, pp. 31–38; M. Davies, L. Stankov, and R.D. Roberts, "Emotional Intelligence: In Search of an Elusive Construct," *Journal of Personality and Social Psychology*, October 1998, pp. 989–1015; and D. Goleman, *Working with Emotional Intelligence* (New York: Bantam, 1999).

33. B.E. Ashforth and R.H. Humphrey, "Emotion in the Workplace," p. 109.

34. Ibid.

35. Ibid., p. 110.

36. Ibid.

37. J.M. George, "Trait and State Affect," p. 162.

38. B.E. Ashforth and R.H. Humphrey, "Emotion in the Workplace," p. 116.

39. S.L. Robinson and R.J. Bennett, "A Typology of Deviant Workplace Behaviors: A Multidimensional Scaling Study," *Academy of Management Journal*, April 1995, p. 555–72.

40. A.G. Bedeian, "Workplace Envy," *Organizational Dynamics*, Spring 1995, p. 50.

41. S. Nelton, "Emotions in the Workplace," *Nation's Business*, February 1996, p. 25.

42. H.M. Weiss and R. Cropanzano, "Affective Events Theory," p. 55.

CHAPTER 4

1. A. Maslow, *Motivation and Personality* (New York: Harper & Row, 1954).

2. D. McGregor, *The Human Side of Enterprise* (New York: McGraw-Hill, 1960).

3. F. Herzberg, B. Mausner, and B. Snyderman, *The Motivation to Work* (New York: Wiley, 1959). See update in M.L. Ambrose and C.T. Kulik, "Old Friends, New Faces: Motivation Research in the 1990s," *Journal of Management*, vol. 25, no. 3, 1999, pp. 233–34.

4. D.C. McClelland, *The Achieving Society* (New York: Van Nostrand Reinhold, 1961); J.W. Atkinson and J.O. Raynor, *Motivation and Achievement* (Washington, DC: Winston, 1974); and R. Kanfer and E.D. Heggestad, "Motivational Traits and Skills: A Person-Centered Approach to Work Motivation," in L.L. Cummings and B.M. Staw (eds.), *Research in Organizational Behavior*, vol. 19 (Greenwich, CT: JAI Press, 1997), pp. 16–24.

5. E.A. Locke, "Toward a Theory of Task Motivation and Incentives," *Organizational Behavior and Human Performance*, May 1968, pp. 157–189; E.A. Locke and G.P. Latham, *A Theory of Goal Setting and Task Performance* (Upper Saddle River, NJ: Prentice Hall, 1990); and E.A. Locke, "Motivation Through Conscious Goal Setting," *Applied and Preventive Psychology*, February 1996, pp. 117–124.

6. F. Luthans and R. Kreitner, *Organizational Behavior Modification and Beyond: An Operant and Social Learning Approach* (Glenview, IL: Scott, Foresman, 1984); and A.D. Stajkovic and F. Luthans, "A Meta-Analysis of the Effects of Organizational Behavior Modification on Task Performance: 1975–95," *Academy of Management Journal*, October 1997, pp. 1122–49.

7. J.S. Adams, "Inequity in Social Exchanges," in L. Berkowitz (ed.), *Advances in Experimental Social Psychology* (New York: Academic Press, 1965), pp. 267–300; and R.T. Mowday, "Equity Theory Predictions of Behavior in Organizations," in R. Steers and L.W. Porter, *Motivation and Work Behavior*, 6th ed. (New York: McGraw-Hill, 1996) pp. 111–131.

8. V. H. Vroom, *Work and Motivation* (New York: Wiley, 1964); and W. Van Eerde and H. Thierry, "Vroom's Expectancy Models and Work-Related Criteria: A Meta-Analysis," *Journal of Applied Psychology*, October 1996, pp. 575–86.

9. See, for instance, N.J. Adler, *International Dimension of Organizational Behavior*, 4th ed. (Cincinnati: Southwestern, 2002), pp. 174–82; C.P. Silverthorne, "Motivation and Management Styles in the Public and Private Sectors in Taiwan and a Comparison with the United States," *Journal of Applied Social Psychology*, December 1996, pp. 1827–37; and A. Sagie, D. Elizur, and H. Yamaguchi, "The Structure and Strength of Achievement Motivation: A Cross-Cultural Comparison," *Journal of Organizational Behavior*, September 1996, pp. 431–44.

CHAPTER 5

1. P.F. Drucker, *The Practice of Management* (New York: Harper & Row, 1954).

2. See, for instance, R. Rodgers and J.E. Hunter, "Impact of Management by Objectives on Organizational Productivity," *Journal of Applied Psychology*, April 1991, pp. 322–326; and R. Rodgers and J.E. Hunter, "A Foundation of Good Management Practice in Government: Management by Objectives," *Public Administration Review*, January–February 1992, pp. 27–39.

3. "At Emery Air Freight: Positive Reinforcement Boosts Performance," *Organizational Dynamics*, Winter 1973, pp. 41–50.

4. See F. Luthans and R. Kreitner, *Organizational Behavior Modification and Beyond: An Operant and Social Learning Approach* (Glenview, IL: Scott, Foresman, 1985); and A.D. Stajkovic and F. Luthans, "A Meta-Analysis of the Effects of Organizational Behavior Modification on Task Performance: 1975–95," *Academy of Management Journal*, October 1997, pp. 1122–1149.

5. F. Luthans and R. Kreitner, "The Management of Behavioral Contingencies," *Personnel*, July–August 1974, pp. 7–16.

6. See Luthans and Kreitner, *Organizational Behavior Modification and Beyond*, Chapter 8; and P.D. Champagne and R.B. McAfee, "Promoting Workplace Safety with Positive Reinforcement," *Performance Management*, vol. 13, no. 2 (1999): pp. 7–11.

7. A.D. Stajkovic and F. Luthans, "A Meta-Analysis of the Effects of Organizational Behavior Modification on Task Performance."

8. Cited in S. Caudron, "The Top 20 Ways to Motivate Employees," *Industry Week*, April 3, 1995, pp. 15–16. See also B. Nelson, "Try Praise," *INC.*, September 1996, p. 115.

9. G. Flynn, "Focus and Flexibility: Prudential's Rewards and Recognition Program in Action," *Workforce*, July 1998, p. 34.

10. "Look, Movie Tickets: With Budgets Tight, Alternatives to Pay Increases Emerge," *Wall Street Journal*, September 27, 1994, p. A1.

11. Cited in *Asian Business*, December 1994, p. 3.

12. J.L. Cotton, *Employee Involvement* (Newbury Park, CA: Sage, 1993), pp. 3, 14.

13. Ibid., p. 3.

14. M. Sashkin, "Participative Management Is an Ethical Imperative," *Organizational Dynamics*, Spring 1984, pp. 5–22.

15. R. Tannenbaum, I.R. Weschler, and F. Massarik, *Leadership and Organization: A Behavioral Science Approach* (New York: McGraw-Hill, 1961), pp. 88–100.

16. See K.L. Miller and P.R. Monge, "Participation, Satisfaction, and Productivity: A Meta-Analytic Review," *Academy of Management Journal*, December 1986, pp. 727–753; J.A. Wagner III, "Participation's Effects on Performance and Satisfaction: A Reconsideration of Research Evidence," *Academy of Management Review*, April 1994, pp. 312–20; and E.A. Locke, M. Alavi, and J.A. Wagner III, "Participation in Decision Making: An Information Exchange Perspective," in G.R. Ferris (ed.), *Research in Personnel and Human Resource Management*, vol. 15 (Greenwich, CT: JAI Press, 1997), pp. 293–331.

17. Cotton, *Employee Involvement*, p. 114.

18. Ibid., p. 140.

19. See, for example, "The Employee Ownership 100." <http://www.nceo.org/library/eo100.html> (June 2000); and L. Zuckerman, "Divided, An Airline Stumbles," *New York Times*, March 14, 2001, p. C1.

20. Cited in "ESOP Benefits Are No Fables," *Business Week*, September 6, 1999, p. 26.

21. "Employee Stock Ownership Plans." <http://www.nceo.org /esops/index.html> (August 2001).

22. Cited in E.E. Potter and A.U. Hattiangadi, "U.S. Wage and Productivity Growth Attainable Through Gainsharing." <http://www.epf.org/press> (March 16, 1998).

23. See Cotton, *Employee Involvement*, pp. 89–113; and W. Imberman, "Boosting Plan Performance with Gainsharing," *Business Horizons*, November–December 1992, p. 79.

24. W. Zellner, "Trickle-Down Is Trickling Down at Work," *Business Week*, March 18, 1996, p. 34; L. Carricaburu, "More Firms Are Linking Pay to Performance," *Salt Lake Tribune*, April 11, 1999; and "What's Wrong with Pay for Performance?" <http://www.home.ximb.ac> (June 17, 2000).

25. D. Beck, "Implementing a Gainsharing Plan: What Companies Need to Know," *Compensation & Benefits Review*, January–February 1992, p. 23.

26. E.E. Lawler III, G.E. Ledford, Jr., and L. Chang, "Who Uses Skill-Based Pay, and Why," *Compensation & Benefits Review*, March–April 1993, p. 22; and A. Podolske, "Seven-Year Update on Skill-Based Pay Plans." <http://www.ioma.com> (July 1999).

27. Cited in E.E. Lawler III, S.A. Mohrman, and G.E. Ledford, Jr., *Creating High Performance Organizations: Practices and Results in the Fortune 1000* (San Francisco: Jossey-Bass, 1995).

28. "Skill-Based Pay Boosts Worker Productivity and Morale," *Wall Street Journal*, June 23, 1992, p. A1.

29. M. Rowland, "It's What You Can Do That Counts," *New York Times*, June 6, 1993, p. F17.

CHAPTER 6

1. For a review of the rational model, see E.F. Harrison, *The Managerial Decision-Making Process*, 5th ed. (Boston: Houghton Mifflin, 1999), pp. 75–102.

2. C.G. Morris, *Psychology: An Introduction*, 9th ed. (Upper Saddle River, NJ: Prentice Hall, 1996), p. 344.

3. This section is based on T.M. Amabile, "Motivating Creativity in Organizations," *California Management Review*, Fall 1997, pp. 42–52.

4. R.W. Woodman, J.E. Sawyer, and R.W. Griffin, "Toward a Theory of Organizational Creativity," *Academy of Management Review*, April 1993, p. 298.

5. W.J.J. Gordon, *Synectics* (New York: Harper & Row, 1961).

6. Cited in T. Stevens, "Creativity Killers," *Industry Week*, January 23, 1995, p. 63.

7. M. Bazerman, *Judgment in Managerial Decision Making*, 3rd ed. (New York: Wiley, 1994), p. 5.

8. See H.A. Simon, *Administrative Behavior*, 3rd ed. (New York: Free Press, 1976); and J. Forester, "Bounded Rationality and the Politics of Muddling Through," *Public Administration Review*, January–February 1984, pp. 23–31.

9. W.H. Agor, ed., *Intuition in Organizations* (Newbury Park, CA: Sage, 1989); and O. Behling and N.L. Eckel, "Making Sense Out of Intuition," *Academy of Management Executive*, February 1991, pp. 46–47; G. Klein, *Sources of Power: How People Make Decisions* (Cambridge: MIT Press, 1998); and P.E. Ross, "Flash of Genius," *Forbes*, November 16, 1998, pp. 98-104.

10. As described in H.A. Simon, "Making Management Decisions: The Role of Intuition and Emotion," *Academy of Management Executive*, February 1987, pp. 59–60.

11. See, for example, M.D. Cohen, J.G. March, and J.P. Olsen, "A Garbage Can Model of Organizational Choice," *Administrative Science Quarterly*, March 1972, pp. 1–25.

12. See J.G. Thompson, *Organizations in Action* (New York: McGraw-Hill, 1967), p. 123.

13. C.E. Lindholm, "The Science of 'Muddling Through,'" *Public Administration Review*, Spring 1959, pp. 79–88.

14. A. Tversky and D. Kahneman, "Judgment Under Uncertainty: Heuristics and Biases," *Science*, September 1974, pp. 1124–31; and J.S. Hammond, R.L. Keeney, and H. Raiffa, "The Hidden Traps in Decision Making," *Harvard Business Review*, September-October 1998, pp. 47–58.

15. See B.M. Staw, "The Escalation of Commitment to a Course of Action," *Academy of Management Review*, October 1981, pp. 577–87; F.D. Schoorman and P.J. Holahan, "Psychological Antecedents of Escalation of Behavior: Effects of Choice, Responsibility, and Decision Consequences," *Journal of Applied Psychology*, December 1996, pp. 786–94; and H. Moon, "Looking Forward and Looking Back: Integrating Completion and Sunk-Cost Effects Within an Escalation-of-Commitment Progress Decision," *Journal of Applied Psychology*, February 2001, pp. 104–13.

16. A.J. Rowe, J.D. Boulgarides, and M.R. McGrath, *Managerial Decision Making, Modules in Management Series* (Chicago: SRA, 1984), pp. 18–22.

17. L. Kohlberg, *Essays in Moral Development: The Philosophy of Moral Development*, vol. 1 (New York: Harper & Row, 1981); and L. Kohlberg, *Essays in Moral Development: The Psychology of Moral Development*, vol. 2 (New York: Harper & Row, 1984).

18. See, for example, J. Weber, "Managers' Moral Reasoning: Assessing Their Responses to Three Moral Dilemmas," *Human Relations*, July 1990, pp. 687–702; and S.B. Knouse and R.A. Giacalone, "Ethical Decision-Making in Business: Behavioral Issues and Concerns," *Journal of Business Ethics*, May 1992, pp. 369–77.

19. S.N. Chakravarty and A. Feldman, "The Road Not Taken," *Forbes*, August 30, 1993, pp. 40–41.

20. A. Wildavsky, *The Politics of the Budgetary Process* (Boston: Little, Brown & Co., 1964).

21. N.J. Adler, *International Dimensions of Organizational Behavior*, 4th ed. (Cincinnati: Southwestern, 2002), pp. 182–89.

22. G.F. Cavanagh, D.J. Moberg, and M. Valasquez, "The Ethics of Organizational Politics," *Academy of Management Journal*, June 1981, pp. 363–74.

CHAPTER 7

1. See, for example, R.K. Merton, *Social Theory and Social Structure* (New York: Free Press, 1968); S.E. Jackson and R.S. Schuler, "A Meta-Analysis and Conceptual Critique of Research on Role Ambiguity and Role Conflict in Work Settings," *Organizational Behavior and Human Decision Processes*, August 1985, pp. 16–78; Y. Fried, H.A. Ben-David, R.B. Tiegs, N. Avital, and U. Yeverechyahu, "The Interactive Effect of Role Conflict and Role Ambiguity on Job Performance," *Journal of Occupational and Organizational Psychology*, March 1998, pp. 19–27; and T.C. Tubre and J.M. Collins, "Jackson and Schuler (1985) Revisited: A Meta-Analysis of the Relationships Between Role Ambiguity, Role Conflict, and Job Performance," *Journal of Management*, vol. 26, no. 1, 2000, pp. 155–69.

2. D.C. Feldman, "The Development and Enforcement of Group Norms," *Academy of Management Review*, January 1984, pp. 47–53; and J.R. Hackman, "Group Influences on Individuals in Organizations," pp. 235–50 in M.D. Dunnette and L.M. Hough (eds.), *Handbook of Industrial and Organizational Psychology*, vol. 3, 2nd ed. (Palo Alto, CA: Consulting Psychologists Press, 1992), pp. 235–250.

3. E. Mayo, *The Human Problems of an Industrial Civilization* (New York: Macmillan, 1933); and F.J. Roethlisberger and W.J. Dickson, *Management and the Worker* (Cambridge, MA: Harvard University Press, 1939).

4. S.E. Asch, "Effects of Group Pressure upon the Modification and Distortion of Judgments," in H. Guetzkow (ed.), *Groups, Leadership and Men*. (Pittsburgh: Carnegie Press, 1951) pp. 177–190.

5. I. Summers, T. Coffelt, and R.E. Horton, "Work-Group Cohesion," *Psychological Reports*, October 1988, pp. 627–36; and B. Mullen and C. Copper, "The Relation between Group Cohesiveness and Performance: An Integration," *Psychological Bulletin*, March 1994, pp. 210–27.

6. Based on J.L. Gibson, J.M. Ivancevich, and J.H. Donnelly, Jr., *Organizations*, 8th ed. (Burr Ridge, IL: Irwin, 1994), p. 323.

7. E.J. Thomas and C.F. Fink, "Effects of Group Size," *Psychological Bulletin*, July 1963, pp. 371–84; A.P. Hare, *Handbook of Small Group Research* (New York: Free Press, 1976); and M.E. Shaw, *Group Dynamics: The Psychology of Small Group Behavior*, 3rd ed. (New York: McGraw Hill, 1981).

8. W. Moede, "Die Richtlinien der Leistungs-Psychologie," *Industrielle Psychotechnik* 4 (1927): pp. 193–207. See also D.A. Kravitz and B. Martin, "Ringelmann Rediscovered: The Original Article," *Journal of Personality and Social Psychology*, May 1986, pp. 936–41.

9. See, for example, J.A. Shepperd, "Productivity Loss in Performance Groups: A Motivation Analysis," *Psychological Bulletin*, January 1993, pp. 67–81; S.J. Karau and K.D. Williams, "Social Loafing: A Meta-Analysis Review and Theoretical Integration," *Journal of Personality and Social Psychology*, October 1993, pp. 681–706; and P.W. Mulvey and H.J. Klein, "The Impact of Perceived Loafing and Collective Efficacy on Group Goal Processes and Group Performance," *Organizational Behavior and Human Decision Processes*, April 1998, pp. 62–87.

10. See, for example, S.E. Jackson, K.E. May, and K. Whitney, "Understanding the Dynamics of Diversity in Decision-Making Teams," in R.A. Guzzo and E. Salas (eds.), *Team Effectiveness and Decision Making in Organizations* (San Francisco: Jossey-Bass, 1995), pp. 204–61; K.Y. Williams and C.A. O'Reilly III, "Demography and Diversity in Organizations: A Review of 40 Years of Research," in B.M. Staw and L.L. Cummings (eds.), *Research in Organizational Behavior*, vol. 20 (Greenwich, CT: JAI Press, 1998), pp. 77–140; and F. Linnehan and A.M. Konrad, "Diluting Diversity," *Journal of Management Inquiry*, December 1999, pp. 399–414.

11. M.E. Shaw, *Contemporary Topics in Social Psychology* (Morristown, NJ: General Learning Press, 1976), p. 356.

12. W.E. Watson, K. Kumar, and L.K. Michaelsen, "Cultural Diversity's Impact on Interaction Process and Performance: Comparing Homogeneous and Diverse Task Groups," *Academy of Management Journal*, June 1993, pp. 590–602.

13. C.A. O'Reilly III, D.F. Caldwell, and W.P. Barnett, "Work Group Demography, Social Integration, and Turnover," *Administrative Science Quarterly*, March 1989, pp. 21–37; S.E. Jackson, J.F. Brett, V.I. Sessa, D.M. Cooper, J.A. Julin, and K. Peyronnin, "Some Differences Make a Difference: Individual Dissimilarity and Group Heterogeneity as Correlates of Recruitment, Promotions, and Turnover," *Journal of Applied Psychology*, August 1991, pp. 675–89; F.J. Milliken and L.L. Martins, "Searching for Common Threads: Understanding the Multiple Effects of Diversity in Organizational Groups," *Academy of Management Review*, April 1996, pp. 402–33; B. Lawrence, "The Black Box of Organizational Demography," *Organizational Science*, February 1997, pp. 1–22; J.B. Sorensen, "The Longitudinal Effects of Group Tenure Composition on Turnover," *American Sociological Review*, April 2000, pp. 298–310; and G.R. Carroll and M.T. Hannan, "Why Corporate Demography Matters: Policy Implications of Organizational Diversity," *California Management Review*, Spring 2000, pp. 148–62.

14. Cited in J.R. Hackman, "Group Influences on Individuals in Organizations," in M.D. Dunnette and L.M. Hough (eds.), *Handbook of Industrial & Organizational Psychology*, 2nd ed., vol. 3 (Palo Alto, CA: Consulting Psychologists Press, 1992), p. 236.

15. O.J. Harvey and C. Consalvi, "Status and Conformity to Pressures in Informal Groups," *Journal of Abnormal and Social Psychology*, Spring 1960, pp. 182–87.

16. J.A. Wiggins, F. Dill, and R.D. Schwartz, "On 'Status-Liability,'" *Sociometry*, April-May 1965, pp. 197–209.

17. J. Greenberg, "Equity and Workplace Status: A Field Experiment," *Journal of Applied Psychology*, November 1988, pp. 606–13.

18. V.H. Vroom and A.G. Jago, *The New Leadership: Managing Participation in Organizations* (Upper Saddle River, NJ: Prentice Hall, 1988).

19. See I.L. Janis, *Groupthink* (Boston: Houghton Mifflin, 1982); S. Smith, "Groupthink and the Hostage Rescue Mission," *British Journal of Political Science* 15 (1984), pp. 117–23; G. Moorhead, R. Ference, and C.P. Neck, "Group Decision Fiascoes Continue: Space Shuttle Challenger and a Revised Framework," *Human Relations*, May 1991, pp. 539–50; and J.N. Choi and M.U. Kim, "The Organizational Application of Groupthink and Its Limits in Organizations," *Journal of Applied Psychology*, April 1999, pp. 297–306.

20. G. Moorhead and J.R. Montanari, "An Empirical Investigation of the Groupthink Phenomenon," *Human Relations*, May 1986, pp. 399–410; and C.P. Neck and G. Moorhead, "Groupthink Remodeled: The Importance of Leadership, Time Pressure, and Methodical Decision-Making Procedures," *Human Relations*, May 1995, pp. 537–57.

21. See, for example, N. Kogan and M.A. Wallach, "Risk Taking as a Function of the Situation, the Person, and the Group," in *New Directions in Psychology*, vol. 3 (New York: Holt, Rinehart and Winston, 1967); and M.A. Wallach, N. Kogan, and D.J. Bem, "Group Influence on Individual Risk Taking," *Journal of Abnormal and Social Psychology* 65 (1962), pp. 75–86.

22. S.G. Harkins and K. Szymanski, "Social Loafing and Group Evaluation," *Journal of Personality and Social Psychology*, December 1989, pp. 934–41.

23. See P.C. Earley, "Social Loafing and Collectivism: A Comparison of the United States and the People's Republic of China," *Administrative Science Quarterly*, December 1989, pp. 565–581; and P.C. Earley, "East Meets West Meets Mideast: Further Explorations of Collectivistic and Individualistic Work Groups," *Academy of Management Journal*, April 1993, pp. 319–48.

CHAPTER 8

1. Based on W. Royal, "Team-Centered Success," *Industry Week*, October 18, 1999, pp. 56–58.

2. Cited in C. Joinson, "Teams at Work," *HRMagazine*, May 1999, p. 30.

3. See, for example, D. Tjosvold, *Team Organization: An Enduring Competitive Advantage* (Chichester, England: Wiley, 1991); J.R. Katzenbach and D.K. Smith, *The Wisdom of Teams* (Boston: Harvard Business School Press, 1993); S.A. Mohrman, S.G. Cohen, and A.M. Mohrman, Jr., *Team-Based Organizations* (San Francisco: Jossey-Bass, 1995); and B.L. Kirkman and B. Rosen, "Powering Up Teams," *Organizational Dynamics*, Winter 2000, pp. 48–66.

4. See, for example, "Teams," *Training*, October 1996, p. 69; and C. Joinson, "Teams at Work".

5. D. Drickhamer, "People-Powered Change," *Industry Week*, October 18, 1999, pp. 76–78.

6. G. Hasek, "The Right Chemistry," *Industry Week*, March 6, 2000, pp. 36–39.

7. C. Dahle, "Extreme Teams," *Fast Company*, November 1999, pp. 310–26.

8. See, for instance, J.L. Cordery, W.S. Mueller, and L.M. Smith, "Attitudinal and Behavioral Effects of Autonomous Group Working: A Longitudinal Field Study," *Academy of Management Journal*, June 1991, pp. 464–76; and P.S. Goodman, R. Davadas, and T.L. Griffith Hughson, "Groups and Productivity: Analyzing the Effectiveness of Self-Managing Teams," in J.P. Campbell, R.J. Campbell, and Associates (eds.), *Productivity in Organizations* (San Francisco: Jossey-Bass, 1988), pp. 295–327

9. R. Maynard, "A Client-Centered Firm's Lessons in Teamwork," *Nation's Business*, March 1997, p. 32.

10. M. Brunelli, "How Harley-Davidson Uses Cross-Functional Teams," *Purchasing Online* <http://www.manufacturing.net/magazine/purchasing/archives/1999> (November 4, 1999).

11. S. Kirsner, "Faster Company," *Fast Company*, May 2000, pp. 162–72.

12. See, for example, A.M. Townsend, S.M. DeMarie, and A.R. Hendrickson, "Virtual Teams: Technology and the Workplace of the Future," *Academy of Management Executive*, August 1998, pp. 17-29; D. Duarte and N.T. Snyder, *Mastering Virtual Teams: Strategies, Tools, and Techniques* (San Francisco: Jossey-Bass, 1999); and K. Kiser, "Working on World Time," *Training*, March 1999, pp. 29–33.

13. K. Kiser, "Working on World Time," p. 30.

14. This model is based on M.A. Campion, E.M. Papper, and G.J. Medsker, "Relations Between Work Team Characteristics and Effectiveness: A Replication and Extension," *Personnel Psychology*, Summer 1996, pp. 429–52; D.E. Hyatt and T.M. Ruddy, "An Examination of the Relationship Between Work Group Characteristics and Performance: Once More into the Breach," *Personnel Psychology*, Autumn 1997, pp. 553–85; S.G. Cohen and D.E. Bailey, "What Makes Teams Work: Group Effectiveness Research from the Shop Floor to the Executive Suite," *Journal of Management*, vol. 23, no. 3 (1997), pp. 239–90; A.D. Shulman, "Putting Group Information Technology in Its Place: Communication and Good Work Group Performance," in S.R. Clegg, C. Hardy, and W.R. Nord (eds.), *Managing Organizations: Current Issues* (London: Sage, 1999), pp. 107–21; G.A. Neuman and J. Wright, "Team Effectiveness: Beyond Skills and Cognitive Ability," *Journal of Applied Psychology*, June 1999, pp. 376–89; P.J. Hinds, K.M. Carley, D. Krackhardt, and D. Wholey, "Choosing Work Group Members: Balancing Similarity, Competence, and Familiarity," *Organizational Behavior and Human Decision Processes*, March 2000, pp. 226–51; and J. Katzenbach, "What Makes Teams Work?" *Fast Company*, November 2000, pp. 109–42.

15. M.A. Campion, E.M. Papper, and G.J. Medsker, "Relations Between Work Team Characteristics and Effectiveness," p. 430.

16. This section is based on M.R. Barrick, G.L. Stewart, M.J. Neubert, and M.K. Mount, "Relating Member Ability and Personality to Work-Team Processes and Team Effectiveness," *Journal of Applied Psychology*, June 1998, pp. 377–91.

17. C. Margerison and D. McCann, *Team Management: Practical New Approaches* (London: Mercury Books, 1990).

18. D.E. Hyatt and T.M. Ruddy, "An Examination of the Relationship Between Work Group Characteristics and Performance," p. 577.

19. R.I. Beekun, "Assessing the Effectiveness of Sociotechnical Interventions: Antidote or Fad?" *Human Relations*, August 1989, pp. 877–97.

20. D. Harrington-Mackin, *The Team Building Tool Kit* (New York: AMACOM, 1994), p. 53.

21. T.D. Schellhardt, "To Be a Star Among Equals, Be a Team Player," *Wall Street Journal*, April 20, 1994, p. B1.

22. C. Hymowitz, "How to Avoid Hiring the Prima Donnas Who Hate Teamwork," *Wall Street Journal*, February 15, 2000, p. B1.

CHAPTER 9

1. See, for example, K.W. Thomas and W.H. Schmidt, "A Survey of Managerial Interests with Respect to Conflict," *Academy of Management Journal*, June 1976, p. 317.

2. See J. Ritter, "Poor Fluency in English Means Mixed

Signals," *USA Today*, January 18, 1996, p. 1A; and A. Kotarumalos, "Pilot Confused Before Deadly Jetliner Crash," *Seattle Post-Intelligencer*, September 30, 1997, p. A2.

3. Cited in "Heard It Through the Grapevine," *Forbes*, February 10, 1997, p. 22.

4. K. Davis, "Management Communication and the Grapevine," *Harvard Business Review*, September–October 1953, pp. 43–49.

5. H. Sutton and L.W. Porter, "A Study of the Grapevine in a Governmental Organization," *Personnel Psychology*, Summer 1968, pp. 223–30.

6. K. Davis, cited in R. Rowan, "Where Did That Rumor Come From?" *Fortune*, August 13, 1979, p. 134.

7. S. Amour, "Boss: It's in the E-Mail," *USA Today*, August 10, 1999, p. 3B.

8. "Ford to Offer Employees Home PCs for $5 a Month." <http://www.informationweek.com> (February 3, 2000).

9. D. Tannen, *You Just Don't Understand: Women and Men in Conversation* (New York: Ballantine Books, 1991); and D. Tannen, *Talking from 9 to 5* (New York: William Morrow, 1995).

10. See E.T. Hall and M.R. Hall, *Understanding Cultural Differences* (Yarmouth, ME: Intercultural Press, 1990); R.E. Dulek, J.S. Fielden, and J.S. Hill, "International Communication: An Executive Primer," *Business Horizons*, January–February 1991, pp. 20–25; and M. Munter, "Cross-Cultural Communication for Managers," *Business Horizons*, May–June 1993, pp. 69–78.

11. This section is based on N.J. Adler, *International Dimensions of Organizational Behavior*, 4th ed. (Cincinnati: Southwestern, 2002), pp. 94–96.

CHAPTER 10

1. S.A. Kirkpatrick and E.A. Locke, "Leadership: Do Traits Matter?" *Academy of Management Executive*, May 1991, pp. 48–60.

2. R.M. Stogdill and A.E. Coons, eds., *Leader Behavior: Its Description and Measurement*, Research Monograph No. 88 (Columbus: Ohio State University, Bureau of Business Research, 1951). This research is updated in C.A. Schriesheim, C.C. Cogliser, and L.L. Neider, "Is It Trustworthy? A Multiple-Levels-of-Analysis Reexamination of an Ohio State Leadership Study, with Implications for Future Research," *Leadership Quarterly*, Summer 1995, pp. 111–45.

3. R. Kahn and D. Katz, "Leadership Practices in Relation to Productivity and Morale," in D. Cartwright and A. Zander (eds.), *Group Dynamics: Research and Theory*, 2nd ed. (Elmsford, NY: Row, Peterson, 1960).

4. R.R. Blake and J.S. Mouton, *The Managerial Grid* (Houston: Gulf, 1964).

5. See, for example, L.L. Larson, J.G. Hunt, and R.N. Osborn, "The Great Hi-Hi Leader Behavior Myth: A Lesson from Occam's Razor," *Academy of Management Journal*, December 1976, pp. 628–641; and P.C. Nystrom, "Managers and the Hi-Hi Leader Myth," *Academy of Management Journal*, June 1978, pp. 325–31.

6. F.E. Fiedler, *A Theory of Leadership Effectiveness* (New York: McGraw-Hill, 1967).

7. Cited in R.J. House and R.N. Aditya, "The Social Scientific Study of Leadership: Quo Vadis?" *Journal of Management* 23, no. 3 (1997), p. 422.

8. C.A. Schriesheim, B.J. Tepper, and L.A. Tetrault, "Least Preferred Co-Worker Score, Situational Control, and Leadership Effectiveness: A Meta-Analysis of Contingency Model Performance Predictions," *Journal of Applied Psychology*, August 1994, pp. 561–73; and R. Ayman, M.M. Chemers, and F. Fiedler, "The Contingency Model of Leadership Effectiveness: Its Levels of Analysis," *Leadership Quarterly*, Summer 1995, pp. 147–67.

9. G.B. Graen and M. Uhl-Bien, "Relationship-Based Approach to Leadership: Development of Leader-Member Exchange (LMX) Theory of Leadership over 25 Years: Applying a Multi-Domain Perspective," *Leadership Quarterly*, Summer 1995, pp. 219–47; T.N. Bauer and S.G. Green, "Development of Leader-Member Exchange: A Longitudinal Test," *Academy of Management Journal*, December 1996, pp. 1538–67; C.R. Gerstner and D.V. Day, "Meta-Analytic Review of Leader-Member Exchange Theory: Correlates and Construct Issues," *Journal of Applied Psychology*, December 1997, pp. 827–44; and C.C. Cogliser and C.A. Schriesheim, "Exploring Work Unit Context and Leader-Member Exchange: A Multi-Level Perspective," *Journal of Organizational Behavior*, August 2000, pp. 487–511.

10. R.J. House, "A Path-Goal Theory of Leader Effectiveness," *Administrative Science Quarterly*, September 1971, pp. 321–38; and R.J. House, "Path-Goal Theory of Leadership: Lessons, Legacy, and a Reformulated Theory," *Leadership Quarterly*, Fall 1996, pp. 323–52.

11. See J.C. Wofford and L.Z. Liska, "Path-Goal Theories of Leadership: A Meta-Analysis," *Journal of Management*, Winter 1993, pp. 857–76.

12. V.H. Vroom and P.W. Yetton, *Leadership and Decision Making* (Pittsburgh: University of Pittsburgh Press, 1973).

13. V.H. Vroom and A.G. Jago, *The New Leadership: Managing Participation in Organizations* (Upper Saddle River, NJ: Prentice Hall, 1988). See also V.H. Vroom and A.G. Jago, "Situation Effects and Levels of Analysis in the Study of Leader Participation," *Leadership Quarterly*, Summer 1995, pp. 169–81.

14. The material in this section is based on J. Grant, "Women as Managers: What They Can Offer to Organizations," *Organizational Dynamics*, Winter 1988, pp. 56–63; S. Helgesen, *The Female Advantage: Women's Ways of Leadership* (New York: Doubleday, 1990); A.H. Eagly and B.T. Johnson, "Gender and Leadership Style: A Meta-Analysis," *Psychological Bulletin*, September 1990, pp. 233–256; A.H. Eagly and S.J. Karau, "Gender and the Emergence of Leaders: A Meta-Analysis," *Journal of*

Personality and Social Psychology, May 1991, pp. 685–710; A.H. Eagly, M.G. Makhijani, and B.G. Klonsky, "Gender and the Evaluation of Leaders: A Meta-Analysis," *Psychological Bulletin*, January 1992, pp. 3–22; J.B. Rosener, *America's Competitive Secret: Women Managers* (New York: Oxford University Press, 1995); R. Sharpe, "As Leaders, Women Rule," *Business Week*, November 20, 2000, pp. 75-84; and "Are Women Better Leaders?" *U.S. News & World Report*, January 29, 2001, p. 10.

15. J.A. Conger and R.N. Kanungo, "Behavioral Dimensions of Charismatic Leadership," pp. 78–97 in J.A. Conger, R.N. Kanungo, and associates (eds.), *Charismatic Leadership* (San Francisco: Jossey-Bass, 1988); and J.A. Conger, "Charismatic and Transformational Leadership in Organizations: An Insider's Perspective on These Developing Streams of Research," *Leadership Quarterly*, Summer 1999, pp. 145–79.

16. R.J. House, J. Woycke, and E.M. Fodor, "Charismatic and Noncharismatic Leaders: Differences in Behavior and Effectiveness," in Conger, Kanungo, and associates (eds.), *Charismatic Leadership*, pp. 103–104; and D.A. Waldman, B.M. Bass, and F.J. Yammarino, "Adding to Contingent-Reward Behavior: The Augmenting Effect of Charismatic Leadership," *Group & Organization Studies*, December 1990, pp. 381–94.

17. J.M. Howell and P.J. Frost, "A Laboratory Study of Charismatic Leadership," *Organizational Behavior and Human Decision Processes*, April 1989, pp. 243–69.

18. This definition is based on M. Sashkin, "The Visionary Leader," in J.A. Conger and R.N. Kanungo (eds.), *Charismatic Leadership*, pp. 124–25; B. Nanus, *Visionary Leadership* (New York: Free Press, 1992), p. 8; N.H. Snyder and M. Graves, "Leadership and Vision," *Business Horizons*, January–February 1994, 1; and J.R. Lucas, "Anatomy of a Vision Statement," *Management Review*, February 1998, pp. 22–26.

19. B. Nanus, *Visionary Leadership*, p. 8.

20. P.C. Nutt and R.W. Backoff, "Crafting Vision," *Journal of Management Inquiry*, December 1997, p. 309.

21. Based on M. Sashkin, "The Visionary Leader," pp. 128–30; and J.R. Baum, E.A. Locke, and S.A. Kirkpatrick, "A Longitudinal Study of the Relation of Vision and Vision Communication to Venture Growth in Entrepreneurial Firms," *Journal of Applied Psychology*, February 1998, pp. 43–54.

22. S. Caminiti, "What Team Leaders Need to Know," *Fortune*, February 20, 1995, p. 93.

23. Ibid., p. 100.

24. R.S. Wellins, W.C. Byham, and G.R. Dixon, *Inside Teams* (San Francisco: Jossey-Bass, 1994), p. 318.

25. N. Steckler and N. Fondas, "Building Team Leader Effectiveness: A Diagnostic Tool," *Organizational Dynamics*, Winter 1995, p. 21.

26. See, for instance, S. Kerr and J.M. Jermier, "Substitutes for Leadership: Their Meaning and Measurement," *Organizational Behavior and Human Performance*, December 1978, pp. 375–403; P.M. Podsakoff, S.B. MacKenzie, and W.H. Bommer, "Meta-Analysis of the Relationships Between Kerr and Jermier's Substitutes for Leadership and Employee Attitudes, Role Perceptions, and Performance," *Journal of Applied Psychology*, August 1996, pp. 380-99; J.M. Jermier and S. Kerr, "Substitutes for Leadership: Their Meaning and Measurement—Contextual Recollections and Current Observations," *Leadership Quarterly* 8, no. 2 (1997), pp. 95–101; and D.A. Waldman, G.R. Ramirez, R.J. House, and P. Puranam, "Does Leadership Matter? CEO Leadership Attributes and Profitability Under Conditions of Perceived Environmental Uncertainty," *Academy of Management Journal*, February 2001, pp. 134–43.

27. Based on S.D. Boon and J.G. Holmes, "The Dynamics of Interpersonal Trust: Resolving Uncertainty in the Face of Risk," in R.A. Hinde and J. Groebel (eds.), *Cooperation and Prosocial Behavior* (Cambridge, UK: Cambridge University Press, 1991), p. 194; D.J. McAllister, "Affect- and Cognition-Based Trust as Foundations for Interpersonal Cooperation in Organizations," *Academy of Management Journal*, February 1995, p. 25; and D.M. Rousseau, S.B. Sitkin, R.S. Burt, and C. Camerer, "Not So Different After All: A Cross-Discipline View of Trust," *Academy of Management Review*, July 1998, pp. 393–404.

28. P.L. Schindler and C.C. Thomas, "The Structure of Interpersonal Trust in the Workplace," *Psychological Reports*, October 1993, pp. 563–73.

29. J.K. Butler, Jr., and R.S. Cantrell, "A Behavioral Decision Theory Approach to Modeling Dyadic Trust in Superiors and Subordinates," *Psychological Reports*, August 1984, pp. 19–28.

30. D. McGregor, *The Professional Manager* (New York: McGraw-Hill, 1967), p. 164.

31. B. Nanus, *The Leader's Edge: The Seven Keys to Leadership in a Turbulent World* (Chicago: Contemporary Books, 1989), p. 102.

32. See K.T. Dirks, "Trust in Leadership and Team Performance: Evidence From NCAA Basketball," *Journal of Applied Psychology*, December 2000, pp. 1004–1012; and K. T. Dirks and D.L. Ferrin, "The Effects of Trust in Leadership on Employee Performance, Behavior, and Attitudes: A Meta-Analysis," paper presented at the Academy of Management Conference; Toronto; August 2000.

33. J.M. Kouzes and B.Z. Posner, *Credibility* (San Francisco: Jossey-Bass, 1993), p. 14.

34. This section is based on D. Shapiro, B.H. Sheppard, and L. Cheraskin, "Business on a Handshake," *Negotiation Journal*, October 1992, pp. 365–77; R.J. Lewicki and B.B. Bunker, "Developing and Maintaining Trust in Work Relationships," in R.M. Kramer and T.R. Tyler (eds.), *Trust in Organizations* (Thousand Oaks, CA: Sage, 1996), pp. 119–24; and R.M. Kramer, "Trust and Distrust in Organizations: Emerging Perspectives, Enduring Questions," in J.T. Spence, J.M. Darley, and D.J. Foss,

eds., *Annual Review of Psychology*, vol. 50 (Palo Alto, CA: Annual Reviews, 1999), pp. 575–81.

35. This section is based on F. Bartolome, "Nobody Trusts the Boss Completely—Now What?" *Harvard Business Review*, March–April 1989, pp. 135–42; J.K. Butler. Jr., "Toward Understanding and Measuring Conditions of Trust: Evolution of a Condition of Trust Inventory," *Journal of Management*, September 1991, pp. 643–63; and R. Zemke, "Can You Manage Trust?" *Training*, February 2000, pp. 76–83.

CHAPTER 11

1. R.M. Kanter, "Power Failure in Management Circuits," *Harvard Business Review*, July–August 1979, p. 65.

2. J.R.P. French, Jr., and B. Raven, "The Bases of Social Power," in D. Cartwright (ed.), *Studies in Social Power* (Ann Arbor: University of Michigan, Institute for Social Research, 1959), pp. 150–167.

3. D. Kipnis, *The Powerholders* (Chicago: University of Chicago Press, 1976), pp. 77–78.

4. R.E. Emerson, "Power-Dependence Relations," *American Sociological Review* 27 (1962), pp. 31–41.

5. H. Mintzberg, *Power In and Around Organizations* (Upper Saddle River, NJ: Prentice Hall, 1983), p. 24.

6. This discussion is based on J.N. Cleveland and M.E. Kerst, "Sexual Harassment and Perceptions of Power: An Under-Articulated Relationship," *Journal of Vocational Behavior*, February 1993, pp. 49–67. See also A.M. O'Leary-Kelly, R.L. Paetzold, and R.W. Griffin, "Sexual Harassment as Aggressive Behavior: An Actor-Based Perspective," *Academy of Management Review*, April 2000, pp. 372–88.

7. D.J. Vredenburgh and J.G. Maurer, "A Process Framework of Organizational Politics," *Human Relations*, January 1984, pp. 47–66.

8. D. Farrell and J.C. Petersen, "Patterns of Political Behavior in Organizations," *Academy of Management Review*, July 1982, p. 405. For a discussion of the controversies underlying the definition of organizational politics, see R.S. Cropanzano, K.M. Kacmar, and D.P. Bozeman, "Organizational Politics, Justice, and Support: Their Differences and Similarities," in R.S. Cropanzano and K.M. Kacmar (eds.), *Organizational Politics, Justice and Support: Managing Social Climate at Work* (Westport, CT: Quorum Books, 1995), pp. 1–18.

9. See, for example, G. Biberman, "Personality and Characteristic Work Attitudes of Persons with High, Moderate, and Low Political Tendencies," *Psychological Reports*, October 1985, pp. 1303–10; G.R. Ferris, G.S. Russ, and P.M. Fandt, "Politics in Organizations," in R.A. Giacalone and P. Rosenfeld, *Impression Management in the Organization* (Hillsdale, NJ: Erlbaum, 1989), pp. 155–56; and K.M. Kacmar, D.P. Bozeman, D.S. Carlson, and W.P. Anthony, "An Examination of the Perceptions of Organizational Politics Model: Replication and Extension," *Human Relations*, March 1999, pp. 383–416.

10. See, for example, Farrell and Petersen, "Patterns of Political Behavior in Organizations," p. 409; P.M. Fandt and G.R. Ferris, "The Management of Information and Impressions: When Employees Behave Opportunistically," *Organizational Behavior and Human Decision Processes*, February 1990, pp. 140–58; and Ferris, Russ, and Fandt, "Politics in Organizations," p. 147.

11. See, for instance, B.R. Schlenker, *Impression Management: The Self-Concept, Social Identity, and Interpersonal Relations* (Monterey, CA: Brooks/Cole, 1980); D.C. Gilmore and G.R. Ferris, "The Effects of Applicant Impression Management Tactics on Interviewer Judgments," *Journal of Management*, December 1989, pp. 557–64; and C.K. Stevens and A.L. Kristof, "Making the Right Impression: A Field Study of Applicant Impression Management During Job Interviews," *Journal of Applied Psychology*, October 1995, pp. 587–606.

12. Based on Schlenker, *Impression Management*; W.L. Gardner and M.J. Martinko, "Impression Management in Organizations," *Journal of Management*, June 1988, p. 332; and R.B. Cladini, "Indirect Tactics of Image Management: Beyond Basking," pp. 45–71 in Giacalone and Rosenfeld, *Impression Management in the Organization*.

13. R.A. Baron, "Impression Management by Applicants during Employment Interviews: The 'Too Much of a Good Thing' Effect," in R.W. Eder and G.R. Ferris, *The Employment Interview: Theory, Research, and Practice* (Newbury Park, CA: Sage, 1989), pp. 204–15; Gilmore and Ferris, "The Effects of Applicant Impression Management Tactics on Interviewer Judgments"; and A.L. Kristof and C.K. Stevens, "Applicant Impression Management Tactics: Effects on Interviewer Evaluations and Interview Outcomes," in D.P. Moore (ed.), *Proceedings of the National Academy of Management Conference* Dallas, August 1994, pp. 127–31.

14. Gilmore and Ferris, "The Effects of Applicant Impression Management Tactics on Interviewer Judgments."

15. G.F. Cavanagh, D.J. Moberg, and M. Valasquez, "The Ethics of Organizational Politics," *Academy of Management Review*, July 1981, pp. 363–74.

CHAPTER 12

1. S.P. Robbins, *Managing Organizational Conflict: A Nontraditional Approach* (Upper Saddle River, NJ: Prentice Hall, 1974).

2. See K.A. Jehn, "A Multimethod Examination of the Benefits and Detriments of Intragroup Conflict," *Administrative Science Quarterly*, June 1995, pp. 256–82; T.L. Simons and R.S. Peterson, "Task Conflict and Relationship Conflict in Top Management Teams: The Pivotal Role of Intragroup Trust," *Journal of Applied Psychology*, February 2000, pp. 102–11; and K.A. Jehn and E.A. Mannix, "The Dynamic Nature of Conflict: A Longitudinal Study of Intragroup Conflict and Group Performance," *Academy of Management Journal*, April 2001, pp. 238–51.

3. This section is based on Robbins, *Managing Organizational Conflict*, pp. 31–55.

4. K.W. Thomas, "Conflict and Negotiation Processes in Organizations," in M.D. Dunnette and L.M. Hough (eds.), *Handbook of Industrial and Organizational Psychology*, vol. 3, 2nd ed. (Palo Alto, CA: Consulting Psychologists Press, 1992), pp. 651–717.

5. See, for instance, C.J. Loomis, "Dinosaurs?" *Fortune*, May 3, 1993, pp. 36–42.

6. I.L. Janis, *Victims of Groupthink* (Boston: Houghton Mifflin, 1972).

7. J. Hall and M.S. Williams, "A Comparison of Decision-Making Performances in Established and Ad-Hoc Groups," *Journal of Personality and Social Psychology*, February 1966, p. 217.

8. R.L. Hoffman, "Homogeneity of Member Personality and Its Effect on Group Problem Solving," *Journal of Abnormal and Social Psychology*, January 1959, pp. 27–32; R.L. Hoffman and N.R.F. Maier, "Quality and Acceptance of Problem Solutions by Members of Homogeneous and Heterogeneous Groups," *Journal of Abnormal and Social Psychology*, March 1961, pp. 401–07.

9. M. Geyelin and E. Felsenthal, "Irreconcilable Differences Force Shea & Gould Closure," *Wall Street Journal*, January 31, 1994, p. B1.

10. J.A. Wall, Jr., *Negotiation: Theory and Practice* (Glenview, IL: Scott, Foresman, 1985).

11. R.E. Walton and R.B. McKersie, *A Behavioral Theory of Labor Negotiations: An Analysis of a Social Interaction System* (New York: McGraw-Hill, 1965).

12. M.H. Bazerman and M.A. Neale, *Negotiating Rationally* (New York: Free Press, 1992), pp. 67–68.

13. J.A. Wall, Jr., and M.W. Blum, "Negotiations," *Journal of Management*, June 1991, pp. 276–78.

14. See N.J. Adler, *International Dimensions of Organizational Behavior*, 4th ed. (Cincinnati: Southwestern, 2002), pp. 208–56; and M.Y. Brannen and J.E. Salk, "Partnering Across Borders: Negotiating Organizational Culture in a German-Japanese Joint Venture," *Human Relations*, April 2000, pp. 451–87.

15. K.D. Schmidt, *Doing Business in France* (Menlo Park, CA: SRI International, 1987).

16. S. Lubman, "Round and Round," *Wall Street Journal*, December 10, 1993, p. R3.

17. E.S. Glenn, D. Witmeyer, and K.A. Stevenson, "Cultural Styles of Persuasion," *Journal of Intercultural Relations*, Fall 1977, pp. 52–66.

18. J. Graham, "The Influence of Culture on Business Negotiations," *Journal of International Business Studies*, Spring 1985, pp. 81–96.

19. K.W. Thomas, "Toward Multidimensional Values in Teaching: The Example of Conflict Behaviors," *Academy of Management Review*, July 1977, p. 487.

20. Based on R. Fisher and W. Ury, *Getting to Yes: Negotiating Agreement without Giving In* (Boston: Houghton Mifflin, 1981); Wall and Blum, "Negotiations," pp. 295–96; and Bazerman and Neale, *Negotiating Rationally*.

CHAPTER 13

1. See, for instance, R.L. Daft, *Organization Theory & Design*, 7th ed. (Cincinnati: Southwestern, 2001).

2. T. Stevens, "Breaking Up Is Profitable to Do," *Industry Week*, June 21, 1999, pp. 28–34.

3. H. Mintzberg, *Structure in Fives: Designing Effective Organizations* (Upper Saddle River, NJ: Prentice Hall, 1983), p. 157.

4. Cited in *At Work*, May–June 1993, p. 3.

5. G. Imperato, "Their Specialty? Teamwork," *Fast Company*, January–February 2000, pp. 54–56.

6. G. Hasek, "The Right Chemistry," *Industry Week*, March 6, 2000, pp. 36–39.

7. C.C. Snow, J. Lipnack, and J. Stamps, "The Virtual Organization: Promises and Payoffs, Large and Small," in C.L. Cooper and D.M. Rousseau (eds.), *The Virtual Organization* (New York: Wiley, 1999), pp. 15–30; and W.F. Cascio, "Managing a Virtual Workplace," *Academy of Management Executive*, August 2000, pp. 81–90.

8. "GE: Just Your Average Everyday $60 Billion Family Grocery Store," *Industry Week*, May 2, 1994, pp. 13–18. See also R. Ashkenas, D. Ulrich, T. Jick, and S. Kerr, *The Boundaryless Organization* (San Francisco: Jossey-Bass, 1995); and R.L. Cross, A. Yan, and M.R. Louis, "Boundary Activities in 'Boundaryless' Organizations: A Case Study of a Transformation to a Team-Based Structure," *Human Relations*, June 2000, pp. 841–68.

9. This analysis is referred to as a contingency approach to organizational design. See, for instance, J.M. Pennings, "Structural Contingency Theory: A Reappraisal," in B.M. Staw and L.L. Cummings (eds.), *Research in Organizational Behavior*, vol. 14 (Greenwich, CT: Jai Press, 1992), pp. 267–309.

10. See R.E. Miles and C.C. Snow, *Organizational Strategy, Structure, and Process* (New York: McGraw-Hill, 1978); D.C. Galunic and K.M. Eisenhardt, "Renewing the Strategy-Structure-Performance Paradigm," pp. 215–255 in B.M. Staw and L.L. Cummings (eds.), *Research in Organizational Behavior*, vol. 16 (Greenwich, CT: Jai Press, 1994); and I.C. Harris and T.W. Ruefli, "The Strategy/Structure Debate: An Examination of the Performance Implications," *Journal of Management Studies*, June 2000, pp. 587–603.

11. See, for instance, P.M. Blau and R.A. Schoenherr, *The Structure of Organizations* (New York: Basic Books, 1971); and R.Z. Gooding and J.A. Wagner III, "A Meta-Analytic Review of the Relationship between Size and Performance: The Productivity and Efficiency of Organizations and Their Subunits," *Administrative Science Quarterly*, December 1985, pp. 462–81.

12. See J. Woodward, *Industrial Organization: Theory and Practice* (London: Oxford University Press, 1965); C. Perrow, "A Framework for the Comparative Analysis of Organizations," *American Sociological Review*, April 1967, pp. 194–208; and C.C. Miller, W.H. Glick, Y. Wang, and G.P. Huber, "Understanding Technology–Structure Relationships: Theory Development and Meta-Analytic Theory Testing," *Academy of Management Journal*, June 1991, pp. 370–99.

13. See F.E. Emery and E. Trist, "The Causal Texture of Organizational Environments," *Human Relations*, February 1965, pp. 21–32; and P. Lawrence and J.W. Lorsch, *Organization and Environment: Managing Differentiation and Integration* (Boston: Harvard Business School, Division of Research, 1967).

14. See, for instance, L.W. Porter and E.E. Lawler III, "Properties of Organization Structure in Relation to Job Attitudes and Job Behavior," *Psychological Bulletin*, July 1965, pp. 23–51; and L.R. James and A.P. Jones, "Organization Structure: A Review of Structural Dimensions and Their Conceptual Relationships with Individual Attitudes and Behavior," *Organizational Behavior and Human Performance*, June 1976, pp. 74–113.

CHAPTER 14

1. See, for example, H.S. Gitlow, *Quality Management Systems: A Practical Guide for Improvement* (Boca Raton, FL: CRC Press, 2001); and J.W. Cortada, *The Quality Yearbook 2001* (New York: McGraw-Hill, 2001).

2. M. Hammer and J. Champy, *Reengineering the Corporation: A Manifesto for Business Revolution* (New York: HarperBusiness, 1993).

3. R. Karlgaard, "ASAP Interview: Mike Hammer," *Forbes ASAP*, September 13, 1993, p. 70.

4. Ibid.

5. W. Kirn, "The 60-Second Book," *Time*, August 1, 1999, p. 45.

6. P. Siekman, "Where 'Build to Order' Works Best," *Fortune*, April 26, 1999, 160C–160V; J. Lardner, "Your Every Command," *U.S. News & World Report*, July 5, 1999, pp. 44–46; and K.A. Crawford, "Customizing for the Masses," *Forbes*, October 16, 2000, p. 168.

7. Cited in J. Thaler, "The Web at Work," *Seattle Times*, April 4, 1999, p. C1. See also A. Cohen, "No Web for You!" *Fortune*, October 30, 2000, F208[B]–F208[L]; and B. Yerak, "Employees' New Coffee Break: Online Shopping," *USA Today*, December 14, 2000, p. 1B.

8. Thaler, "The Web at Work."

9. Cited in M. Conlin, "Workers, Surf at Your Own Risk," *Business Week*, June 12, 2000, p. 105.

10. Ibid., 106.

11. T. Spencer, "Paycheck, Health Benefits, and a Mercedes," *Fortune*, June 26, 2000, p. 336.

12. E. Ackerman, "Optionaires, Beware!" *U.S. News & World Report*, March 6, 2000, pp. 36–38; E. McDonald, "Breathing Underwater," *Forbes*, May 15, 2000, p. 188; L. Lavelle, "When Good Options Go Bad," *Business Week E.Biz*, December 11, 2000, pp. EB96-98; and E. Corcoran, "Promises, Promises," *Forbes*, February 19, 2001, pp. 54–56.

13. See, for instance, M.J. McCarthy, "You Assumed 'Erase' Wiped Out That Rant Against the Boss? Nope," *Wall Street Journal*, March 7, 2000, p. A1; S. Boehle, "They're Watching You: Workplace Privacy is Going . . . Going . . . " *Training*, August 2000, pp. 50-60; K. Weisul, "How Should You Police Employees Goofing Off on the Net? Very Carefully," *Business Week Frontier*, February 5, 2001, pp. F18-20; and "Keeping Tabs on Employees Online," *Business Week*, February 19, 2001, p. 16.

14. L. Guernsey, "The Web: New Ticket to a Pink Slip," *New York Times*, December 16, 1999, p. D1+.

15. American Management Association Survey of 2,133 corporations; January 2000.

16. J. Fonstad, "It's the Business Model, Stupid!" *Red Herring*, February 2000, pp. 70–72; and G. Dalton, "Ways of Doing Business," *The Industry Standard*, March 13, 2000, pp. 92–95.

17. A. Cohen, "Click Here for a Hot Rumor About Your Boss," *Time*, September 11, 2000, p. 48.

18. Cited in "Communication 'Inflation' Affecting Worker Performance," *Manpower Argus*, March 2000, p. 7.

19. P. Labarre, "Leaders.com," *Fast Company*, June 1999, p. 96.

20. Ibid., p. 104.

21. Ibid., p. 100.

22. Ibid.

23. Ibid., p. 104.

24. Cited in *Red Herring*, December 1999, p. 37.

25. Reported in J. Markoff, "A Newer, Lonelier Crowd Emerges in Internet Study," *New York Times*, February 16, 2000, p. A1.

26. Reported in G. Koretz, "The Web's Chilling Trend?" *Business Week*, June 5, 2000, p. 36.

27. J.R. Hackman and G.R. Oldham, "Motivation Through the Design of Work: Test of a Theory," *Organizational Behavior and Human Performance*, August 1976, pp. 250–79.

28. See B.T. Loher, R.A. Noe, N.L. Moeller, and M.P. Fitzgerald, "A Meta-Analysis of the Relation of Job Characteristics to Job Satisfaction," *Journal of Applied Psychology*, May 1985, pp. 280–89; Y. Fried and G.R. Ferris, "The Validity of the Job Characteristics Model: A Review and Meta-Analysis," *Personnel Psychology*, Summer 1987, pp. 287–322; R.W. Renn and R.J. Vandenberg, "The Critical Psychological States: An Underrepresented Component in Job Characteristics Model Research," *Journal of Management* 21, no. 2 (1995), pp. 279–303; J.R. Rentsch and R.P. Steel, "Testing the Durability of Job Characteristics As Predictors of Absenteeism Over a Six-Year Period," *Personnel Psychology*, Spring 1998, pp. 165-90.

29. J.R. Hackman, "Work Design," in J.R. Hackman and J.L. Suttle (eds.), *Improving Life at Work* (Santa Monica, CA: Goodyear, 1977), pp. 132–33.

30. Ibid., pp. 96–162.

31. G.R. Salancik and J. Pfeffer, "A Social Information Processing Approach to Job Attitudes and Task Design," *Administrative Science Quarterly*, June 1978, pp. 224–53; and J.G. Thomas and R.W. Griffin, "The Power of Social Information in the Workplace," *Organizational Dynamics*, Autumn 1989, pp. 63–75.

32. See, for instance, J. Thomas and R.W. Griffin, "The Social Information Processing Model of Task Design: A Review of the Literature," *Academy of Management Journal*, October 1983, pp. 672–82; M.D. Zalesny and J.K. Ford, "Extending the Social Information Processing Perspective: New Links to Attitudes, Behaviors, and Perceptions," *Organizational Behavior and Human Decision Processes*, December 1990, pp. 205–46; G.W. Meyer, "Social Information Processing and Social Networks: A Test of Social Influence Mechanisms," *Human Relations*, September 1994, pp. 1013-45; and K.J. Klein, A.B. Conn, D.B. Smith, and J.S. Sorra, "Is Everyone in Agreement? An Exploration of Within-Group Agreement in Employee Perceptions of the Work Environment," *Journal of Applied Psychology*, February 2001, pp. 3–16.

33. C. Garfield, "Creating Successful Partnerships with Employees," *At Work*, May/June 1992, p. 8.

34. See, for instance, data on task enlargement described in M.A. Campion and C.L. McClelland, "Follow-Up and Extension of the Interdisciplinary Costs and Benefits of Enlarged Jobs," *Journal of Applied Psychology*, June 1993, pp. 339–51.

35. J.R. Hackman, "Work Design," pp. 132–33.

36. See, for example, J.R. Hackman and G.R. Oldham, *Work Redesign* (Reading, MA: Addison-Wesley, 1980); J.B. Miner, *Theories of Organizational Behavior* (Hinsdale, IL: Dryden Press, 1980), pp. 231–266; R.W. Griffin, "Effects of Work Redesign on Employee Perceptions, Attitudes, and Behaviors: A Long-Term Investigation," *Academy of Management Journal*, June 1991, pp. 425–35; and J.L. Cotton, *Employee Involvement* (Newbury Park, CA: Sage, 1993), pp. 141–72.

37. J.R. Hackman, "The Design of Work Teams," in J.W. Lorsch (ed.), *Handbook of Organizational Behavior* (Upper Saddle River, NJ: Prentice Hall, 1987), pp. 324–27.

38. T.M. Beers, "Flexible Schedules and Shift Work: Replacing the '9-to-5' Workday?" *Monthly Labor Review*, June 2000, pp. 33–40

39. L. Rubis, "Fourth of Full-Timers Enjoy Flexible Hours," *HRMagazine*, June 1998, pp. 26–28.

40. D.R. Dalton and D.J. Mesch, "The Impact of Flexible Scheduling on Employee Attendance and Turnover," *Administrative Science Quarterly*, June 1990, pp. 370–87; and K.S. Kush and L.K. Stroh, "Flextime: Myth or Reality," *Business Horizons*, September–October 1994, p. 53.

41. B.B. Baltes, T.E. Briggs, J.W. Huff, J.A. Wright, and G.A. Neuman, "Flexible and Compressed Workweek Schedules: A Meta-Analysis of Their Effects on Work-Related Criteria," *Journal of Applied Psychology*, August 1999, pp. 496–513.

42. Cited in S. Armour, "Telecommuting Gets Stuck in the Slow Lane," *USA Today*, June 25, 2001, p. 2A.

43. "Telecommuting As a Way of Life," *Fortune*, January 12, 1998, p. 94.

44. Cited in R.W. Judy and C. D'Amico, *Workforce 2020* (Indianapolis: Hudson Institute, 1997), p. 58.

45. E.C. Baig, "Saying Adios to the Office," *Business Week*, October 12, 1998, pp. 152–53; A. Tergesen, "Making Stay-at-Homes Feel Welcome," *Business Week*, October 12, 1998, pp. 155–56; C.A.L. Dannhauser, "The Invisible Worker," *Working Woman*, November 1998, p. 38; and "Biggest U.S. Workplace Trend Is Telecommuting," *Manpower Argus*, July 2000, p. 3.

CHAPTER 15

1. See, for example, J. Pfeffer, *Competitive Advantage Through People: Unleashing the Power of the Work Force* (Boston: Harvard Business School Press, 1996); M.A. Huselid, S.E. Jackson, and R.S. Schuler, "Technical and Strategic Human Resource Management Effectiveness as Determinants of Firm Performance," *Academy of Management Journal*, February 1997, pp. 171–88; and L. Gratton, *Living Strategy: Putting People at the Heart of Corporate Business* (London: Financial Times/Prentice Hall, 2000).

2. L. Yoo-Lim, "More Companies Rely on Employee Interviews," *Business Korea*, November 1994, pp. 22–23.

3. Ibid.

4. T.J. Hanson and J.C. Balestreri-Spero, "An Alternative to Interviews," *Personnel Journal*, June 1985, p. 114. See also T.W. Dougherty, D.B. Turban, and J.C. Callender, "Confirming First Impressions in the Employment Interview: A Field Study of Interviewer Behavior," *Journal of Applied Psychology*, October 1994, pp. 659–65.

5. See A.I. Huffcutt and W. Arthur Jr., "Hunter and Hunter (1984) Revisited: Interview Validity for Entry-Level Jobs," *Journal of Applied Psychology*, April 1994, pp. 184–90; M.A. McDaniel, D.L. Whetzel, F.L. Schmidt, and S.D. Maurer, "The Validity of Employment Interviews: A Comprehensive Review and Meta-Analysis," *Journal of Applied Psychology*, August 1994, pp. 599–616; J.M. Conway, R.A. Jako, and D.F. Goodman, "A Meta-Analysis of Interrater and Internal Consistency Reliability of Selection Interviews," *Journal of Applied Psychology*, October 1995, pp. 565–79; M.A. Campion, D.K. Palmer, and J.E. Campion, "A Review of Structure in the Selection Interview," *Personnel Psychology*, Autumn 1997, pp. 655–702; and F.L. Schmidt and J.E. Hunter, "The Validity and Utility of Selection Methods in Personnel Psychology: Practical and Theoretical Implications of 85 Years of Research Findings," *Psychological Bulletin*, September 1998, pp. 262–74.

6. R.L. Dipboye, *Selection Interviews: Process Perspectives* (Cincinnati: South-Western Publishing, 1992), pp. 42–44.

7. W.F. Cascio, *Applied Psychology in Personnel Management*, 4th ed. (Upper Saddle River, NJ: Prentice Hall, 1991), p. 271.

8. See G.A. Adams, T.C. Elacqua, and S.M. Colarelli, "The Employment Interview as a Sociometric Selection Technique," *Journal of Group Psychotherapy*, Fall 1994, pp. 99–113; R.L. Dipboye, "Structured and Unstructured Selection Interviews: Beyond the Job-Fit Model," *Research in Personnel Human Resource Management* 12 (1994), pp. 79–123; and B. Schneider, D.B. Smith, S. Taylor, and J. Fleenor, "Personality and Organizations: A Test of the Homogeneity of Personality Hypothesis," *Journal of Applied Psychology*, June 1998, pp. 462–70.

9. E.E. Ghiselli, "The Validity of Aptitude Tests in Personnel Selection," *Personnel Psychology*, Winter 1973, p. 475.

10. R.J. Herrnstein and C. Murray, *The Bell Curve: Intelligence and Class Structure in American Life* (New York: Free Press, 1994); and M.J. Ree, J.A. Earles, and M.S. Teachout, "Predicting Job Performance: Not Much More Than g," *Journal of Applied Psychology*, August 1994, pp. 518–24.

11. J. Flint, "Can You Tell Applesauce from Pickles?" *Forbes*, October 9, 1995, pp. 106–08.

12. D.S. Ones, C. Viswesvaran, and F.L. Schmidt, "Comprehensive Meta-Analysis of Integrity Test Validities: Findings and Implications for Personnel Selection and Theories of Job Performance," *Journal of Applied Psychology*, August 1993, pp. 679–703; P.R. Sackett and J.E. Wanek, "New Developments in the Use of Measures of Honesty, Integrity, Conscientiousness, Dependability, Trustworthiness, and Reliability for Personnel Selection," *Personnel Psychology*, Winter 1996, pp. 787–829; and F.L. Schmidt and J.E. Hunter, "The Validity and Utility of Selection Methods in Personnel Psychology."

13. P. Carbonara, "Hire for Attitude, Train for Skill," *Fast Company, Greatest Hits* 1 (1997), p. 68.

14. J.J. Asher and J.A. Sciarrino, "Realistic Work Sample Tests: A Review," *Personnel Psychology*, Winter 1974, pp. 519–33; and I.T. Robertson and R.S. Kandola, "Work Sample Tests: Validity, Adverse Impact and Applicant Reaction," *Journal of Occupational Psychology*, Spring 1982, pp. 171–82.

15. See, for instance, A.C. Spychalski, M.A. Quinones, B.B. Gaugler, and K. Pohley, "A Survey of Assessment Center Practices in Organizations in the United States," *Personnel Psychology*, Spring 1997, pp. 71–90.

16. G.C. Thornton, *Assessment Centers in Human Resource Management* (Reading, MA: Addison-Wesley, 1992); W.F. Cascio, *Applied Psychology in Human Resource Management*, 5th ed. (Upper Saddle River, NJ: Prentice Hall, 1998), pp. 238–42; and W. Arthur Jr., D.J. Woehr, R. Maldegen, "Convergent and Discriminant Validity of Assessment Center Dimensions: A Conceptual and Empirical Reexamination of the Assessment Center Construct-Related Validity Paradox," *Journal of Management* 26, no. 4 (2000), pp. 813–35.

17. Cited in *Training*, October 2000, p. 52.

18. Cited in J.C. Szabo, "Training Workers for Tomorrow," *Nation's Business*, March 1993, pp. 22–32.

19. Cited in M. Hequet, "The Union Push for Lifelong Learning," *Training*, March 1994, p. 31; and D. Baynton, "America's $60 Billion Problem," *Training*, May 2001, pp. 51–6.

20. Reported in *From School to Work* (Princeton, NJ: Educational Testing Service, 1990).

21. "U.S. Business Takes Up Challenge of Training Its Rawest Recruits," *Manpower Argus*, July 1999, p. 6.

22. Cited in "Survey Shows 75% of Large Corporations Support Diversity Programs," *Fortune*, July 6, 1998, p. S14.

23. See, for example, S. Nelton, "Nurturing Diversity," *Nation's Business*, June 1995, pp. 25–27; J.K. Ford and S. Fisher, "The Role of Training in a Changing Workplace and Workforce: New Perspectives and Approaches," in E.E. Kossek and S.A. Lobel, eds., *Managing Diversity* (Cambridge, MA: Blackwell Publishers, 1996), pp. 164–93.

24. B. Hynes-Grace, "To Thrive, Not Merely Survive," in *Textbook Authors Conference Presentations*, sponsored by the American Association of Retired Persons, Washington, DC, October 21, 1992, p. 12.

25. "Teaching Diversity: Business Schools Search for Model Approaches," *Newsline*, Fall 1992, p. 21.

26. G.R. Weaver, L.K. Trevino, and P.L. Cochran, "Corporate Ethics Practices in the Mid-1990's: An Empirical Study of the Fortune 1000," *Journal of Business Ethics*, February 1999, pp. 283–94.

27. K. Dobbs, "The U.S. Department of Labor Estimates That 70 Percent of Workplace Learning Occurs Informally," *Sales & Marketing Management*, November 2000, pp. 94–8.

28. S.J. Wells, "Forget the Formal Training. Try Chatting at the Water Cooler," *New York Times*, May 10, 1998, p. BU-11.

29. D. Schaaf, "Inside Hamburger University," *Training*, December 1994, pp. 18–24.

30. P.M. Blau, *The Dynamics of Bureaucracy*, rev. ed. (Chicago: University of Chicago Press, 1963).

31. "The Cop-Out Cops," *National Observer*, August 3, 1974.

32. G.P. Latham and K.N. Wexley, *Increasing Productivity Through Performance Appraisal* (Reading, MA: Addison-Wesley, 1981), p. 80.

33. See review in R.D. Bretz, Jr., G.T. Milkovich, and W. Read, "The Current State of Performance Appraisal Research and Practice: Concerns, Directions, and Implications," *Journal of Management*, June 1992, p. 326.

34. See, for instance, R. Lepsinger and A.D. Lucia, "360-Degree Feedback and Performance Appraisal," *Training*, September 1997, pp. 62–70; W.W. Tornow and M. London (eds.), *Maximizing the Value of 360-Degree Feedback*

(San Francisco: Jossey-Bass, 1998); J. Ghorpade, "Managing Five Paradoxes of 360-Degree Feedback," *Academy of Management Executive*, February 2000, pp. 140–50; and A.S. Wellner, "Everyone's a Critic," *Business Week Small Biz*, April 2, 2001, p. 18.

35. Cited in C. Hymowitz, "Do '360' Job Reviews by Colleagues Promote Honesty or Insults?" *Wall Street Journal*, December 12, 2000, p. B1.

36. A.S. DeNisi and L.H. Peters, "Organization of Information in Memory and the Performance Appraisal Process: Evidence from the Field," *Journal of Applied Psychology*, December 1996, pp. 717–37.

37. See, for instance, J.W. Hedge and W.C. Borman, "Changing Conceptions and Practices in Performance Appraisal," in A. Howard, ed., *The Changing Nature of Work* (San Francisco: Jossey-Bass, 1995), pp. 453–59.

38. See, for instance, D.E. Smith, "Training Programs for Performance Appraisal: A Review," *Academy of Management Review*, January 1986, pp. 22–40; T.R. Athey and R.M. McIntyre, "Effect of Rater Training on Rater Accuracy: Levels-of-Processing Theory and Social Facilitation Theory Perspectives," *Journal of Applied Psychology*, November 1987, pp. 567–72; and D.J. Woehr, "Understanding Frame-of-Reference Training: The Impact of Training on the Recall of Performance Information," *Journal of Applied Psychology*, August 1994, pp. 525–34.

39. H.J. Bernardin, "The Effects of Rater Training on Leniency and Halo Errors in Student Rating of Instructors," *Journal of Applied Psychology*, June 1978, pp. 301–08.

40. Ibid.; and J.M. Ivancevich, "Longitudinal Study of the Effects of Rater Training on Psychometric Error in Ratings," *Journal of Applied Psychology*, October 1979, pp. 502–08.

41. M.S. Taylor, K.B. Tracy, M.K. Renard, J.K. Harrison, and S.J. Carroll, "Due Process in Performance Appraisal: A Quasi-Experiment in Procedural Justice," *Administrative Science Quarterly*, September 1995, pp. 495–523.

42. J.S. Lublin, "It's Shape-Up Time for Performance Reviews," *Wall Street Journal*, October 3, 1994, p. B1.

43. Much of this section is based on H.H. Meyer, "A Solution to the Performance Appraisal Feedback Enigma," *Academy of Management Executive*, February 1991, pp. 68–76.

44. B. Gates, *The Road Ahead* (New York: Viking, 1995), p. 86.

45. T.D. Schelhardt, "It's Time to Evaluate Your Work, and All Involved Are Groaning," *Wall Street Journal*, November 19, 1996, p. A1.

46. R.J. Burke, "Why Performance Appraisal Systems Fail," *Personnel Administration*, June 1972, pp. 32–40.

47. B.R. Nathan, A.M. Mohrman, Jr., and J. Milliman, "Interpersonal Relations as a Context for the Effects of Appraisal Interviews on Performance and Satisfaction: A Longitudinal Study," *Academy of Management Journal*, June 1991, pp. 352–69. See also B.D. Cawley, L.M. Keeping, and P.E. Levy, "Participation in the Performance Appraisal Process and Employee Reactions: A Meta-Analytic Review of Field Investigations," *Journal of Applied Psychology*, August 1998, pp. 615–33.

48. J. Zigon, "Making Performance Appraisal Work for Teams," *Training*, June 1994, pp. 58–63.

CHAPTER 16

1. See, for example, E.H. Schein, *Organizational Culture and Leadership* (San Francisco: Jossey-Bass, 1985), p. 168.

2. This seven-item description is based on C.A. O'Reilly III, J. Chatman, and D.F. Caldwell, "People and Organizational Culture: A Profile Comparison Approach to Assessing Person-Organization Fit," *Academy of Management Journal*, September 1991, pp. 487–516; and J.A. Chatman and K.A. Jehn, "Assessing the Relationship Between Industry Characteristics and Organizational Culture: How Different Can You Be?" *Academy of Management Journal*, June 1994, pp. 522–53. For a review of cultural dimensions, see N.M. Ashkanasy, L.E. Broadfoot, and S. Falkus, "Questionnaire Measures of Organizational Culture," in N.M. Ashkanasy, C.P.M. Wilderom, and M.F. Peterson (eds.), *Handbook of Organizational Culture and Climate* (Thousand Oaks, CA: Sage, 2000), pp. 131–45.

3. Y. Wiener, "Forms of Value Systems: A Focus on Organizational Effectiveness and Cultural Change and Maintenance," *Academy of Management Review*, October 1988, p. 536.

4. T.E. Deal and A.A. Kennedy, "Culture: A New Look through Old Lenses," *Journal of Applied Behavioral Science*, November 1983, p. 501.

5. E.H. Schein, "The Role of the Founder in Creating Organizational Culture," *Organizational Dynamics*, Summer 1983, pp. 13–28.

6. See, for example, J.R. Harrison and G.R. Carroll, "Keeping the Faith: A Model of Cultural Transmission in Formal Organizations," *Administrative Science Quarterly*, December 1991, pp. 552–82.

7. L. Grensing-Pophal, "Hiring to Fit Your Corporate Culture," *HRMagazine*, August 1999, pp. 50–54.

8. R.C. Alexander, "Can Xerox Duplicate Its Original Success?" *Wall Street Journal*, May 17, 2000, p. A26; P.L. Moore, "Xerox: Rick Thoman Speaks Up for Himself," *Business Week*, May 29, 2000, pp. 51-52; and A. Bianco and P.L. Moore, "Downfall: The Inside Story of the Management Fiasco at Xerox," *Business Week*, March 5, 2001, pp. 82–92.

9. J. Van Maanen and E.H. Schein, "Career Development," in J.R. Hackman and J. L. Suttle (eds.), *Improving Life at Work* (Santa Monica, CA: Goodyear, 1977), p. 59.

10. E. Ransdell, "The Nike Story? Just Tell It!" *Fast Company*, January-February 2000, pp. 44–46.

11. "DCACronyms," April 1997, Rev. D (Seattle, WA: The Boeing Co., 1997).

12. See R.H. Kilmann, M.J. Saxton, and R. Serpa, eds, *Gaining Control of the Corporate Culture* (San Francisco: Jossey-Bass, 1985); T.H. Fitzgerald, "Can Change in Organizational Culture Really Be Managed?" *Organizational Dynamics*, Autumn 1988, pp. 5–15; B. Dumaine, "Creating a New Company Culture," *Fortune*, January 15, 1990, pp. 127–31; J.P. Kotter and J.L. Heskett, *Corporate Culture and Performance* (New York: Free Press, 1992), pp. 83–106; and H.M. Trice and J.M. Beyer, *The Cultures of Work Organizations* (Upper Saddle River, NJ: Prentice Hall, 1993), pp. 393–428.

13. B. Victor and J.B. Cullen, "The Organizational Bases of Ethical Work Climates," *Administrative Science Quarterly*, March 1988, pp. 101–25; L.K. Trevino, "A Cultural Perspective on Changing and Developing Organizational Ethics," in W.A. Pasmore and R.W. Woodman (eds.), *Research in Organizational Change and Development*, vol. 4 (Greenwich, CT: JAI Press, 1990); and R.R. Sims, "The Challenge of Ethical Behavior in Organizations," *Journal of Business Ethics*, July 1992, pp. 505–13.

14. D.P. Ashmos and D. Duchon, "Spirituality at Work: A Conceptualization and Measure," *Journal of Management Inquiry*, June 2000, p. 139.

15. This section is based on I.A. Mitroff and E.A. Denton, *A Spiritual Audit of Corporate America: A Hard Look at Spirituality, Religion, and Values in the Workplace* (San Francisco: Jossey-Bass, 1999); J. Milliman, J. Ferguson, D. Trickett, and B. Condemi, "Spirit and Community at Southwest Airlines: An Investigation of a Spiritual Values-Based Model," *Journal of Organizational Change Management* 12, no. 3 (1999), pp. 221–33; E.H. Burack, "Spirituality in the Workplace," *Journal of Organizational Change Management* 12, no. 3 (1999), pp. 280–91; and F. Wagner-Marsh and J. Conley, "The Fourth Wave: The Spiritually-Based Firm," *Journal of Organizational Change Management* 12, no. 3 (1999), pp. 292–302.

16. Cited in F. Wagner-Marsh and J. Conley, "The Fourth Wave," p. 295.

17. M. Conlin, "Religion in the Workplace: The Growing Presence of Spirituality in Corporate America," *Business Week*, November 1, 1999, pp. 151–58.

18. Cited in Ibid., p. 153.

19. C.P. Neck and J.F. Milliman, "Thought Self-Leadership: Finding Spiritual Fulfillment in Organizational Life," *Journal of Managerial Psychology* 9, no. 8 (1994), p. 9.

20. D.W. McCormick, "Spirituality and Management," *Journal of Managerial Psychology* 9, no. 6 (1994), p. 5; E. Brandt, "Corporate Pioneers Explore Spiritual Peace," *HRMagazine* 41, no. 4 (1996), p. 82; P. Leigh, "The New Spirit at Work," *Training and Development* 51, no. 3 (1997), p. 26; and P.H. Mirvis, "Soul Work in Organizations," *Organization Science* 8, no. 2 (1997), p. 193.

21. Cited in J. Milliman, et al, "Spirit and Community at Southwest Airlines."

22. N.J. Adler, *International Dimensions of Organizational Behavior*, 4th ed. (Cincinnati: Southwestern, 2002), pp. 67–69.

23. See C. Lindsay, "Paradoxes of Organizational Diversity: Living Within the Paradoxes," in L.R. Jauch and J.L. Wall (eds.), *Proceedings of the 50th Academy of Management Conference*, San Francisco, 1990, pp. 374-78; and T. Cox, Jr., *Cultural Diversity in Organizations: Theory, Research & Practice* (San Francisco: Berrett-Koehler, 1993), pp. 162–70.

CHAPTER 17

1. These similes were developed by P.B. Vaill, *Managing As a Performing Art: New Ideas for a World of Chaotic Change* (San Francisco: Jossey-Bass, 1989).

2. K. Lewin, "Group Decision and Social Change," in G. E. Swanson, T. M. Newcome, and E. L. Hartle (eds.), *Readings in Social Psychology*, 2nd ed. (New York: Holt, 1952), pp. 459–73.

3. T. Peters, *Thriving on Chaos* (New York: Alfred A. Knopf, 1987), p. 3.

4. R.H. Hall, *Organization: Structures, Processes, and Outcomes*, 4th ed. (Upper Saddle River, NJ: Prentice Hall, 1987), p. 29.

5. See, for example, C. Argyris and D.A. Schoen, *Organizational Learning II* (Reading, MA: Addison Wesley, 1996); L. Baird, P. Holland, and S. Deacon, "Imbedding More Learning into the Performance Fast Enough to Make a Difference," *Organizational Dynamics*, Spring 1999, pp. 19–32; and R.S. Snell, "Moral Foundations of the Learning Organization," *Human Relations*, March 2001, pp. 319–42.

6. For a sampling of various OD definitions, see J.I. Porras and P.J. Robertson, "Organizational Development: Theory, Practice, and Research," in M.D. Dunnette and L.M. Hough (eds.), *Handbook of Industrial & Organizational Psychology*, 2nd ed., vol. 3 (Palo Alto: Consulting Psychologists Press, 1992), pp. 721–23; N. Nicholson (ed.), *Encyclopedic Dictionary of Organizational Behavior* (Malden, MA: Blackwell, 1998), pp. 359-61; and G. Farias and H. Johnson, "Organizational Development and Change Management," *Journal of Applied Behavioral Science*, September 2000, pp. 376–79.

7. See, for instance, W.A. Pasmore and M.R. Fagans, "Participation, Individual Development, and Organizational Change: A Review and Synthesis," *Journal of Management*, June 1992, pp. 375–97; T.G. Cummings and C.G. Worley, *Organization Development and Change*, 5th ed. (Minneapolis: West, 1993); and W.W. Burke, *Organization Development: A Process of Learning and Changing*, 2nd ed. (Reading, MA: Addison-Wesley, 1994).

8. R.T. Golembiewski and A. Blumberg, eds., *Sensitivity Training and the Laboratory Approach*, 2nd ed. (Itasca, IL: Peacock, 1973).

9. J.E. Edwards and M.D. Thomas, "The Organizational Survey Process: General Steps and Practical Considerations," in P. Rosenfeld, J.E. Edwards, and M.D. Thomas (eds.), *Improving Organizational Surveys: New Directions, Methods, and Applications* (Newbury Park, CA: Sage, 1993), pp. 3–28.

10. E.H. Schein, *Process Consultation Revisited: Building the Helpful Relationship* (Reading, MA: Addison-Wesley, 1999), p. 9.

11. Ibid.

12. W. Dyer, *Team Building: Issues and Alternatives* (Reading, MA: Addison-Wesley, 1994).

13. N. Margulies and J. Wallace, *Organizational Change: Techniques and Applications* (Glenview, IL: Scott, Foresman, 1973), pp. 99–100.

14. R.R. Blake, J.S. Mouton, and R.L. Sloma, "The Union–Management Intergroup Laboratory: Strategy for Resolving Intergroup Conflict," *Journal of Applied Behavioral Science* 1 (1965), pp. 25–57.

15. Adapted from R.S. Schuler, "Definition and Conceptualization of Stress in Organizations," *Organizational Behavior and Human Performance*, April 1980, p. 189.

16. M.A. Verespej, "Stressed Out," *Industry Week*, February 21, 2000, pp. 31–34.

17. Cited in *Fast Company*, March 2000, p. 219

18. See, for example, S.M. Jex, *Stress and Job Performance: Theory, Research, and Implications for Managerial Practice* (Thousand Oaks, CA: Sage, 1998).

19. Discussions of the 3M Co. in this section are based on T. Stevens, "Tool Kit for Innovators," *Industry Week*, June 5, 1995, pp. 28–31; T.A. Stewart, "3M Fights Back," *Fortune*, February 5, 1996, pp. 94–99; B. O'Reilly, "The Secrets of America's Most Admired Corporations: New Ideas, New Products," *Fortune*, March 3, 1997, pp. 60–64; B. Filipczak, "Innovation Drivers," *Training*, May 1997, p. 36; M. Conlin, "Too Much Doodle?" *Forbes*, October 19, 1998, pp. 54–55; and D. Weimer, "3M: The Heat Is on the Boss," *Business Week*, March 15, 1999, pp. 82–84.

20. F. Damanpour, "Organizational Innovation: A Meta-Analysis of Effects of Determinants and Moderators," *Academy of Management Journal*, September 1991, pp. 555–90.

21. See J. Ewing, "Sharing the Wealth," *BusinessWeek e.biz*, March 19, 2001, pp. EB36–40; and D. Tapscott, D. Ticoll, and A. Lowy, *Digital Capital: Harnessing the Power of Business Webs* (Boston: Harvard Business School Press, 2000).

22. B. Roberts, "Pick Employees' Brains," *HRMagazine*, February 2000, p. 115.

23. Ibid., pp. 115–16; B. Fryer, "Get Smart," *INC. Technolgy 1999* 3, p. 65; and D. Zielinski, "Have You Shared a Bright Idea Today?" *Training*, July 2000, p. 65.

24. B. Fryer, "Get Smart," p. 63.

25. B. Roberts, "Pick Employees' Brains," p. 117; and D.W. DeLong and L. Fahey, "Diagnosing Cultural Barriers to Knowledge Management," *Academy of Management Executive*, November 2000, pp. 113–27.

26. J. Gordon, "Intellectual Capital and You," *Training*, September 1999, p. 33.

27. D. Zielinksi, "Have You Shared a Bright Idea Today?" pp. 65–67.

Glindex

Definitions are shown in *italics*; numbers in **bold** indicate additional display material.

Ability, and team composition, 106
Absenteeism, employee, 2
Acclaiming, impression management, 160
Accommodation in conflict process, 169, 176
Achievement need. *See* Need for achievement (nAch)
Achievement-oriented leader, 138
Advanced Filtration Systems, Inc., 197
Aetna Life, 103
Affect
    A generic term that encompasses both emotions and moods, 36
Affiliation need. *See* Need for affiliation
Age of organization and change, 242
Aggression in organizational culture, 231
Agreeableness, 31
Alcoa, 10, 181, 223
All-channel network communication, 119
Allaire, Paul, 236
Ally McBeal (television program), 87
Amabile, T. M., **72**
Amazon.com, 9, 201, 202
Ambiguity
    decision making, 77
    grapevine communication, 120
America Online (AOL), 142
America West Airlines, 209
American Management Association, 65, 203, 213
American Safety Razor, 66
American Steel & Wire, 66
Analytical decision-making style, 77–78
Anchoring, decision-making biases, 174
Andersen Corp., 63
Anger, as universal emotion, 38
Anthropology
    The study of societies to learn about human beings and their activities, 3–4
AOL (America Online), 142
Apple Computer, 31, 65, 101, 190
Appraisal, performance. *See* Performance appraisal
Armstrong, C. Michael, 64
Asch, Solomon E., 89–90
Ash, Mary Kay, 142, 235
Assessment centers
    Centers where line executives, supervisors, and/or trained psychologists evaluate candidates as they go through one to several days of exercises that simulate real problems that they would confront on the job, 217–18
Assimilation and workplace diversity, 8
Assumed similarity and perception, 25

AT&T, 31, 64, 101, 110, 189, 190, 213, 223
Attitude
    attitude/behavior relationship, 22–23
    defined, 19
    dissonance reduction, 21–22
    individual behavior, 19–23, 28
    job satisfaction, 19–21
    and systematic study of OB, 2
    two-factor theory, 45–47
Attractiveness in expectancy theory, 52
Attribution theory, 23–25
Australian Airlines, 101
Authority
    The rights inherent in a managerial position to give orders and expect the orders to be obeyed, 182
Autonomy in job characteristic model, 206, **207**
Availability heuristic
    The tendency for people to base their judgments on information that is readily available to them, 76
Avoidance in conflict process, 169, 176

Balance work/life conflicts, 10–11
Barclays, 11
Behavior
    behavioral approach to leadership, 131–33, **134**
    in conflict process, 168–69
    decision-making style, 77–78
    modification of, 58, **59**, 60
    in performance appraisal, 225
    See also Organizational behavior (OB)
Behavior, group, 85–99
    basic group concepts, 85–94
    classification of, 85
    contributing disciplines to study of, 3–5
    defined, 84
    group decision making, 94–98
    implications for managers, 98–99
Behavior, individual, 14–29
    attitudes, 19–23
    contributing disciplines to study of, 3–5
    in e-organization, 201–3
    implications for managers, 27–29
    learning, 26–27, 29
    perception, 23–25
    values, 14–19
Behaviorally anchored rating scales
    An appraisal method where actual job-related behaviors are rated along a continuum, 224
Bell, Alexander Graham, 72

Bell & Howell, 66
Ben & Jerry's Homemade, 243, 244
Benson, Rick, 64
Bias
    decision making, 173–74
    in interviews, 216
Big 5 Model
    The five basic dimensions underlying personality are extroversion, agreeableness, conscientiousness, emotional stability, and openness to experience, 31–32
Blake, Robert R., 133, **134**
Blockage and conflict, 163, 164
BMC Software, 60
BMW, 104, 217
Board representatives
    A form of representative participation; employees sit on a company's board of directors and represent the interests of the firm's employees, 63
Body language, 117–18
Boeing, 101, 105, 254
Boomers, as cohort, work values of, 16–17
Boulgarides, J. D., **78**
Boundaryless organization
    An organization that seeks to eliminate the chain of command, have limitless spans of control, and replace departments with empowered teams, 190–91
Bounded rationality
    A decision-making approach whereby individuals construct simplified models that extract the essential features from problems without capturing all their complexity, 73–74
Bowerman, Bill, 239
Boy Scouts, 131
Brainstorming
    An idea-generating process that specifically encourages any and all alternatives while withholding any criticism of those alternatives, 97
Branson, Richard, 235
Broadcast.com, 205
Bureaucracy
    A structure with highly routine operating tasks achieved through specialization, very formalized rules and regulations, tasks that are grouped into functional departments, centralized authority, narrow spans of control, and decision making that follows the chain of command, 186

Calm-waters simile, 251–52
Campbell, Laura, 85–86, 87
Case, Steve, 142
Case Corp., 199, 200
Caterpillar Corporation, 10, 192
Cavanagh, G. F., **162**
Center for the Study of Work Teams, 101
Centralization
    The degree to which decision making is concentrated at a single point in the organization, 184
Cessna Aircraft, 180
Chain, in network communication, 119
Chain of command
    An unbroken line of authority that extends from the top of the organization to the lowest echelon and clarifies who reports to whom, 182–83

Challenger (space shuttle), 96
Chambers, John, 142
Champion Spark Plug, 66
Change
    Making things different, 250
Change, organizational, 248–65
    contemporary issues in, 260–64
    forces for, 248–50
    implications for managers, 264–65
    management of planned, 250–51
    management through organizational development (OD), 257–60
    resistance to, 253–56
    stimulation of, 9–10
    views of, 251–53
Change agents
    Persons who act as catalysts and assume the responsibility for managing change activities, 251
Channels in communication process, 114–15, 119, 127
Charismatic leadership
    Inspires followers to transcend their own self-interests for the good of the organization; capable of having a profound and extraordinary effect on followers, 141, 144
Childress Buick, 61
Churchill, Winston, 131, 141
Cigna Corp., 66
Cincinnati Milacron, 66
Cisco Systems, 142, 189, 201, 213, 264
Citizenship, organizational. *See* Organizational citizenship
Clancy, Tom, 199
Client relationship establishment and job enrichment, 211
Coaches, team leaders as, 143
Coalitions, 155–56
Coercive power
    Power that is based on fear, 152–53
Cognition and conflict process, 168
Cognitive dissonance, 21–22
Cohesiveness
    The degree to which members of a group are attracted to each other and are motivated to stay in the group, 90, **91**
Cohort
    A group of individuals who hold a common attribute, 15–17, 92
Collaboration in conflict process, 168, 176
Collectivism, and cultural assessment, 18, **19**
Command group, 85
Common purpose, team creation process, 109
Communication
    The transference and understanding of meaning, 112–29
    barriers to effective, 122–24
    as conflict source, 164, 166–67
    cross-cultural, 124–26
    direction of, 115–16
    ethics in, 126
    functions of, 114
    implications for managers, 126–27
    interpersonal, 116–18
    process of, 114–15
    resistance to change, 255
    stress reduction, 262
    technology and work/life conflicts, 10

Communication, within organizations, 119–22
    computer-aided, 121–22
    formal small-group networks, 119
    grapevine, 119–21, 129
    organizational behavior in e-world, 204–5
Communication process
    The steps between a source and a receiver that result in the transference and understanding of meaning, 114–15, 127–28
Competence and trust, 145, 148
Competency-based pay, 66
Competition
    in conflict process, 168, 176
    organizational change and, 249
Composition
    creation of effective teams, 105, 106–8
    group, 92–93
Compromise in conflict process, 169, 176
Computer-aided communication, 121–22
Conceptual decision-making style, 77–78
Conflict
    A process in which an effort is purposely made by A to offset the efforts of B by some form of blocking that will result in frustrating B in attaining his or her goals or furthering his or her interests, 163–77
    bureaucracy and, 186
    emotions and, 40–41
    functional vs. dysfunctional, 165, 171, 260
    human relations view of, 164, 165
    implications for managers, 176
    interactionist view, 164, 165
    managing, 176
    negotiation and, 171–76
    team creation process, 109–10
    team leaders as managers of, 143
    traditional view of, 164–65
Conflict process
    Four stages: potential opposition or incompatibility; cognition and personalization; behavior; and outcomes, 166–71
    behavior, 168–69
    cognition and personalization, 168
    outcomes, 169–71
    potential opposition, 166–67
Conformity, 89–90, 93, 160
Conscientiousness, 31
Consideration
    The extent to which a leader is likely to have job relationships characterized by mutual trust, respect for subordinates' ideas and regard for subordinates' feelings, 132
Consistency
    attribution theory, 24
    trust, 145, 148
Contemporary work cohorts and values, 16–17
Context
    creation of effective teams, 105, 108–9
    cultural, and communication, 125
Contingency theories of leadership, 134–41
    Fiedler model, 135–37
    gender as contingency variable, 139–41
    leader-member exchange (LMX) theory, 137
    leader-participation model, 139
    path-goal theory, 137–39
Continuous improvement process, 198
Control
    as goal of OB, 5
    locus of (*See* Locus of control)
    span of (*See* Span of control)
Conventional level, moral development, 79–80
Coors Brewing, 103
Cost-minimization strategy
    A strategy of tightly controlling costs, refraining from incurring unnecessary innovation or marketing expenses, and cutting prices in selling a basic product, 192
Counseling and stress reduction, 262
Crawford, Cindy, 154
Creative potential, 71, 73
Creative-thinking skills, 72
Creativity
    The ability to produce novel and useful ideas, 71–72
Crisis and change in organizational culture, 242
Critical incidents as performance appraisal method, 223
Cross-cultural issues. *See* Cultures, national, and cross-cultural issues
Cross-functional teams
    Employees from about the same hierarchical level but from different work areas who come together to accomplish a task, **102**, *104*, 256
Cross-training, 209
Cuban, Mark, 205
Cultures, national, and cross-cultural issues
    assessment framework, 18
    communication, 124–26
    in conflict process, 169
    decision making, effect on, 81
    emotions, 39
    globalization, 8–9, 10, **249**, 250
    group composition, 92–93
    motivation theories, 53–54
    in negotiation, 174
    OB concepts, 8–9
    vs. organizational culture, 246
    performance appraisal, 228–29
    personality, 33–34
    values, 17–18
    See also Organizational culture
Custom Research Inc., 104
Customer departmentalization, 181–82
Customers and quality management, **7**
Cyberloafing, 202

DaimlerChrysler, 101, 104
Decentralization, 184
Decision making
    Making choices from among two or more alternatives, 69
    biases, and negotiation, 173–74
    constraints on, 80–81
    e-world behavior, 203–4
    intuitive, 74–75
    political behavior, 158
    satisficing model of, 73

Decision making *(cont.)*
    See also Group decision making; individual decision making
Decoding, in communication process, 114–15
Dell Computer, 198
Delphi Automotive Systems, 6–7
Departmentalization
    The basis by which jobs are grouped together, 181–82
Dependency and power, 154–55
Deterrence-based trust
    Trust based on fear of reprisal if the trust is violated, 146
Development, organizational. *See* Organizational development (OD)
Deviant workplace behaviors, 41
Diary keeping and performance appraisals, 225
Dillinger, John, 152
Directive decision-making style, 77–78
Directive leader, 137
Disgust, as universal emotion, 38
Walt Disney Co., 65, 216, 234
Walt Disney Imagineering, 60
Walt Disney World, 234
Disneyland, 234, 236
Displayed emotions
    Organizationally required and appropriate emotions, 37
Dissonance reduction and attitude, 21–22
Distinctiveness of behavior and attribution theory, 24
Distributive bargaining
    Negotiation that seeks to divide up a fixed amount of resources; a win-lose situation, 171–73
Diversity
    of group members, 92
    paradox of, 246–47
    training, 219
    workforce, 7–8
    See also Gender issues
Division of labor, 179
Dole, Bob, 154
Domino's Pizza, 9
Dot.com stock collapse, 202–3
Downward communication, 115
Driving force, in calm-waters simile, 252
Due process in performance appraisal, 226
Dulck, R. E., **125**
Dysfunctional conflict, 165, 171, 260

E-business
    The full breadth of activities included in a successful Internet-based enterprise, 200
E-commerce
    The sales side of electronic business, 200
E-mail communication, 121–22
E-organization (e-org)
    Applications of e-business concepts to all organizations, 200–201
E-world, organizational behavior in, 200–206
    about, 200–201
    communication, 204
    decision making, 203–4
    ethics, 201–3
    group behavior, implications for, 203–5
    individual behavior, implications for, 201–3
    leadership, 204–5
    motivation, 201–3
    politics and networking, 205
    relationship redefinition, 205–6
Eastern Airlines, 9
Eastman Kodak, 65, 81, 186
Eaton-Aeroquip, 100, 103
Eaton Corp., 66, 100
eBay, 201, 202, 204
Economic change, 249, 254
Edison, Thomas, 42
Education and resistance to change, 256
Effect, law of, 26
Efficacy, team creation process, 109
Effort, expectancy theory, 52
EI. *See* Emotional intelligence (EI)
Einstein, Albert, 72
Eisner, Michael, 65
Electronic-mail communication, 121–22
Electronic meeting
    A group decision-making technique that allows participants to comment and vote on issues by using networked computers, 97–98
Elements of organization, structural, 178–85
    about, 178–79
    centralization and decentralization, 184
    chain of command, 182–83
    departmentalization, 181–82
    formalization, 184–85
    span of control, 183–84, 194
    work specialization, 179–81
Emerson Electric, 111
Emery Air Freight, 58, 60
Emotional intelligence (EI)
    An assortment of noncognitive skills, capabilities, and competencies that influence a person's ability to succeed in coping with environmental demands and pressures, 39–40
Emotional labor
    The expression of organizationally desired emotions during interpersonal transactions, 37
Emotional stability, 31
Emotions, 36–41
    Intense feelings directed at someone or something, 36–37
    communication, 114, 124, 129
    culture and, 39
    feelings and trust, 148
    felt vs. displayed, 37
    gender, 39
    implications for managers, 41
    OB applications, 39–41
    six universal, 38
Empathy, in emotional intelligence, 39
Employee deviance
    Voluntary actions that violate established norms and that threaten the organization, its members, or both, 41
Employee involvement
    A participative process that uses the entire capacity of employees and is designed to encourage increased commitment to the organization's success, 61–62

Employee involvement programs, 61–64
  employee stock ownership plans (ESOPs), 63, 64
  motivation theories, 63
  participative management, 62
  in practice, 63–64
  representative participation, 62–63
Employee recognition programs, 60–61
Employee stock ownership plans (ESOPs)
  Company-established benefit plans in which employees acquire stock as part of their benefits, 63, 64
Employees
  balance work/life conflicts, 10–11
  behavior and organization structure, 193–94
  emotions and, 39–41
  empowerment, **7**, *9*, 245
  equity theory, 50–52
  innovation and change stimulation, 9–10
  loyalty of, 11
  participation vs. involvement, 62
  process reengineering, 198–99
  recognition programs, 60–61
  selection of, 215–18, 235
  spirituality, 245
  "temporariness" in workplace, 10
  Theory X and Theory Y, 45
  tolerance and organizational spirituality, 245
  turnover of, 2
Empowerment
  Increasing the decision-making discretion of workers, **7**, *9*, 245
Encoding, in communication process, 114–15
Encounter stage, socialization, 236, 237
Environment
  in path-goal theory, 138
  uncertainty in, and organizational structure, 193
Equity and status, 93–94
Equity theory
  Individuals compare their job inputs and outcomes with those of others and then respond so as to eliminate any inequities, 50–52, 93–94
Erie Insurance, 213
Escalation of commitment
  An increased commitment to a previous decision, often in spite of negative information, 76–77, 173
ESOPs. *See* Employee stock ownership plans (ESOPs)
Etensity, 202
Ethical dilemmas
  Situations in which organizational members are required to define right and wrong conduct, 11–12
Ethical issues
  cohort dominant work values, 17
  creation of ethical organizational culture, 242–43
  decision making, individual, 82
  e-organization, 201–3
  ethical behavior, 11–12
  training, 219–20
Ethnicity and workforce diversity, 7–8
Expectancy theory
  The strength of a tendency to act in a certain way depends on the strength of an expectation that the act will be followed by a given outcome and on the attractiveness of that outcome to the individual, 52–53, 65–66

Expert power
  Influence based on special skills or knowledge, 153
Expertise
  change as threat to, 255
  in creative model, 72
Explanations of behavior, 5
Externally-caused behaviors and attribution theory, 24
Extranet
  Extended intranets, accessible only to selected employees and authorized outsiders, 122, 200, **201**
Extroversion, 31
ExxonMobil, 8

Facial expression as nonverbal communication, 118
Falbe, C. M., **152**
Fear, as universal emotion, 38
Fear of unknown and resistance to change, 254
Federal Express. *See* FedEx
FedEx (Federal Express), 31, 58, 101, 116, 235, 256
Feedback
  in communication process, 114–15, 127–28
  job characteristic model, 206, **207**
  job enrichment, 211
  management by objectives (MBO), 57
  360-degree evaluations, 223
Felt emotions
  An individual's actual emotions, 37
Fiedler, Fred E., 134, 135–37
Fiedler leadership model
  A theory that proposes that effective groups depend upon a proper match between a leader's style of interacting with subordinates and the degree to which the situation gives control and influence to the leader, 135–37
Fielden, J. S., **125**
Filtering
  A sender's manipulation of information so that it will be seen more favorably by the receiver, 123
Firestone Tire, 66
Flexibility
  team composition, 108
  work/life conflicts, 11, 212
Flextime
  Short for "flexible working hours," 212
Florida Power & Light, 101
Ford, Henry, 179
Ford, Henry, II, 239
Ford Motor Co., 8, 10, 104, 105, 110, 121, 179, 192, 197, 199, 239, 255, 256
Formal groups, 85
Formal small-group network communication, 119
Formal training, 220
Formalization
  The degree to which jobs within the organization are standardized, 184–85
Fortune 500, 101
Fortune 1000, 67
Fox Television, 9
Framing negotiations, decision-making biases, 174
French, John R. P., Jr., 152
Friendship groups, 85
Frito-Lay, 66

Fullers (restaurant), 240–41
Functional conflict, 197
Functional departmentalization, 181
Functional outcomes in conflict process, 169–70
Fundamental attribution error, 25

Gainsharing
  An incentive plan in which improvements in group productivity determine the total amount of money that is allocated, 65
Gates, Bill, 227, 235
GE. *See* General Electric
Gender issues
  communication style, 123–24
  emotion and, 39
  leadership, contingency theories of, 139–41
  in workforce, 8
  See also Diversity
General Electric (GE), 31, 60, 61, 101, 186, 190, 256
General Foods, 101
General Mills, 60
General Motors (GM), 8, 80, 103, 104, 122, 170
Geographic departmentalization, 181
Gimbel's, 9
Globalization
  politics and organizational change, **249**, 250
  response to, 8–9
  work/life conflicts, 10
  See also Cultures, national, and cross-cultural issues
GM. *See* General Motors
Goal achievement, as reason to join groups, **86**
Goal-setting theory
  The theory that specific and difficult goals lead to higher performance, 48–49, 54, 262
Goals, team creation process, 109
W. L. Gore & Associates, 103, 223, 235
W. T. Grant, 9
Grapevine
  An informal communication network within a group or organization, 119–21, 129
Graphic rating scales
  An appraisal method in which the evaluator rates performance factors on an incremental scale, 224
Graybar Electric, 63
Great Plains Software, 213
www.greedyassociates.com, 204
Group decision making, 94–98
  brainstorming, 97
  electronic meetings, 97–98
  groupshift, 96
  groupthink, 95–96
  vs. individual, 94–95
  techniques for, 97–98
Group demography
  The degree to which members of a group share a common demographic attribute, such as age, sex, race, educational level, or length of service in the organization, and the impact of this attribute on turnover and satisfaction, 92
Group order ranking, 224
Group(s)
  Two or more individuals, interacting and interdependent, who come together to achieve particular objectives, 84–85

  behavior of (*See* Behavior, group)
  coalition power, 155–56
  cohesiveness, 90, **91**
  composition, 92–93
  decision making, 94–98
  inertia, 255
  norms, 87–90
  reasons to join, 85, **86**
  roles, 85–87
  size, 90–92
  status, 93–94
  vs. teams, 101–2
Groupshift
  A change in decision risk between the group's decision and the individual decision that members within the group would make; can be toward either conservatism or greater risk, 96
Groupthink
  Phenomenon in which the norm for consensus overrides the realistic appraisal of alternative courses of action, 95–96, 170

Habit and resistance to change, 253–54
Hackman, J. Richard, 206, 208, **210**
Hall, E. T., **125**
Halo effects and perception, 25
Hamburger University, McDonald's, 220
Hammer, Michael, 198
Happiness, as universal emotion, 38
Harassment, sexual. *See* Sexual harassment
Harley-Davidson, 104
Hasbro, 204
Hawthorne studies, 87–89, 164
Herzberg, Frederick, 45–47
Heuristics
  Judgmental shortcuts in decision making, 76
Hewlett-Packard, 101, 103, 105, 190, 243, 244, 264
Hierarchy of needs theory
  Abraham Maslow provided hierarchy of five needs—physiological, safety, social, esteem, and self-actualization—and as each need is sequentially satisfied, the next need becomes dominant, 43–44, 53
High-context culture
  Culture that relies heavily on nonverbal and subtle situational cues, 125
Hill, J. S., **125**
Hiring of employees, 215–18, 235
Historical precedents, organizational constraints, 81
Hofstede, Geert, 18, **19**
Holland, John L., **35**
Honda Motors, 31, 104
Honesty and trust, 146
Honeywell, 103
Hooker Chemical, 66
Horizontal boundaries, structural organization, 190
House, Robert J., 137
HR. *See* Human resource (HR) policies and practices
Human relations view of conflict, 164, 165
Human resource (HR) policies and practices, 215–29
  employee selection, 215–18
  implications for managers, 228–29
  innovation stimulation, 263

performance appraisal, 220–28
training programs, 218–20
Hygiene factors, two-factor theory
Those factors—such as company policy and administration, supervision, and salary—that when adequate in a job, placate workers. When these factors are adequate, people will not be dissatisfied, 46

IBM, 18, 66, 104, 186, 192, 197, 246
Identification-based trust
The highest level of trust, achieved when there is an emotional connection between the parties, 147
Illinois Tool Works, 184, 186
IM. *See* Impression management (IM)
Imitation strategy
A strategy of minimizing risk and maximizing opportunities for profit by following the lead of other organizations, 192
Importance and dependency, 154–55
Impression management (IM)
The process by which individuals attempt to control the impression others form of them, 160–61
Improvement
continual, and quality management, 6–7
continuous improvement process, 198
performance appraisal, 225–26
Incentives. *See* Motivation
Incompatibility and conflict, 163
Individual decision making, 69–83
about, 69–70
actual process of, 73–81
alternative development, 75–76
bounded rationality, 73–74
choices and heuristics, 76–77
creativity in, 71–72
cultural influences on, 81
differences between individuals, 77–80
emotions, 40
ethics, 82
vs. group, 94–95
implications for managers, 83
individual differences, 77–80
intentional process of, 70–73
intuition, 74–75
problem identification, 75
rational model, 70–71
styles, 77–79
Individualism, 18, **19,** 53
Individual(s)
behavior of, implications for managers, 27–29
focus on development of, 244–45
political behavior factors, 158
ranking, 224
resistance to change, 253–54
into team players, 110–12
See also Behavior, individual
Industrial Light & Magic, 103
Influence. *See* Power
Informal groups, 85
Informal training, 220
Information
communication of, 114

decision-making biases, 174
selective processing of, 254
Information overload
The phenomenon that occurs when the information we have to work with exceeds our processing capacity, 123
Initiating structure
The extent to which a leader is likely to define and structure his or her role and those of subordinates in the search for goal attainment, 132
Innovation
in organizational culture, 231
stimulation of, 9–10, 260, 262–63
Innovation strategy
A strategy for meaningful and unique innovations, 192
www.insidetheweb.com, 204
Instrumental values
Preferable modes of behavior or means of achieving terminal values, 15, **16**
Integrative bargaining
Negotiation that seeks one or more settlements that can create a win-win solution, 173
Integrity and trust, 145, 148
Intel Corp., 154–55, 264
Interactionist view of conflict, 164, 165
Interest groups, 85
Intergroup development
OD efforts to change the attitudes, stereotypes, and perceptions that groups have of each other, 260
Internally-caused behaviors and attribution theory, 24
Internet
A worldwide network of interconnected computers, 200, **201,** 202
Internet time, 204–5
Interpersonal communication, 116–18
nonverbal, 117–18
oral, 116–17
written, 117
Interpersonal skills, 219
Interview process in employee selection, 216
Intonation as nonverbal communication, 118
Intranet
An organization's private Internet, 61, 122, **200**
Intrinsic task motivation, creative model, 72–73
Intuition and intuitive decision making, 74–75
Involvement, employee. *See* Employee involvement

J. Peterman, 9
Jackson, Jesse, 141
Jago, Arthur G., 139, **140**
Jargon and communication effectiveness, 124, 128, 241
JCM. *See* Job characteristics model
JCPenney, 184
Jesus Christ, 131
Job characteristics model (JCM)
Identifies five job characteristics and their relationship to personal and work outcomes, 206–7
Job enlargement
Expanding jobs horizontally, 210
Job enrichment
Vertical expansion of jobs, 210–11

Job rotation
The periodic shifting of a worker from one task to another, 209
Job satisfaction
concern with, 2
defined, 19
determinants of, 19–20
personality, 32, 34–36
satisfaction, productivity and OCB, 20–21
two-factor theory, 45–47
work stress, 261–62
See also under Work
Jobs, Steve, 65
John Deere, 66, 101
Johns, G., **207**
Johnson & Johnson, 101, 178, 242–43, 264
Jordan, Michael, 154
Judgment shortcuts and perception, 25
Justice and decision making, 82

Kearns, David T., 236
Kennedy, John F., 131
Kinesics
The academic study of body motions, 117–21
King, Martin Luther, Jr., 131, 133
King, Stephen, 199
KM. *See* Knowledge management (KM)
Knight-Ridder Information, 241
Knowledge-based trust
Trust based on the behavioral predictability that comes from a history of interaction, 146–47
Knowledge management (KM)
Process of organizing and distributing an organization's collective wisdom so the right information gets to the right people at the right time, 263–64
Kodak, 81
Kohlberg, Lawrence, **79**
Krupp-Hoesch, 11

Lampreia (restaurant), 240–41
Language and communication effectiveness, 124, 128, 241
Lateral communication, 116
Law of effect, 26
Leader-member exchange (LMX) theory
Theory that argues that leaders establish a special relationship with a small group of their followers, 137
Leader-member relations
The degree of confidence, trust, and respect subordinates have in their leader, 135–36
Leader-participation model
A leadership theory that provides a set of rules to determine the form and amount of participative decision making in different situations, 139
Leadership, 130–49
The ability to influence a group toward the achievement of goals, 130
behavioral approach to, 131–33, **134**
change in organizational culture, 242
charismatic, 141
contingency theories, 134–41
emotions, 40
implications for managers, 148–89

managerial grid, 133
Ohio State studies, 132
organizational behavior in e-world, 204–5
vs. power, 151
as relevant, 143–44
team creation by, 108
teams for, 142–43
trait theories, 131, 141
trust and, 144–48
University of Michigan studies, 133
visionary, 142
See also Management
Learning
defined, 26
individual behavior, 26–27, 29
organizational culture, 239–41
organizational spirituality, 244
Learning organization
An organization that has developed the continuous capacity to adapt and change, 256
Least preferred co-worker (LPC) questionnaire
An instrument that purports to measure whether a person is task- or relationship-oriented, 135–37
Legitimate power
The power a person receives as a result of his or her position in the formal hierarchy of an organization, 153
Levi Strauss, 65, 122, 199–200, 223
Levittown, 199
Lewicki, R. J., **172**
Lewin, Kurt, 251–52
Life, quantity vs. quality of, and cultural assessment, 18, **19**
Ling, Gary, 209
Listening, active, 128–29
Literacy skills, 218
Litterer, J. A., **172**
Liz Claiborne (company), 189
LMX theory. *See* Leader-member exchange (LMX) theory
Lockheed-Martin, 111
Locus of control
A personality attribute that measures the degree to which people believe they are masters of their own fate, 32
Long-term vs. short-term orientation, and cultural assessment, 18, **19**
Low-context culture
Culture that relies essentially on words to convey meaning, 125
Loyalty, 11, 17, 145
LPC questionnaire. *See* Least preferred co-worker (LPC) questionnaire
Lying, 126

MacArthur, Douglas, 141
Mach. *See* Machiavellianism (Mach)
Machiavellianism (Mach)
The degree to which an individual is pragmatic, maintains emotional distance, and believes that ends can justify means, 32
MAD TV (television program), 9
Malcolm Baldridge National Quality Award, 116
Management
change, planned, 250–51

change, through organizational development (OD), 257–60
groupthink, 96
organization structure, **179**
organizational culture, 235–38
of organizational culture, 241–42
"temporariness" in workplace, 10
Theory X and Theory Y, 45
See also Leadership; Managers, implications for
Management by objectives (MBO)
A program that encompasses specific goals, participatively set, for an explicit period, with feedback on progress toward the goal, 55–58
Managerial grid
A nine-by-nine matrix outlining eighty-one different leadership styles, 133, **134**
Managers, implications for
behavior, group, 98–99
behavior, individual, 27–29
change, organizational, 264–65
communication, 126–27
conflict, 176
culture, organizational, 247
decision making, individual, 83
e-world, organizational behavior, 201–5
emotions, 41
human resource (HR) policies and practices, 228–29
individual behavior, 27–29
leadership, 148–89
motivation, 54, 68
negotiation, 177
personality, 41
political behavior, 162
power, 162
structure of organization, 195
teams, 112
technology and work design, 213–14
trust, 189
values, 27–28
Mandela, Nelson, 131
Margerison, C., **107**
Marks & Spencer, 85, 192
Mary Kay Cosmetics, 142, 235, 240
Maslow, Abraham, 43–44, 53, 244
Mass customization
Production processes that are flexible enough to create products and services that are individually tailored to individual customers, 199–200
Mass production
Using division of labor, standardization, and automated processes to manufacture products in large quantities, 199
Material symbols in organizational culture, 240–41
Matrix structure
A structure that creates dual lines of authority; combines functional and product departmentalization, 187–88
Matsushita, 186
Mayo, Elton, 87
MBO. *See* Management by objectives (MBO)
MBTI. *See* Myers-Briggs Type Indicator (MBTI)
McCann, D., **107**
McClelland, David, 47–53

McClelland's Theory of Needs
The needs for achievement, power, and affiliation are the major needs to be met in the workplace, 47–48
McColough, C. Peter, 236
McDonald's, 8, 19, 180, 220
McGregor, Douglas, 45
Mead Paper, 66
Mechanistic model
A structure characterized by extensive departmentalization, high formalization, a limited information network, and centralization, 191
Melting pot assumption, 8
Men. *See* Gender issues
Merrill Lynch, 64
Message, in communication process, 114–15
Metamorphosis stage, socialization, 236, 237–38
Michigan, Survey Research Center at University of, 133
Microsoft, 31, 216, 227, 235
Military veterans, as cohort, work values of, 16–17
M&M / Mars, 103
Moberg, D., **162**
Modeling behavior, 26
Montgomery Ward, 9
Moods
Feelings that tend to be less intense than emotions and that lack a contextual stimulus, 36
Moral development and decision-making style, 79–80
Morita, Akio, 235
Mother Teresa, 131
Motivation, 42–68
The willingness to do something, conditioned by this action's ability to satisfy some need for the individual, 43
behavior modification, 58, **59**, 60
communication of, 114
cultural issues, 53–54
e-organization, 201–3
employee involvement programs, 61–64
employee recognition programs, 60–61
equity theory, 50–52
expectancy theory, 52–53
goal-setting theory, 48–49
implications for managers, 54, 68
individual behavior, 27
management by objectives (MBO), 55–58
Maslow's hierarchy of needs theory, 43–44, 53
McClelland's theory of needs, 47–48
path-goal theory of leadership, 137
performance appraisal, 221
reinforcement theory, 49–50
skill-based pay programs, 66–67
theories of, 43–54
Theory X and Theory Y, 45
two-factor theory, 45–47
variable-pay programs, 64–66
Motivation-hygiene theory, 45
Motorola, 101, 110, 190, 256
Mouton, Jane S., 133, **134**
Multiperson comparison as performance appraisal method, 224–25
Multiple channels in communication process, 127
Multiple evaluators in performance appraisal, 225

Myers-Briggs Type Indicator (MBTI)
   A personality test that taps four characteristics and classifies people into one of sixteen personality types, 31
Myth of rationality, 36

nAch. *See* Need for achievement
Nader, Ralph, 133
nAff. *See* Need for affiliation (nAff)
NASA, 60
National cultures. *See* Cultures, national, and cross-cultural issues
National Steel Corp., 189
Nature of workforce, organizational change, 249
NEC Corp., 190
Need
   A physiological or psychological deficiency that makes certain outcomes appear attractive, 43
Need for achievement (nAch)
   The drive to excel, 47–48, 53
Need for affiliation (nAff)
   The desire for good interpersonal relationships, 47, 48, **86**
Need for power (nPow)
   The need to make others do what they otherwise would otherwise not do, 47, 48
Negotiation, 171–77
   A process in which two or more parties exchange goods or services and attempt to agree on the exchange rate for them, 171
   bargaining strategies, 171–73
   conflict and, 171–76
   implications for managers, 177
   issues in, 173–76
Networks
   for communication, 97–98, 119
   e-world organizational behavior, 205
Nexters, as cohort, work values of, 17
Nike, 189, 239
Nissan, 60, 104
Nominal group technique
   A group decision-making method in which individual members meet face-to-face to pool their judgments in a systematic but independent fashion, 97
Nonverbal communication, 117–18
Nordstrom, 233, 239
Nordstrom, John W., 239
Norms
   Acceptable standards of behavior within a group that are shared by the group's members, 87–90
   conformity and Asch studies, 89–90
   Hawthorne studies, 87–89
   status and, 93
nPow. *See* Need for power (nPow)

OB. *See* Organizational behavior (OB)
OB Mod
   A program in which managers identify performance-related employee behaviors and then implement an intervention strategy to strengthen desirable performance behaviors and weaken undesirable behaviors, 58, **59**, 60
OCB. *See* organizational citizenship behavior
OD. *See* Organizational development (OD)

Off-the-job training, 220
O'Hare Airport (Chicago, IL), 197
Ohio State leadership studies, 132, 137, 138
Oldham, Greg R., 206
On-the-job training, 220
Openness
   to experience, 31
   organizational spirituality, 245
   trust, 145, 147
Opposition and conflict, 163, 164
Oral communication, 116–17
Organic model
   A structure that is flat, uses cross-hierarchical and cross-functional teams, has low formalization, possesses a comprehensive information network, and relies on participative decision making, 191
Organization
   A formal structure of planned coordination, involving two or more people, in order to achieve a common goal, 2–3
Organization structure, 178–95
   How job tasks are formally divided, grouped, and coordinated, 178
   in conflict process, 167
   constraints on decision making, 80–81
   design of, 185–88
   differences in, 191–93
   elements of, 178–85
   employee behavior, 193–94
   implications for managers, 195
   inertia, 254–55
   innovation stimulation, 262–63
   resistance to change, 254–56
   team creation, 108
   types of, new, 188–91
Organizational behavior (OB), 1–13
   The systematic study of the actions and attitudes that people exhibit within organizations, 1–3
   contributing disciplines, 3–5
   cross-cultural considerations, 18–19
   in e-world, 200–206
   field of, 2–5
   goals of, 5
   managerial challenges and opportunities, 6–12
Organizational change. *See* Change, organizational
Organizational citizenship
   Discretionary behavior that is not part of an employee's formal job requirements but that nevertheless promotes the effective functioning of the organization, 2
Organizational citizenship behavior (OCB), 2, 20–21
Organizational culture, 230–47
   A system of shared meaning held by members that distinguish the organization from other organizations, 231
   creation and sustaining of, 234–38, **239**
   defined, 230–33
   employees learning of, 239–41
   ethical, 242–43
   functions of, 233–34
   implications for managers, 247
   innovation stimulation, 263

as liability, 234
    management of change, 241–42
    vs. national culture, 246
    paradox of diversity amid, 246–47
    political behavior factors, 158–60
    socialization, 236–38
    spirituality and, 243–46
Organizational development (OD)
    A collection of planned-change interventions, built on humanistic-democratic values, that seek to improve organizational effectiveness and employee well-being, 257
    intergroup development, 260
    managing change through, 257–60
    process consultation, 258–59
    sensitivity training, 257–58
    survey feedback, 258
    team building, 259–60
Organizational improvement, 7
Outcome orientation in organizational culture, 231
Overconfidence, decision-making biases, 174

Paired comparison evaluation, 224–25
Paradox of diversity, 246–47
Participation and resistance to change, 255–56
Participative leadership, 138
Participative management
    A process in which subordinates share a significant degree of decision-making power with their immediate superiors, 62
Patagonia, 213
Path-goal theory
    The theory that a leader's behavior is acceptable to subordinates insofar as they view it as a source of either immediate or future satisfaction, 137–39
Pay
    equity theory, 51
    skill-based, 66–67
    status, 94
    variable, 64–66
PC. *See* Process consultation (PC)
Peer evaluation, 222
JCPenney, 184
People, empowerment of, 9
People orientation in organizational culture, 231
People skills, 1, 7
PeopleSoft, 213
PepsiCo, 103
Perception
    attribution theory, 23–24
    of conflict, 163–64
    factors which influence, 23
    as individual behavior, 23–25, 28–29
    judgment shortcuts, 25
    selective, 123
Performance
    evaluation of, 80, 159
    expectancy theory, 52
    management by objectives (MBO), 57
    pay-for-performance, 66
    systematic study of OB, 2
    team creation, 108–9

Performance appraisal, 220–28
    of behaviors, 222
    criteria, 221–22
    evaluators, 222–23
    feedback, 226–27
    in global context, 228
    in human resource (HR) policies and practices, 220–28
    improvement of, 225–26
    of individual task outcomes, 221
    methods, 223–25
    motivation, 221
    of team, 227–28
    of traits, 222
Performance-simulation tests, 217–18
Personal variables in conflict process, 167
Personality, 30–36
    The sum total of psychological traits that define how an individual reacts and interacts with others, 30
    Big-Five Model, 31–32
    culture and, 33–34
    implications for managers, 41
    job matching, 34–36
    locus of control, 32
    Machiavellianism, 32
    Meyers-Briggs Type Indicator (MBTI), 31
    in negotiation, 174
    risk propensity, 33, 54
    self-esteem, 32–33
    self-monitoring, 33
    team composition, 107
    Type A, 33, 34
Personalization and conflict process, 168
J. Peterman, 9
Peters, Tom, 253
Physical distance as nonverbal communication, 118
Physiological needs, 44, 53
Picasso, 72
Piece-rate pay plans
    Workers are paid a fixed sum for each unit of production completed, 64–65
Pizza Hut, 66
Planned change
    Change activities that are intentional and goal-oriented, 250–51
Political behavior, 157–62
    Activities that are not required as part of one's formal role in the organization, but that influence, or attempt to influence, the distribution of advantages and disadvantages within the organization, 157–58
    e-world organizational behavior, 205
    ethics of, 161–62
    factors contributing to, 158–60
    global, and organizational change, **249**, 250
    implications for managers, 162
    impression management, 160–61
Political science
    The study of the behavior of individuals and groups within a political environment, 4–5
Politics. *See* Political behavior

Position power
: *The degree of influence a leader has over power variables such as hiring, firing, discipline, promotions, and salary increases,* 135–36

Potential opposition in conflict process, 166–67
Powell, Colin, 131
Power, 150–62
: *A capacity that A has to influence the behavior of B so that B do what they otherwise would not do,* 150
  bases of, 152–54
  dependency, 154–55
  distance, and cultural assessment, 18, **19**
  empowerment, 7, 9, 245
  group, 92–93, 155–56
  implications for managers, 162
  vs. leadership, 151
  politics (*See* Political behavior)
  position, in Fiedler Model, 135–36
  as reason to join groups, **86**
  sexual harassment, 156–57
  spirituality, 245
  threat to established power relationships, 255

Power-Cable Corp., 103
The Practice (television program), 87
Prearrival stage, socialization, 236, 237
Preconventional level, moral development, 79
Prediction of behavior, 5
Preferences of member and team composition, 108
Prefontaine, Steve, 239
Prentice Hall, 8
Price Club, 31
PriceLine.com, 205
Principled level, moral development, 79, **80**
Print on Demand, 199
Problem identification, 75
Problem-solving skills, 219
Problem-solving teams
: *Groups of five to twelve employees from the same department who meet for a few hours each week to discuss ways of improving quality, efficiency, and the work environment,* 102–3

Process conflict
: *Conflict that relates to how work gets done,* 165

Process consultation (PC)
: *An outside consultant assists a client, usually a manager, to perceive, understand, and act on process events with which he or she must deal,* 258–59

Process departmentalization, 181
Process reengineering
: *Asks managers to reconsider how work would be done and their organization structured if they were starting over,* 6–7, 198–99

Procter & Gamble, 154–55, 181, 216
Productivity, 2, 20–21
Profit-sharing plans
: *Organization-wide programs that distribute compensation based on some established formula designed around a company's profitability,* 65

Prudential Insurance, 61

Psychology
: *The science that seeks to measure, explain, and sometimes change the behavior of humans and other animals,* 3, **4**

Publix Supermarkets, 63

Quality, improvement of, 6–7
Quality circles
: *A work group of eight to ten employees and supervisors who meet regularly to discuss their quality problems, investigate causes, recommend solutions, and take corrective actions,* 103

Quality management
: *A philosophy of management that is driven by the constant attainment of customer satisfaction through the continuous improvement of all organizational processes,* 6–7

Quality of life, and cultural assessment, 18, **19**

Race and workforce diversity, 7–8
: *See also* Diversity

Rational decision-making model, 70–71
Rational (decisions)
: *Choices that are consistent and value-maximizing within specified constraints,* 70

Raven, Bertram, 152
Reading skills, 218
Receiver, in communication process, 114–15
Recognition programs, employee, 60–61
Redesign, work, 209–11, 262
Reebok, 189
Reengineering, process, 6–7, 198–99
Referent power
: *Influence based on possession by an individual of desirable resources or personal traits,* 157–58

Reinforcement theory
: *A behavioristic approach, which argues that reinforcement conditions behavior,* 49–50, 60, 61

Relationship conflict
: *Conflict that focuses on interpersonal relationships,* 165

Relationships, e-organization redefinition of, 205–6
Representative heuristic
: *The tendency for people to judge probability of a future outcome by trying to match it with a preexisting category,* 76

Representative participation
: *Workers participate in organizational decision making through a small group of representative employees,* 62–63

Resistance point, distributive bargaining, 172
Resistance to change, 253–56
  individual, 253–54
  organizational, 254–55
  overcoming, 255–56
Resource allocations, threat to, 255
Resources availability, team creation, 108
Reward
  acceptance and resistance to change, 256
  dissonance reduction, 22
  equity theory, 51
  expectancy theory, 52
  system as organizational constraint, 80
Reward power
: *Compliance achieved based on the ability to distribute rewards that others view as valuable,* 153

Rights and decision making, 82
Ringlemann, Max, 91
Ringlemann effect, 91
Risk propensity
    An individual's willingness to take chances, 33, 54
Risk taking in organizational culture, 231
Rituals
    Repetitive sequences of activities that express and reinforce the key values of the organization, what goals are most important, which people are important and which are expendable, 240
Rokeach, Milton, 15
Rokeach Value Survey (RVS), 15
Roles
    A set of expected behavior patterns that are attributed to occupying a given position in a social unit, 85–87
Roosevelt, Franklin Delano, 141
Routineness, degree of, 193
Rowe, A. J., **78**
Royal Bank of Canada, 264
Royal Dutch Shell, 105, 186
Rumors and grapevine communication, 120–21
(RVS) Rokeach Value Survey, 15

Sadness, as universal emotion, 38
Safety needs, 44, 53
San Diego Zoo, 101
Satisfaction, job. *See* Job satisfaction
Satisficing model of decision making, 73
Saturn Corporation, 181
Scarcity
    conflict and, 163, 164
    dependency and, 155
Scheduling options, 211–13
Schendell, Laura, 60
Sears, 184
Security, 254
    as reason to join groups, **86**
    resistance to change, 254
Selection of employees, 215–18, 235
Selective information processing, 254
Selective participation, as barrier to effective communication, 123
Selectivity and perception, 25
Self-actualization, 44, 53, 244
Self-awareness, in emotional intelligence, 39
Self-esteem
    The degree to which people like or dislike themselves, 32–33, **86**
Self-evaluation, performance appraisal, 222–23
Self-managed work teams
    Groups of ten to fifteen people who take on responsibilities of their former supervisors, 103
Self-management, in emotional intelligence, 39
Self-monitoring
    An individual's ability to adjust his or her behavior to external, situational factors, 33
Self-motivation, in emotional intelligence, 39
Self-serving bias, 25
Senge, P. M., 256

Sensitivity training
    Training groups that seek to change behavior through unstructured group interaction, 257–58
Sexual harassment
    Unwelcome advances, requests for sexual favors, and other verbal or physical conduct, whether overt or subtle, of a sexual nature, 156–57
Shaping behavior, 26
Shea & Gould, 171
Shenandoah Life Insurance Co., 101
Shiseido, 101
Short-term vs. long-term orientation, and cultural assessment, 18, **19**
Siemens, 11, 220, 263–64
Simple structure
    A structure characterized by a low degree of departmentalization, wide spans of control, authority centralized in a single person, and little formalization, 185–86
The Simpsons (television program), 9
SIP model. *See* Social information-processing (SIP) model
Six-personality-types model
    A model that relates an employee's job satisfaction with his or her personality type, 34
Size
    of groups, and group behavior, 90–92
    organizational culture and, 242
    organizational structure and, 192
    of team and team composition, 107–8
Skill-based pay
    Pay levels are based on how many skills employees have or how many jobs they can do, 66–67
Skills
    feedback, 127–28
    listening, active, 128–29
    negotiation, 176
    people, 1, 8
    training programs, 218–20
    variety of, in job characteristic model, 206, **207**
Small-group network communication, 119
Smith, Fred, 235
Smith Corona, 9
Social information-processing (SIP) model
    Employees adopt attitudes and behaviors in response to the social cues provided by others with whom they have contact, 208–9
Social loafing
    The tendency for individuals to expend less effort when working collectively than when working individually, 91, 110
Social needs, 44, 53
Social psychology
    An area within psychology that focuses on the influence of people on one another, 3, **4**
Social skills, in emotional intelligence, 39
Social trends and organizational change, 249, 250
Socialization
    The process that adapts employees to the organizations culture, 236–38
Sociology
    A discipline that studies people in relation to their fellow human beings, 3, **4**

Sony, 31, 235
Southwest Airlines, 216, 243, 244, 245, 246
Span of control
  The number of subordinates a manager can efficiently and effectively direct, 183–84, 194
Specialization. *See* Work specialization
Spirituality and organizational culture, 243–46
Sprint, 223
Stability in organizational culture, 231
Stanford University study, 205–6
Status
  A prestige grading, position, or rank within a group, **86**, 93–94
Stereotyping and perception, 25
Stories, and learning culture, 239
Stress
  A dynamic condition in which an individual is confronted with an opportunity, constraint, or demand related to what he or she desires and for which the outcome is perceived to be both uncertain and important, 261–62
Strong culture
  A culture in which the core values are intensely held and widely shared, 233
Structure of organization. *See* Organization structure
Subordinates
  path-goal theory, 138–39
  performance appraisals, 223
  sexual harassment by, 156–57
Superiors
  performance appraisals, 222
  sexual harassment by, 156–57
Supportive leader, 137
Surprise, as universal emotion, 38
Survey feedback
  An assessment tool in which questionnaire data become the springboard for identifying and clarifying organizational issues and problems, 258
Suttle, J. L., 208, **210**
Symbols, material, in organizational culture, 240–41
System-imposed time constraints, 80
Systematic study
  The use of scientific evidence gathered under controlled conditions and measured and interpreted in a reasonably rigorous manner to attribute cause and effect, 2

T-groups (training groups), 257–58
Target point, distributive bargaining, 172
Task characteristics theories, 206–9
Task conflict
  Conflict that relates to the content and goals of the work, 165
Task force, 104
Task groups, 85
Task identity in job characteristic model, 206, **207**
Task significance in job characteristic model, 206, **207**
Task structure
  The degree to which job assignments are structured or unstructured, 135–36
Team building
  High interaction among team members to increase trust and openness, 259–60

Team players, 110–12
Teams, 100–112
  building, 259–60
  creation of effective, 105–10
  efficacy of, 109
  vs. groups, 101–2
  implications for managers, 112
  individuals into, 110–12
  leadership by, 142–43
  orientation toward, 231
  popularity of, 101
  problem-solving, 102–3
  structure of, 188–89
  types of, 102–5
Technical skills, 218–19
Technology
  How an organization transfers its inputs into outputs, 192–93
Technology and work design, 196–214
  implications for managers, 213–14
  organizational behavior in e-world, 200–206
  organizational change, 249
  scheduling options, 211–13
  work design, 206–3
  work redesign, 209–11
  in workplace, 196–200
Telecommuting
  Doing work at home at least two days a week on a computer that is linked to an office, 212–13
"Temporariness" in workplace, 10
Terminal values
  Desirable end-states of existence, 15, **16**
Theory X
  The assumption that employees dislike work, are lazy, dislike responsibility, and must be coerced to perform, 45, 63
Theory Y
  The assumption that employees like work, are creative, seek responsibility, and can exercise self-direction, 45, 63
Thinking style and decision making, 77
Thoman, Rick, 236
360-degree evaluations
  Performance feedback from the full circle of an employee's daily contacts in an organization, 223
Three-component model of creativity
  Individual creativity essentially requires expertise, creative-thinking skills, and intrinsic task motivation, 71–72
3M Co., 31, 101, 192, 262, 263
Time, Internet, 204–5
Time constraints, system-imposed, 80
Time-management program, 262
Time Warner, 142
Tolerance
  ambiguity and decision making, 77
  organizational spirituality, 245
Tom's of Maine, 243, 244
Toyota Motor Co., 8, 101, 104
Traditional view of conflict, 164–65
Training
  cross-training, 209
  of evaluator, performance appraisal, 226

human resource (HR) policies and practices, 218–20
 sensitivity training, 257–58
 team players, 111–12
Trait approach to leadership, 131, 141
Traits in performance appraisal, 225
Transactional leaders
 Leaders who guide or motivate their followers in the direction of established goals by by clarifying role and task requirements, 141
Transformational leaders
 Leaders who inspire their followers to transcend their own self-interests for the good of the organization; they can have a profound or extraordinary effect on their followers, 141
Trouble-shooters, team leaders as, 143
www.truckinlife.com, 204
Trust
 A positive expectation that another will not act opportunistically, 144–46
 building, 147–48
 implications for managers, 189
 leadership, 144–48
 organizational spirituality, 245
 types of, 146–47
Turnover, employee, 2
Two-factor theory
 Motivator factors are related to job satisfaction, while hygiene factors are associated with dissatisfaction, 45–47
Type A personality
 A competitive, impatient, ambitious person, 33

Uncertainty avoidance, and cultural assessment, 18, **19**
Uniformity of organizational culture, 231–33
Unisys, 181
United Airlines, 63
United Parcel Service (UPS), 223
Unity of command principle
 A person should have one and only one superior to whom he or she is directly responsible, 182
University of Michigan Survey Research Center, 133
UPS (United Parcel Service), 223
Upward communication, 115–16
U.S. Post Office, 197
Utilitarianism
 System in which decisions are made solely on the basis of their outcomes or consequences, 82

Valasquez, M., **162**
Value systems
 Systems that represent a prioritizing of individual values, 15
Values, 14–19
 Basic convictions that specific modes of conduct or end-states of existence are preferable to opposite or converse modes of conduct or end-states of existence, 14
 across cultures, 17–19
 implications for managers, 27–28
 loyalty and ethical behavior, 17
 terminal, 15, **16**
 types of, 15–17

Van Maanen, J., **238**
Variable-pay programs
 A portion of an employee's pay is based on some individual and/or organizational measure of performance, 64–66
VeriFone, 105
Vertical boundaries in structural organization, 190
Vertical job expansion and job enrichment, 211
Veterans, as cohort, work values of, 16–17
Viant, 236
Videoconferencing, 122
Virgin Group, 235
Virtual office, 212
Virtual organization
 A small, core organization that outsources major business functions, 189, **190**
Virtual teams
 Teams that use computer technology to tie together physically dispersed members to achieve a common goal, **102**, 104–5
Visionary leadership
 The ability to create and articulate a realistic, credible, and attractive vision of the future for an organization or organization unit that grows out of and improves on the present, 142, 205
Vocational Preference Inventory, 34
Volkswagen, 186, 264
Volvo, 8, 101
Vroom, Victor, 139, **140**

W. L. Gore & Associates, 103, 223, 235
W. T. Grant, 9
Wal-Mart, 22, 66, 192, 201, 256
Walt Disney Co., 65, 216, 234
Walt Disney Imagineering, 60
Weak culture, 233, 242
Weather Channel, 202
Weatherill Associates, 243
Welch, Jack, 190
Western Electric Company, 87
Weyerhauser, 60
Wheel, in network communication, 119
Whirlpool, 264
White-water rapids simile, 252
Whitman, Meg, 204
Wilson, Joseph C., 235–36
Winner's curse, 174
Women. *See* Gender issues
Wood, Peter, 6
Woodworth, R. D., **38**
Work design, 206–13
 redesign, 209–11, 262
 scheduling options, 211–13
 task characteristics theories, 206–9
 teams, creation of effective, 105
 See also under Jobs; Technology and work design
Work group
 A group who interacts primarily to share information and to make decisions to help each other perform within his or her area of responsibility, 101, **102**
Work redesign, 209–11, 262

Work sampling tests
: *Hands-on simulations of part or all of the job that must be performed by applicants,* 217

Work specialization
: *The degree to which tasks in the organization are subdivided into separate jobs,* 179–81, 194

Work team
: *A group whose individual efforts result in a level of performance that is greater than the sum of the individual inputs,* 101–2

Workforce diversity
: *Organizations have become more heterogeneous in terms of gender, race, and ethnicity,* 7–8

Workplace spirituality
: *The recognition that people have an inner life that nourishes and is nourished by meaningful work that takes place in the context of community,* 243

Works councils
: *Groups of nominated or elected employees who must be consulted when management makes decisions involving personnel,* 62–63

World politics and organizational change, **249**, 250
Written communication, 117
Written essay as performance appraisal method, 223
Written tests for employee selection, 217
www.greedyassociates.com, 204
www.insidetheweb.com, 204
www.truckinlife.com, 204

The X-Files (television program), 9
Xerox, 60, 103, 181, 203, 213, 218, 235
Xers, as cohort, work values of, 16–17

Yetton, Phillip W., 139, **140**
Yukl, G., **152**